JEAN–PAUL SARTRE AND HIS CRITICS:

AN INTERNATIONAL BIBLIOGRAPHY (1938–1975)

BIBLIOGRAPHIES OF FAMOUS PHILOSOPHERS

The Philosophy Documentation Center is publishing a series of
BIBLIOGRAPHIES OF FAMOUS PHILOSOPHERS, edited by
Richard H. Lineback. **HENRI BERGSON: A BIBLIOGRAPHY**
was the first bibliography in the series. **JEAN–PAUL SARTRE**
is the second bibliography in the series.

JEAN-PAUL SARTRE AND HIS CRITICS

AN INTERNATIONAL BIBLIOGRAPHY

(1938 - 1975)

François Lapointe

Claire Lapointe

PHILOSOPHY DOCUMENTATION CENTER
BOWLING GREEN STATE UNIVERSITY
BOWLING GREEN, OHIO 43403
U.S.A.

Library of Congress Card Number: 75-27725

ISBN 0-912632-32-1

CONTENTS

INTRODUCTION

INTRODUCTION

On June 20, 1975, Jean-Paul Sartre celebrated his seventieth
birthday. One of the chief witnesses of our age, a controversial
figure not only because of his philosophy, but because of the con-
clusions he drew as a writer who combined his work with political
activism, Sartre has now entered a period of reduced productivity.
His output much reduced by weariness, age, and an affliction of the
optic nerve, Sartre is withdrawing into himself. His name has now
disappeared from the daily paper Libération and from all other remaining publications to which he used to lend his name as Directeur
in order to shield them from government reprisals. But now he no
longer wants to be identified with publications which he scarcely
reads any more. He has difficulty walking more than half a mile or
so, and he has had treatment for high blood pressure as well. But
the real problem, Sartre said in an interview published in Le Nouvel Observateur (30 juin 1975), is that his vision is failing. "My
career as a writer is completely destroyed," said Sartre. "I have
had hemorrhages behind my left eye, the one with which I could see."
(He lost the sight in his right eye from leucoma at age three.)
"As a consequence, I can neither read nor write." "I can still
talk," he said, adding that if French television could find the fi-
nancial backing, he hoped to do "a series of programs where I will
try to talk about the seventy-five years of this century."

What are the personal plans of Sartre? In 1974, during a
series of conversations with two young French revolutionaries, Philippe Gavi, the editor of Libération, and Pierre Vicot, the leader
of the 'Maoists', they suggested that Sartre ought to write a popular novel instead of going on with the fourth volume of his Flaubert. Sartre objected: "I have already written three volumes and
the fourth needs to be done. A popular novel? I should first have
to find out what that is. When have popular novels ever aroused
revolutionary fervor in their readers?" And then he added: "You
are asking a lot of me, and I work that much less. I shall think
myself lucky if I finish my Flaubert . . ." The writing of a novel
means being in sympathy with its hero's future, he went on; it means
expressing one's own feelings about the shape of things to come
through his experiences. "But for me the future is a sealed book--
and then you expect me to start a new literary career."

In June 1973, in an interview granted to Francis Jeanson and
reproduced in the concluding part of his book Sartre dans sa vie
(1974) discussing his future literary projects, Sartre mentioned the
fourth volume of his work on Flaubert, L'Idiot de la famille, as
well as "des préfaces pour des livres politiques." As to the Critique de la raison dialectique (1960), he did not think that he
would finish it. In the first part, he said, he had given the the-

oretical foundations of what he had wanted to do. But in the second
part, he would have to explain what history is, "et je considère que
je ne sais pas assez d'histoire pour entreprendre ça." ("And I feel
that I do not know enough history to undertake that.").

So it is clear that the second volume of the Critique de la
raison dialectique will not be written, any more than the treatise
on ethics which Sartre once promised. And so it is perhaps all the
more understandable that Sartre does not want to leave his Flaubert
as a limbless torso, and will go on working on it as long as his
strength allows. Sartre now appears to be convinced that his political ideas will not remain valid for very long, but that his book
on Gustave Flaubert will be read for a long time to come.

Although Sartre's work has been widely read and reviewed, and
has exerted a significant influence on contemporary thought, yet no
comprehensive bibliography of the wide range of critical response to
his writings has appeared to date. Since bibliography is an essential tool at some stage of most scholarly endeavors, and certainly
an essential tool of philosophy and literature as a kind of scholar-
ship, we hope that his compilation of secondary materials will give
Sartre scholars some assistance.

With over 5000 titles devoted to Sartre, surely a Sartre bibliography needs no lengthy justification. We have long been aware
of the need for a full, detailed, and accurate list of the reactions
of Sartre's critics. There can be little doubt that Sartre has re-
ceived, and is still receiving, the sort of attention given only to
great writers. Arduous as the task has sometimes been, it was
worthwhile, and we can only hope that others will come to share our
view when they see the sheer bulk of the data available, and becoming available, on the works of Sartre. The works listed here show
that Sartre's ideas are constantly being examined in new ways, in
new contexts, and using new resources uncovered by investigations
in a variety of fields. This bibliography provides continuing proof
that Sartre's work is still found fresh and exciting by a new generation of scholars.

Bibliography always serves a utilitarian purpose. Some order
had to be imposed on this chaos. To compile as complete a collection of items as possible is one thing. To provide a useful arrangement of this collection is another thing. The major task of
the bibliographer should be to bring order out of the chaos of al-
phabetic or chronological listing. After long deliberation, we have
decided to distribute the material in six sections. Part One con-
tains books devoted to Sartre (or almost exclusively so), and the
books are classified by language. Part Two lists unpublished dis-

sertations and theses, also indicating the entries, when available, in <u>Dissertation Abstracts International</u>. In Part Three we have listed books and articles devoted to a single work of Sartre, beginning with the novels, then the plays, and finally essays and philosophical works proper. In Part Four, we have listed other items by proper names. This section includes material in which Sartre is being compared or contrasted with major figures in philosophy or literature. The remaining items are arranged by subject. A final section includes book reviews. Entries found in the Appendix arrived too late to be included in the body of the manuscript.

The bibliography is intended to be as complete as is technically feasible. Our purpose is to provide an accurate, reasonably complete and useful arrangement of materials for those interested in Sartre's thought and life. Although no bibliography can claim to be exhaustive, every attempt at completeness and accuracy has been made. All of the standard reference works known to us were consulted, and many periodicals and books were searched individually. Items through May 1975 are included.

Although we have made every effort to compile an accurate, up-to-date, and reasonably complete bibliography, we are fully aware of the provisional nature of our work and feel no obligation to apologize for this. As is well known to bibliographers, publication constitutes a stage in the movement toward completeness, a more or less 'complete' starting point for further work. Our hope is that eventually we can come closer to our ideal of completeness in a supplementary volume, or a second edition, which will continue this one beyond 1974, and which will include earlier important items we were regrettably unable to include, as well as corrections of possible errors.

It is impossible in an extensive bibliography to remove all errors and make good all gaps of information. Since we intend to issue a supplementary volume, or a revised second edition, we urgently sollicit the help of those who use this bibliography. Please send us corrections, leads, and information. We would be pleased to hear from students of Sartre, especially those in Scandanavia as well as Central and East Europe who are frustrated by our omissions.

We would like to thank the staff of the **Philosophy Documentation Center** for their help and especially **Michael R. Linkins** for his preparation of the manuscript.

François and Claire Lapointe
Tuskegee Institute, Alabama   36088
U.S.A.

PART I

BOOKS DEVOTED TO SARTRE

BOOKS IN ENGLISH

1   Adereth, Maxwell. Commitment in Modern French Literature, Politics, and Society in Péguy, Aragon and Sartre. New York: Schocken, 1967, 127-191.

2   Albérès, René-Marill. Jean-Paul Sartre, Philosopher Without Faith. Trans. from the French by Wade Baskin. New York: Philosophical Library, 1961.

3   Barnes, Hazel E. Humanistic Existentialism: The Literature of Possibility. Lincoln: Univ. of Nebraska Pr., 1959.

4   Barnes, Hazel E. Sartre. New York: Lippincott, 1973.

5   Bauer, George H. Sartre and the Artist. Chicago: Univ. of Chicago Pr., 1969.

6   Belkind, Allan. Jean-Paul Sartre: Sartre and Existentialism in English, A Bibliographic Guide. Kent, Ohio: Kent State Univ. Pr., 1969.

7   Brée, Germaine. Camus and Sartre: Crises and Commitment. New York: Delta Books, 1972.

8   Burnier, Michel-Antoine. Choice of Action: The French Existentialists on the Political Front Line. Trans. from the French by B. Murchland. New York: Random House, 1968.

9   Carson, Ronald A. Sartre. Guilford and London: Lutterworth Pr., 1974.

10   Catalano, Joseph. A Commentary on Sartre's 'Being and Nothingness'. New York: Harper, 1974.

11   Champigny, Robert. Humanism and Human Racism: A Critical Study of Essays by Sartre and Camus. The Hague: Mouton, 1972.

12   Champigny, Robert. Stages on Sartre's Way, 1939-1952. Bloomington, Indiana: Indiana Univ. Pr., 1959.

13   Contat, Michel and Rybalka, Michel. The Writings of Sartre. Two volumes. Trans. from the French. Evanston, Illinois: Northwestern Univ. Pr., 1974.

14   Cranston, Maurice W. Jean-Paul Sartre. New York: Grove Pr.; Edinburgh: Oliver and Boyd, 1962.

15   Cranston, Maurice W. The Quintessence of Sartre. Montreal:
      Harvest House, 1970.

16   Cumming, Robert D., ed. The Philosophy of Jean-Paul Sartre.
      New York: Random House, 1965.

17   Dempsey, Peter. The Psychology of Sartre. Westminster,
      Maryland: Newman Pr., 1950.

18   Desan, Wilfrid. The Marxism of Sartre. Garden City, New
      York: Doubleday, Anchor Books, 1965.

19   Desan, Wilfrid. The Tragic Finale: An Essay on the Philos-
      ophy of Sartre. Cambridge, Massachusetts: Harvard Univ.
      Pr., 1954.

20   Falk, Eugene H. Types of Thematic Structures: The Nature
      and Function of Motifs in Gide, Camus and Sartre. Chi-
      cago: Univ. of Chicago Pr., 117-176.

21   Fell, Joseph J. Emotion in the Thought of Sartre. New York:
      Columbia Univ. Pr., 1965.

22   Fields, Belden. An Examination of the Ontological Founda-
      tions of the Political Theory of Sartre. New York, 1961.

23   Gore, Keith O. Sartre, La Nausée et Les Mouches. (Studies
      in French Literature, 17) London: Edward Arnold, 1970.

24   Greene, Norman N. Jean-Paul Sartre: The Existentialist Ethic.
      Ann Arbor: Univ. of Michigan Pr., 1960.

25   Greene, Marjorie. Sartre. New York: New Viewpoints, 1973.

26   Hartmann, Klaus. Sartre's Ontology: A Study of 'Being and
      Nothingness' in the Light of Hegel's Logic. Trans. from
      the German. Evanston, Illinois: Northwestern Univ. Pr.,
      1966.

27   Jameson, Fredric R. Sartre: The Orgins of a Style. New
      Haven: Yale Univ. Pr., 1961.

28   Jolivet, Régis. Sartre or the Theology of the Absurd.
      Trans. from the French by Wesley C. Piersol. New York:
      Newman Press, 1968.

29   Kaelin, Eugene F. An Existentialist Aesthetic: The Theories
      of Sartre and Merleau-Ponty. Madison, Wisconsin: Univ. of
      Wisconsin Pr., 1962.

30   Kern, Edith, ed. Sartre: A Collection of Critical Essays.
      Englewood Cliffs, New Jersey: Prentice-Hall, 1962.

31   Kern, Edith Existential Thought and Fictional Technique:
      Kierkegaard, Sartre, Beckett. New Haven: Yale Univ. Pr.,
      1970.

32   King, Thomas M. Sartre and the Sacred. Chicago: Univ. of
      Chicago Pr., 1974.

33   Lafarge, René. Jean-Paul Sartre: His Philosophy. Trans.
      from the French by Marina Smyth-Kok. Notre Dame, Indiana:
      Univ. of Notre Dame Pr., 1970.

34   Laing, R. D., and Cooper, D. G. Reason and Violence: A
      Decade of Sartre's Philosophy, 1950-1960. Revised with an
      expanded introduction. Foreward by Sartre. London:
      Tavistock, 1971.

35   Manser, A. R. Sartre: A Philosophic Study. London: Oxford
      Univ. Pr., 1966.

36   Martin, Vincent. Existentialism: Kierkegaard, Sartre and
      Camus. Washington, D.C.: Thomist Pr., 1962.

37   Masters, Brian. A Student's Guide to Sartre. London: Heine-
      mann Educational Books, 1970.

38   Masters, Brian. Sartre: A Study. Rowman and Littlefield,
      1974.

39   McBride, William L. Fundamental Change in Law and Society:
      Hart and Sartre on Revolution (Studies in the Social Sci-
      ences, 6). The Hague: Mouton, 1970; New York: Humanities
      Press, 1971.

40   McCall, Dorothy. The Theater of Jean-Paul Sartre. New York:
      Columbia Univ. Pr., 1969.

41   McMahon, Joseph J. Humans Being: The World of Jean-Paul
      Sartre. Chicago: Univ. of Chicago Pr., 1971.

42   Molnar, Thomas. Sartre, Ideologue of Our Time. New York:
      Funk and Wagnall, 1968.

43   Murdoch, Iris. Sartre, Romantic Realist. New Haven: Yale
      Univ. Pr., 1953.

44   Natanson, Maurice. A Critique of Jean-Paul Sartre's On-
      tology. Lincoln, Nebraska: Univ. of Nebraska Pr., 1951;
      The Hague: Nijhoff, 1973.

45   Odajnyk, Walter. Marxism and Existentialism. Garden City,
      New York: Doubleday, Anchor Books, 1965.

46   Peyre, Henri. Jean-Paul Sartre (Columbia Essays on Modern
      Writers, 31). New York: Columbia Univ. Pr., 1968.

47   Pollman, Leo. Sartre and Camus: Literature of Existence.
      Trans. from the German by Helen and Gregor Sebba. New
      York: Frederick Ungar, 1970.

48   Richter, Liselotte. Jean-Paul Sartre. Trans. from the
      German by Freud D. Wieck. New York: Frederick Ungar, 1970.

49   Salvan, Jacques L. To Be Or Not To Be. Detroit: Wayne State
      Univ. Pr., 1962.

50   Salvan, Jacques L. The Scandalous Ghost: Sartre's Existen-
      tialism as Related to Vitalism, Humanism, Mysticism and
      Marxism. Detroit: Wayne State Univ. Pr., 1967.

51   Savage, Catherine. Malraux, Sartre and Aragon as Political
      Novelists. Gainesville: Univ. of Florida Monographas,
      Humanities, No. 17, 1964. "Sartre and the Road to Liberty",
      17-42.

52   Schaldenbrand, Sister Mary Aloysius. Prenomenologie of Free-
      dom: An Essay on the Philosophies of Sartre and G. Marcel.
      Washington, D.C.: Catholic Univ. of America. Philosophical
      Study No. 91, 1960.

53   Seznec, Jean. On Two Definitions of Literature. Oxford:
      Claredon Pr., 1952.

54   Sheridan, James F. Sartre: The Radical Conversion. Athens,
      Ohio: Ohio Univ. Pr., 1969.

55   Sheridan, James F. Once More From the Middle: A Philosophi-
      cal Anthropology. Athens, Ohio: Ohio Univ. Pr., 1973.

56   Shouery, Imad T. Ambiguity and Relevance in Sartre's Exis-
      tentialism. Beirut, Lebanon: Librairie du Liban, 1973.

57   Stern, Alfred. Sartre: His Philosophy and Psycholanalysis.
      2nd rev. ed. New York: Liberal Arts Pr., 1967.

58   Streller-Justus, J. Jean-Paul Sartre: To Freedom Condemned.
      Trans. from the German by Wade Baskin. New York: Philo-
      sophical Library, 1960.

59   Suhl, Benjamin. Jean-Paul Sartre: The Philosopher as a
      Literary Critic. New York: Columbia Univ. Pr., 1970.

60   Thody, Philip. Jean-Paul Sartre: A Literary and Political
      Study. New York: Macmillan, 1961.

61   Thody, Philip. Sartre: A Biographical Introduction (Lead-
      ers of Modern Thought Series). London: Studio Vista,
      1971; New York: Scribner's, 1972.

62   Ussher, Arland. Journey Through Dread: A Study of Kier-
      kegaard, Heidegger and Sartre. London: Dawren-Finlayson,
      1955; New York: Devin-Adair, 1959.

63   Warnock, Mary. The Philosophy of Sartre. New York: Hillary
      House, 1965; London: Hutchison and Company, 1965.

64   Warnock, Mary, ed. Sartre: A Collection of Critical Essays.
      Garden City, New York: Doubleday, 1971.

65   Zuidema, Sytse Ulbe. Jean-Paul Sartre. Trans. from the
      Dutch by Dirk Jellema. Philadelphia: Presbyterian and
      Reformed Pub., 1960.

BOOKS IN FRENCH

66   Albérès, René-Marill. Jean-Paul Sartre. 7e éd. (Classiques
      du XXe siècle, 11). Paris: Editions Universitaires, 1965.

67   Arnold, James A. et Piriou, Jean-Pierre. 'Les Mots' de Jean-
      Paul Sartre: Genèse et critique d'une autobiographie.
      Paris: Minard, Archives des Lettres Modernes, No. 144, 1973.

68   Audry, Colette, ed. Pour ou contre l'existentialisme. Paris:
      Atlas, 1948.

69   Audry, Colette. Connaissance de Sartre. Cahiers de la Com-
      pagnie Madeleine Renaud--Jean-Louis Barrault, 3, No. 13,
      octobre 1955.

70   Audry, Colette. Jean-Paul Sartre et la réalité humaine.
      (Coll. "Philosophes de tous les temps", 23). Paris: Seghers,
      1966.

71   Beigbeder, Marc. L'homme Sartre: essai de dévoilement pré-
      existentiel. Paris: Bordas, 1947.

72   Belkind, Allan. Sartre: la critique anglo-saxonne. Paris:
      Minard, 1971.

73   Bolle, Louis. Les lettres et l'absolu: Valéry, Sartre,
      Proust. Genève: Perret-Gentil, 1959.

74   Bonnet, Henri. De Malherbe à Sartre: essai sur les pro-
      grès de la conscience esthétique. Paris: A.G. Nizet,
      1968.

75   Borel, Pierre-Louis. De Péguy à Sartre: paradoxes du XXe
      siècle. Neuchâtel: H. Messeiller, 1964.

76   Boros, Marie-Denise. Un Séquestré: l'homme sartrien, étude
      du thème de la séquestration dans l'oeuvre de Sartre.
      Paris: A.G. Nizet, 1968.

77   Boutang, Pierre, et Pingaud, Bernard. Sartre est-il possédé?
      2e éd. Paris: Editions de la Table Ronde, 1950.

78   Burnier, Michel-Antoine. Les Existentialistes et la poli-
      tique. Paris: Gallimard, 1966.

79   Campbell, Robert. Jean-Paul Sartre ou une littérature phi-
      losophique. 2e éd. revisé et augmenté. Paris: Pierre
      Ardent, 1965.

80   Carette, R. Sartre et la philosophie du possible. Gand:
      Editions J.D.S., 1953.

81   Champigny, Robert. Humanisme et racisme humain. Paris:
      Saint Germain-des-Prés, 1972.

82   Contat, Michel. Explication des 'Séquestrés d'Altona' de
      Sartre. Paris: Minard, Lettres Modernes, 1968.

83   Contat, Michel et Rybalka, Michel. Les Ecrits de Sartre:
      Chronologie, bibliographie commentée. Suivies de 'Textes
      retrouvés'. Lettre-préface de Sartre. Paris: Gallimard,
      1970.

84   Contat, Michel et Rybalka, Michel. Jean-Paul Sartre: un
      théâtre de situation. (Coll. "Idées"). Textes rassemblés,
      établis, présentés et annotés par Contat et Rybalka.
      Paris, Gallimard, 1973.

85   Cormeau, Nelly. Littérature existentialiste: le roman et le
      théâtre de Sartre. Liège: Thone, 1950.

86   Cranston, Maurice W. La quintessence de Sartre. Montréal:
      Harvest House, 1970.

87   Daniélou, Jean. Dialogue avec les existentialistes. Paris:
      Le Portulan, 1948.

88   Dauphin, E.J. Ekécrate: dialogue sur l'existentialisme, ré-
      ponse à M. Sartre. Montpellier: Causse, Graille et Castel-
      nau, 1947.

89   Durand, R.P. Sartre ou la liberté sans Dieu. Marseille:
      Conférence C.I.T.A., 1963.

90   Ferrier, Jean-Louis. La Pensée anhistorique de Sartre.
      Basel: Verlag für Recht und Gesellschaft, 1952. Also
      Studia Philosophica, 12, 1952, 4-17.

91   Gagnebin, Laurent. Connaître Sartre. Paris: Editions
      Resna, 1972.

92   Garaudy, Roger. Questions à Jean-Paul Sartre, précédées
      d'une lettre ouverte. Paris: Provence, 1960.

93   Guindey, Guillaume. Le Drame de la pensée dialectique: Hegel,
      Marx, Sartre. (Coll. Problèmes et controverses). Paris:
      Vrin, 1974, 160 pp.

94   Gutwirth, Rudolf. La Phénoménologie de Jean-Paul Sartre.
      (Coll. Sentiers). Paris: Privat, 1974, 288 pp.

95   Hayen, E. Henri. Sartre contre l'homme. Annemasse: Editions
      l'Effort Humain, 1947.

96   Hervé, Pierre. Lettre à Sartre et à quelques autres par la
      même occasion. Paris: Editions de la Table Ronde, 1956.

97   Houbart, Jacques. Un Père dénaturé: essai critique sur la
      philosophie de Sartre. Paris: Julliard, 1964.

98   Hoy, Peter C. Sartre et les bibliographes. (Coll. "Biblio-
      notes"). Paris: Minard, 1972.

99   Idt, Geneviève. 'Le Mur' de Jean-Paul Sartre: techniques et
      contexte d'une provocation. Paris: Librairie Larousse,
      1972.

100   Idt, Geneviève. _Sartre, La Nausée: analyse critique_. Paris:
       Hatier, 1971.

101   Jeanson, Francis. _Le Problème moral et la pensée de Sartre_.
       2e éd. avec un nouveau chapitre "Un quidam nommé Sartre".
       Lettre-préface de Sartre. Paris: Editions du Seuil, 1965.

102   Jeanson, Francis. _Sartre par lui-même_. 2e éd. (Coll.
       "Microcosme"). Paris: Editions du Seuil, 1967.

103   Jeanson, Francis. _Jean-Paul Sartre_. (Coll. "Les Ecrivains
       devant Dieu", 9). Paris: Desclée de Brouwer, 1966.

104   Jeanson, Francis. _Sartre dans sa vie_. Paris: Editions du
       Seuil, 1974.

105   Jolivet, Régis. _Les Doctrines existentialistes de Kierk-
       egaard à Sartre_. Abbaye de Saint Wandrille: Editions de
       Fontenelle, 1948, 144-230.

106   Jolivet, Régis. _Le Problème de la mort chez Heidegger et
       Sartre_. Abbaye de Saint Wandrille: Editions de Fontenelle,
       1950.

107   Jolivet, Régis, _Sartre ou la théologie de l'absurde_. Paris:
       Arthème Fayard, 1965.

108   Joubert, Ingrid. _Aliénation et la liberté dans 'Les Chemins
       de la liberté' de Sartre_. Paris: Didier, 1973.

109   Juin, Hubert. _Jean-Paul Sartre ou la condition humaine_.
       Bruxelles: Editions de la Boétie, 1946.

110   Kanapa, Jean. _Comme si la lutte entière_. Paris: Nagel, 1946.

111   Kanapa, Jean. _L'Existentialisme n'est pas un humanisme_.
       Paris: Editions Socialses, 1947.

112   Lafarge, René. _La Philosophie de Sartre_. Toulouse: Privat,
       1967.

113   Laing, Ronald David et Cooper, David Graham. _Raison et vi-
       olence: dix ans de la philosophie de Sartre, 1950-1960_.
       Avant-propos de Sartre. Paris: Payot, 1972.

114   Las Vergnas, Raymond. _L'Affaire Sartre_. Paris: Haumont,
       1946.

115   Launay, Claude. Sartre, 'Le Diable et le bon Dieu': analyse
      critique. ("Profil d'une oeuvre", No. 15). Paris: Hatier,
      1970.

116   Laurent, Jacques. Paul (Bourget) et Jean-Paul (Sartre).
      Paris: Grasset, 1951.

117   Lacarme, Jacques, éd. Les Critiques de notre temps et
      Sartre. Paris: Garnier, 1973.

118   Lecherbonnier, Bernard. Huis Clos, Jean-Paul Sartre: analyse
      critique. Paris: Hatier, 1972.

119   Lecoeur, Yves. L'Escalier de Jean-Paul Sartre. Paris,
      Gallimard, 1956.

120   Lefebre, Luc J. L'Existentialisme est-il une philosophie?
      Paris: Editions Alsatia, 1946.

121   Lilar, Suzanne. A Propos de Sartre et de l'amour. Paris:
      Grasset, 1967.

122   Llech-Walter, Colette. Héros existentialistes dans l'oeuvre
      de Sartre. Perpignan: Centre Culturel Espérantiste, n.d.

123   Louis, Chanoine Michel. Humanisme et réligion, I: L'experi-
      ence athée, Nietzche, Sartre, Malraux. Paris: Aunônerie
      Catholique du Lycée Jeanson De Sailly, 1965.

124   Martin-Deslias, Noël. Jean-Paul Sartre ou la conscience
      ambiguë. Paris: Nagel, 1972.

125   Merleau-Ponty, Maurice. Les Aventures de la dialectique.
      Paris: Gallimard, 1955, 131-273.

126   Molnar, Thomas. Sartre, philosophe de la contestation.
      Paris: Editions de la Table Ronde, 1972.

127   Monthaye, Gaston. L'Athéisme, le communisme, et l'existen-
      tialisme. Paris: Librairie Mercure, 1949.

128   Mougin, Henri. La Sainte famille existentialiste. Paris:
      Editions Sociales, 1947.

129   Nahas, Helen. Etude de la femme dans la littérature fran-
      çaise: Jean-Paul Sartre et Simone de Beauvoir. Paris:
      Presses Universitaires de France, 1957.

130   Niel, André. Jean-Paul Sartre, héros et victime de la 'con-
       science malheureuse': essai sur le drame de la pensée oc-
       cidentale. Paris: Courrier du Livre, 1966.

131   Niel, André. Les grands appels de l'humanisme contemporain.
       Paris: Courrier du Livre, 1966.

132   Paissac, Henri. Le Dieu de Sartre. Paris: Arthaud, 1950.

133   Patté, Daniel. L'Athéisme d'un chrétien ou un chrétien à
       l'écoute de Sartre. Préface de Frantz J. Leenhardt.
       Paris: Nouvelles Editions Latines, 1965.

134   Presseault, Jacques. L'Etre-pour-autrui dans la philosophie
       de Sartre. Paris: Desclée de Brouwer; Montréal: Les
       Editions Bellarmin, 1970.

135   Prince, Gérald J. Métaphysique et technique dans l'oeuvre
       romanesque de Sartre. Genève: Droz, 1968.

136   Pruche, Benoît. Existentialisme et acte d'être. Paris:
       Arthaud, 1947.

137   Pruche, Benoît. L'Homme de Sartre. Paris: Arthaud,
       1949.

138   Raillard, Georges. 'La Nausée' de Jean-Paul Sartre. Paris:
       Classiques Hachette, 1972.

139   Royle, Peter. Sartre, L'Enfer et la liberté: études de 'Huis
       Clos' et des 'Mouches'. Québec: Presses de l'Université
       Laval, 1973.

140   Sébille, J., éd. Jean-Paul Sartre. 2e éd. (Coll. "Prob-
       lèmes", 2). Paris: Nathan, 1966.

141   Suhl, Benjamin. Jean-Paul Sartre, critique littéraire.
       Trans. from the English by Jean-Pierre Cottereau. Paris:
       Editions Universitaires, 1971.

142   Sulzer, Elisabeth. L'Engagement et le personnage chez
       Sartre. Winterthur: Hans Schellenberg, 1972.

143   Troisfontaines, Roger. Le Choix de Jean-Paul Sartre: exposé
       et critique de "L'Etre et le Néant". Paris: Aubier, 1945.

144   Varet, Gilbert. L'Ontologie de Sartre. Paris: Presses
       Universitaires de France, 1948.

145   Verstraeten, Pierre. Violence et éthique: esquisse d'une
       critique de la morale dialectique à partir du théâtre
       politique de Sartre. Paris: Gallimard, 1972.

146   Werner, Eric. De la violence au totalitarisme: essai sur la
       pensée de Camus et de Sartre. (Liberté de l'Esprit).
       Paris: Calmann-Levy, 1972.

                        BOOKS IN GERMAN

147   Biemel, Walter. Jean-Paul Sartre in Selbstzeugnissen und
       Bilddokumenten. Dargestellt von Walter Biemel. (Rowohlts
       Monographien, 87). Reinbek bei Hamburg: Rowohlt, 1967.

148   Galler, Dieter. Kretschmers Typologie in den dramatischen
       Charakteren Sartres. München: Huebner, 1967.

149   Gauger, Rosemarie. 'Littérature engagée' in Frankreich zur
       Zeit des Zweiten Weltkriegs. Die literarische Auseinan-
       dersetzung Sartres, Camus', Argons und Saint Exuperys mit
       der politischen Situation ihres Landes. Göttingen: Alfred
       Kümmerle, 1971.

150   Goldstein, Walter D. Jean-Paul Sartre und Martin Buber: Eine
       vergleischende Betrachtung von Existentialismus und Dialogik.
       Jerusalem: Mass, 1965.

151   Hana, Ghanam-George. Freiheit und Person: Eine Auseinander-
       setzung mit d. Darstellung Sartres. Müchen: Beck, 1965.

152   Hartmann, Klaus. Grundzüge der Ontologie Sartres in ihrem
       Verhältnis zu 'L'Etre et le néant'. Berlin: de Gruyter,
       1963.

153   Hartmann, Klaus. Sartres Sozialphilosophie: Eine Unter-
       suchung zu 'Critique de la raison dialectique'. Berlin:
       de Gruyter, 1966.

154   Hasenhüttl, Gotthold. Gott ohne Gott: Ein Dialog mit Jean-
       Paul Sartre, mit d. Weihnachtsspiel 'Bariona oder der
       Donnersohn' von Jean-Paul Sartre. Ubers. von Gotthold
       Hasenhüttl. Graz: Styria, 1972.

155   Haug, Wolfgang F. Jean-Paul Sartre und die Konstrukion des
       Absurden. Frankfurt am Main: Suhrkamp, 1966.

156   Holz, Hans Heinz. Jean-Paul Sartre: Darstellung und Kritik
      seiner Philosophie. Meisenheim am Glan: Westkulturverlag,
      Anton Hain, 1951.

157   Knecht, Ingbert. Sartres Theorie der Entfremdung. Bonn:
      Selbstverlag, 1972, 375 pp.

158   Kohut, Karl. 'Was ist Literatur'? Die Theorie der 'litté-
      rature engagée' bei Sartre. Marburg: Kohut, 1965.

159   Krauss, Henning. Die Praxis der 'Littérature engagée' im
      Werk Sartres, 1938-1949. (Studia Romanica, 20). Heidel-
      berg: C. Winter, 1970.

160   Krosigk, Frederich von. Philosophie und politische Aktion
      bei Sartre. München: Beck, 1969.

161   Kummer, Bernhard. Fehlentscheidung des deutschen Theaters:
      Jean-Paul Sartre, Kritik und Warnung. (Forschungsfragen
      unserer Zeit). Zeven, 1960.

162   Lausberg, Heinrich. Interpretationen dramatischer Dich-
      tungen, 2 volumes, München: Max Hueber, 1964. (Vol. I:
      Les Séquestrés; II: Huis-clos et La Putain respectueuse).

163   Moeller, Joseph. Absurdes Sein? Eine Auseinandersetzung
      mit der Ontologie Sartres. Stuttgart: Kohlhammer, 1959.

164   Mayer, Hans. Annerkungen zu Sartre. Robert Minder z. 70.
      Geburtstag gewidmet (Opuscula aux Wissenschaft und Dich-
      tung, 29). Pfullingen: Neske, 1972.

165   Otto, Maria. Reue und Freiheit: Versuch über ihre Bezie-
      hung im Ausgang von Sartres Drama (Symposium Philoso-
      phische Schriften, 6). Freiburg: Alber, 1961.

166   Panou, S. Dialektisches Denken: Sartre, Bloch, Garaudy.
      München: Uni-Cruck, 1973.

167   Pollman, Leo. Sartre und Camus: Literatur der Existenz.
      Stuttgart: Kohlhammer, 1967.

168   Richter, Liselotte. Jean-Paul Sartre; oder Die Philo-
      sophie des Zweipalts: Ein Vortrag mit Exkursen. Berlin:
      Chrono, 1949.

169   Roosli, Joseph. Die Existenzphilosophie: Anthropologie von
      Jean-Paul Sartre. (Annalen der philosophischen Gesell-

schaften Inner-Schweiz und Ostschweiz). V, No. 1-2, 1949.
Wed bei Eschenz, 1949.

170   Seel, Gerhard. Sartres Dialektik: Zur Methode und Begründung seiner Philosophie unter besonderer Berücksichtigung
der Subjekts-, Zeit- und Werttheorie. Bonn: Bouvier Verlag
H. Grundmann, 1971.

171   Streller-Justus, J. Zur Freiheit verurteilt: Ein Grundriss
der Philosophie Sartres. Hamburg, 1952.

172   Schwarz, Theodor. Jean-Paul Sartres 'Kritik der dialektischen Vernunft'. Berlin: Deutscher Verlag der Wissen-
schaften, 1967.

173   Spoerri, Theophil. Aufruf zum Widerstand: Die Herausfor-
derung Sartres. Konstanz: Bahm, 1965.

174   Vietta, Egon. Theologie ohne Gott: Versuch über die menschliche Existenz in der modernen französischen Philosophie. (Mit einem Anhang: 'Der Begriff der Freiheit bie
Sartre'). Hamburg: Hauswedell, 1948.

175   Vogel, Heinrich. Freiheit und Reise: Das Evangelium und
'Die Fliegen' von Sartre. Berlin: 1948.

176   Zehm, Günther Albrecht. Historische Vernunft und direkte
Aktion: Zur Politik und Philosophie Sartres. (Frankfurter
Studien z. Wissenschaft, von d. Politik, I). Stuttgart:
Klett, 1964.

177   Zehm, Günther Albrecht. Jean-Paul Sartre. (Friedrichs
Dramatiker des Welttheater, 8). Velber B. Hannover:
Friedrich, 1965.

BOOKS IN ITALIAN

178   Bausola, Adriano. Libertà e relazioni interpersonali.
Milano: Vita e Pensiero, 1973, 143 pp.

179   Bausola, Adriano. Il problema della libertà. Introduzione
a Sartre. Milano: CELUC, 1971, 152 pp.

180   Borello, Oreste. Studi su Sartre. (Biblioteca di Cultura
Filosofica, 29). Bologna: Capelli, 1964.

181   Canilli, Adele. Sartre e la ragione dialettica. (Sguardi
       su la filosofia contemporanea, 25). Torino: Edizione di
       Filosofia, 1961.

182   Cavaciuti, Santino. L'Ontologia di Jean-Paul Sartre. Pub-
       blicazione dell'Istituto di Filososofia, Facoltà di Ma-
       gister dell'Università di Genova, 7). Milano: Marzorati,
       1969.

183   Cera, Giovanni. Sartre tra ideologia e storia. (Biblioteca
       di cultura moderna, 723). Bari: Laterza, 1972.

184   Chieppa, Vincenzo. Pirandello e Sartre. Firenze: Kursaal,
       1967.

185   Chiodi, Pietro. Sartre e il marxismo. Milano: Feltrinelli,
       1965.

186   Clava, Giorgio. Gratutito nichilismo di Sartre. (Sguardi
       su la filosofia contemporanea, 56). Torino: Edizione di
       'Filosofia', 1964.

187   Cortese, Luigi. Il problema della prassi in Sartre. Roma:
       Clatanisetta, S. Sciascia, 1966.

188   D'Alberti, Sarah. Momenti dell'esistenzialismo europea:
       crisi dell'esistenza in Marcel, Sartre, Abbagnano e suoi
       riflessi nel marxismo. (Collana di saggi e monografie,
       30). Palermo: S.F. Flaccovio, 1972.

189   Falconi, Carlo. Jean-Paul Sartre. Modena: Guanda, 1949.

190   Faucitano, Filiberto. 'L'Essere e il nulla' di Jean-Paul
       Sartre. Napoli: S. Iodice, 1959.

191   Fé, Franco. Sartre e il comunismo. (Nostro tempo, 15).
       Firenze: La Nuova Italia, 1970.

192   Jeanson, Francis. Sartre. Traduzione di Pietro Lazagna.
       Bologna: Dehoniane, 1971, 196 pp.

193   Gentiloni, Silveri F. Jean-Paul Sartre contro la speranza.
       Roma: Civilta Cattolica, 1952.

194   Manno, Ambrogio. L'Esistenzialismo di Jean-Paul Sartre.
       Napoli: Istituto Superiore di Scienze e Lettere, 1958.

195   Moravia, Sergio. Introduzione a Sartre. Bari: Laterza,
       1973, 175 pp.

196   Pagano, Giacoma Maria. Sartre e la dialettica. Napoli:
       Giannini, 1970.

197   Papone, Annagrazia. Esistenze e corporeità in Sartre: Dalle
       prime opera all' 'Essere e il nulla'. (Istituto di Filoso-
       fia della Facoltà de Lettere e Filosofia dell'Università
       de Genova). Firenze: F. Le Monnier, 1969.

198   Pellegrino, Giuseppe. Gli operai della nostra storia:
       Nietzsche, Freud, Sartre. (Segui dei tempi, 1971).
       Fossano: Esperienze, 1971.

199   Rovalti, Pier Aldo. Che Cosa ha veramente detto Sartre?
       Roma, Ubaldini, 1969.

200   Senofonte, Ciro. Sartre e Merleau-Ponty. (Università degli
       studi di Salerno. Collana di studi et testi, 9). Napoli:
       Libreria scientifica Editrice, 1972.

201   Stefanini, Mario. La Libertà esistenziale in Jean-Paul
       Sartre. Milano: Vita e Pensiero, 1949.

BOOKS IN SPANISH

202   Brufau-Prats, Jaime. Lineas fondamentales de la ontología
       y antropología de Sartre en 'L'Etre et le néant'. Sala-
       manca: Universidad de Salamanca, 1971.

203   Brufau-Prats, Jaime. Moral, vida social y derecho en Jean-
       Paul Sartre. (Coll. "Acta Salmanlicensis", 20). Sala-
       ca: Universidad de Salamanca, 1967.

204   Chariot, Pierre. Sartre y el existencialismo. (Enciclopedia
       Popular Illustrada). Barcelona: Plaza and James, 1963.

205   Dalma, Juan. Jean-Paul Sartre. Buenos Aires: Centro Editor
       de America Latina, 1968.

206   Desan, Wilfrid. El marxismo de Jean-Paul Sartre. Buenos
       Aires: Paidos, 1971.

207   Fantone, Vicente. El existencialismo y la libertad creadora:
      Una critica al existencialismo de Sartre. Buenos Aires:
      Argos, 1948.

208   Frutos, Eugenio. El humanismo y la moral de Sartre. Sara-
      gossa, 1949.

209   Gallo, Blas Raul. Jean-Paul Sartre y el marxismo. Buenos
      Aires: Quetzal, 1966.

210   Garcia-Sabell, D. Tres sintomas de Europa: J. Joyce, V. van
      Gogh, Jean-Paul Sartre. Madrid: Revista de Occidente, 1968.

211   Garmendia, Guillermina. Jean-Paul Sartre. Buenos Aires:
      Centro Editor de America Latina, 1967.

212   Gonzales Mas, Ezequiel. Sartre y Camus: el nuevo espíritu de
      la literatura francesa. Universidad de Guayaquil, 1959.

213   Herra, R.A. Sartre y los prolegómenos a la antropología.
      (Universidad de Costa Rica, ser. Filosofia, 28). San José:
      Ciudad Univ. Rodrigo Facio, 1968.

214   Maciel, Luis Carlos. Sartre, vida y obra. Rio de Janeiro:
      José Alvaro, 1967.

215   Marin Ibanez, Ricardo. Libertad y compromiso en Sartre.
      Valencia, 1959. Disputacion provincial de Valencia, 1959.

216   Pintos, Juan Luis. El ateismo del ultimo Sartre: La linea
      evolutiva de su actitud atea. Madrid: Razón y Fé Editorial,
      1968.

217   Quiles, Ismael. Sartre y su existencialismo. Madrid: Espasa-
      Calpe, 1967.

218   Quiles, Ismael. Jean-Paul Sartre: El existencialismo del
      absurdo. 2nd ed. (La Filosofia de nuestro tiempo, 5).
      Buenos Aires: Espasa-Calpe.

219   Riu, Federico. Ensayos sobre Sartre. Caracas: Monte Avila,
      1968.

220   Sanchez, Villaseñor, José. Introducción al pensamiento de
      Sartre. Mexico: Editorial Jus, 1950.

221   Seijas, Rudolfo. Carta a Sartre, y otros ensayos. Buenos
      Aires: Editorial Goyanarte, 1962.

222   Sotelo, Ignacio. Sartre y la razón dialectica. Madrid:
       Tecnos, 1967.

223   Stern, Alfred. La filosofia de Sartre y el psisoanalisis
       existencialista. 2a. ed. revisida y ampliada por el autor.
       Buenos Aires: Co. General Fabril, 1962.

224   Troisfontaines, Roger. El existencialismo ateo de Sartre.
       Alcoy: Marfil, 1949.

225   Vidiella, J. De Kierkegaard a Sartre. Barcelona: Bruguera,
       1963.

226   Virasoro, Rafael. Existencialismo y moral: Heidegger y
       Sartre. Sante Fé, Argentina: Libreria y Editorial
       Castellivi, 1957.

BOOKS IN DUTCH

227   Arntz, Joseph. De liefde in de ontologie van Sartre.
       Nijmegen: Drukkerij Gebr. Janssen, 1960.

228   Bauters, Paul. Jean-Paul Sartre. (Ontmoetingen, 51).
       Bruges: Desclée de Brouwer, 1964.

229   Carp, E.A.D.E. Teilhard, Jung, en Sartre over evolutie.
       (Aula-boeken, 426). Utrecht: Het Spectrum, 1969.

230   Carp, E.A.D.E. Zelfonthulling in het mensbeeld van Sartre.
       Antwerpen: Standaard Wetenschappelijke Uitgeverij; Rotter-
       dam: Universitaire Pers Rotterdam, 1970.

231   Eeden, H. van. De Roschach-proef en de verbeeldings-phenome-
       nologie van Sartre. Nijmegen: Dekker and Van de Vegt, 1949.

232   Flam, Leopold. De walg van Jean-Paul Sartre. Vilvoorde:
       Dethier, 1960.

233   Miskotte, Kornelis H. Barth over Sartre. Dies-College.
       Leiden: Universitaire Pers Leiden, 1951.

234   Nauta, Lolle W. Jean-Paul Sartre. Baarn: Het Wereldvenster,
       1966.

235   Niftrik, Gerrit Cornilis van. De Boodschap van Sartre.
       Nijkerk: G.F. Callenbach, 1967.

236   Plessen, Jacques. Inleiding tot het denken van Sartre.
       7th dr. (Hoofdfiguren van het menselijk denken, 5).
       Assen: Born, 1959.

237   Struyker Boudier, C.E.M. Jean-Paul Sartre: Een inleiding
       tot zijn denken. Tielt-Den Haag: Lannoo, 1967.

238   Verhoeff, Johan Peter. Sartre als toneelschrijver: Een
       literairkritische studie. Amsterdam: Groningen, 1962.

239   Zuidema, Sytse Ulbe. Nacht zonder dageraad naar aanleiding
       van het atheistisch en nihilistisch existentialisme van
       Sartre. Franeker: Wever, 1948.

BOOKS IN OTHER LANGUAGES

240   al-Didi, 'Abd al-Fattah. Falsafat Sartar ma'a tarjamat min
       a'malih. 1971.

241   al'Hifni, 'Abd al Mun 'im. al-Wujudiyah fi. hayat Sartar.
       1967, 136 pp.

242   Amaral Veira, Roberto Attila do. Sartre e a revolta do
       nosso tempo. Rio: Forense, 1967, 116 pp.

243   Bornheim, Gerd. A. Sartre: Metafisica e existencialismo.
       Sao Paulo: Perspectiva, 1971.

244   Garaudy, Roger. Jean-Paul Sartre ve Marxisme. Ceviren:
       Selahattin Hilav. 2.Baski. Istanbul, 1965.

245   Gemmer, Anders. Jean-Paul Sartre Ecksistentialism em
       kritisk Vurdering. Copenhagen: Munsgaard, 1947.

246   Gemmer, Anders. Czlowiek, swiat rzezy, Bog w filozofil
       Sartre'a. Warszawa: Panstwowe Wydawnicintwo Naukowe,
       1969.

247   Kamil, Fu'ad. al-Ghayr fifalsafat Sartar, 1967, 87 pp.

248   Kuznetov, Vatalii Nikolaevich. Zan-Pol Sartr o ekzisten-
       tializm. Moscow: Izd. MGU, 1969, 286 pp.

249   Tarabishi, Jurj. Sartar wa-al-Markisiyah, 1964, 189 pp.

PART II

DOCTORAL DISSERTATIONS

DOCTORAL DISSERTATIONS

250   Andrews, Jeffery. "Romantic Myth in the Works of Sartre."
       Dissertation, Illinois Univ.

251   Archer, Raymond Hardy. "Hume and Sartre on the Self." Dis-
       sertation Abstracts, 34, No. 3, September 1973, pp. 1317-
       1318A (Rice Univ.).

252   Aronson, Alan R. "Art and Freedom in Sartre." Dissertation
       Abstracts, 29, No. 8, 1969, p. 2747A (Brandeis Univ.,
       1968).

253   Arras, John D. "A Critique of Existential Ethics." Disser-
       tation Abstracts, 33, No. 10, April 1973, p. 5771A (North-
       western Univ., 1972).

254   Aycock, Charles B. "The Journal of Dislodgement: The Possi-
       bilities and Their Use by Rilke and Sartre." Dissertation
       Abstracts, 32, No. 6, December 1971, p. 3289A.

255   Bauer, George H. "Art and the Artist in the Creative Works
       and Critical Essays of Sartre." Dissertation Abstracts,
       28, No 6, December 1971, p. 2236A (Indiana Univ., 1967).

256   Beard, Donald B. "A House of Conceits: A Study of the Drama
       of Sartre, Camus, Ionesco and Beckett." Dissertation Ab-
       stracts, 29, 1969, p. 198A (Univ. of Redlands, 1969).

257   Bell, Linda Ann. "An Analysis of Moral Judgment in Connection
       with Bad Faith and Inauthenticity in the Early Philosophy
       of Jean-Paul Sartre." Dissertation Abstracts, 34, No. 2,
       August 1973, pp. 817-818A (Emory Univ.).

258   Belli, Angela. "The Use of Greek Mythological Themes and
       Characters in Twentieth Century Drama." Dissertation Ab-
       stracts, 27, No. 11, May 1967, p. 3832A.

259   Bettler, Alan R. "A Chronicle of the Beginnings of French
       Existentialism." Dissertation Abstracts, 31, No. 5, No-
       vember 1970, p. 2432A.

260   Bhadra, Mrinal K. "A Critical Study of Sartre's Ontology of
       Consciousness." Dissertation Abstracts, 32, No. 4, 1971,
       p. 2128A (Univ. of Oklahoma, 1971).

261   Bingham, William L. "The Journal as Literary Form." Disser-
       tation Abstracts, 30, No. 4, October 1969, p. 1552A.

262   Bluestone, Natalie S.H.   "Time and Consciousness in Sartre
       and William James." Dissertation Abstracts, 1963, p. 143A
       (John Hopkins Univ., 1962).

263   Blundo, Virginia C.   "Sartre's Concept of Bad Faith: Philo-
       sophical, Literary and Psychological Interpretations."
       Dissertation Abstracts, 35, No. 1, July 1974, p. 510A.

264   Boros, Marie-Denise.   "Le thème de la séquestration dans
       l'oeuvre littéraire de Sartre." Dissertation Abstracts,
       25, December 1964, pp. 3565-3566A (Univ. of California at
       Los Angeles, 1964).

265   Boudreaux, Michael M.   "Nothingness: The Adventures of the
       For-Itself." Dissertation Abstracts, 34, May 1974, p.
       7275A (Univ. of Missouri at Columbia, 1973).

266   Brantl, George E.   "The Tragic Commitment: An Essay in Exis-
       tentialist Metaphysics." Dissertation Abstracts, 17, 1957,
       p. 1783A (Columbia Univ.).

267   Bremen, Rudolph S.   "Free Man's Responsibilities in the The-
       ater of Sartre." Dissertation Abstracts, 21, No. 3, Septem-
       ber 1960, p. 619A (Univ. of Pittsburgh, 1960).

268   Brooks, Rolph P., Jr.   "Sartre's Existential Psychoanalysis."
       Dissertation Abstracts, 29, 1968, p. 243A (Duquesne Univ.,
       1968).

269   Bryant, D.S.   "Bases for Educational Theory in the Philosophy
       of Sartre." Dissertation Abstracts, 27, No. 7, 1966, p.
       2003A (Stanford Univ., 1966).

270   Bukala, Casimir R.   "Intersubjectivity in Sartre's Dramatic
       Philosophy." Dissertation Abstracts, 31, No. 9, 1970,
       p. 4834A (Boston College, 1970).

271   Burian, Jarka M.   "A Study of Twentieth Century Adaptation
       of the Greek Atreidae Dramas." Dissertation Abstracts, 15,
       1955, p. 2524A (Cornell Univ., 1954).

272   Burke, David R.   "An Examination of Sartre's Conception of
       Freedom." Dissertation Abstracts, 26, No. 8, February 1966,
       pp. 4725-4726A (Michigan State Univ., 1965).

273   Campbell, Karlyn K.   "The Rhetorical Implications of the Phi-
       losophy of Sartre." Dissertation Abstracts, 29, No. 9
       April 1969, p. 3701A (Univ. of Minnesota, 1968).

274   Carandang, A.L. "Sartre and His Atheism." Dissertation Ab-
      stracts, 27, No. 8, February 1967, p. 2555A (Univ. of Notre
      Dame, 1966).

275   Carricaburu, Joseph. "Sartre et Marx." Dissertation, Univ.
      of Southern California at Los Angeles.

276   Chung, Ha Eun. "Alienation in the Writings of Hegel, Marx,
      and the Existentialists." Dissertation Abstracts, 23, 1962,
      p. 162A (Pittsburgh Theological Seminary, 1961).

277   Coleman, Michael. "Beyond Sartre: Toward a Phenomenologi-
      cally Evolving Consciousness." Univ. of California, Santa
      Barbara, 1972.

278   Colwell, Charles C. "The Judgment of Literature." Disserta-
      tion Abstracts, 20, No. 5, November 1959, pp. 1782-1783A
      (Emory Univ., 1958).

279   Cording, Richard A. "Sartre's Theory of Freedom." Disserta-
      tion Abstracts, 30, No. 4, October 1969, pp. 1595-1596A
      (Univ. of Missouri at Columbia, 1969).

280   Craver, Samuel M. "Individuality and Education: A Compara-
      tive Study of the Philosophies of John Dewey and Sartre."
      Dissertation Abstracts, 32, No. 9, 1972, p. 4831A
      (Univ. of North Carolina at Chapel Hill, 1971).

281   Crawford, Maria A. "An Existential Vision of Man in the
      Fiction of Witold Gombrowicz and Selected Novels by Sartre,
      Sarraute, Robbe-Grillet and Michel Butor." Dissertation
      Abstracts, 33, No. 11, 1971, p. 6107A (Catholic Univ. of
      America).

282   Cronkite, Roland F. "The Metaphysics of Love in Contempor-
      ary Existentialism with Special Emphasis on Sartre." Dis-
      sertation Abstracts, 31, No. 11, 1971, p. 6107A (Catholic
      Univ. of America).

283   Culbertson, Diana. "Twentieth Century Autobiography: Yeats,
      Sartre, and Nabokov: Studies in Structure and Form." Dis-
      sertation Abstracts, 32, No. 12, 1972, p. 6968A (Univ. of
      North Carolina at Chapel Hill, 1971).

284   Delue, Steven M. "On the Marxism of Sartre in the Light of
      Jean-Jacques Rousseau: An Analysis of 'Critique de la raison
      dialectique'." Dissertation Abstracts, 32, No. 8, February
      1972, p. 4674A (Univ. of Washington, 1971).

285   Desan, Wilfrid. "The Ontology of Sartre: Essay of Systemati-
       zation and Critique." Harvard Univ., 1951.

286   Dickenson, Donald H. "Problems of Religion and Myth in Mod-
       ern Drama, 1914-1950." Dissertation Abstracts, 22, No. 10,
       April 1962, p. 3773A (Northwestern Univ.).

287   Dina, Stephen. "Causality and Consciousness in Sartre's
       Theory of Knowledge." Dissertation Abstracts, 35, No. 2,
       August 1974, p. 1156A (Marquette Univ., 1974).

288   Doherty, Cyril M. "The Theme of Culpability in the Literary
       Works of Sartre." Dissertation Abstracts, 34, April 1974,
       p. 6635A (Univ. of Wisconsin, 1973).

289   Donovan, Josephine C. "Gnosticism in Modern Literature: A
       Study of Selected Works of Camus, Sartre, Hesse and Kafka."
       Dissertation Abstracts, 32, No. 10, April 1972, p. 5784A
       (Univ. of Wisconsin, 1971).

290   Dunne, R. "The Validity of Merleau-Ponty's Criticism of
       Sartre's Marxism." Univ. of Ottawa, 1972.

291   Easterling, Ilda M. "L'humour de Sartre." Dissertation Ab-
       stracts, 29, No. 9, March 1969, pp. 3132-3133A (Brigham
       Young Univ., 1968).

292   Eberbach, Margaret L. "The Role of the Reader: A Study of Ten
       French Novels of the Twentieth Century." Dissertation Ab-
       stracts, 27, 1966, pp. 769-770A (New York Univ.).

293   Edmondson, P.E. "Sartrean Freedom: A Changing Perspective."
       Dissertation Abstracts, 28, No. 9, March 1968, p. 3726A
       (Duke Univ., 1967).

294   Elveton, R.O. "The Concept of Phenomenon." Dissertation Ab-
       stracts, 28, 1968, p. 3712A (Northwestern Univ., 1967).

295   Ellis, Helen E. "Sunday School and Sartre: The Tension in
       Robert Penn Warren's Novels." Dissertation Abstracts, 34,
       January 1974, p. 4257A (Univ. of Massachusetts, 1973).

296   Emonet, Pierre-Marie, O.P. "Le thème de la liberté dans la
       philosophie de Sartre." Angelicum, Rome, 1949.

297   Fell, Joseph J. "A Critique of Sartre's Theory of Emotion."
       Dissertation Abstracts, 28, No. 11, May 1968, p. 4663A
       (Columbia Univ., 1963).

298 Fisher, Rosemary F. "Man and Freedom in Sartre: Two Stages in His Thought." _Dissertation Abstracts_, 33, No. 3, September 1972, p. 1195A (St. Louis Univ., 1972).

299 Flynn, Bernard C. "Sartre's Doctrine of Freedom: The Development of Sartre's Philosophy from Ontology to Philosophical Anthropology." Duquesne Univ., 1968.

300 Flynn, Thomas R. "'We Are All Assassins': Sartre and the Problem of Collective Responsibility." Columbia Univ., 1971.

301 Fort, Keith. "Beyond Despair: A Comparative Study of Four Novels." _Dissertation Abstracts_, 25, 1964, p. 2511A (Univ. of Minnesota, 1964).

302 Franks, Thomas H. "Sartre's Concept of Sincerity." _Dissertation Abstracts_, 32, No. 11, May 1972, p. 6487A (Univ. of Michigan, 1971).

303 Fu, Charles. "Contemporary Ethical Autonomism: A Critical Study of Sartre and Hare." _Dissertation Abstracts_, 30, No. 7, 1970, p. 3053A (Univ. of Illinois, Urbana, 1968).

304 Furhmann, Gunther. "Der Atriden-Mythos im modernen Drama." Wurzburg Univ., 1950.

305 Gahamanyi, Celestin. "La conception de la liberté chez Sartre et Merleau-Ponty." Thèse de Lettres, Univ. de Fribourg, Suisse, 1967.

306 Gaither, Mary E. "Ancient and Modern Concepts of the Tragic Hero." _Dissertation Abstracts_, 13, 1953, p. 547A (Indiana Univ.).

307 Garris, N. Norman. "Education as Existential Liberation: A Study of the Educational Significance of Sartrean Authenticity." _Dissertation Abstracts_, 32, No. 8, February 1972, p. 4488A (Univ. of California at Los Angeles, 1971).

308 Gerrard, Charlotte F. "Heresy on the French Stage, 1950-1952, in Le Profanateur, Malatesta, Le Diable et le bon Dieu and Bacchus." _Dissertation Abstracts_, 27, 1966, p. 772A (Univ. of Pittsburgh, 1965).

309 Greene, Norman J. "Sartre as Critic of Political Ideologies." _Dissertation Abstracts_, 20, No. 5, 1959, p. 1847A (Univ. of Michigan, 1958).

310   Halpern, Joseph. "Sartre's Critical Itinerary, 1931-1972."
       Dissertation Abstracts, 33, No. 5, November 1972, p. 2375A
       (Stanford Univ., 1972).

310a   Handler, Philip L.   "Joyce in France, 1920-1959." Disserta-
       tion Abstracts, 27, p. 476 (Columbia Univ., 1966).

311   Hanly, C.M.T.   "The Nature of Freedom in the Philosophy of
       Sartre." Dissertation Abstracts, 27, No. 3, September
       1966, p. 798A (Univ. of Toronto, 1964).

312   Harrington, Catherine S.   "Southern Fiction and the Quest for
       Identity." Dissertation Abstracts, 25, 1964, pp. 1210-
       1211A (Univ. of Washington, 1963).

313   Hellerich, G.   "An Investigation into the Education Implica-
       tions of Sartre's Notion of 'Being-With' and the Reaction
       of Martin Buber." Dissertation Abstracts, 28, No. 12,
       June 1968, p. 4951A (Univ. of Kansas, 1967).

314   Hitz, Hermann.   "Der Character des sartreschen Humanismus in
       begriffsanslytischer Hinsicht: Die Funktion des Theorems vom
       Urentwurf." Univ. of Wurzburg, 1959.

315   Hoffman, K.   "Existential Philosophy: A Study of Its Past and
       Present Form." Harvard Univ., 1949.

316   Hoy, Nancy.   "The Theme of Nostalgia for the Lost Paradise of
       Childhood in Sartre's Fiction." Dissertation Abstracts, 32,
       No. 10, April 1972, p. 5791A (New York Univ., 1971).

317   Jameson, Fredric.   "The Origins of Sartre's Style." Yale
       Univ., 1959.

318   Jaquette, William A.   "Value, Nothingness and Sartre." Dis-
       sertation Abstracts, 30, No. 8, February 1970, p. 3503A.

319   John, S.   "The Literary Technique of Sartre, with Special Ref-
       erence to Imagery." Wales Univ., 1958.

320   Jones, Robert E.   "The Exile Hero in Contemporary Drama."
       Dissertation Abstracts, 14, 1954, pp. 1724-1725A (Columbia
       Univ., 1954).

321   Jones, William.   "The Development of the Social Philosophy of
       Sartre." Dissertation Abstracts, 31, No. 9, 1971, p. 4840A
       (Univ. of Notre Dame, 1970).

322   Jones, William R. "Sartre's Philosophical Anthropology in
       Relation to His Ethics: A Criticism of Selected Critics."
       Dissertation Abstracts, 31, No. 1, July 1970, p. 425A (Brown
       Univ., 1969).

323   Joubert, Ingrid. "Aliénation et liberté dans 'Les Chemins de
       la liberté de Sartre." Dissertation Abstracts, 31, January
       1971, pp. 3552-3553A (Univ. of Oregon, 1970).

324   Kazanian, Sonia. "Sartre en Roumanie." Dissertation, Univ.
       of Califcrnia at Los Angeles.

325   Kenevan, Phillis B. "Time Consciousness, and the Ego in the
       Philosophy of Sartre." Dissertation Abstracts, 30, No. 7,
       1970, p. 3054A (Northwestern Univ., 1969).

326   Kennard, Jean E. "Towards a Novel of the Absurd: A Study of
       the Relationship Between the Concept of the Absurd as De-
       fined in the Works of Sartre and Camus and Ideas and Forms
       in the Fiction of Barth, Beckett, N. Dennis Hiller, J.
       Purdy." Dissertation Abstracts, 29, 1968, p. 3144A (Ber-
       keley, California).

327   Kingston, F. Temple. "A Comparison of Christian and Non-
       Christian Existentialism as Exemplified by the Works of
       Contemporary French Writers." Oxford, Christ Church, 1954.

328   Klein, Maxine. "Theater of Crisis: A Study of the Plays of
       Sartre and Camus." Dissertation Abstracts, 24, No. 9, March
       1964, p. 3881A (Cornell Univ., 1963).

329   Kohut, Karl. "Was ist Literatur? Die Theorie der 'littérature
       engagée' bei Sartre." Inaugural dissertation, Marburg
       Univ., 1965.

330   Kowatzki, Irmgard. "Der Begriff des Spiels als aesthetisches
       Phaenomen von Schiller bis Sartre." Dissertation Abstracts,
       30, No. 12, 1970, p. 5448A (Stanford Univ., 1969).

331   Kripinski, Wlodnemierz. "Essai d'analyse des structures thé-
       matiques chez Pirandello et chez certains écrivains fran-
       çais." Univ. de Strasbourg, 1967.

332   Leefmans, Bert M.P. "Modern Tragedy: Five Adaptations of 'Or-
       esteia' and 'Oedipus the King'." Dissertation Abstracts,
       14, 1954, pp. 127-128A (Columbia Univ.).

333   Lehan, Richard. "Existentialism and the Modern American
       Novel." Dissertation Abstracts, 20, No. 2, October 1959,
       p. 1365A (Univ. of Wisconsin, 1958).

334   Leiner, Jacqueline. "Nizan et Sartre." Univ. de Paris, 1968.

335   Lessing, Arthur. "Man is Free: A Critical Study of the Con-
       ception of Human Freedom in the Philosophies of Heidegger
       and Sartre." Dissertation Abstracts. 28, 1967, p. 1470A
       (Tulane Univ., 1966).

336   Lindermayer, Eric Ray. "Jean-Paul Sartre: Original Choice."
       Dissertation Abstracts, 35, No. 10, April 1975, p. 6762A
       (Columbia Univ.).

337   Long, Madeleine. "Sartrean Themes in Contemporary American
       Literature." Dissertation Abstracts, 28, No. 4, 1967, p.
       1439A (Columbia Univ.).

338   Lovitt, C.W. "Sartre: Saint Genet, comédien et martyr,
       Sartre's Use of Genet." Dissertation Abstracts, 27, 1966,
       p. 506A.

339   Lucio, Luellen Gold. "The Writer as Public Figure: Mailer,
       Sartre, Solzhenitsyn, An Essay in the Sociology of Litera-
       ture." Dissertation Abstracts, 34, No. 6, December 1973,
       p. 3411A (Yale Univ.).

340   Malhotra, Ashok K. "'Nausea': An Expression of Sartre's
       Existential Philosophy." Dissertation Abstracts, 30, No.
       12, 1970, p. 5483A (Univ. of Hawaii).

341   Markus, Thomas B. "The Concept of Communion in the Modern
       French Theater." Dissertation Abstracts, 23, No. 11, May
       1963, pp. 4460-4461A (Tulane Univ.).

342   McBride, William L. "The Concept of Fundamental Change in Law
       and Society." Dissertation Abstracts, 25, No. 11, May 1965,
       pp. 6684-6685A (Yale Univ., 1964).

343   McCall, Dorothy K. "Action and Its Image: A Critical Study of
       the Plays of Sartre." Dissertation Abstracts, 28, No. 2,
       August 1967, p. 684A (Columbia Univ., 1967).

344   McClusky, John E. "A Dilemma of Existential Political Theory:
       An Analysis of Political Cohesion and Freedom in the Wri-
       tings of Sartre and H. Arendt." Univ. of Southern Califor-
       nia at Berkeley, 1971.

345   McIlvain, Betty T.   "Point of View in Three Contemporary Works
        of Fiction." Dissertation Abstracts, 29, No. 2, August
        1968, p. 610A.

346   McIntire, Russel M.   "Some Implications of Sartre's Concept of
        Consciousness For a Theory of Human Action." Dissertation
        Abstracts, 33, No. 12, June 1973, p. 6968A (Vanderbilt
        Univ., 1972).

347   McKenna, Andrew J.   "Baudelaire and Sartre: A Study in Com-
        parative Analysis." Dissertation Abstracts, 31, No. 7,
        January 1971, p. 3556A (Johns Hopkins Univ.).

348   Mehlman, Jeffrey.   "A Structural Study of Autobiography:
        Proust, Leiris, Sartre, Lévi-Strauss." Dissertation Ab-
        stracts, 33, No. 1, July 1972, p. 320A (Yale Univ., 1971).

349   Miedzianogora, Miriam.   "Gilbert Ryle and Sartre: A Compara-
        tive Study of Two Theories of Mind." Dissertation Ab-
        stracts, 26, No. 8, February 1966, p. 4732A (Columbia Univ.,
        1964).

350   Molnar, Thomas S.   "Fictional Philosophy in France: The Mod-
        ern Approach to Philosophy." Dissertation Abstracts, 13,
        No. 1, February 1953, pp. 98-99A (Columbia Univ.).

351   Morea, Rachelle.   "Viscosity and Violence in Sartre's Novels."
        Dissertation Abstracts, 34, No. 12, June 1974, p. 7769A
        (New York Univ., 1973).

352   Morris, Phyllis A.S.   "Sartre's Concept of a Person." Dis-
        sertation Abstracts, 30, No. 5, November 1969, p. 2081A
        (Univ. of Michigan, 1969).

353   Moyano, Pedro B.   "L'homme libre à la lumière de la phénomé-
        nologie ontologique." Louvain Univ., 1954.

354   Murphy, Richard T.   "Phenomenology and the Dialectic: A Study
        of Pre-Reflexive Consciousness in the Phenomenological
        Theories of Husserl, Sartre and Merleau-Ponty." Disserta-
        tion Abstracts, 24, No. 2, August 1963, pp. 779-780A (Ford-
        ham Univ.).

355   Nahas, Helen.   "Etude de la femme dans la littérature existen-
        tielle française: Sartre et Simone de Beauvoir." Disserta-
        tion Abstracts, 14, No. 8, 1954, p. 1220A (Univ. of Minne-
        sota, 1954).

356   Nasaw, David George. "Jean-Paul Sartre: Apprenticeship in
      History (1925-1945)" Dissertation Abstracts, 34, No. 6,
      December 1973, pp. 3314-3315A (Columbia Univ.).

357   Natanson, Maurice. "A Critical Analysis of the Foundations
      and Phenomenological Structure of the Ontology of Sartre."
      Univ. of Nebraska, 1950.

358   Nordstrom, Louis D. "Sartre and Evil: A Study of Saint Genet,
      Artist and Martyr." Columbia Univ., 1974.

359   O'Brien, Robert J. "Ego, Self and Person: A Study in Sartre's
      Phenomenological Psychology and Ontology." Dissertation Ab-
      stracts, 33, No. 12, June 1973, p. 6970A (Univ. of Califor-
      nia, Santa Cruz, 1971).

360   Odini, Eleni M. "Sartre's Contribution to the Phenomenology
      of Marxism." Dissertation Abstracts, 35, No. 1, July 1974,
      p. 539A.

361   O'Neill, William F. "Sartre's Concept of Freedom and its Im-
      plications for American Education." Univ. of Southern Cal-
      ifornia, 1958.

362   Overholt, George E. "Freedom, Facticity and Education: The
      Educational Implications of Sartrean Existentialism." Dis-
      sertation Abstracts, 30, No. 10, 1970, p. 4336A (Ohio State
      Univ., 1969).

363   Paribatra, Marsi. "Le romantisme contemporain." Univ. de
      Paris, 1954.

364   Patterson, Olanda. "Solitude and Communication in the Works
      of Sartre and Camus." Dissertation Abstracts, 25, No. 7,
      January 1965, p. 4154A (Stanford Univ. 1964).

365   Penick, Edwin A. "A Theological Critique of the Interpreta-
      tion of Man in the Fiction and Drama of Faulkner, Heming-
      way, Sartre and Camus." Yale Univ., 1954.

366   Plank, William G. "Sartre and Surrealism." Dissertation Ab-
      stracts, 33, No. 8, February 1973, p. 4429A (Univ. of Wash-
      ington, 1972).

367   Ponasse, Lorris R. "Sartre dramaturge." Univ. of Chicago,
      1972.

368   Portman, Stephen G. "The Problem of Values and Jean-Paul
       Sartre's Existential Psychoanalysis." Dissertation Ab-
       stracts, 32, No. 7, January 1972, p. 4066A (Univ. of New
       Mexico).

369   Powell, Elton George. "The Thematic Structure of Jean-Paul
       Sartre's Les Chemins de la liberté." Dissertation Ab-
       stracts, 34, No. 1, July 1973, pp. 333-334A (Univ. of North
       Carolina).

370   Pranger, R. "The Problem of Citizenship in the Action
       Theories of Modern Social Sciences and Existentialism."
       Berkeley, California, 1961.

371   Prince, Gérald J. "Métaphysique et technique dans l'oeuvre
       romanesque de Sartre." Dissertation Abstracts, 30, No. 1,
       July 1969, pp. 335-336A (Brown Univ., 1967).

372   Quinn, Bernard J. "Sartre on Violence: A Political, Philo-
       sophical and Literary Study." Dissertation Abstracts, 31,
       1971, p. 4177A (Louisiana State Univ.).

373   Ramwez, Alain Daniel. "Jean-Paul Sartre's Review 'Les Temps
       Modernes' (1945-1952): A Literary History." Dissertation
       Abstracts, 35, No. 9, March 1975, p. 6155A (Univ. of Mis-
       souri at Columbia, 1974).

374   Ratanaku, Pinit. "The Self is Freedom: A Critical Study of
       Sartre's Philosophy of Freedom." Dissertation Abstracts,
       31, No. 7, 1971, p. 3601A (Yale Univ., 1970).

375   Rauch, Leo. "Intentionality and Its Development in the Phe-
       nomenological Psychology of Edmund Husserl." Dissertation
       Abstracts, 29, 1968, pp. 937-938A (New York Univ., 1968).

376   Ray, F.L. "An Analytical Study of Three Representative Exis-
       tential Dramas of Sartre in Terms of Aristotelian Structural
       Criteria of Tragedy." Dissertation Abstracts, 27, 1967, p.
       2652A (Univ. of Southern California, 1966).

377   Reid, Joel O. "Existentialism in Black American Literature."
       Dissertation Abstracts, 35, No. 3, September 1974, p. 1708A
       (Claremont Graduate School, 1973).

378   Richards, Lewis A. "The Literary Styles of Sartre and Faulk-
       ner: An Analysis, Comparison and Contrast." Dissertation
       Abstracts, 24, No. 9, March 1964, pp. 3755-3756A (Univ. of
       California at Los Angeles, 1963).

379   Rico, Lucien A. "Le réalisme littéraire de Sartre: Etude sur
       le concept phénoménologique de l'apparition et sa transposi-
       tion dans la technique de la fiction narrative." Disserta-
       tion Abstracts, 31, No. 12, June 1971, p. 6628A (Univ. of
       California at Los Angeles, 1970).

380   Sanchez, Ray. "John Dewey, Sartre and the Modern Metaphysics
       of Value." Columbia Univ., 1961.

380a   Schact, Richard L. "The Category of Alienation." Disserta-
       tion Abstracts, 28, p. 516A (Princeton Univ., 1968).

381   Schaldenbrand, Mary Aloysius, Sr. "Phenomenologies of Free-
       dom: An Essay in the Philosophies of Sartre and G. Marcel."
       Catholic Univ. of America, 1960.

382   Schlisske, Gunter. "Die Ontologie Sartres als subjektiver
       Idealismus." Munich Univ., 1961.

383   Scorer, P. "A Comparison of Dramatic Methods and the Pres-
       entation of Ideas in the Plays of Sartre and Anouilh, with
       Special Reference to Les Mouches and Antigone." Univ. of
       Manchester, 1953.

384   Shearson, William S. "The Notion of Encounter in Existential-
       ist Metaphysics: An Inquiry into the Nature and Structure
       of Existential Knowledge in Kierkegaard, Sartre and Buber."
       Dissertation Abstracts, 32, No. 6, 1972, p. 3374A (Univ. of
       Toronto, 1970).

385   Shefner, Helena. "Spiritual Crisis in French Prose Litera-
       ture, 1940-1944." Columbia Univ., 1961.

386   Shephard, Leslie A. "The Implosion of Personality in the
       Modern Novel." Dissertation Abstracts, 31, 1970, p. 340A
       (New York Univ.).

387   Shouery, Imad T. "The Psychological Origins of Sartre's Con-
       cept of Freedom." Dissertation Abstracts, 28, 1968, p.
       4668A (Univ. of Oklahoma, 1968).

388   Silvermann, Hugh J. "Existential Ambiguity: A Phenomenology
       of Human Nature." Dissertation Abstracts, 34, No. 6, Decem-
       ber 1973, pp. 3473-3474A (Stanford Univ.).

389   Simon, John K. "The Glance of the Idiot: A Thematic Study of
       Faulkner and Modern French Fiction." Dissertation Ab-
       stracts, 25, No. 2, August 1964, p. 1120A (Yale Univ.,
       1964).

390   Sist, Arthur J. "Non-Alienated Society: An Appraisal of Its
       Possibility in the Light of the Sartrean Problematic and of
       the Responses of the Pluralistic and Participatory Theories
       of Democracy." Dissertation Abstracts, 32, No. 3, 1971, p.
       1570A (Yale Univ., 1971).

391   Skloot, Robert. "The Uses of Time in Modern Drama." Disser-
       tation Abstracts, 29, No. 8, February 1969, pp. 2829-2839A
       (Univ. of Minnesota, 1969).

392   Smoot, R. William. "A Critical Study of the Ethical Theory
       of Sartre." Dissertation Abstracts, 34, No. 6, December
       1973, p. 3474A (Northwestern Univ., 1972).

393   Soper, William W. "The Self and Its World in R.B. Perry, E.
       Scheffield Brightman, Sartre, and Kierkegaard." Disserta-
       tion Abstracts, 23, 1962, pp. 1042-1043A (Boston Univ.).

394   Stone, Robert W. "The Self as Agent-in-the-World: An Alter-
       native to Husserl's and Sartre's Accounts of the Ego."
       Dissertation Abstracts, 34, No. 10, March 1974, p. 6051A
       (Univ. of Texas at Austin, 1972).

395   Stur, Eduard J. "Der Begriff der Freiheit bei Sartre." Wien
       Univ., 1950.

396   Suhl, Benjamin. "Jean-Paul Sartre: The Philosopher as a Lit-
       erary Critic." Dissertation Abstracts, 32, No. 1, July
       1971, p. 457A (Columbia Univ.).

397   Taylor, Hawley C. "The Philosophical Novel." Dissertation
       Abstracts, 30, No. 5, November 1969, p. 2045A.

398   Texier, Louis Henri Jean. "Etude de langue et de style, évo-
       lution de la structure de la phrase dans l'oeuvre romanesque
       de Jean-Paul Sartre. Montpellier, 1970, 232 pp.

399   Thomas, J.J. "The Image of Man in the Literary Heroes of
       Sartre and Three American Novelists: Saul Bellow, J. Barth,
       and Ken Kesey, A Theological Evaluation." Dissertation Ab-
       stracts, 28, No. 6, December 1967, p. 2333A (Northwestern
       Univ., 1967).

400   Ungar, Steven Ronald. "Poetry and the Evolution of Sartre's
       Poetics," <u>Dissertation Abstracts</u>, 34, No. 3, September
       1973, p. 1298A (Cornell Univ.).

401   Upchurch, N. "The Theater of Sartre: Myth, Freedom, and Com-
       mitment." <u>Dissertation Abstracts</u>, 27, No. 11, May 1967,
       p. 3885A (Duke Univ., 1966).

402   Wang, Joan P. "Joseph Conrad, Proto-Existentialist: A Com-
       parative Study of Conrad, Camus and Sartre." <u>Dissertation
       Abstracts</u>, 26, No. 2, August 1965, pp. 1051-1052A (Indiana
       Univ., 1964).

403   Welsbacher, R.C. "Four Projections of Absurd Existence in the
       Modern Theater." <u>Dissertation Abstracts</u>, 25, No. 12, June
       1965, pp. 7423-7424 (Ohio State Univ., 1964).

404   Whitmore, Sara G. "History Versus the Novel: A Sartrean Con-
       cern and Its French Antecedents." <u>Dissertation Abstracts</u>,
       35, No. 8, February 1975, p. 5433A (Univ. of Washington,
       1974).

405   Williams, David V. "A Study of Existential Philosophy and
       Its Relationship to Principles of Counseling." <u>Disserta-
       tion Abstracts</u>, 34, No. 3, September 1973, p. 1091A (Univ.
       of Tulsa).

406   Williams, John S. "The Far Side of Despair: Sartre's Hidden
       Ethics and the Death of God, A Literary and Theological
       Study of Sartre's Drama." Univ. of Chicago, 1968.

407   Wisadavet, Wit. "Sartre's and the Buddhist Concept of Man."
       <u>Dissertation Abstracts</u>, 25, 1964, p. 544A (Indiana Univ.,
       1963).

408   Woodle, Garly L. "Sartre's Political Development, 1928-
       1952." <u>Dissertation Abstracts</u>, 31, 1970, pp. 2946-2947A
       (Univ. of Colorado).

409   Yon, André-François. "Contemporary French Philosophical Lit-
       erary Criticism." <u>Dissertation Abstracts</u>, 20, No. 5, No-
       vember 1959, pp. 1798-1799A (Pennsylvania State Univ.).

410   Young, Marlene. "The Political Implications of Phenomeno-
       logical Existentialism." <u>Dissertation Abstracts</u>, 34, No.
       5, November 1973, p. 2733A (Georgetown Univ.).

411   Zimmermann, Eugenia N. "Metaphysics and Technique in the Ex-
       pository Prose of Sartre, 1936-1960." _Dissertation_ Ab-
       stracts, 26, No. 6, December 1965, p. 3358A (Univ. of Wis-
       consin, 1965).

412   Zivanovic, Judith K. "Humanism in the Drama of Bertold Brecht
       and Sartre." _Dissertation_ Abstracts, 30, No. 1, July 1969,
       p. 433A (Univ. of Wisconsin).

M. A. THESES

413   Adereth, Maxwell. "The Emergence of the Concept of 'Littéra-
       ture engagée' in Contemporary French Literature with Special
       Reference to Péguy, Aragon and Sartre." Birbeck College,
       London, 1961.

414   Beardsworth, P. "A Comparison of Dramatic Methods and the
       Presentation of Ideas in the Plays of Sartre and Anouilh."
       Manchester Univ., 1953.

415   Binnie, Donald J. "Art, Freedom, and Morality in the Phi-
       losophy of Sartre." McMaster Univ. (Canada), 1961.

416   Gore, Keith O. "The Treatment of Personal Relations in the
       Plays of Sartre." Wales Univ., 1957-1958.

417   Grant, Nigel J. "Some Phenomenological and Existential Ap-
       proaches to Psychology with an Analysis of the Status of
       Explanations Framed in Phenomenological Terms." Univ. of
       Edinburgh, 1966.

418   Leddy, Joseph J. "A Critical Analysis of Sartre's Existen-
       tial Humanism with Particular Emphasis Upon His Concept of
       Freedom and Its Moral Implications." Univ. of Windsor
       (Canada), 1963.

419   Margadat, Ted W. "Camus and Sartre: A Study in Revolt and
       Revolution on the Left." Harvard Univ., 1962.

420   Pranger, B. "Sartre and Camus: Politics of Action." Univ.
       of California at Berkeley, 1957.

421   Schaepman, P.M. "The Philosophy of Existence." London
       Univ., Univ. College, 1958-1958.

422   Thody, Philip. "The Vogue of the American Novel in France After 1944: A Study of Its Nature, Origins and Literary Influence." London Univ., King's College, 1952-1953.

PART III

STUDIES OF INDIVIDUAL WORKS OF SARTRE

LA NAUSEE

STUDIES IN ENGLISH

423   Allen, Diogenes. "Two Experiences of Existence: Sartre and
        Iris Murdoch." International Philosophical Quarterly, 14,
        June 1974, 181-187.

424   Arnold, James A. "La Nausée Revisited." French Review, 39,
        No. 2, November 1965, 199-213.

425   Axtheim, Peter M. The Modern Confessional Novel. New Haven:
        Yale Univ. Press, 1967.

        Bingham, William L. see 261.

426   Camus, Albert. "Sartre's La Nausée," Yale French Studies,
        Spring-Summer 1948, 1, No. 1, 62-65.

427   Cohn, Robert G. "Sartre's First Novel: La Nausée and La Voix
        royale." Forum for Modern Language Studies, 4, No. 4, Octo-
        ber 1968, 335-346.

429   Davis, John F. "La Nausée: Imagery and Use of the Diary
        Form." Nottingham French Studies, 10, No. 1, May 1971,
        33-46.

        Donovan, Josephine C. see 289.

        Eberbach, Margaret L. see 292.

430   Edwards, Michael. "La Nausée: A Symbolist Novel." Adam:
        International Review, 35, No. 343-345, 1970, 9-21.

        Falk, Eugene H. see 20.

431   Filler, Louis. "Book Notes." Antioch Review, IX, No.
        2, Summer 1949, 252-254.

432   Finkelstein, Sydney. "Sickness (imported)." Masses and
        Mainstream, II, No. 6, June 1949, 75-76.

433   Fletcher, Dennis J. "Sartre and Barrès: Some Notes on La
        Nausée." Forum for Modern Language Studies, 4, No. 4,

434   Fletcher, Dennis J. "Use of Color in La Nausée." Modern Language Review, LXIII, No. 2, April 1968, 370-380.

Fort, Keith. see 301.

435   Frohock, Wilbur M. "First-Person Narrative." Style and Temper. Cambridge, Massachusetts: Harvard Univ. Press, 1967, 78-111.

436   Frohock, Wilbur M. "The Prolapsed World of Sartre." Accent, VII, No. 2, Fall 1946, 3-13.

437   Goldthorphe, Rhiannon. "The Presentation of Consciousness in Sartre's La Nausée and Its Theoretical Basis, II: Transcendence and Intentionality." French Studies, XXV, January 1971, 32-46.

438   Goldthorpe, Rhiannon. "The Representation of Consciousness in Sartre's La Nausée and its Theoretical Basis: Reflexion and Facticity." French Studies, XXII, No. 2, April 1968, 114-132.

Gore, Keith O. see 23.

439   Greene, Francis J. "Louis Guilloux's Le Sang Noir: A Prefiguration of Sartre's La Nausée." French Review, XL, No. 2, December 1969, 205-214.

440   Grossvogel, David I. "Sartre: La Nausée." Limits of the Novel. Ithaca, New York: Cornell Univ. Press, 1967, 226-255.

441   Jameson, Fredric. "The Laughter of Nausea." Yale French Review, No. 23, Summer 1959, 26-32.

Jameson, Fredric. see 27.

442   Johnson, Patricia J. "Empty Gesture: Descriptive Technique in Sartre's La Nausée." Romance Notes, XIV, No. 3, Spring 1973, 421-424.

443   Kellman, Steven G. "Sartre's La Nausée as Self-Begetting Novel." Symposium, 27, No. 4, Winter 1974, 303-314.

444   Kermode, Frank. "Literary Fiction and Reality." Sense of an Ending. London-New York: Oxford Univ. Pr., 127-152.

445   Marcel, Gabriel. "Existence and Human Freedom." The Philos-
        ophy of Existence." London: Harvill Pr., 1948; New York:
        Philosophical Library, 1949, 32-66.

446   Mason, H.A. "Existentialism and Literature." Scrutiny, XIII,
        No. 2, September 1945, 82-95.

      McIlvain, Betty Thomas. see 345.

447   Mendel, Sydney. "The Descent into Solitude: On Existence
        Real, Certain and Incurable." Forum (Huston), III, No. 8,
        Fall 1961, 19-24.

448   Moravevich, June. "La Nausée and Les Mots: Vision and Re-
        vision." Studies in Philology, LXX, No. 2, April 1973,
        222-232.

449   Mueller, William R. "A Portrait of the Existentialist."
        Celebration of Life: Studies in Modern Fiction. New York:
        Sheed, 1972, 30-49.

450   Mullett, Charles F. "The Novelist Confronts Clio." South
        Atlantic Quarterly, LX, Winter 1960, 56-70.

451   Oxenhandler, Neal. "The Metaphor of Metaphor in La Nausée."
        Chicago Review, XV, No. 4, Summer-Autumn 1962, 47-54.

452   Somers, Paul F. "Camus, Si, Sartre, No, or The Delightful M.
        Mersault." French Review, XLII, April 1969, 693-700.

453   Swingewood, Alan. "Alienation, Refication and the Novel."
        The Sociology of Literature by Diana T. Laurenson and Alan
        Swingewood. New York: Schocken, 1972, 207-248.

454   Taubman, Robert. "Early Sartre." New Statesman, No. 1635,
        13 July 1962, 53.

      Taylor, Hawley C. see 397.

455   Toynbee, Philip. "Growing Isolation." The Observer, No.
        9087, 29 August 1965, 21.

456   Vernon, John. The Gold Garden and the Map: Schizophrenia in
        Twentieth Century Literature and Culture. Urbana: Univ. of
        Illinois Press, 1973, 75-84.

457   Vickery, John B. "The Dillemas of Language: Sartre's La
      Nausée and Iris Murdoch's Under The Net." Journal of Nar-
      ration Technique, I, 1971, 69-76.

458   Walker, Margaret. "The Nausea of Sartre." Yale Review, XLII,
      No. 2, Winter 1953, 251-261.

459   Watson, Graeme. "Roquentin in Indo-China." Journal of the
      Australasian University Language and Literature Association,
      No. 22, November 1964, 277-281.

460   Wilson, Clotilde. "Sartre's Graveyard of Chimeras: La Nausée
      and Mort de quelqu'un." French Review, XXXVIII, May 1965,
      744-753.

461   Zimmermann, Eugenia N. "La Nausée and the Avators (sic) of
      Being." Mosaic, V, No. 3, 1972, 151-157.

462   Zimmermann, Eugenia N. "Some of These Days: Sartre's 'Petite
      Phrase'." Contemporary Literature, XI, Summer 1970, 375-
      381.

STUDIES IN FRENCH

463   Arland, Marcel. "La Nausée." Nouvelle Revue Française, XXVI,
      No. 298, 1938, 129-133.

464   Bost, Pierre. "Proust devant une sonate, Sartre devant un air
      de jazz entendent une seule vois." Figaro Littéraire, IV,
      No. 142, 1949, pp. 1, 3.

465   Boutet de Monvel, Denis. "Du Voyage au bout de la nuit à La
      Nausée." L'Action Nationale, LX, No. 2, octobre 1970, 168-
      172.

466   Champigny, Robert. "Sens de La Nausée." Publications of
      Modern Language Association PMLA, LXX, 1955, 37-46.

467   Chonez, Claudine. "Jean-Paul Sartre, Romancier Philosophe."
      (article-interview). Marianne, 23 novembre 1938.

468   Chonez, Claudine. "A qui les lauriers des Goncourt, Fémina,
      Renaudot, Interallié?" Marianne, 7 décembre 1938.

469   Cottier, Georges. "L'homme de la facticité: Notes sur La
      Nausée de Sartre." Lettres (Genève), III, No. 1, 1945,
      33-45.

470   Daniélou, Jean. "La Nausée." Etudes, Tome CCCXXVII, octobre
      1938, 140-142.

471   Dionne, René. "La nausée d'Antoine Roquentin." Collège et
      Famille, XXVI, 1964, 8-27.

472   Fitch, Brian T. "L'Evocation du réel dans La Nausée de
      Sartre." Le Réel dans la littérature et dans la langue.
      Actes du Dixième Congrès de la Fédération Internationale
      des Langues et Littératures Modernes. Strasbourg: 29 août-
      3 septembre 1966. Publiés avec un avant-propos par Paul
      Vernois. Paris: C. Klincksieck, 1967.

473   Fitch, Brian T. "Le mirage du moi idéal: La Nausée de
      Sartre." Le Sentiment d'étrangeté chez Malraux, Sartre,
      Camus et de Beauvoir: Etranger à moi-même et à ce monde.
      Paris: Minard, 1964, 93-139.

474   Garelli, Jacques. "Antoine Roquentin ou la faillité de
      l'adequatio rei intellectu," et "Existence et ontologie dans
      l'oeuvre de Sartre." La Gravitation poétique. Paris: Mer-
      cure de France, 1966, 52-57.

475   Guignet, Jean. "Deux romans existentialistes: La Nausée et
      L'Etranger." French Review, XXIII, No. 2, décembre 1949,
      86-91.

476   Guyot, Charly. "Sartre et l'experience de l'angoisse."
      Labyrinthe (Genève), No. 4, 1945, pp. 6, 9.

477   Jaloux, Edmond. "La Nausée" Nouvelles Littéraires, 18 juin
      1938, No. 818, 4.

478   Idt, Geneviève. La Nausée: Analyse Critique. Paris: Hatier,
      1971.

479   Idt, Geneviève. "Les mots, sans les choses, sans let mots,
      La Nausée." Degrés, 1, No. 3, 1973, 1-117.

480   Lasry, José-Henri. "A propos de La Nausée de Sartre." Fon-
      taine, No. 9, mai-juin 1940, 15-18.

481   Leclerc, Annie. "De Roquentin à Mathieu." L'Arc: Sartre
      aujourd'hui, No. 30, décembre 1966, 71-76.

482   Magny, Claude-Edmonde. "Sartre ou la duplicité de l'être:
       Ascèse et mythoamnie." Les Sandales d'Empédoclé: Essai
       sur les limites de la littérature. Neuchâtel: Editions
       de la Baconnière, 1945, 105-172.

483   Maire, Gilbert. "De Roquentin à Jean-Paul Sartre," pp. 377-
       380; "Roquentin, créature et disciple de Sartre," pp. 357-
       376; et "Situations privilégiés et situation acquise," pp.
       391-409, dans Les Instants privilégiés. Préface de Jean
       Guitton. Paris: Aubier-Montaigne, 1962.

484   Marcel, Barbiel. "La Nausée par Jean-Paul Sartre." Carrefour,
       janvier 1939, 12-14.

485   Morris, Madeleine. "Faust à Bouville." Revue de Littérature
       Comparée, XLII, 1968, 534-548.

486   Mingelgrün, Albert. "L'air de jazz dans La Nausée: Un chemin-
       ement proustien." Revue de l'Université de Bruxelles, No.
       1, 1972.

487   Nizan, Paul. "La Nausée." Le Soir, 16 mai 1938, 12. Reim-
       primé "La Nausée, un roman de Jean-Paul Sartre". Pour une
       nouvelle culture. Susan Suleiman, ed. Paris: Grasset,
       1971.

488   Noth, Ernst Erich. "La Nausée et Le Mur, par Jean-Paul
       Sartre." Le Point (Colmar), IV, No. 20, 1939, 41-97.

489   Onimus, Jean. "Folantin, Salavin, Roquentin, trois étapes
       de la conscience malheureuse." Face au monde réel. Bruges:
       Desclée de Brouwer, 1962, 99-116. First published in
       Etudes, CCXCVI, 1956, 106-128.

490   Pellegrin, Jean. "L'objet à deux faces dans La Nausée."
       Revue des Sciences Humaines, n.s., Fasicule 113, janvier-
       mars 1964, 87-97.

491   Poulet, Georges. "La 'nausée' de Sartre et le 'cogito' car-
       tésien." Studi Francesi, V, No. 15, septembre-décembre
       1961, 454-462.

492   Poulet, Georges. "La Nausée de Sartre." Le Point de départ:
       Etudes sur le temps humain, III. Paris: Plon, 1964, 216-
       236.

493   Raillard, Georges. "Actualité de La Nausée." Le Français
       dans la Monde, No. 39, mars 1966, 6-13.

494   Raillard, Georges. <u>La</u> <u>Nausée</u> <u>de</u> Jean-Paul <u>Sartre</u>. Paris:
       Classiques Hachette, 1972.

495   Seifert, Stéfanie. "Quelques éléments semblables chez Sartre
       et chez Proust dans <u>La</u> <u>Nausée</u> et dans <u>A</u> <u>la</u> <u>recherche</u> <u>du</u>
       <u>temps</u> <u>perdu</u>." <u>Bulletin</u> <u>de</u> <u>la</u> <u>Société</u> <u>des</u> <u>Amis</u> <u>de</u> <u>Marcel</u>
       <u>Proust</u> <u>et</u> <u>des</u> <u>Amis</u> <u>de</u> <u>Combray</u>, No. 22, 1972, 1428-1433.

496   Robbe-Grillet, Alain. "Nature, humanisme, tragédie." <u>Nou-</u>
       <u>velle</u> <u>Revue</u> <u>Française</u>, No. 70, 1958, 580-604. Reimprimé
       <u>Pour</u> <u>un</u> <u>nouveau</u> roman. Paris: Editions de Minuit, 1963,
       55-84.

497   Robin, Armand. "Jean-Paul Sartre, <u>La</u> <u>Nausée</u>." <u>Esprit</u>, VI,
       No. 70, 1938, 574-575.

498   Saisselin, Remy G. "Bouville ou l'anti-Combray." <u>French</u> <u>Re-</u>
       <u>view</u>, XXXIII, janvier 1960, 68-73.

499   Strinhamber, P. Louis. "Sur <u>La</u> <u>Nausée</u> de Sartre." <u>Syn-</u>
       <u>thèses</u>, V, No. 55, décembre 1950, 68-73.

500   Tison-Braun, Micheline. <u>La</u> <u>Crise</u> <u>de</u> l'humanisme: Le <u>conflit</u>
       <u>de</u> <u>l'individu</u> <u>et</u> <u>de</u> <u>la</u> <u>société</u> <u>dans</u> <u>la</u> <u>littérature</u> <u>française</u>
       <u>moderne</u>, <u>Tome</u> <u>II</u>: <u>1914-1939</u>. Paris: Librairie Nizet, 1967,
       402-414.

501   Wahl, Jean. "Note sur <u>La</u> <u>Nausée</u>." <u>Poésie</u>, <u>pensée</u>, <u>percep-</u>
       tio. Paris: Calmann-Levy, 1948.

STUDIES IN GERMAN, ITALIAN AND SPANISH

502   Accaputo, Nino. "A proposito di '<u>La</u> <u>Nausée</u>' di Jean-Paul
       Sartre." <u>Di</u> <u>Alcuni</u> <u>contemporanei</u> <u>della</u> <u>letteratura</u> <u>fran-</u>
       <u>cese</u>. Napoli: Pellerano-del Gaudio, 1955.

503   Funke, Hans-Wolfgang. "Die geschichtslose Welt des Antoine
       Roquentin: Kritische Bemerkungen zum existentialistischen
       Lebensbild von Sartres Roman <u>La</u> <u>Nausée</u>." Beiträge zur
       <u>Romanischer</u> <u>Philologie</u>, Heft 2, 1970.

504   Horst, Karl August. "Die Abenteuer der Faszination in 'La
       Nausée'." <u>Das</u> <u>Spektrum</u> <u>des</u> <u>modernen</u> <u>Romans</u>. München: C.H.
       Beck, 1964, 110-118.

505   Hühnerfeld, Paul. "Philosophen prägen das Bild der Zeit:
       Sartre und Jaspers in neuen Büchern." Die Zeit, IV, No.
       48, 1949, 9.

506   Kruse, M. "Philosophie und Dichtung in Sartres La Nausée."
       Romantisches Jahrbuch, IX, 1958, 214-225.

507   MacGregor, Joaquín. "Jean-Paul Sartre, La Nausée." Filoso-
       fía y Letras, XV, No. 30, 1948, 350-354.

508   Pohl, Gerhart. "Sartres Seelkrankheit." Aufbau, VI, No. 2,
       1950, 170-172.

509   Serrano-Plato, Arturo. "Nausea y Niebla." Revista de Occi-
       dente, No. 78, September 1969, 295-328.

510   Tagliaferri, Aldo. Beckett e l'iperdeterminazione letteraria.
       Milano: Feltrinelli, 1967, 158-161.

511   Violato, Gabriella. "La Nausée e il romanzo esistenzialista."
       Annali della Facoltà de Lettere, Filosofia dell'Università
       di Macerata, III-IV, 1970-1971, 365-383.

LE MUR

STUDIES IN ENGLISH

512   Ames, Van Meter. "Back to the Wall." Chicago Review, XIII,
       No. 2, 1958, 128-143.

513   Braun, Sidney D. "Source and Psychology of Sartre's Le Mur."
       Criticism, VII, Winter 1965, 45-51.

514   Camus, Albert. "Sartre's Le Mur and Other Studies." Lyrical
       and Critical Essays. New York: Knopf, 1968, 202-206.

515   Frid, Y. "A Philosophy of Unbelief and Indifference: Jean-
       Paul Sartre and Contemporary Bourgeois Individualism."
       Modern Quarterly, II, No. 3, Summer 1947, 215-223. Also in
       American Review, U.S.S.R., VIII, October 1947, 11-19.

516   McLaughlin, Richard. "The Wall and Other Stories." Saturday
       Review of Literature, XXXII, No. 6, 5 February 1949, 29-39.

STUDIES IN FRENCH

517   Brasillach, Robert. "Le Mur." L'Action Française, 13 avril
       1939.

518   Gilles, Françoise. "Entretien avec Jean-Paul Sartre." Com-
       bat, 8 septembre 1967. (On film version of Le Mur. Cf.
       Les Ecrits de Sartre, Contat and Rybalka, 451-452.)

519   Idt, Geneviève. "Le Mur" de Jean-Paul Sartre: Techniques et
       contexte d'une provocation. Paris: Larousse, 1972.

520   Marcel, Gabriel. "Le Mur, par Jean-Paul Sartre." Carrefour,
       juin-juillet 1939.

521   Noth, Ernst Erich. "La Nausée et Le Mur par Jean-Paul Sar-
       tre." Le Point (Colmar), IV, No. 20, 1939, 41-97.

522   Py, Albert. "Le recours à la nouvelle chez Jean-Paul Sartre:
       Etude du Mur." Studies in Short Fiction, III, 1966, 246-
       252.

523   Thérive, André. "Sur Le Mur de Jean-Paul Sartre." Le Temps,
       31 mars 1939, 3.

STUDIES IN GERMAN

524   Kaiser, Joachim. "Menschen, Triebe, Perversionen: Sartres
       humanistische Höllenwanderung (zur deutschen Ausgabe von
       Le Mur bei Rowohlt)." Die Zeit, XVI, No. 45, 1961, 19.

La Chambre

525   Buch, Stratton. "The Uses of Madness." Tennessee Studies in
       Literature, III, 1958, 63-71 (Parallel between La Chambre
       and Balzac's Louis Lambert).

526   Greenlee, James. "Sartre's Chambre: The Story of Eve."
       Modern Fiction Studies, XVI, Spring 1970, 77-84.

527   Simon, John K. "Madness in Sartre: Sequestration and The
       Room." Yale French Studies, No. 30, Fall-Winter 1962-1963,
       63-67.

528   Simon, John K. "Sartre's Room." Modern Language Notes,
       LXXVIV, December 1964, 526-536.

529   Sternberg, Jacques. "La chambre noire." Nouvel Observateur,
       n.s., No. 6, 24 décembre 1964, 34.

530   Virtanen, Reino. "La Chambre and Louis Lambert: A Brief Com-
       parison." Symposium, VIII, No. 2, Winter 1954, 327-330.

L'Enfance d'un chef

531   Cohn, Dorrit. "Narrated Monologue: Definition of a Fiction-
       al Style." Comparative Literature, XVIII, Spring 1966, 97-
       112.

532   Elmquist, Claire. "Lucien, Jean-Paul et la mauvaise foi: Une
       étude sur Sartre." Orbis Litterarum, XXVI, 1971, 220-231.

533   Smith, Madeleine. "The Making of a Leader." Yale French
       Studies, No. 1, Spring-Summer 1949, 80-83.

Intimité

534   Anonymous. "A propos d'Intimité." Nouvelle Revue Française,
       No. 308, mai 1939, 808.

535   Morris, Edward. "On Intimacy." Yale French Studies, No. 1,
       Spring-Summer 1949, 73-79.

Erostrate

536   Rom, Paul, and Ansbacher, Heinz. "An Adlerian Case or a Char-
       acter by Sartre?" Journal of Individual Psychology, XXI,
       May 1965, 32-41.

LES CHEMINS DE LA LIBERTE

STUDIES IN ENGLISH

537 Beach, Joseph Warren. "Sartre's Roads To Freedom and The Re-
     prieve." Western Review, XII, No. 3, Spring 1948, 180-191.

538 Blotner, Joseph L. "Jean-Paul Sartre: The Shadow of Munich."
     The Political Novel. New York: Doubleday, 1949.

539 Borbasm, Laszlo. "The Bourgeoisie in the Post-War Novel."
     French Review, XXVIII, 1954, 35-43.

540 Brombert, Victor. "Sartre and the Existential Novel: The
     Intellectual as 'Impossible Hero'." The Intellectual Hero:
     Studies in the French Novel, 1880-1955. Philadelphia: Lip-
     pincott, 1961, 181-203.

541 Church, Margaret. "Jean-Paul Sartre: Flight into the Future."
     Time and Reality: Studies in Contemporary Fiction. Chapel
     Hill: Univ. of North Carolina, 1963, 253-276.

542 Cranston, Maurice W. "Introduction and Appreciation." The
     Age of Reason. Eric Sutton, trans. London: Heron Books,
     1970.

543 Douglas, Kenneth N. "Sartre and the Self-Inflicted Wound."
     Yale French Studies, No. 9, Spring 1952, 123-132. Reprinted
     Sartre: A Collection of Critical Essays, Edith Kern, ed.
     Englewood Cliffs, New Jersey: Prentice-Hall, 1962, 39-46.

544 Edinborough, A. "Sartre and the Existentialist Novel."
     Queen's Quarterly, LVI, No. 1, Spring 1949, 105-112.

545 Eoff, Charles A. "The Challenge of Absurdity: Sartre, L'Age
     de raison." New York: New York Univ. Pr., 1961, 213-254.

546 Fowlie, Wallace. "Existentialist Hero: A Study of L'Age de
     raison." Yale French Studies, I, No. 1, Spring-Summer 1948,
     53-61.

547 Fowlie, Wallace. A Guide to Contemporary Literature from
     Valéry to Sartre. New York: Meridian Books, 1957.

548   Frid, Y.   "A Philosophy of Unbelief and Indifference: Sartre
      and Contemporary Bourgeois Individualism."   Modern Quarter-
      ly, II, No. 3, Summer 1947, 215-223.

549   Gibson, A. Boyce.   "Death in the Soul."   Meanjin Quarterly,
      XI, 1952, 262-272.

550   Glicksberg, Charles I.   "Sartre: Existentialism in Fiction."
      Prairie Schooner, XXIII, No. 1, Spring 1949, 12-18.

551   Hardwick, Elizabeth.   "Fiction Chronicle: The Age of Reason
      by Jean-Paul Sartre."   Partisan Review, XIV, No. 5, Septem-
      ber-October 1947, 533-535.

      Harrington, Catherine S.   see 312.

552   Lehan, Richard.   "The Trilogies of Sartre and Dos Passos."
      Iowa English Yearbook, No. 9, 1964, 60-64.

553   Lichtenstein, Heinz.   "The Age of Reason, Jean-Paul Sartre."
      Philosophy and Phenomenological Research, IX, No. 1, 1948,
      148-153.

554   Mason, H.A.   "Les Chemins de la liberté, I and II."   Scru-
      tiny, XIV, No. 1, Summer 1946, 2-15.

555   Matthews, H.J.   "Sartre: Roads to Freedom."   The Hard Journey:
      The Myth of Man's Rebirth.   London: Chatto and Windus, 1968,
      97-113.

556   McLaughlin, Richard.   "The Age of Reason."   Saturday Review of
      Literature, XXX, No. 29, December 1947, 13, 24-25.

557   O'Brien, Justin.   "The Reprieve."   New York Times Book Review,
      13 July 1947, 4, and Ibid., 23 November 1947, 26.

558   O'Brien, Justin.   "Sartre: Roads to Freedom."   The French Lit-
      erary Horizon.   New Brunswick, New Jersey: Rutgers Univ.
      Pr., 1967, 313-316.

559   Peterson, Virginia.   "The Age of Reason: Jean-Paul Sartre."
      The Commonwealth, XLVI, No. 15, 25 July 1947, 360.

560   Peyre, Henri.   "Existentialism and French Literature."   The
      Contemporary French Novel.   London: Oxford Univ. Pr., 1955,
      216-239.   Reprinted Sartre: A Collection of Critical Essays.

Edith Kern, ed. Englewood Cliffs, New Jersey: Prentice-
Hall, 1962, 31-38.

Powell, Elton G. see 369.

561   Spender, Stephen. "Sartre's Existential Comedy'." The Na-
       tion, CLXVL, No. 9, 28 February 1948, 239-241.

562   Tarbox, R. "Exhaustion Psychology and Sartre's The Age of
       Reason." American Image, XXX, Spring 1973, 80-96.

563   Trilling, Diana. "Sartre's Research." The Nation, CLXV,
       No. 6, 9 August 1947, 146-147.

564   Ullman, Stephen. "Image in the Modern Novel." Style in the
       French Novel. Oxford: Basil Blackwell, 1964, 210-262.

565   Vassilieff, Elizabeth. "Sartre: Roads to Freedom." Meanjin
       Quarterly, XII, 1953, 79-92.

566   Wardman, Harold W. "Sartre and the Literature of 'Praxis':
       Les Chemins de la liberté." Essays in French Literature
       (Univ. of Western Australia), IV, 1967, 44-68.

567   Wilson, Edmund. "L'Age de raison." New Yorker, XXIII, 2
       August 1947, 60-63.

568   Wilson, Edmund. "Jean-Paul Sartre: The Novelist and the Ex-
       istentialist." Classics and Commercials: A Literary Chron-
       icle of the Forties. New York: Farrar, Strauss and Cudahy,
       1950, 393-403. Reprinted Sartre: A Collection of Critical
       Essays. Edith Kern, ed. Englewood Cliffs, New Jersey:
       Prentice-Hall, 1962, 47-53.

                        STUDIES IN FRENCH

569   Abraham, Pierre. "La liberté et ses chemins." Europe,
       XXVIII, No. 51, février 1950, 54-61.

570   Anonymous. Interview with Sartre on Mathieu Delarue of Les
       Chemins de la liberté." Figaro Littéraire, 13 avril 1946,
       8.

571   Anonymous. "Sur 'France-Culture': Les Chemins de la liberté."
       Le Figaro, 11 juillet 1972, 17.

572   Béguin, Albert. "L'Age de raison." Esprit, XIII, No 12,
       1945, 969-971.

573   Béguin, Albert. "Le sursis." Esprit, XIII, No. 12, 1945,
       969-971.

574   Blanchot, Maurice. "Les romans de Sartre." L'Arche. No.
       10, octobre 1945, 121-134. Reimprimé La Part du feu.
       Paris: Gallimard, 1949, 195-211.

575   Bory, Jean-Louis. "Les Chemins de la liberté." Arts et Let-
       tres, No. 1, mars 1946, 80-82.

576   Bousquet, Jöe. "Le cabinet de lecture." Cahiers du Sud. No.
       274, 1945, 845-849.

577   Bruch, Jean-Louis. "Jean-Paul Sartre: La Mort dans l'âme."
       Revue du Caire, XII, No. 126, janvier 1950, 243-247.

578   Catesson, Jean. "Les Chemins de la liberté I et II." Cahiers
       du Sud, No. 279, 1946, 287-294.

579   Celly, Raoul. "Roman existentialiste: L'Age de raison."
       Revue de la Méditerranée, III, No. 12, mars-avril 1946, 219-
       223.

580   Debray, Pierre. "Du roman psychologique au roman de la condi-
       tion humaine." Cahiers du Monde Nouveau, IV, No. 3, mars
       1948, 63-69.

581   Grisoli, Christian. "Les Chemins de la liberté, par Jean-
       Paul Sartre." Paru, No. 13, 1945, 11-17.

582   Grisoli, Christian. "Entretien avec Sartre." Paru, No. 13,
       décembre 1945, 5-10.

583   Hell, Henri. "Les Chemins de la liberté, II, par Jean-Paul
       Sartre." Fontaine, No. 48-49, janvier-février 1946, 352-
       357.

584   Hoog, Armand. "Les Chemins de la liberté de Jean-Paul Sar-
       tre." Carrefour, II, No. 61, 19 octobre 1945, 6.

       Joubert, Ingrid. see 323.

585   Joubert, Ingrid. <u>Aliénation et liberté dans 'Les Chemins de la liberté' de Sartre</u>. Paris: Didier, 1973, 318 pp.

586   Kemp, Robert. "Jean-Paul Sartre - Simone de Beauvoir." <u>Nouvelles Littéraires</u>, No. 951, 1945, 3-4.

587   Kemp, Robert. "Sartre contre Sartre." <u>Nouvelles Littéraires</u>, No. 1154, 1949, 2.

588   Las Vergnas, Raymond. <u>L'Affaire Sartre</u>. Paris: Haumont, 1946.

589   Le Clech, Guy S. "Sur les chemins de la liberté: <u>Le Sursis</u>." <u>La Nef</u>, III, No. 19, 1946, 93-96.

590   Leclerc, Annie. "De Roquentin à Mathieu." <u>L'Arc</u>. No. 30, 1966, 71-76.

591   Magny, Claude-Edmonde. "<u>Les Chemins de la liberté</u>." <u>Poésie 45</u>, 1945.

592   Magny, Claude-Edmonde. "Existentialisme et littérature: <u>L'Age de raison et Le Sursis</u>." <u>Clartés</u>, 19 octobre 1945. Also in <u>Poésie 46</u>, janvier 1946, No. 29, 58-67.

593   Magny, Claude-Edmonde. "<u>Le Sursis</u>." <u>Poésie 46</u>, No. 29, janvier 1946, 58-67.

594   Marcel, Gabriel. "Sartre: <u>Les Chemins de la liberté</u>." <u>La Nef</u>, décembre 1945, 130-133.

595   Maulet, Pierre. "<u>Les Chemins de la liberté I et II</u>." <u>Renaissance</u>, décembre 1945, No. 17, 146.

596   Maulnier, Thierry. "<u>Les Chemins de la liberté</u>." <u>Vingtième Siècle</u>, 8-15 novembre 1945, 4.

597   Maulnier, Thierry. "Feuilleton littéraire: Le mal du milieu du siècle." <u>Hommes et Mondes</u>. No. 41, décembre 1949, 590-595.

598   Nadeau, Maurice. "A propos de Louis Guilloux et de Jean-Paul Sartre: Le romancier et ses personnages." <u>Mercure de France</u>, CCCVII, No. 1036, décembre 1949, 698-707.

599   Parrot, Louis. "<u>Les Chemins de la liberté</u>." <u>Lettres Françaises</u>. No 79, 1945, 5.

600   Picard, Raymond. "L'art de Jean-Paul Sartre et les 'hommes de mauvaise volonté'." France Libre, XI, No. 64, 15 février 1946, 289-296.

601   Picon, Gaëtan. "Sartre et le roman contemporain." Confluences, V, No. 8, octobre 1945, 883-891.

602   Pingaud, Bernard. "Un univers figé." Sartre est-il possédé? 2e éd. Paris: Editions de la Table Ronde, 1950.

603   Rousseaux, André. "La Mort dans l'âme." Figaro Littéraire. No. 183, 1949, 2.

604   Thiébault, Marcel. "Le Sursis." Revue de Paris, LII, No. 9, décembre 1945, 103-107.

605   Waelhens, Alphonse de. "Le roman existentialiste." Essais et Etudes Universitaires, II, 1946, 107-117.

606   Wurmser, André. "Les falsificateurs de l'histoire contre le roman." Lettres Françaises. No. 284, 1949, 3.

607   Yafine. "Les Chemins de la liberté I et II." Esprit, XIII, 1945, 971-973.

STUDIES IN OTHER LANGUAGES

608   Backholm, Karl Gustav. "Kott och i ideromanen." Nya Argus, LIX, 1953, 153-157.

609   Boer, J. "De nieuwe roman van Jean-Paul Sartre." Erasme, I, 1946, 22-24.

610   Ergmann, Raoul. "Jean-Paul Sartre, Les Chemins de la liberté." Schweizer Annalen, III, 1946-1947, No. 6-7, 344-350.

611   Kühn, Rheinhard. "Jean-Paul Sartre: Les Chemins de la liberté." Der moderne französische Roman. Walter Pabst, ed. Berlin: Erich Schmidt, 1968, 198-212.

612   LeWalter, Christian E. "Die entzelzliche Freiheit: Zu Jean Paul Sartres 'aufschub'." Die Zeit, V, No. 25, 1950, 4.

613   Meyer, Rudolf. "L'Age de raison de Monsieur Sartre." Hamburgische Akademische Rundschau, II, 1947-1948, 501-513.

614   Ott, Karl August. "Sartre Appell an ausere Freiheit." <u>Aussprache</u> (Biberach/Riss). No. 1, 1950, 100-103.

GENERAL STUDIES OF SARTRE'S FICTION

STUDIES IN ENGLISH

615   Alexander, Ian W. "The Phenomenological Philosophy in France: An Analysis of Its Themes and Implications." <u>Currents of Thought in French Literature: Essays in Memory of G.T. Clapton</u>. T.V. Benn, ed. Oxford: Basil Blackwell, 1965, 325-351. Reprinted <u>Sartre: A Collection of Critical Essays</u>. Mary Warnock, ed. Garden City, New York: Doubleday, 1971, 63-101.

616   Barnes, Hazel A. "Literature as Salvation in the Work of Sartre." <u>American Catholic Philosophical Association Proceedings</u>, XXXIX, 1965, 53-68.

617   Batt, Jean C. "Contemporary French Literature." <u>Contemporary Review</u>. No. 1091, November 1956, 276-279.

618   Brée, Germaine and Guiton, M.O. "Jean-Paul Sartre: The Search for Identity." <u>Age of Fiction</u>. New Brunswick, New Jersey: Rutgers Univ. Pr., 1957, 203-218.

619   Brée, Germaine and Guiton, M.O. <u>The French Novel from Gide to Camus</u>. New York: Harcourt, Brace and World, 1962.

620   Berger, Gaston. "Existentialism and Literature in Action." <u>University of Buffalo Studies</u>, XVIII, No. 4, 1948.

621   Bruneau, Jean. "Existentialism and the American Novel." <u>Yale French Studies</u>, I, No. 1, 1949, 66-72.

622   Champigny, Robert. "Existentialism in the Modern French Novel." <u>Thought</u>, XXXI, No. 122, Autumn 1956, 365-384.

623   Copleston, Frederick C. "The Philosophy of the Absurd." <u>The Month</u>, CLXIII, No. 957, March 1949, 157-164.

624   Cruickshank, John. "Existentialism After Twelve Years--An Evaluation." <u>Dublin Review</u>, CCXXXI, Summer 1957, 52-67.

625   Davis, Richard. "American Literature in the World Today." <u>Tennessee Studies in Literature</u>, VIII, 1963, 119-139.

626   Evans, Oliver. "The Rise of Existentialism." South Atlantic
       Quarterly, XLVII, No. 2, April 1948, 152-156.

627   "Existentialism and Literature." Chicago Review, XIII, 1959.

628   Fowlie, Wallace. "Existentialism." Climate of Violence: The
       French Literary Tradition from Baudelaire to the Present.
       New York: Macmillan, 1967, Chapter 13.

629   Gibson, A. Boyce. "Existentialism: An Interim Report."
       Meanjin Quarterly, VII, No. 1, Autumn 1948, 41-52.

630   Glicksberg, Charles I. "Literary Existentialism." Arizona
       Quarterly, IX, No. 1, Spring 1953, 24-39.

631   Greenwood, E.B. "Literature and Philosophy." Essays in Crit-
       icism, XX, No. 1, January 1970, 5-18.

632   Hardré, Jacques. "The Existentialism of Jean-Paul Sartre."
       Carolina Quarterly, I, No. 2, March 1949, 49-55.

633   Hatzfeld, Helmut. "Existentialist Engagement." Trends and
       Styles in Twentieth Century French Literature. Washington:
       Catholic University of America Pr., 1957, 137-159.

634   Heppenstall, Rayner. "Jean-Paul Sartre." Quarterly Review
       of Literature, IV, No. 4, 1949, 416-429.

635   Holthusen, Hans Egon. "Meaning and Destiny in European Lit-
       erature." Chicago Review, XIV, No. 4, Spring 1961, 1-19.

636   Kern, Edith, ed. Sartre: A Collection of Critical Essays.
       Englewood Cliffs, New Jersey: Prentice-Hall, 1962.

637   Kleppner, Amy M. "Philosophy and the Literary Medium: The
       Existentialist Predicament." Journal of Aesthetics and
       Art Criticism, XXIII, No. 2, Winter 1964, 207-217.

638   Kronegger, Maria F. "The Multiplication of the Self from
       Flaubert to Sartre." L'Esprit Créateur, XIII, No. 4, Win-
       ter 1973, 310-319.

639   Laurenson, Diana and Swingewood, Alan. The Sociology of Lit-
       erature. London: MacGibbon and Kee, 1971.

640   Maurois, André. "Jean-Paul Sartre." From Proust to Camus:
       Profiles of Modern French Writers. New York: Doubleday,
       1966, 299-324.

641   McElroy, David D.   Existentialism and Modern Literature: An
      Essay in Existential Criticism.   New York: Greenwood Pr.,
      1968.

642   Little, Arthur.   "Existentialism and the New Literature."
      Studies, XXXV, No. 140, December 1946, 459-467.

643   McEachran, F.   "The Literature of Existentialism."   Contem-
      porary Review, May 1963, 257-264.

644   Moore, T.H.   "The Continuation of Existentialism."   Twentieth
      Century French Literature Since World II.   Carbondale,
      Illinois: Southern Illinois Univ. Pr., 1966, 34-73.

645   Mortimer, Raymond.   "Emergence of Jean-Paul Sartre."   New
      Statesman and Nation, XXX, No. 355, 24 November 1945, 355-
      356.

646   Murray, John.   "A Mirror of France."   The Month, CLXXXI, No.
      948, November-December 1945, 393-403.

647   Peyre, Henri.   "Existentialism--A Literature of Despair?"
      Yale French Studies, I, No. 1, Spring-Summer 1948, 21-32.

648   Peyre, Henri.   "The Resistance and Literary Revival in
      France."   Yale Review, XXXV, No. 1, September 1945, 84-92.

649   Pucciani, Orestes F.   "Existentialism."   Modern Language
      Forum, XXXV, No. 1-2, March-June 1950, 1-13.

650   Radford, Jocelyn.   "Existentialism in Modern French Litera-
      ture."   Manitoba Arts Review, X, 1956, 16-31.

651   Spivak, Charlotte.   "The Estranged Hero of Modern Literature."
      North Dakota Quarterly, XXIX, Winter 1961, 13-19.

652   Vial, Fernand.   "Existentialism in France."   American Society
      Legion of Honor Magazine, XIX, No. 1, Spring 1948, 33-52.

653   Votan, A.   "Literature of Extreme Situations: Existentialism
      and the Romantic Protest."   Horizon, XX, Summer 1949, 145-
      150.

STUDIES IN FRENCH

654   Bellème, Laurence.   "Notes sur une littérature d'action."
      Comprendre (Venise), XV, mars 1956, 165-167.

655   Bersani, Jacques, et al. La Littérature en France depuis
      1945. Paris: Bordas, 1970.

656   Bourbousson, Edouard. "La littérature existentialiste et son
      influence." French Review, XXIII, No. 6, mai 1950, 36-48.

657   Brodin, Pierre. Présences contemporaines: Cours de littéra-
      ture française contemporaine. Première série. Paris: De-
      bresse, 1954, 347-367.

658   Brodin, Pierre. Présences contemporaines: Courants et thèmes
      principaux de la littérature française contemporaine. Tome
      3. Paris: Debresse, 1957.

659   Chaigne, Louis. "Jean-Paul Sartre." Vies et oeuvres d'écri-
      vains. 2e éd., 4e série. Paris: Lanore, 1954, 49-101.

660   Chaigne, Louis. Notre littérature d'aujourd'hui. Paris,
      Lanore, 1949.

661   Chaigne, Louis. Notre littérature vivante, Tome 6: XXe
      siècle. Paris: 1959.

662   Cuénot, Claude. "Littérature et philosophie chez Sartre."
      Renaissances, No. 21, mai 1946, 49-61.

663   Jans, Adrien. "Vers un nouveau message de la littérature
      française--d'Aragon à Sartre." Revue Générale Belge, No. 1,
      novembre 1945, 119-123.

664   Junod, Roger-Louis. "Jean-Paul Sartre." Ecrivains français
      du XXe siècle. Lausanne: Payot, 1963, 117-139.

665   Koefoed, Oleg. "L'oeuvre littéraire de Sartre: Essai d'inter-
      prétation." Orbis Litterarum, VI, No. 34, 1948, 209-272;
      Ibid., VII, 61-141.

666   Las Vergnas, Raymond. "En marge d'un snobisme." Nouvelles
      Littéraires, No. 965, 1946, 1-2.

667   Las Vergnas, Raymond. "Pour un snobisme de la beauté." Nou-
      velles Littéraires, No. 961, 1946, 6.

668   Las Vergnas, Raymond. "Snobisme de la laideur." Nouvelles
      Littéraires, No. 960, 1945, 1, 8.

669   Lemarchand, Jacques. "L'existentialisme vu de la terrasse."
       Rencontres, No. 1, 1946.

670   Lobet, Marcel. "Que faut-il penser de l'existentialisme lit-
       téraire?" Revue Générale Belge, No. 5, mars 1946, 551-559.

671   Lobet, Marcel. La Science du bien et du mal: Essai sur la
       connaissance littéraire. Paris: La Nef de Paris, 1954.

672   Magny, Claude-Edmonde. "La littérature française depuis
       1940." France Libre (London), 15 décembre 1945.

673   Magny, Claude-Edmonde. "Système de Sartre." Esprit, XIII,
       No. 4, 1945, 564-580; Ibid., 709-724. Reimprimé Littérature
       et critique." Paris: Payot, 1971, 60-89.

674   Maurois, André. Nouvelles directions de la littérature fran-
       çaise. Oxford: Claredon Pr., 1967.

675   Moeller, Charles. "De la littérature existentialiste à l'ex-
       ploration du monde." Revue Nouvelle, X, 15 décembre 1954,
       588-601.

676   Montigny, R. Jean-Paul Sartre et l'existentialisme ou le
       problème de la littérature philosophique. Lindau Im
       Bodensee: Frish und Perneder, 1948.

677   Mueller, Fernand-Lucien. "La nouvelle philosophie de l'exis-
       tence." Présence (Genève), V, No. 1, avril 1946, 20-42.

678   Ouy, Achille. "Déclin de l'existentialisme." Mercure de
       France, No. 1002, 1947, 359-363.

679   Picon, Gaëtan. Panorama de la nouvelle littérature française.
       Paris: Gallimard, 1960.

680   Rousseaux, André. Littérature du vingtième siècle, Tome 5:
       Paris: Albin Michel, 1955.

681   Royle, Peter. "Vers une interprétation cohérente de l'oeuvre
       littéraire de Sartre." Revue de l'Université Laurentienne,
       I, No. 1, June 1968, 73-76.

682   Simon, Pierre-Henri. L'homme en procès. 6e éd. Neuchâtel:
       Editions de la Baconnière; Paris: SFL, 1962.

683   Simon, Pierre-Henri. Les témoins de l'homme: La condition
       humaine dans la littérature du vingtième siècle. édition
       révisé. Paris: Payot, 1967.

684   Simon, Pierre-Henri. Les témoins de l'homme. Paris: A.
       Colin, 1951.

685   Sylvestre, Guy. "Existentialisme et littérature." Revue de
       l'Université Laval, I, No. 6, février 1947, 423-433.

       STUDIES IN OTHER LANGUAGES

686   Bo, Carlo. Della Lettura e altri saggi. Firenze: Vallecchi,
       1953.

687   Buhl, Wolfgang. "Revolution der Literatur." Erlanger Univer-
       sitat, II, No. 3-4, 1948, 32-33.

688   Caminero, Nemesio G. "Panorama existencialista." Pensa-
       miento, XVI, 1948, 66-74.

689   Champly, Henry. "Brochazos sobre el existencialisme sartri-
       ano." Revista Universitaria de Buenos Aires, No. 8, 1948,
       449-472.

690   Dresden, S. Existentialisme en literatur beschouwing.
       Amsterdam: Meidenhoff, 1946.

691   Fanizza, Franco. Letteratura come filosofia. Firenze: La
       Nuova Italia, 1964.

692   Fredericia, W. "Bestätigen Jean-Paul Sartres Dramen und
       Romane sein existenzialistisches Denken?" Die Zeit, V, No.
       17, 1950, 4.

693   Kohut, Karl. "Jean-Paul Sartre." Französische Literatur der
       Gegenwart: In Einzeldarstellungen. Herausgegeben von Wolf-
       Dieter Lange. Stuttgart: Alfred Kröner, 1971, 159-192.

694   Mondrome, D. "L'operà letterarià di Jean-Paul Sartre." Ci-
       viltà Cattólica, LXLIX, No. 1, 1948, 476-490.

695   Squadrilli, Rosa Alba. "Jean-Paul Sartre." Quaderni di Roma,
       II, Facscilolo 5-6, October 1948, 404-413.

696   Torre, Guillermo de. "El existencialismo en la literatura."
       Cuadernos Americanos, XXXVII, No. 1, January-February 1948,
       253-272; Ibid., No. 2, March-April 1948, 223-234.

697   Torre, Guillermo de. Valoración literaria del existencialis-
       mo. Buenos Aires: Editorial Losada, 1948.

NOVEL

STUDIES IN ENGLISH

698   Albérès, René-Marill. "Is There a New Ethic in Fiction?"
       What's Novel in the Novel? Yale French Studies, No. 8,
       1951, 9-16.

699   Barnes, Hazel E. "Modes of Aesthetic Consciousness in Fic-
       tion." Bucknell Review, XII, No. 1, March 1964, 82-93.

700   Beja Morris, ed. Psychological Fiction. Glenview, Illinois:
       Scott, Foresman and Company, 1971.

701   Bergonzi, Bernard. The Situation of the Novel. London: Mac-
       millan, 1970.

702   Booth, Wayne C. The Rhetoric of Fiction. Chicago: Univ. of
       Chicago Pr., 1961.

703   Brée, Germaine. "The Writer of Our Time: Malraux, Sartre,
       Camus." Varieties of Literary Experience. S. Burnshaw, ed.
       New York: New York Univ. Pr., 1962, 75-94.

704   Cook, Albert. The Meaning of Fiction. Detroit: Wayne State
       Univ. Pr., 1960.

705   Correa, Gustavo. "The Modern Spanish Novel." Hispanic Re-
       view, XXXI, April 1963, 177-180.

706   Cruickshank, John. The Novelist as Philosopher. London:
       Oxford Univ. Pr., 1962.

707   Fauconmier, R.L. "French Novelists in Revolt." Queens Quar-
       terly, LXIII, Winter 1957, 608-617.

       Hoy, Nancy. see 316.

708   Jameson, Storm. "The Novelist Today." Virginia Quarterly Re-
       view, XXV, No. 4, Autumn 1949, 562-574.

709   Josipivici, Gabriel. "Sartre and the 'Nouveau roman'." Adam
       International Review, XXXV, No. 343-345, 1970, 98-99.

710   Kahler, Eric. "The Transformation of Modern Fiction." Com-
       parative Literature, VII, No. 2, Spring 1965, 121-128.

711   Lehan, Richard J. A Dangerous Crossing: French Literary Exis-
       tentialism and the Modern American Novel. Carbondale, Il-
       linois: Southern Illinois Univ. Pr., 1973.

       Lehan, Richard J. see 333.

712   Lehan, Richard J. "Existentialism in Recent American Fiction:
       The Demonic Quest." Texas Studies in Literature and Lan-
       guage, I, No. 2, Summer 1959, 181-202.

713   LeSage, Laurent. "French Literature Since World War II, Crit-
       icism and Research, 3: The Novel." Symposium, XI, Spring
       1957, 16-24.

       Morea, Rachelle. see 350.

714   Murdoch, Iris. "The Novelist as Metaphysician." The Listen-
       er, XLIII, 16 March 1950, 473-476.

715   Nadeau, Maurice. French Novel Since the War. London: Met-
       huen, 1963.

716   Panichas, George A., ed. The Politics of Twentieth Century
       Novelists. New York: Hawthorn Books, 1971.

717   Reck, Rima Drell. "Jean-Paul Sartre: Ambiguity of Moral
       Choice." Literature and Responsibility: The French Novel-
       ists in the Twentieth Century. Baton Rouge: Louisiana State
       Univ. Pr., 1970, 3-41.

       Shephard, Leslie A. see 385.

718   Szanto, George H. Narrative Consciousness: Structure and Per-
       ception in the Fiction of Kafka, Beckett, and Robbe-Grillet.
       Austin: Univ. of Texas Pr., 1972.

719   Thomas, J. James. "The Sartrean Hero." The Revolutionary
       Hero: A Phenomenological Investigation of the Literature of
       Jean-Paul Sartre and Four American Novelists. Michigan:
       University Center, 1971, 17-24.

Thomas, J. James. see 398.

720   Ullmann, Stephen. "Image in the Modern Novel." Style in the
       French Novel. Oxford: Basil Blackwell, 1964, 210-262 (La
       Mort dans l'âme).

721   Ullmann, Stephen. Language and Style: Collected Papers. Ox-
       ford: Basil Blackwell, 1964.

722   Ullmann, Stephen. "Style and Personality." Review of English
       Literature, VI, No. 2, April 1965, 21-31.

723   Weightman, John. "Jean-Paul Sartre." The Novelist as Philos-
       opher: Studies in French Fiction 1935-1960. John Cruil-
       shank, ed. London: Oxford Univ. Pr., 1962, 102-127.

724   West, Paul. The Modern Novel. London: Hutchinson, 1963, 164-
       170.

725   Wyatt, Kathryn Day. Unanumistic Imagery in Twentieth Century
       Literature. University, Mississippi: Romance Monographs,
       1974.

726   Zéraffa, Michel. "The Young Novelists' Problem of Style and
       Technique." Yale French Studies, No. 8, Winter 1951-1952,
       2-8.

STUDIES IN FRENCH

727   Albérès, René-Marill. "Jean-Paul Sartre." La révolte des
       écrivains d'aujourd'hui. Paris: Correa, 1949, 183-208.

728   Albérès, René-Marill. Métamorphoses du roman. Paris: Albin
       Michel, 1966.

729   Albérès, René-Marill. "Aux sources du 'nouveau roman": L'im-
       pressionisme anglais." Revue de Paris, LXIX, No. 5, mai
       962, 74-86.

730   Barilli, Renato. "De Sartre à Robbe-Grillet." Un nouveau
       roman: recherches et traditions; la critique étrangère.
       J.H. Matthews, ed. Paris: Minard, 1964, 105-128.

731   Barrère, Jean-Bertrand. La Cure d'amaigrissement du roman.
       Paris: Albin Michel, 1964.

732   Champigny, Robert. _Le Genre romanesque_. Monte Carlo: Regain, 1963.

733   Curtis, Jean-Louis. "Sartre et le roman." _Haute Ecole_. Paris: René Julliard, 1950, 165-205.

734   Haedens, Kléber. _Paradoxe sur le roman_. Paris: Grasset, 1964.

735   Jansen, Conrad. "Sur le roman." _Cahiers des Saisons_. No. 22, été 1960, 170-187.

736   Lalou, Etienne. "Le dernier roman existentialiste." _L'Express_. No. 984, 18-24 mai 1970, 63-64.

737   Marzac, Nicole A.D. "Le thème du 'pays perdu' dans le roman contemporain." _Revue des Sciences Humaines_. Fascicule 119, juillet-septembre 1965, 431-440.

738   Monnier, Jean-Paul. _L'Age ingrat du roman_. Neuchâtel: Editions de la Baconnière, 1967.

739   Morrissette, Bruce. "Problèmes du roman cinématographique." _Cahiers de l'Association Internationale des Etudes Françaises_. No. 20, mai 1968, 275-289.

740   Nadeau, Maurice. _Le Roman français depuis la guerre_. Paris: Gallimard, 1963.

741   Pingaud, Bernard. "L'année dernière à Leningrad." _Esprit_, July 1964. Introduction aux interventions de divers écrivains au Colloque sur le roman qui s'est tenu en août 1963, en U.R.S.S.

742   Pingaud, Bernard. "De Sartre à Robbe-Grillet." _Education Nationale_. No. 20, 31 mai 1962, 16-18.

743   Prince, Gerald J. "Le comique dans l'oeuvre romanesque de Jean-Paul Sartre." _PMLA_, LXXXVI, March 1972, 295-303.

744   Prince, Gerald J. "La main et la menace de l'en-soi dans l'oeuvre romanesque de Sartre." _Romance Notes_, X, Autumn 1968, 7-10.

Prince, Gerald J. see 371.

745   Prince, Gerald J. _Métaphysique et technique dans l'oeuvre romanesque de Sartre_. Genève: Droz, 1968.

746   Prince, Gerald J. "Le symbolisme des noms dans l'oeuvre ro-
       manesque de Sartre." Papers on Language and Literature,
       IV, No. 3, Winter 1969, 316-321.

747   Ricardou, Jean. Pour une théorie du nouveau roman. Paris:
       Editions du Seuil, 1971.

748   Ricardou, Jean. Problèmes du nouveau roman. Paris: Edit-
       ions du Seuil, 1967.

749   Robbe-Grillet, Alain. "Nature, humanisme, tragédie." Nou-
       velle Revue Française. No. 70, 1958, 580-604. Reimprimé
       Pour un nouveau roman. Paris: Editions du Seuil, 1963,
       55-84.

750   Robichon, Jacques. "Libérons le roman français de M. Sar-
       tre." Liberté de l'Esprit. No. 16, décembre 1950, 263-
       267.

751   Roy, Claude. "Descriptions critique: Jean-Paul Sartre."
       Poésie 47, VIII, No. 38, mars 1947, 35-49. Reimprimé
       Descriptions critiques. Paris: Gallimard, 1949, 161-
       189.

752   Zéraffa, Michel. Personne et personnage: Le romanesque
       des années 1920 aux années 1950. Paris: Klincksieck, 1969.

753   Zéraffa, Michel. Roman et société. Paris: Presses Univer-
       sitaires de France, 1971.

STUDIES IN OTHER LANGUAGES

754   Bo, Carlo. "Il romanziere e il mondo vischioso." Aut Aut.
       No. 51, 1959, 169-179.

755   Dneprow, W. "Ist die klassiche Kunst überholt? Aus den
       Erfahrungen des westlichen Romans." Kunst und Literatur,
       XIII, No. 9, September 1965, 939-967.

756   Fortini, Franco. "Guidizi su Sartre romanziere." Pensiero
       Critico, I, No. 1, 1950, 74-78.

757   Horst, Karl. Das Spektrum des modernen Romans. Munich: Beck,
       1960, 83-89, 97-105.

758   Lotti, L. "Esistenzialismo ed esistenzialismo sartriano come
       presupposti ideologici del romanzo italiano del dopoguerra."
       L'Italia Franciscana: Rivista di Cultura, Roma, XLI, No. 3,
       1966, 179-187.

759   Migner, Karl. Theorie des modernen Romans: Eine Einführung.
       Stuttgart: Alfred Kröner, 1970.

760   Pales, A. "Sartre, novela y teatro." Nueva Etapa, X, 1956,
       8-15.

761   Pollmann, Leo. Der französische Roman im 20. Jahrhundert.
       Stuttgart: Kohlhammer, 1970.

762   Pollmann, Leo. Der neue Roman in Frankreich und Lateinamer-
       ika. Stuttgart: Kohlhammer, 1970.

763   Pongs, Hermann. Romanschaffen im Umbruch der Zeit: Eine
       Chronik von 1952 bis 1962. Tübingen: Verlag der Deutschen
       Hochschullerhrerzeitung, 1963.

764   Roy, Claude. "Jean-Paul Sartre." Revista de las Indias (Bo-
       gotá), XXXIII, No. 105, September 1948, 427-449.

765   Sabato, Ernesto. "Sartre contra Sartre o la misión trascen-
       dente de la novela." Sur. No. 329, July-December 1971,
       268-282. Reprinted Sur. No. 311, March-April 1968, 31-45.

766   Sinko, Erwin. Roman eines Romans. Koln, 1962.

767   Varela Jácome, Benito. "Problemática de las novelas de Jean-
       Paul Sartre." Renovación de la novela en el siglo XX. Bar-
       celona: Edición Destino, 1967, 343-362.

768   Waelhens, Alphonse de. "Der Roman des Existentialismus."
       Universitas, I, No. 8, November 1948, 945-951.

769   Zeltner-Neukomm, Gerda. "Das Problem der Existenz." Das
       Wagnis des französischen Gegenwartsromans: Die neue Welter-
       fahrung in der Literatur. Hamburg: Rowohlt, 1960, 40-49.

PLAYS

BARIONA

770   Esslin, Martin. "Sartre's Nativity Play." Adam International
      Review, XXXV, No. 343-345, 1970, 36.

771   Hassenhüttl, Gotthold. Gott öhne Gott: Ein Dialog mit Jean-
      Paul Sartre. Mit d. Weihnachtsspiel 'Bariona oder der Don-
      nersohn' von Jean-Paul Sartre. Ubers. von Gotthold Hasen-
      hüttl. Graz: Styria, 1972, 336 pp.

772   Krauss, Henning. "Bariona: Sartres Theaterauffassung im Spie-
      gel seines ersten Dramas." Germanisch-Romanische Monat-
      schrift, N.F., XIX, No. 2, April 1969, 179-194.

773   Mohanty, Christine. "Bariona, The Germination of Sartrean
      Theater." French Review, XLVII, No. 6, May 1974, 1094-1109.

774   Quinn, Bernard. J. "The Politics of Despair Versus the Pol-
      itics of Hope: A Look at Bariona, Sartre's First pièce en-
      gagée." French Review, Special Issue, XLV, No. 4, Spring
      1972, 95-105.

775   Quinn, Bernard J. "Sarah: A Refreshing Addition to Sartre's
      Gallery of Dramatic Heroines." Proceedings: Pacific North-
      west Conference on Foreign Languages. Corvallis, Oregon:
      State Univ., 1973, 175-177.

776   Quinn, Bernard J. "Sarah, Wife of Bariona: Sartre's First
      Dramatic Heroine." Language Quarterly, 12, No. 1-2, 1973,
      pp. 8, 46, 55.

777   Roure, Rémy, "Sartre a sauvé une âme (Noël 40)." Figaro
      Littéraire. 26 mars 1961, 1 (Cf. Les Ecrits de Sartre,
      Contat et Rybalka, 374).

778   Stenström, Thure. "Jean-Paul Sartre's First Play." Orbis
      Litterarum, XXII, 1967, 173-190.

LES MOUCHES

STUDIES IN ENGLISH

779   Abrahamson, E. "Contemporary French Plays From Ancient
       Sources: Sartre's Les Mouches." The Adventures of Odys-
       seus. St. Louis: n.p., 1960, 57-65.

780   Allen, Marcus. "Character Development in the Oreste of Vol-
       taire and Les Mouches of Jean-Paul Sartre." College Lan-
       guage Association Journal, XVIII, No. 1, September 1974,
       1-21.

781   Anonymous. "The Flies." New Statesman and Nation, XLII,
       1 December 1951, 620-621.

782   Artinian, Robert W. "Foul Winds in Argos: Sartre's Les
       Mouches." Romance Notes, XIV, 1972, 7-12.

       Bearsworth, P. see 414.

783   Belli, Angela. "Jean-Paul Sartre: Les Mouches." Ancient
       Greek Myths and Modern Drama: A Study in Continuity. New
       York: New York Univ. Pr.; London: Univ. of London Pr., 1968,
       70-87.

       Belli, Angela see 258.

784   Bentley, Eric. "Jean-Paul Sartre, Dramatist." Kenyon Review,
       VIII, No. 1, Winter 1946, 66-79.

785   Blake, Patricia. "Sartre's Theater: No Exit and The Flies."
       Partisan Review, XIV, No. 3, 1947, 313-316.

786   Buckley, Michael J. "Les Mouches: Antinomies Within Atheis-
       tic Humanism." Cithara, III, No. 1, November 1963, 1-15.

787   Bukala, C.R. "Sartre's Orestes: An Instance of Freedom as
       Creativity." Philosophy Today, XVII, Spring 1973, 40-51.

788   Burdick, Dolores M. "Concept of Character in Giraudoux's
       Electre and Sartre's Les Mouches." French Review, XXXIII,
       December 1959, 131-136.

789   Burdick, Dolores M. "Imagery of the 'Plight' in Sartre's Les
       Mouches." French Review, XXXII, 1958, 242-246.

Burian, Jarka M.   see 271.

790   Conacher, D.J.   "Orestes as Existential Hero."   Philological Quarterly, XXXIII, October 1954, 407-417.

791   Conradie, Pieter Jacobus.   The Treatment of Greek Myths in Modern French Drama: A Study of the 'Classical' Plays of Anouilh, Cocteau, Giraudoux, Sartre.   Stellenbosch Universiteit Annale, Series B, XXIX, No. 2, 1963.

792   Debusscher, G.   "Modern Masks of Orestes: The Flies and the Prodigal."   Modern Drama, XII, Decmeber 1969, 308-318.

793   Dickenson, Donald H.   "Jean-Paul Sartre: Myth and Anti-Myth."   Myth In The Modern Stage.   Urbana: Univ. of Illinois Pr., 1969, 219-247.

Dickenson, Donald H.   see 286.

794   Fauve, Jacques.   "A Drama of Essence: Salacrou and Others."   Yale French Studies, No. 14, Winter 1954-1955, 30-40.

795   Freeze, Donald J.   "Zeus, Orestes, and Sartre."   New Scholasticism, XLIV, No. 2, Spring 1970, 249-264.

Gaither, Mary E.   see 306.

796   Gassner, John.   The Theater in Our Time: A Survey of the Men, Materials, and Movements in the Modern Theater.   New York: Crown, 1954.

797   Glicksberg, Charles.   "Nihilism in Contemporary Literature."   Nineteenth Century and After, CLXIV, October 1949, 214-222.

798   Gore, Keith O.   Sartre: La Nausée and Les Mouches.   London: Edward Arnold, 1970.

799   Green-Armytage, A.H.N.   "Eumenides: Two Modern French Plays."   Downside Review, LXX, October 1952, 394-403.

800   Grossvogel, David I.   "Further Perils of Debate."   The Self-Conscious Stage in Modern French Drama.   New York: Columbia Univ. Pr., 1958, 123-146.

801   Hamburger, Kate.   From Sophocles to Sartre: Figures from Greek Tragedy, Classical and Modern.   Trans. from the German by Helen Sebba.   New York: Ungar, 1969.

802   Hanzeli, Victor E.   "The Progeny of Atreus."   Modern Drama,
       III, May 1960, 75-81.

803   Hastings, Pat G.   "Symbolism in the Adaptations of Greek Myth
       by Modern French Dramatists."   Nottingham French Studies,
       II, No. 1, May 1963, 25-34.

804   Heilman, Robert Bechtold.   The Iceman, the Arsonist, and the
       Troubled Agent: Tragedy, Melodrama on the Modern Stage.
       Seattle: Univ. of Washington Pr., 1973.

805   Henn, T.R.   "The Transmigration of the Greeks."   The Harvest
       of Tragedy.   London: Methuen, 1956, 233-243.

806   Highet, Gilbert.   "The Reinterpretation of Myths."   Virginia
       Quarterly Review, XXV, Winter 1949, 99-115.

807   Juhasz, Leslie A.   Sartre: No Exit, The Flies, and Other
       Works.   New York: Monarch Pr., 1965.

808   Kaufmann, Walter.   "Euripides, Nietzsche, Sartre."   Tragedy
       and Philosophy.   Garden City, New York: Doubleday, 1968,
       283-315.

809   Kaufmann, Walter.   "Nietzsche Between Homer and Sartre: Five
       Treatements of the Orestes Story."   Revue Internationale de
       Philosophie, XVIII, No. 67, 1964, 50-73.

810   Kaufmann, Walter.   "Sartre as Playwright: The Flies and Dirty
       Hands."   Tragedy and Philosophy.   New York: Doubleday, 1968.
       Reprinted Sartre: A Collection of Critical Essays.   Mary
       Warnock, ed.   Garden City, New York: Doubleday, Anchor
       Books, 1971, 244-259.

       Leefmans, Bert M.P.   see 352.

811   Leites, Nathan.   "Trends in Moral Temper."   American Imago,
       1948, 3-37.

812   Lerner, Max.   "Sartre's Orestes: The Free Man in an Age of
       Fear."   Actions and Passions.   New York: Simon and Schuster,
       1959, 49-51.

813   Mason, H.A.   "Existentialism and Literature."   Scrutiny,
       XIII, No. 2, September 1945, 82-98.

814   McClaren, James C. "Identical Contents: Greek Myth, Modern
       French Drama." Renascence, XXI, No. 1, Autumn 1968, 32-
       40.

815   Pocock, J.G.A. "The Flies." Cambridge Review, LXXIX, No.
       1926, 22 February 1958, 379, 381.

816   Richman, H.P. "The Death of God." Hibbert Journal, LIX,
       April 1961, 220-226.

817   Royle, Peter. "The Ontological Significance of Les Mouches."
       French Studies, XXVI, No. 1, January 1972, 42-53.

818   Russell, John. "The Existentialist Theater." Horizon, XI,
       No. 65, May 1945, 319-328.

819   Seidlin, Oskar. "The Oresteia Today: A Myth Dehumanized."
       Thought, XXXIV, Autumn 1959, 434-452.

820   Slochower, Harry. "The Function of Myth in Existentialism."
       Yale French Studies, I, No. 1, Spring-Summer 1948, 42-52.

821   Spoerri, Theophil. "The Structure of Existence: The Flies."
       Sartre: A Collection of Critical Essays. Edith Kern, ed.
       Englewood Cliffs, New Jersey: Prentice-Hall, 1962, 54-61.

822   Stamm, Rudolf. "The Orestes Theme in Three Plays by Eugene
       O'Neill, T.S. Eliot, and Jean-Paul Sartre." English Studies
       (Amsterdam), 30, 1949, 244-255.

823   Weisert, John J. "Two Recent Variations on the Orestes
       Theme." Modern Language Journal, XXXV, No. 5, May 1951,
       356-363.

STUDIES IN FRENCH

824   Bespaloff, Rachel. "Réflexions sur l'esprit de la tragédie."
       Deucalion, II, 1947, 169-193.

825   Bory, Jean-Louis. "Du crépuscule des dieux au crépuscule des
       hommes." Gazette des Lettres, VII, No. 5, n.s., 15 février
       1951, 88-91.

826   Cases, Ida Petazzoni, ed. Les Mouches. Roma: A. Signorelli,
       1972, 159 pp.

827   Castelot, André. "Les Mouches." La Gerbe, 17 juin 1943, 6.

828   Cawdrey, Michel. "Les Mouches de Sartre: Interprétation du
       symbolisme." French Review, XLII, 1968, 50-54.

829   Defradas, Jean. "D'Homère à Jean-Louis Barrault: Esquisse
       d'une histoire de l'Orestie." L'Information Littéraire,
       IX, No. 1, janvier-février 1957, 17-24.

830   De Lattre, Alain. "Destin et liberté dans l'Orestie." An-
       nales d'Esthétique, 11-12, 1972-1973, 40-62.

831   Domenach, Jean-Marie. "Résurrection de la tragédie, I: Le
       Second Romantisme." Le Retour du tragique. Paris: Editions
       du Seuil, 1967, 215-233.

832   Etiemble, René. "Les Mouches." Bibliographie, XVIII, No. 5,
       mai-juin 1950, 6-7.

833   Etiemble, René. "Les Mouches, par Jean-Paul Sartre." Va-
       leurs. No. 1, 1945, 78-80.

834   Frèches, Claude-Henri. "Les Mouches de Sartre: Tragédie des
       remords." La Liberté tragique et le thème du rachat de
       Sophocle à Sartre. Sao Paulo: n.p., 1958, 57-72.

835   Guyon, Bernard. "Sartre et le mythe d'Oreste." Congrès
       d'Aix-en-Provence, avril 1963. Actes du Congrès. Associ-
       ation Guillaume Budé. Paris: Minard, 1964.

836   Kemp, Robert. "Les Mouches." La Vie du théâtre. Paris: Al-
       bin Michel, 1956, 231-233.

837   Laubreaux, Alain. "Les Mouches." Je Suis Partout. 11 juin
       1943.

838   Laubreaux, Alain. "Les Mouches." L'Oeuvre, 7 juin 1943.

839   Laubreaux, Alain. "Les Mouches." Le Petit Parisien. 5 juin
       1943.

840   Leiris, Michel. "Les Mouches." Lettres Françaises (clandes-
       tines). No. 12. Réimprimé avec des modifications Brisées.
       Paris: Mercure de France, 1966, 74-78.

841   Lusset, M. et al. "Jean-Paul Sartre à Berlin: Discussion au-
       tour des Mouches." Verger, I, No. 5, 1948, 109-123.
       M. Lusset, Sartre, Weisenborn, Theunissen, Roditi, Karsch,

Zimmermann, Steinhoff, Fehling prennent part à la discussion.

842   Marcel, Gabriel. "Les Mouches." Chercher Bien, 1943.

843   Marcel, Gabriel. "Les Mouches." Confluences, III, No. 85, 1943, 514-519.

844   Marcel, Gabriel. "Les Mouches, par Jean-Paul Sartre." Nouvelles Littéraires. 18 janvier 1951.

845   Maulnier, Thierry. "Les Mouches." France Libre (London), 15 mars 1944, 397-401.

846   Maulnier, Thierry. "Les Mouches." Revue Universelle. No. 62, 25 juillet 1943, 155-158.

847   Merleau-Ponty, Maurice. "Les Mouches." Confluences, No. 25, septembre-octobre 1943, 514-519.

848   Neveux, Georges. "Les Mouches." Cahiers du Sud, XIX, No. 260, octobre 1943, 825-828.

849   Novy, Yvon. "Ce que nous dit Jean-Paul Sartre de sa première pièce." Interview. Comoedia, III, No. 95, 24 avril 1943, 1.

850   Purnal, Roland. "Au Théâtre de la Cité, Les Mouches." Comoedia, 12 juin 1943.

851   Roulet, Lionel de. "Jean-Paul Sartre, Les Mouches." La France Libre, VII, No. 41, mars 1949, 397-398.

852   Royle, Peter. Sartre: L'Enfer et la liberté: Etudes de 'Huis Clos' et des 'Mouches'. Quebec: Presses de l'Université Laval, 1973, 258 pp.

853   Sarrochi, Jean. "Sartre dramaturge: Les Mouches et Les Séquestrés d'Altona." Travaux de linguistique et de littérature. (Etudes littéraires) Publié par le Centre de philologie et de littérature romanes de l'Université de Strasbourg, VIII, No. 2, Strasbourg-Paris: Librairie C. Klincksieck, 1970, 157-172.

854   Spoerri, Theophil. "Les Mouches de Jean-Paul Sartre." Lettres (Genève), III, No. 1, 1945, 11-28.

855   Sueur, Georges. "Les Mouches de Sartre au Centre dramatique
      du Nord." Le Monde, No. 7736, 27 novembre 1969, 21.

856   Van Laere, François. "La liberté sur le vif, Sartre et Les
      Mouches aujourd'hui." Synthèses, XXII, No. 256-257, octo-
      bre-novembre 1967, 21-31.

STUDIES IN OTHER LANGUAGES

857   Anonymous. "Unterrichtsentwurf zu Jean-Paul Sartre, Die
      Fliegen." Religionspädagogische Projektgruppe Lahr-Frei-
      burg: Religionspädagogisches Institut der Evang. Lanes-
      kirche in Baden, n.d.

858   Barzel, W. "Blinde Freiheit: Zu einem Stück von Sartre."
      Stimmen der Zeit, 141, 1947, 217-223.

859   Baurle, Wilhelm. "Die menschliche Freiheit in Sartre's
      Fliegen: Blätter der Frehiheit (Heidelberg), I, No. 13,
      1949, 9-10.

860   Birkenfeld, G. "Sartre gegen Sartre." Horizont (Berlin),
      III, No. 2, 1948, 17-18.

861   Deml, F. "Die Fliegenplage droht Berlin." Rundfunk (Berlin),
      III, No. 4, 1949, 4.

862   Dietrich, Margaret. "Jean-Paul Sartre und seine existentiel-
      len Dramen: von den Fliegen bis zu den Eingeschlossenen."
      Universitas, XXIII, 1968, 795-799.

863   Ekman, Hans Göran. "Jean-Paul Sartres Les Mouches." Edda,
      LV, No. 6, 1968, 372-379.

864   Ergmann, Raoul. "Uraufführung des Schauspiels Die Fliegen."
      Bühnenkritik (Augsburg).

865   Eylau, H.Y., und Scheidt, B. "Die Freiheit, ein Morder zu
      sein? Eine Kontroverse um Sartres Fliegen." Quelle, II,
      No. 4, 1948, 110-114.

      Fuhrmann, Gunther. see 304.

866   Hamburger, Kate. Von Sophokles zu Sartre: Griechisch Dramen-
      figuren antik und modern. Stuttgart: Kohlhammer, 1962.

867   Herbst, W. "Die Fliegen: Gedanken zu Sartres Drama." Kirche
      (Berlin-Dahlem), III, No. 10, 1948, 1-2.

868   Hofer, W. "Deutsche Erstaufführung von Sartres 'Fliegen' in
      Düsseldorf." Rheinischer Merkur (Koblenz), II, No. 43,
      1947, 3-4.

869   Jakel, Werner. "Antike Stätte in einigen Dramen der Gegen-
      wart." Sammlung, XIII, 1958, 178-195.

870   Kohut, Karl. "Jean-Paul Sartre, Les Mouches." Das moderne
      französische Drama: Interpretationen Herausgegeben von
      Walter Pabst. Berlin: Erich Schmidt, 1971, 154-173.

871   Kuchler, Walther. "Gedanken zu Sartres Les Mouches." Neue-
      philologische Zeitschrift, I, 1949, 16-31.

872   Lasso de la Vega, José S. "Teatro griego y teatro contem-
      poraneo." Revista de la Universidad de Madrid, XIII, No.
      51, 1964, 415-464.

873   Lennig, W. "Der Abfall vom Menschen (Sartres Die Fliegen im
      Hebbeltheater unter Jurgen Fehlings Regie)." Sonntag (Ber-
      lin), III, No. 2, 1948, 7.

874   Macchia, Giovanni. "Sartre ed Eschilo." La Nuova Europa, II,
      No. 52, 31 December 1945, 7.

875   Neuhaus, R., und Bahr, J. "Die Fliegen: Freiheit gegen Glau-
      ben." Göttinger Universitätszeitung, III, No. 6, 1948, 9-
      11.

876   Nordheim, Werner von. "Drei Atriden-Dramen von Euripides,
      Hauptmann, und Sartre--verglichen mit Goethes Iphigenie."
      Wirkendes Wort, XI, 1961, 162-172.

877   Schmauch, Jochen. "Die Freiheit und Die Fliegen von Jean-
      Paul Sartre." Seele (Regensburg), XXVIII, 1952, 35-38.

878   Spoerri, Theophil. "Die verfehten Strukturen: Jean-Paul
      Sartre und der Existentialismus." Die Struktur des Exis-
      tenz. Zurich: R. Romer Speer, 1951.

879   Stenström, Thure. "Sartres Les Mouches." Existentialismen:
      Studier idess ide-tradition och litterara yttringar. Stock-
      holm: Natur och Kultur, 1966,190-261.

880   Stockum, Th. C. van. "Jean-Paul Sartre's drama (1943) en de moderne hernieuwing van de Orestes-mythe." Levende Talen, No. 224, 1964, 72-88.

881   Straub, Frédérique. "Les Mouches." Pariser Zeitung, 17 June 1943.

882   Vietta, Egon. "Sartres Fliegen und das existentielle Philosophieren." Hamburgische Akademische Rundschau, II, 1947-1948, 513-524.

883   Vogel, Geinrich. "Freiheit und Reise: Das Evangelium und 'die Fliegen' von Sartre." Berlin, n.p., 1948.

884   Weber, C.A. "Sartre, Die Fliegen." Literarische Revue (Munchen), III, No. 2, 1948, 111-115.

885   Werrie, J. "Jean-Paul Sartre y su teatro existencialisto." Arbor, XXVIII, 1948, 589-596.

886   Wiemken, H. "Der 50 jahrige Jean-Paul Sartre." Voksbühne (Hamburg), V, No. 12, 1955, 224-226.

887   Wildenhoff, U. "Jean-Paul Sartres Existentialismus in katholischer Sicht." Unitas (Köln), LXLIX, No. 1, 1959, 15-20.

HUIS CLOS

STUDIES IN ENGLISH

888   Astruc, Alexandre. "The European Audience: Jean-Paul Sartre and Huis-Clos." New Writing and Daylight, VI. London: Hogarth Pr., 1945, 136-142.

889   Ayer, A.J. "Secret Session." Polemic, No. 2, January 1946, 60-63.

890   Bentley, Eric. "Jean-Paul Sartre, Dramatist: The Thinker As Playwright." Kenyon Review, VIII, No. 1, Winter 1946, 66-79.

891   Bentley, Eric. "Their Punishment Fits Their Crime." New York Times Book Review, 2 February 1947.

Blake, Patricia. see 785.

892   Bliltgen, Sister M.J.   "No Exit: The Sartrean Idea of Hell."
       Renascence, XIX, 1967, 59-63.

893   Brown, J.M.   "The Unbeautiful and the Damned."   Seeing More
       Things.   New York: McGraw-Hill, 1948, 85-91.

894   Cargo, Robert T.   "Sartre's Huis Clos."   Explicator, XXIV,
       Item 76, 1966.

895   Cate, Hollis L.   "The Final Line of Sartre's No Exit."   Notes
       on Contemporary Literature, II, 1972, 9-10.

896   Cohn, Ruby.   "Dialogues of Cruelty."   Southern Review, III,
       No. 2, Spring 1967, 322-340.

897   Cohn, Ruby.   "Four Stages of Absurdism."   Drama Survey, IV,
       No. 3, Winter 1965, 195-208.

898   Cohn, Ruby.   "Hell On The Twentieth Century Stage."   Wisconsin
       Studies in Comparative Literature, V, No. 1, Winter-Spring
       1964, 48-53.

899   Falk, Eugene H.   "No Exit and Who's Afraid of Virginia Woolf:
       A Thematic Comparison."   Studies in Philology, LXVII, July
       1970, 406-417.

900   Foulkes, S.H. and Anthony, E.J.   "The Rational History of the
       Therapeutic Group, 3: A Literary Example of a Closed Group."
       Group Psychotherapy: The Psychoanalytic Approach.   Hamonds-
       worth, Middlesex: Penguin, 1965.

901   Fowlie, Wallace.   A Guide to Contemporary French Literature
       from Valéry to Sartre.   New York: Meridian Books, 1957.

902   Hardee, A. Maynor.   "Garcin and Sisyphus."   Discourse, XII,
       1960, 226-230.

903   Jeanson, Francis.   "Pessimism and Optimism in Sartre's
       Thought."   Sartre: A Collection of Critical Essays.   Mary
       Warnock, ed.   Garden City, New York: Doubleday, Anchor
       Books, 1971, 176-185.

       Juhasz, Leslie A.   see 807.

904   Loeb, E.   "Sartre's No Exit and Brecht's The Good Woman of
       Setzvan: A Comparison."   Modern Language Quarterly, XII,
       No. 3, September 1961, 283-291.

905   Mankowitz, Wolf. "Hell is Other People." Politics and
         Letters, I, No. 1, Summer 1947, 68-70.

906   Mendel, Sydney. "The Descent Into Solitude: On Existence
         Real, Certain and Incurable." Forum (Houston), III, No. 8,
         Fall 1961, 19-24.

907   Parsons, Howard L. "Existential Hell." Journal of Religious
         Thought, XXI, No. 1, 1964-1965, 25-42.

908   Raine, Kathleen. "Closed Session." New English Review, XII,
         No. 2, February 1946, 181-183.

909   Sakharoff, Micheline. "The Polyvalence of the Theatrical Lan-
         guage of No Exit." Modern Drama, XVI, No. 2, September
         1973, 199-206.

STUDIES IN FRENCH

910   Astruc, Alexandre. "Huis-clos." Poésie 44, No. 21, novembre-
         décembre 1944, 99-107.

911   Cottier, Georges. "Les 'autres' de Jean-Paul Sartre." Laby-
         rinthe (Genève), No. 9, 1945, 11-12.

912   Gaillard, Pol. "Pièces noires." Pensée, No. 1, octobre-dé-
         cembre 1944, 108-117.

913   Gomel, Jacques. "Procès à huis clos." Cahiers de Notre
         Jeunesse. No. 20, février 1945, 49-55.

914   Hanoteau, Guillaume. Ces nuits qui ont fait Paris: Un demi-
         siècle de théâtre d'Ubu à Huis Clos. Paris: Fayard, 1971.

915   Kanters, Robert. "Huis clos." Cahiers du Sud, XXII, No. 269,
         janvier-février 1945, 100-104.

916   Legay, Jacques. "Le cinéma: Huis Clos." La Revue Nouvelle,
         XI, No. 3, 15 mars 1955, 308-310.

917   Marcel, Gabriel. "Huis clos et La Putain respectueuse de
         Jean-Paul Sartre." Nouvelles Littéraires, 21 mai 1953.

918   Marcel, Gabriel. "Huis clos et le visage infernal de l'ex-
         périence humaine." Horizons (Nantes). No. 1, 1945, 60-64.

919   Marcel, Gabriel. "Huis clos par Jean-Paul Sartre." Nouvelles
      Littéraires, 26 avril 1945.

920   Marcel, Gabriel. "Reflexions du critique." Revue Théâtrale,
      février 1947.

921   Marcel, Gabriel. "Le théâtre." Hommes et mondes. No. 4,
      novembre 1946, 195-198.

922   Pingaud, Bernard. "Huis clos ou la téléfraction." Les Temps
      Modernes, XXI, No. 235, décembre 1965, 1144-1146.

923   Pons, Christian. "Eliot et Sartre: De Huis clos à Fin de car-
      rière ou de la liberté de la pureté." Cahiers du Sud, LII,
      No. 383-384, août-septembre 1965.

      Royle, Peter. see 852.

924   Sandier, Gilles. "Socrate dramaturge." L'Arc, Sartre aujourd'
      hui. No. 30, décembre 1966, 77-86.

925   Sartre, Jean-Paul. "Sartre donne les clefs de 'L'enfer, c'est
      les autres'." Figaro Littéraire, 7-13 janvier 1965. Préface
      parlée à l'enrégistrement de Huis clos.

926   Thoroval, Jean, et Leo, Maurice. "Jean-Paul Sartre: Huis
      clos." Le Commentaire des textes littéraires. Paris:
      Bordas, 1971, 97-103.

927   Troyat, Henri. "Huis clos." La Nef, II, No. 4, 1945, 154-
      155.

928   Truchet, Jacques. "Huis clos et L'Etat de siège, signes
      avant-coureurs de l'anti-théâtre." Le Théâtre moderne, II:
      Depuis la deuxième guerre mondiale. Etudes de J. Robichez,
      et al. Paris: Editions du Centre National de la Recherche
      Scientifique, 1967, 29-36.

929   Vague, Jean. "Huis clos." Lettres. No. 1, 1945, 76-78.

930   Valogne, Catherine. "Huis clos revu par Jacqueline Audry."
      Lettres Françaises, 16 septembre 1954. On the film version
      of Huis clos.

STUDIES IN OTHER LANGUAGES

931   Beyerle, Marianne. "Die Modernisierung der Hölle in Sartres
       Huis-clos." Aufassätze zur Themen- und Motivgeschichte: Fest-
       schrift für Hellmut Petroconi zum 70. Gebürtstag am April
       1965 von seinem Hamgurger Schülern. Hamburg: Cram. de
       Gruyther und Co. in Komm., 1965, 171-188.

932   Braun, Hanns. "Sartre in und um München: Notizen zu zweimal
       'Huis-clos." Rheinischer Merkur (Koblenz), V, No. 17, 1950,
       6.

933   B.M.V. "Theologie der Hölle: Anmerkungen zu Sartres Hinter
       verschlossen Türen." Gegenwart, V, No. 10, 15 May 1950, 19-
       20.

934   Drese, Claud Helmut. "Die Hölle des Bewussteins: Zu Sartres
       'Geschlossener Gesellschaft' und Eliot's 'Cocktail Party'."
       Das Literarische Deutschland (Heidelberg), II, No. 20,
       1951, 3.

935   Flügel, Heinz. "Sartres Hölle." Hochland (München), XLIII,
       1951-1952, 365-373.

936   Gehlen, Arnold. "Über Huis-clos von Jean-Paul Sartre."
       Wiener Literarisches Echo, I, October-December 1949, 4-7.

937   Holzamer, Karl. "Die Wahrheit in Scherben." Rheinischer
       Merkur (Koblenz), IV, No. 29, 1949, 3-4.

938   Lausberg, Heinrich. Interpretationen Dramatischer Dichtun-
       gen, Volume 2. München: Max Hueber, 1964.

939   Mello Alvarenga, Octavio. "Huis clos e o apocalipse." Re-
       vista do Livro, II, No. 8, 1957, 225-228.

940   Miró Quesada, Francisco. "El existencialismo, Sartre y Huis-
       clos." El Comercio (Lima), 18 June 1948.

941   Wasintynski, Jeremi. "Symbolikhen i Sartres 'Stengte Doren'."
       Vinduet, XII, No. 4, 1958, 306-314.

MORTS SANS SEPULTURE

STUDIES IN ENGLISH

942   Abraham, Claude K. "A Study in Auto-Hypocrisy: Morts sans
      sépulture." Modern Drama, III, February 1961, 343-347.

943   Gabriel, Gilbert W. "The Victors and the Venial." Theatre
      Arts, XXXIX, No. 2, 1949, 17.

STUDIES IN FRENCH

944   Anonymous. "Incident au Théâtre Antoine." Le Monde, 9 novem-
      bre 1946, 6.

945   Anonymous. "Morts sans sépulture." Le Monde, 9 novembre
      1946. Scandal of first representation in Paris.

946   Anonymous. "Morts sans sépulture n'est pas une pièce sur la
      Résistance', nous dit Jean-Paul Sartre." Combat, 30 octo-
      bre 1946, 4.

947   Anonymous. "Scandale à Paris." France-Dimanche, 17 novembre
      1946. Première représentation.

948   Augagneur, Marcel. "Au Théâtre Antoine: Deux pièces de Jean-
      Paul Sartre." France-Soir, 20 novembre 1946, 2.

949   Boll, Christiane. "En relisant Morts sans sépulture." Margi-
      nales, XXIV, No. 124, février 1969, 64-66.

950   Brisson, Pierre. "Le cas de Sartre et le théâtre." Figaro
      Littéraire, 4 octobre 1947, No. 76, 1, 3.

951   Brisson, Pierre. "Le cas Sartre." Propos de théâtre. Paris:
      Gallimard, 1957, 21-53.

952   Brunot, Henriette. "Le théâtre: Morts sans sépulture de Jean-
      Paul Sartre." Psyché, I, No. 2, décembre 1946, 258-262.

953   Carat, Jacques. "Théâtre Antoine: Morts sans sépulture et La
      P . . . respectueuse." Paru, janvier 1947, No. 26, 42-45.

954   Gandrey-Rety, Jean. "Morts sans sépulture." Arts, 29 novembre 1946, No. 95, 7.

955   Gandrey-Rety, Jean. "Morts sans sépulture ou la putain scandalisée." Arts, 22 novembre 1946, No. 94, 7.

956   Gautier, Jean-Jacques. "Au Théâtre Antoine: Morts sans sépulture et La Putain respectueuse." Le Figaro, 14 novembre 1946, 4.

957   H.K. "Les deux pièces de M. Sartre." Le Monde, 5 novembre 1946, 6.

958   Kemp, Robert. "Morts sans sépulture au Théâtre Antoine." Le Monde, 15 novembre 1946, 6.

959   Kemp, Robert. "Une affaire classée: Les deux pièces de Sartre." Le Monde, 22 novembre 1946, 3.

960   Leclerc, Guy. "Au Théâtre Antoine, Morts sans sépulture, La Putain respectueuse." L'Humanité, 20 novembre 1946, 3.

961   Lemarchand, Jacques. "Morts sans sépulture et La putain respectueuse au Théâtre Antoine." Combat, 10 novembre 1946, 3.

962   Marcel, Gabriel. "Deux pièces de Jean-Paul Sartre." Hommes et Mondes, No. 6, janvier 1947, 192-196.

963   Marcel, Gabriel. "Deux pièces nouvelles de Jean-Paul Sartre." Nouvelles Littéraires, 21 novembre 1946.

964   Marcel, Gabriel. "Réflexions du critique." Revue Théâtrale, février 1947.

965   Marcel, Gabriel. "Réflexions sur la saison théâtrale parisienne." Revue Théâtrale, juin-août 1947, 364-366.

966   Paulus, Claude. "Notes sur Morts sans sépulture de Jean-Paul Sartre." Synthèses, II, No. 10, 1948, 113-117.

967   Rinieri, J.J. "Jean-Paul Sartre: Morts sans sépulture--La Putain respectueuse." La Nef, No. 26, janvier 1947, 155-158.

968   S., C.W. "Morts sans sépulture a eu à Copenhage une première mouvementée." Le Figaro, 6 novembre 1946, 4.

969   Sion, Georges. "Sartre, et puis Shakespeare." Revue Générale
      Belge, octobre 1947, 932-938.

970   Touchard, Pierre Aimé. "Spectacle Jean-Paul Sartre au Théâtre
      Antoine." Opéra, 13 novembre 1946, No. 79, 3.

971   Warnod, André. "La torture pose le problème de la liberté hu-
      maine', nous dit Jean-Paul Sartre." Le Figaro, 1 novembre
      1946. Interview.

STUDIES IN GERMAN

972   Anonymous. "Sartre unter Vorzensur: Tote ohne Begrabnis in
      Hamburg." Die Zeit, V, No. 20, 1950, 3.

973   Bohne, Regine. "Tote ohne Begrabnis: Ein Stück von Sartre
      und eine Diskussion in Hamburg." Frankfurter Hefte, V,
      No. 7, 1950, 781.

974   Gaillard, Pol. "Romane und Philosophie enttäuschen, Komö-
      dien und Dramen--das ist ihr Weg." Theater der Zeit (Ber-
      lin), II, No. 3, 1947, 15.

975   Pouillon, Jean. "Philosophisches Theater." Umschau (Mainz),
      II, 1947, 425-432.

976   Siewert, Eva. "Sartre in Berlin." Neues Europa (Stuttgart),
      III, No. 6, 1948, 2.

977   Varloot, Jean. "Sobismus modernsten Stils: Nihilismus."
      Theater der Zeit (Berlin), No. 3, 1947, 17.

LA PUTAIN RESPECTUEUSE

STUDIES IN ENGLISH

978   Bentley, Eric. "Sartre's Struggle for Existenz." Kenyon Re-
      view, X, No. 2, Spring 1948, 328-334. Reprinted Sartre: A
      Collection of Critical Essays. Edith Kern, ed. Englewood
      Cliffs, New Jersey: Prentice-Hall, 1962, 73-79.

979   Carr, Philip. "The Theater in Paris." World Review, Decem-
      ber 1947, 41-45.

980   Ewing, James M.   "Sartre's Existentialism and The Respectful
      Prostitute."   Southern Quarterly (Univ. of Southern Mississ-
      ippi), VII, No. 2, January 1969, 167-174.

981   Jack, Homer A.   "Censoring Sartre."   The Nation, CLXVIII, No.
      11, 12 March 1949, 305.

982   Nathan, George J.   "The Respectful Prostitute."   Theater Book
      of the Year 1947-1948.   New York: Knopf, 1948, 30-33, 258-
      261.

983   O'Keefe, C.   "'Tis Pity She's Respectful: Respectful Prostit-
      ute Banned in Chicago."   Theater Arts, No. 33, March 1949,
      49-50.

984   Wilson, Edmund,   "Jean-Paul Sartre: The Novelist and the Exis-
      tentialist."   Classics and Commercials: A Literary Chronicle
      of the Forties.   New York: Farrar, Strauss and Cudahy, 1950,
      393-403.   Reprinted Sartre: A Collection of Critical Essays,
      Edith Kern, ed.   Englewood Cliffs, New Jersey: Prentice-
      Hall, 1962, 47-53.

985   Wright, Richard.   "Introductory Note to The Respectful Pros-
      titute: Art and Action.   New York: Twice a Year Press,
      1948, 14-16.

STUDIES IN FRENCH

986   Anonymous.   "La Putain respectueuse a été présentée par M. Du-
      pont au Conseil Municipal."   Combat, 6 décembre 1946, 3.

987   Anonymous.   "Le scandale de La Putain respectueuse."   Le
      Figaro, 21 novembre 1946.

988   Augagneur, Marcel.   "Au Théâtre Antoine: Deux pièces de M.
      Sartre."   France-Soir, 20 novembre 1946, 2.

989   Blanquet, Marc.   "Jean-Paul Sartre installe l'existentialisme
      chez Antoine."   Opéra, 6 novembre 1946, 3.

990   Cadieu, Martine.   "Une 'comédie musicale': La P . . . respec-
      tueuse au Théâtre-Maison de la Culture à Caen."   Lettres
      Françaises, No. 1205, 25-31 octobre 1972, 22.

991   Carat, Jacques. "Théâtre Antoine: <u>Morts sans sépulture</u> et <u>La</u>
       <u>P . . . respectueuse</u>." <u>Paru</u>, janvier 1947, 42-45.

992   Cohen, François. "De la vérité à l'écran ou le fils de Taft
       n'est pas un conquérant solitaire." <u>Nouvelle Critique</u>, IV,
       No. 40, Nov. 1952, 103-109. On the film version.

993   Dutourd, Jean. "<u>La P . . . respectueuse</u>." <u>Le Paradoxe du</u>
       <u>critique</u> suivi <u>Sept saisons</u>: <u>Impressions de théâtre</u>. Paris:
       Flammarion, 1972, 162-163.

994   Fayrol, André. "La peur des mots." <u>Le Monde</u>, 10 novembre
       1946, 1.

995   Gautier, Jean-Jacques. "Au Théâtre Antoine: <u>Morts sans sépul-</u>
       <u>ture</u> et <u>La P . . . respectueuse</u>." <u>Le Figaro</u>, 14 novembre
       1946, 4.

996   H.K. "Les deux pièces de M. Sartre." <u>Le Monde</u>, 5 novembre
       1946, 6.

997   Kemp, Robert. "Une affaire classée: Les deux pièces de Sar-
       tre." <u>Le Monde</u>, 22 novembre 1946, 3.

998   Lang, Renée B. "Sartre: <u>La Putain respectueuse</u>." <u>French Re-</u>
       <u>view</u>, XX, No. 6, 1947, 490-491.

999   Leclerc, Guy. "Au Théâtre Antoine: <u>Morts sans sépulture</u>, <u>La</u>
       <u>P . . . respectueuse</u>." L'Humanité, 20 novembre 1946, 4.

1000   Lemarchand, Jacques. "<u>Morts sans sépulture</u> et <u>La Putain</u> re-
       <u>spectueuse</u> au Théâtre Antoine." <u>Combat</u>, 10 novembre 1946,
       3.

1001   Marcel, Gabriel. "Deux pièces de Jean-Paul Sartre." <u>Hommes</u>
       <u>et Mondes</u>. No. 6, janvier 1947, 192-196.

1002   Marcel, Gabriel. "Deux pièces nouvelles de Jean-Paul Sartre."
       <u>Nouvelles Littéraires</u>, 21 novembre 1946.

1003   Marcel, Gabriel. <u>L'Heure théâtrale</u>: <u>De Giraudoux à Jean-Paul</u>
       <u>Sartre</u>. Paris: Plon, 1959.

1004   Marcerou, Jacques. "Jean-Paul Sartre va faire ses débuts de
       metteur en scène avec <u>La Putain respectueuse</u>." <u>Libération</u>,
       30 octobre 1946.

1005 Maulnier, Thierry. "La Putain respectueuse." Spectateur, 19 novembre 1946.

1006 Rinieri, J.J. "Jean-Paul Sartre: Morts sans sépulture--La Putain respectueuse." La Nef. No. 26, janvier 1947, 155-158.

1007 Sakari, A. "Jean-Paul Sartre: Néologiste malgré lui." Neuphilologische Mitteilungen (Helsinki), LI, 1950, 130-132.

STUDIES IN GERMAN

1008 Erdmann, C. "Die ehrbare Dirne'--Jean-Paul Sartres Bekenntnis zur Zukunft." Unsere Universität (Greifswald), No. 1, 1953-1954, 10-11.

1009 Erpenbeck, Fritz. "Die ehrbare Dirne von Jean-Paul Sartre in den Kammerspielen der Städtischen Theater Lepizig." Theater der Zeit (Berlin), IX, No. 5, 1954, 40-43.

1010 Guthke, Karl. "Kleists Zerbrochener Krug und Sartres La Putain respectueuse." Die Neueren Sprachen, N.F., 1959, 466-470.

1011 Heer, Friedrich. "Sartre sieht Amerika." Die Osterreichische Furche (Wien), VI, No. 5, 1950, 7.

1012 Hensel, Georg. "Die Erhbare Anklage." Neue Literarische Welt (Heidelberg), IV, No. 9, 1953, 9.

1013 Honig, H.C. "Sartres Schauspiel-meisterhaft dargestellt: Zur Aufführung der Ehrbaren Dirne in den Kammerspielen der Städtischen Theater Leipzig." Heute und Morgen (Schwerin), No. 5, 1954, 300-301.

1014 Lausberg, Heinrich. Interpretationen Dramatischer Dichtungen, Vol. 2. München: Max Hueber, 1964.

1015 Zimmermann, Hans-Joachin. "Noch einmal: Kleists Zerbrochener Krug und Sartres La Putain respectueuse." Die Neueren Sprachen, 1960, 484-488.

LES MAINS SALES

STUDIES IN ENGLISH

1016   Anonymous. "Boyer on Broadway." Life, XXVI, No. 1, 3 January 1949, 49-52.

1017   Clurman, Harold. "Red Gloves." New Republic, 20 December 1948, 28-29.

1018   Daniel, George. "Hoederer versus Hugo in Les Mains sales of Sartre." South Atlantic Bulletin, XX, May 1954, 11-14.

1019   Ferguson, Francis. "Sartre as Playwright." Partisan Review, XVI, No. 4, April 1949, 409-411.

1020   Glicksberg, Charles I. "Existentialism Versus Marxism." Nineteenth Century and After, CXLVII, May 1950, 335-341. Reprinted The Tragic Vision in Twentieth Century Literature. Carbondale: Southern Illinois Univ. Pr., 1963, 335-341.

1021   Grossvogel, David I. "Further Perils of Debate." The Self-Conscious Stage in Modern French Drama. New York: Columbia Univ. Pr., 1958, 123-146.

1022   Fleming, Peter. "Crime Passionel by Jean-Paul Sartre." The Spectator, CLXXXI, 13 August 1948, 205.

1023   J.G.W. "Les Mains sales." Twentieth Century, CLII, No. 908, October 1952, 363-364.

1024   Kahler, Eric. "Doctor Faustus from Adam to Sartre." Comparative Drama, I, No. 2, Summer 1967, 75-92.

1025   Kaufmann, Walter. "Euripides, Nietzsche, Sartre." Tragedy and Philosophy. Garden City, New York: Doubleday, 1968, 283-315.

1026   MacArthur, Roderick. "Author! Author!" Theater Arts. No. 33, March 1949, 11-13. Cf. Les Ecrits de Sartre, Contat and Rybalka, 181-182.

1027   Mendel, Sydney. "The Ambiguity of the Rebellious Son." Forum (Houston), Spring 1966, 32-36.

1028   Nathan, George J. "Dirty Hands." Theater Book of the Year: 1948-1949. New York: Knopf, 1949, 193, 221-223.

1029   Pucciani, Oreste F. "Introduction to Les Mains sales." The French Theater Since 1930. Boston: Ginn and Co., 1954.

1030   Sauvage, Leo. "Crime passionel." New Statesman and Nation, XXXV, June 1948, 520.

1031   Sauvage, Leo. "Crime passionel." The Spectator, 13 August 1948, 144-145.

1032   Sauvage, Leo. "'Red Gloves' and 'Dirty Hands'." The Nation, CLXVIII, No. 1, 1 January 1949, 19-20.

1033   Schneider, Isidor. "Dirty Hands." Masses and Mainstream, II, No. 1, January 1949, 88-92.

1034   Styan, J.L. "Les Mains sales." The Elements of Drama. Cambridge: Univ. Pr., 1965, 239-243.

1035   Walzer, Michael. "Political Action: The Problem of Dirty Hands." Philosophy and Public Affairs, II, Winter 1973, 160-180.

STUDIES IN FRENCH

1036   Alter, André. "Au Théâtre Antoine: Les Mains sales de Jean-Paul Sartre." L'Aube, VII, No. 4, 1948, 2.

1037   Ambrière, Francis. "Les Mains sales au Théâtre Antoine." Opéra, VII, No. 4, 1948, No. 151, 1, 3.

1038   Anex, G. "Les Mains sales par Jean-Paul Sartre." Formes et Couleurs, No. 4, 1948.

1039   Anonymous. "A propos des Mains sales de Jean-Paul Sartre." Conseil de Vigilance doctrinaire du Diocèse de Besançon, 1949.

1040   Anonymous. "Le 'Crime passionel' projeté par Jean-Paul Sartre." Arts, 26 mars 1948. Cf. Les Ecrits de Sartre, p. 179.

1041   Baude, Pierre-André; "Demain, au Théâtre Antoine, Jean-Paul Sartre prendra position devant le problème de l'engagement politique." L'Aube, 7 avril 1948, 2.

1042 Biermez, Jean. "Les Mains sales." Les Temps Modernes, No.
      36, septembre 1948, 574-576.

1043 Carat, Jacques. "Les Mains sales." Paru. No. 42, 1948, 130-
      132.

1044 Delpech, Jeannine. "Les Mains sales." Nouvelles Littéraires.
      No. 1076, 15 avril 1948, 8.

1045 Dornand, Guy. "Drame politique puis crime passionel . . .
      Jean-Paul Sartre nous parle de sa prochaine pièce." Franc-
      Tireur, 25 mars 1948. Interview.

1046 Duras, Marguerite. "Sartre et l'humour involontaire."
      Action, April 1948.

1047 Dussane, B. "Les Mains sales." Mercure de France, CCCIII,
      No. 1018, 7 juin 1948, 314-317.

1048 Gauthier, Jean-Jacques. "La vie théâtrale: Les Mains sales."
      Hommes et Mondes. No. 23, juin 1948, 342-345.

1049 Gordon, René. "Avant la création des Mains sales, Jean-Paul
      Sartre nous dit." L'Ordre, 31 mars 1948.

1050 Gouhier, Henri. "Les Mains sales." Vie Intellectuelle. No.
      7, 1948, 121-123.

1051 Grandrey-Rety, Jean. "Les Mains sales." Arts, No. 161, 9
      avril 1948, 7.

1052 Grandrey-Rety, Jean. "Sartre et le parti prolétarien--Les
      Mains sales, II." Arts. No. 163, 23 avril 1948, 7.

1053 Grin, Nevin. "Les Américains s'ennuient aux Mains sales."
      Opéra. No. 188, 5 janvier 1949, 3.

1054 Guilly, René. "Dans Les Mains sales, Jean-Paul Sartre pose le
      problème de la fin et des moyens." Combat, 31 mars 1948, 2.

1055 Gutwirth, Marcel. "Jean-Paul Sartre à l'école de Pierre Cor-
      neille." Modern Language Notes, LXXIX, mai 1964, 257-264.

1056 Jeener, J.B. "Quand Cocteau, le poète, met en scène le philo-
      sophe Jean-Paul Sartre." Le Figaro, 30 mars 1948, 4.

1057 Kemp, Robert. "Les Mains sales." Le Monde, 20 avril 1948, 7.

1058   Kemp, Robert. "Les Mains sales." La Vie du Théâtre. Paris:
        Albin Michel, 1956, 225-230.

1059   Kemp, Robert. "Les Mains sales au Théâtre Antoine." Le
        Monde, 4-5 avril, 1948.

1060   Laforgue, René. "A propos de la pièce de Sartre, Les Mains
        sales." Psyché, III, No. 20, juin 1948, 652-654.

1061   Leclerc, Guy. "Monsieur Sartre a les mains sales." L'Human-
        ité, 7 avril 1948, 4.

1062   Kourilsky, Françoise. "Le brouillon des Mains sales." Nouvel
        Observateur. No. 226, 10-16 mars 1969, 56.

1063   Lemarchand, Jacques. "Les Mains sales." Caliban, juin 1948,
        52-53.

1064   Lemarchand, Jacques. "Les Mains sales au Théâtre Antoine."
        Combat, 6 avril 1948, 2.

1065   Magnan, Henri. "Avec Jean-Paul Sartre avant la première des
        Mains sales." Le Monde, 25 mars 1948, 6.

1066   Marcel, Gabriel. "Les Mains sales de Jean-Paul Sartre." Nou-
        velles Littéraires, 23 avril 1948.

1067   Mauduit, Jean. "Les Mains sales." Liaison, II, No. 15, mai
        1948, 291-293.

1068   Maulnier, Thierry. "Avec Les Mains sales, Jean-Paul Sartre
        ouvre un débat de conscience qui est interdit aux militants
        communistes." Figaro Littéraire, 10 avril 1948.

1069   Maulnier, Thierry. "Les Mains sales." Revue de la Pensée
        Française, VII, No. 6, juin 1948, 39-42.

1070   Meyer, Gaston, ed. Les Mains sales. Paris: Bordas; Brux-
        elles: Asedi; Lausanne: Spes, 1971.

1071   Outié, Claude. "Peut-on entrer dans un parti quelconque sans
        se salir les mains? nous demande Jean-Paul Sartre, écrivain
        'engagé'." L'Aurore, 30 mars, 1948.

1072   Patri, Aimé. "Les Mains sales." Arche, III, No. 18-19, août-
        septembre 1948, 198-199.

1073   Pingaud, Raymond.   "Le théâtre et le monde réel: Les Mains
       sales." Table Ronde, I, No. 6, juin 1948, 1033-1037.

1074   Rinieri, J.J.   "Les Mains sales." La Nef, V, No. 42, mai
       1948, 139-142.

1075   Vinet, J.P.   "On joue en Amerique une pièce de moi dont j'ig-
       nore le texte." Combat, 27-28 novembre 1948. Red Gloves
       with Charles Boyer as Hoederer. Interview. Cf. Les Ecrits
       de Sartre, 180-181.

                    STUDIES IN OTHER LANGUAGES

1076   Brückner, Rodelinde.   "Jean-Paul Sartre: Les Mains sales,
       Ihre Verwendbarkeit im Hinblick auf lernzielorientiertes
       Testen." Die Neueren Sprachen, N.S., Heft 5, May 1973,
       266-272.

1077   Dalhaus, Carl.   "Sartres 'Schmutzige Hände'." Blätter des
       Deutschen Theaters in Göttingen. No. 5, 1950-1951.

1078   Jacobi, Johannes.   "Schmutzige Hände. Sartre-Aufführung in
       Berlin." Die Zeit, IV, No. 4, 1949, 3.

1079   Lasky, Melvin J.   "Die vertauschten Hände." Der Monat, I, No.
       4, 1948-1949, 102-105.

1080   Lattmann, Dieter.   "Schmutzige Hände." Die Neue Schau
       (Kassel), X, 1949, 245.

1081   Rivera de Ventosa, F.   "Sartre: Les Mains sales y la Critique
       de la raison dialectique." Punto Europa. No. 102, 1964,
       62-66.

1082   Sturani, Enrico.   "Le Mani sporche di Sartre." Belfagor,
       XIX, No. 3, 31 May 1964, 351-354.

                      LES JEUX SONT FAITS

                      STUDIES IN ENGLISH

1083   Baskin, William H.   "The Circle as a Symbol of the Absurd in
       Les Jeux sont faits." Romance Notes, I, No. 1, November
       1959, 13-17.

1084   Bower, Anthony. "Films." The Nation, CLXVIII, No. 8, 12
        February 1949, 193.

1085   Forkey, Leo O. "Jean-Paul Sartre: Les Jeux sont faits."
        French Review, XXII, No. 1, October 1948, 53-54.

1086   Guerard, Albert J. "The Diderot of Our Age." The Nation,
        CLXVII, No. 22, 27 November 1948, 608-609.

STUDIES IN FRENCH

1087   Carrier, Denise. "Les Jeux sont faits." Paru. No. 40, 1948,
        123-125.

1088   Carrière, Paul. "Les Jeux sont faits? 'Tout le contraire
        d'une pièce existentialiste, nous dit Jean-Paul Sartre."
        Le Figaro, 29 avril 1947, 8.

1089   Castelli, Enrico. "Philosophie et cinéma: A propos d'un film
        de Sartre." Revue Internationale de Filmologie, I, 1948,
        339-342.

1090   Charenson, Guy. "Les Jeux sont faits." Nouvelles Litte-
        raires. No. 1058, 1947, 6.

1091   Debrix, Jean. "Jean-Paul Sartre au cinéma: Les Jeux sont
        faits." Revue de la Pensée Française, VII, No. 3, 1948,
        41-48.

1092   Delannoy, Jean. "Les Jeux sont faits." Combat, 15 avril
        1947. Interview.

1093   Marion, Denis. "Jean-Paul Sartre à Camus." Combat, 20 sep-
        tembre 1947, 2.

1094   Petit, L. "Les Jeux sont faits." Vie Intellectuelle. No. 7,
        1948, 123-126.

1095   Rybalka, Michel. "Sartre et le cinéma." L'Esprit Créateur,
        VIII, No. 4, Fall 1968, 284-292.

1096   Saint-Pierre, Michel de. "Autour d'un film de Jean-Paul
        Sartre." Etudes, Tome CCLVI, 1948, 252-262.

STUDIES IN GERMAN

1097 Hünnerfeld, Paul. "Das Spiel ist aus." Die Zeit, IV, No. 16, 1949, 3.

1098 Lausberg, Heinrich. "Einführung in Sartres Les Jeux sont faits." Archiv für das Studium der Neueren Sprachen, CLXLVI, No. 1, July 1959, 16-35.

1099 Schauder, Karl Heinz. "Im Raderwerk von Macht und Gewalt: Sartre und der Film." Kultur (München), VI, No. 105, 1957-1958, 13.

1100 Stobbe, Rudolf, "Sartres Lebensthese in Das Spiel ist aus." Die Volksbühne (Hamburg), XV, No. 4, 1964-1965, 73-74.

1101 Zeltner, Gerda. "Bemerkungen zu Sartres Les Jeux sont faits." Neue Schweizer Rundschau, N.F., 1949-1950, 581-586.

L'ENGRENAGE

STUDIES IN FRENCH

1102 Bastide, François-Régis. "L'Engrenage de Jean-Paul Sartre." Nouvelles Littéraires, XLVII, No. 2163, 6 mars 1969, 13.

1103 Dutourd, Jean. "L'Engrenage." Le Paradoxe du critique suivi de Sept saisons: Impressions de théâtre. Paris: Flammarion, 1972, 345-346.

1104 Jaubert, Jacques. "Raymond Pellegrin, le tyran de Sartre, n'est plus un inconditionel du théâtre." Figaro Littéraire. No. 1191, 3-9 mars 1969, 39.

1105 Judrin, Roger. "Un cathare," et "Une pureté fabuleuse." Moralites littéraires. Paris: Gallimard, 1966, 160-168.

1106 Lemarchand, Jacques. "L'Engrenage au Théâtre de la Ville." Figaro Littéraire. No. 1192, 10-16 mars, 1969, 29.

1107 Olivier, Claude. "Un pauvre théâtre." Lettres Françaises. No. 1273, 13-18 mars 1969, 13.

1108   Patri, Aimé. "L'Engrenage de Jean-Paul Sartre." Paru. No.
       52, 1949, 37-39.

1109   Pingaud, Bernard. "'J'ai pensé à un pays où on ne pourrait
       vraiment rien faire d'autre'." Théâtre de la Ville-Journal.
       No. 2, novembre 1968, 27. Propos recueillis par Bernard
       Pingaud. Cf. Les Ecrits de Sartre, 472.

1110   Poirot-Delpech, Bertrand. "L'Engrenage de Jean-Paul Sartre."
       Le Monde. No. 7504, 27 février 1969, 23.

STUDY IN GERMAN

1111   Colberg, Klaus. "Sartre-Film auf dem Theater. Uraufführung
       im Zürcher Schauspielhaus." Neue Literarische Welt (Heidel-
       berg), III, No. 24, 1952, 8.

LE DIABLE ET LE BON DIEU

STUDIES IN ENGLISH

1112   Champigny, Robert. Stages on Sartre's Way: 1938-1952. Bloom-
       inton, Indiana: Indiana Univ. Pr., 1959. "Comedian et mar-
       tyr." reprinted Sartre: A Collection of Critical Essays:
       Edith Kern, ed. Englewood Cliffs, New Jersey: Prentice-
       Hall, 1962, 80-92.

1113   Conlon, D.J., ed. "Sartre, Jean-Paul: Le Diable et le Bon
       Dieu. London: Methuen, 1971, 167 pp.

1114   Fauve, Jacques. "A Drama of Essence: Salacrou and Others."
       Yale French Studies. No. 14, Winter 1954-1955, 30-40.

1115   Flint, Martha, and Gerrard, Charlotte. "Le Diable et le bon
       Dieu and an Angry Young Luther." Journal of European
       Studies, II, No. 3, September 1972, 247-255.

1116   Frank, Joseph. "God, Man and Jean-Paul Sartre." Partisan Re-
       view, XIX, March 1952, 202-210.

       Gerrard, Charlotte F. see 308.

1117 Lewis, A. "The French Theater--Giraudoux, Sartre, Camus."
      The Contemporary Theater. New York: Crown, 1962, 191-217.

1118 Lüthy, Herbert. "The Devil and the Good Lord." Twentieth
      Century, XL, September 1951, 435-437.

1119 Mermier, G. "Cervantes El Rufian dichoso and Sartre's Le Di-
      able et le bon Dieu." Modern Languages (London), XLVIII,
      No. 4, December 1967, 143-147.

1120 Ricoeur, Paul. "Sartre's Lucifer and the Lord." Yale French
      Studies. No. 14, Winter 1954-1955, 85-93.

1121 Ridge, George R. "Le Diable et le bon Dieu: Sartre's Concept
      of Freedom." Shennendoah, IX, No. 2, Winter 1958, 35-38.

1122 Russell, John. "Sartre and Claudel." World Review, January
      1952, 34-38.

1123 Weales, Gerald. "Whatever Happened to Jean-Paul Sartre?"
      Hudson Review, XIII, No. 3, Autumn 1960, 465-469.

1124 Weber, Eugen. "The Surrender of Goetz." Symposium, XIII,
      Spring 1959, 106-111.

STUDIES IN FRENCH

1125 Abram, Paul. "Le Diable et le bon Dieu de M. Jean-Paul Sartre
      au Théâtre Antoine." Liberation, XII, No. 6, 1951, 2.

1126 Almont, Maxime. "240 minutes durant, M. Sartre distille le
      désespoir et l'ennui." Combat, 14 juin 1951, 112-119.

1127 Alter, André. "D'un théâtre qui se veut athée: 'Le Diable et
      le bon Dieu' de Sartre." Terre Humaine. No. 7, juillet
      1951, 112-119.

1128 Anonymous. "Jean-Paul Sartre repond à la critique et offre
      un guide au spectateur pour suivre Le Diable et le bon
      Dieu." Figaro Littéraire, 20 juin 1951, 4.

1129 Anonymous. "Jean-Paul Sartre et le siècle d'or." Arts. No.
      315, 15 juin 1951, 1.

1130   Anonymous. "'Le Diable et le bon Dieu: Ma pièce est avant
        tout une pièce de foules'." Le Monde, 31 mai 1951, 7.
        Interview.

1131   Anonymous. "Le Diable et le bon Dieu." France Illustrée,
        VII, No. 700, 30 juin 1951.

1132   Bastide, François-Régis. "Le Diable et le bon Dieu de Jean-
        Paul Sartre. Nouvelles Littéraires, XLVI, No. 2149, 28
        novembre, 13.

1133   Blanchet, André. "Comment Jean-Paul Sartre se représente Le
        Diable et le bon Dieu." Etudes, Tome CCLXX, 1951, 230-241.
        Reimprimé La Littérature et le spirituel. Paris: Aubier,
        1959, 253-266.

1134   Brulé, Claude. "La nouvelle pièce de Sartre: Le Diable et
        le bon Dieu." Opéra. No. 302, 25 avril 1951, 1, 5.

1135   "Entre le ciel et la terre, Pierre Brasseur tiendra la scène
        quatre heures pour Le Diable et le bon Dieu." Combat, 5
        juin 1951, 2.

1136   B., J.F. "Le Diable et le bon Dieu (selon Jean-Paul Sartre)
        2.

1137   C., B. "Maria Casarès entre le diable Brasseur et le dieu
        Sartre." Opéra, 31 mai 1951, No. 307, 5.

1138   Chauffier, Louis-Martin, et al. "Entretien avec Sartre: 'Dès
        que deux personnes s'aiment, elles s'aiment contre Dieu."
        Paris-Presse: Intransigeant, 7 juin 1951. Cf. Les Ecrits
        de Sartre, 239.

1139   Chonez, Claudine. "Si Dieu existe, nous dit Sartre à propos
        de sa pièce, le Bien et le Mal sont identiques." L'Observa-
        teur, 31 mai 1951, 6.

1140   Cogniat, Raymond. "Le Diable et le bon Dieu." Arts. No.
        316, 22 juin 1951, 7.

1141   Contat, Michel et Rybalka, Michel. "Le Diable et le bon
        Dieu devant la critique." Cahiers Littéraires (de l'O.R.T.
        F.), VIII, No. 17, 7-20 juin 1970, 25-27.

1142   Daniel-Rops, Daniel. "Le blasphème dérisoire." L'Aurore,
        9-10 juin 1951.

1143 Duché, Jean. "Sartre répond à la critique dramatique et
      offre un guide au spectateur pour suivre Le Diable et le
      bon Dieu." Figaro Littéraire, 20 juin 1951, 4.

1144 Duméry, Henry et Auxias, J.M. "Réflexions complémentaires sur
      Le Diable et le bon Dieu." Esprit, XX, No. 1, janvier 1952,
      118-128.

1145 Dutourd, Jean. "Le Diable et le bon Dieu." Le paradoxe du
      critique suivi de Sept Saisons: Impressions de théâtre.
      Paris: Flammarion, 1972, 322-325.

1146 Féral, Roger. "Il a fallu 19,4000 heures de travail pour que
      Le Diable et le bon Dieu puissent se disputer Pierre Bras-
      seur chaque soir pendant quatre heures." France-Soir, 31
      mai 1951, 2.

1147 Forestier, Jacques. "Jouvet attend Sartre." Opéra, 7 février
      1951, No. 291, 1.

1148 Forestier, Jacques. "Sartre: Le Diable et le bon Dieu."
      Opéra, 3 janvier 1951, No. 286, 1, 5.

1149 Gautier, Jean-Jacques. "Le Diable et le bon Dieu de Jean-
      Paul Sartre." Hommes et Mondes, VI, No. 60, juillet 1951,
      286-291.

1150 Gautier, Jean-Jacques. "Au Théâtre Antoine: Le Diable et le
      bon Dieu de Jean-Paul Sartre." Le Figaro, 13 juin 1951, 6.

1151 Hautefeuille, François d'. "Jean-Paul Sartre et Lucifer."
      Ecrits de Paris, No. 215, June 1963, 53-59.

1152 Jeener, J.B. "Avec Le Diable de le bon Die c'est une chro-
      nique dramatique que veut nous offrir Jean-Paul Sartre."
      Le Figaro, 23 juin 1951.

1153 Kanters, Robert. "De la passion selon Saint Sartr au Vray
      mystère de la Passion." Gazette des Lettres, VII, n.s., No.
      10, 15 juillet 1951, 101-104.

1154 Kanters, Robert. "Le Diable et le bon Dieu." Cahiers du
      Sud. No. 307, 1951, 503-505.

1155 Kanters, Robert. "Dieu devant Sartre." Figaro Littéraire.
      No. 1071, 27 octobre 1966, 5.

1156 Kanters, Robert. "L'enfant de Zevaco et de Saint Thomas."
      L'Express. No. 907, 25 novembre-1 décembre 1968, 46-47.

1157 Kemp, Robert. "Le Diable et le bon Dieu." Le Monde, 13 juin
      1951, 9.

1158 Kemp, Robert. "Le Diable et le bon Dieu." La Vie du théâtre.
      Paris: Albin Michel, 1956, 234-238.

1159 Launay, Claude. Sartre: Le Diable et le bon Dieu, Analyse
      critique. (Profil d'une oeuvre, 15) Paris: Hatier, 1970.

1160 LeGrix, François. "Spectacle d'un temps: Le Diable et le bon
      Dieu de Sartre, ou: la preuve par l'absurde." Ecrits de
      Paris. No. 81, juillet 1951, 103-115.

1161 Lemarchand, Jacques. "Le Diable et le bon Dieu de Jean-Paul
      Sartre au Théâtre Antoine." Figaro Littéraire, 16 juin
      1951, No. 269, 10.

1162 Lemarchand, Jacques. "Le Diable et le bon Dieu au Théâtre
      National Populaire et Nekrassov au Théâtre National de
      Strasbourg." Figaro Littéraire. No. 1178, 2-8 décembre,
      1969, 29.

1163 Lemarchand, Jacques. "Le festival enviravignonné." Figaro
      Littéraire, No. 1263, 3-9 août 1970, 38.

1164 Marcel, Gabriel. "Au coin du sacrilège." Nouvelles Litté-
      raires, XLVI, No. 2153, 26 décembre 1968, 13.

1165 Marcel, Gabriel. "Le Diable et le bon Dieu par Jean-Paul
      Sartre." Nouvelles Littéraires, 14 juin 1951.

1166 Maulnier, Thierry. "Y a pas d'bon Dieu." Combat, 16-17 juin
      1951, 2, and Ibid., 25 juin, 1951, 6.

1167 Maulnier, Thierry. "Du premier au dernier Sartre." Théâtre
      de France. Paris: Les Publications de France, 1951, 64-75.

1168 Mauriac, François. "Jean-Paul Sartre, l'athée providentiel."
      Le Figaro, 26 juin 1951, 1.

1169 Mouillaud, Maurice. "Le Diable et le bon Dieu." Nouvelle
      Critique, No. 29, septembre-octobre 1951, 78-83.

1170 Nimier, Roger. "Roger Nimier a vu avant vous Le Diable et le
      bon Dieu." Opéra, 13 juin 1951, No. 309, 5.

1171 Olivier, Claude. "Le jeu des mots." Lettres Françaises, No.
      1261, 11-17 décembre 1968, 14.

1172 Peju, Marcel. "Le Diable et le bon Dieu, nous dit Sartre,
      c'est la même chose . . . moi je choisis l'homme." Samedi-
      Soir, 2-8 juin 1951. Cf. Les Ecrits de Sartre, 237-238.

1173 Poirot-Delpech, Bertrand. "Le Diable et le bon Dieu au T.N.
      P." Le Monde. No. 7504, 27 février 1969, 23.

1174 Poirot-Delpech, Bertrand. "Le Diable et le bon Dieu de Jean-
      Paul Sartre." Au Soir le soir: Théâtre 1960-1970. Paris:
      Mercure de France, 1969, 255-259.

1175 Portal, Georges. "Un pauvre diable et un faux dieu." Ecrits
      de Paris, février 1969, 124-128.

1176 Ricoeur, Paul. "Réflexions sur Le Diable et le bon Dieu."
      Esprit, XIX, novembre 1951, 711-719.

1177 Rivoyre, Christine de. "Jean-Paul Sartre nous présente Le
      Diable et le bon Dieu." Le Monde, 31 mai 1951. Cf. Les
      Ecrits de Sartre, 236.

1178 Robichon, Jacques. "Dieu, le Diable, et M. Sartre, ou la
      partie perdue." Liberté de l'Esprit, III, No. 23, juillet-
      septembre 1951, 220-222.

1179 Rosbo, Patrick Kerlero de. "Au Théâtre National Populaire:
      Le Diable et le bon Dieu de Jean-Paul Sartre (mise en scène
      de Georges Wilson)." Paris-Théâtre. No. 261-262, 1969,
      36-37.

1180 Sartre, Jean-Paul. "Je n'en pense pas moins." Opéra, 9 mai
      1951, No. 304, 1.

1181 Simon, Alfred. "Sartriens et batraciens." Esprit, XXXVI,
      No. 377, janvier 1969, 106-108.

1182 Tanneguy de Quénetain. "Jean-Paul Sartre: Le Diable et le
      bon Dieu." Réalités. No. 179, décembre 1960, 116-122,
      153 ff.

1183 Triolet, Elsa. "Le Diable et le bon Dieu." Lettres Fran-
      çaises, 14 juin 1951.

1184 Trooz, Charles de. "Littérature et impiété." Revue Générale
      Belge, LXL, No. 4, 15 avril 1954, 893-905. Reimprimé Le
      Concert dans la bibliothèque. Bruxelles, 1959, 137-151.

1185 Vier, Jacques. "Le Diable et le bon Dieu." Littérature à
      l'emporté-pièce. 2e série. Paris: Edition du Cèdre, 1961,
      87-92.

                    STUDIES IN OTHER LANGUAGES

1186 Anonymous. "La parte del diavolo." Illustrazione Italiana,
      X, 1959, 27-30.

1187 Anonymous. "Sartre antwortet der Kritik." Geistiges Fran-
      kreich (Wien), V, 1951, 212.

1188 Bab, Julius. "Sartres Götz von Berlichingen." Uber den Tag
      hinaus: Kritische Betrachtungen. Heidelberg, 1960, 251-
      252.

1189 Beckmann, Heinz. "Drama gegen Gott: Zu Sartres neuem Büh-
      nenstück, der Teufel und der liebe Gott." Rheinischer
      Merkur (Koblenz), VI, No. 45, 1951, 7.

1190 Bock, Harmut. "Ein negatives Lutherdrama: Zu Jean-Paul Sar-
      tres Stück: Der Teufel und der liebe Gott." Zeichen der
      Zeit (Berlin), X, No. 2, 1956, 65-69.

1191 Bondy, François. "Der Teufel und der liebe Gott. Zur Urauf-
      führung von Jean-Paul Sartre: Le Diable et le bon Dieu."
      Weltwoche (Zürch), No. 919, 1951, 5.

1192 Colberg, Klaus. "Sartre streitet wider Gott." Neues Abend-
      land (Augsburg), VII, No. 1, 1952, 58-60.

1193 Collazo, Celso. "Que es Le Diable et le bon Dieu?" Insula,
      VII, No. 73, January 1952, 11-12.

1194 Doblhoff, Lily. "Sartres neues Drama: Zur Uraufführung von
      Sartres Der Teufel und der liebe Gott in Paris." Universi-
      tas (Stuttgart), VI, 1951, 1273-1274.

1195 Dürrenmatt, Friedrich. "Der Teufel and der liebe Gott:
      Schauspiel von Sartre." Theater-Schriften und Reden.
      Zürich: Im Verlag der Arche, 1966, 311-313.

1196   Ellmer, Paul. "Sartres Götz von Berlichingen." Le Diable et
       le bon Dieu." Die Zeit, VI, No. 25, 1951, 5.

1197   Fagone, Virgilio. "Il diavolo e il Buon Dio." Civiltà Cattó-
       lica, CXIV, 1963, 360-373.

1198   Fergnani, Franco. "Le Diable et le bon Dieu nell'evoluzione
       filosofica di Jean-Paul Sartre." Rivista di Filosofía, LIV,
       No. 1, January-March 1963, 65-89.

1199   Hambro, Carl. "Sartres nye skuespill: Le Diable et le bon
       Dieu." Vinduet, V, No. 7, 1951, 547-556.

1200   Horst, Karl A. "Sartre oder die Kunst im Vakuum." Merkur,
       VI, No. 8, 1952, 744-757.

1201   John, Robert L. "Jean-Paul Sartres atheistisches Bühnencredo."
       Maske und Kothurn (Graz-Wien), II, 1956, 292-300.

1202   Junge, Hermann. "Der Teufel und der liebe Gott." Die Neue
       Furche (Tübingen), VI, 1952, 346-348.

1203   Leese, Kurt. "Betrachtungen zu Sartres Der Teufel und der
       liebe Gott." Ethische und religiose Grundfragen im Denken
       der Gegenwart. Stuttgart: Schriften zur Zeit, 1956, 21-
       39.

1204   Lüthy, Herbert. "Jean-Paul Sartre und Der liebe Gott."
       Christ und Welt, IV, No. 27, 1951, 8.

1205   Magana Esquivel, Antonio. "Teatro." Hispanoamericano, LVII,
       No. 1481, 21 September 1970, 51.

1206   Ramona Rey, Maria. "La última pieza de Sartre y su moral."
       Revista de Guatemala, 2e epoca, año 1, 4, January-March
       1952, 215-224.

1207   Sartre, Jean-Paul "Bekenntnis zum Bart." Der Spiegel, V,
       No. 24, 1951, 36-37.

1208   Wisser, Richard. "Jean-Paul Sartre und der 'liebe Gott':
       Aktualisierte Geistesgeschichte--Ideologisierte Religions-
       geschichte." Zeitschrift für Religion und Geistesgeschichte
       (Koln), XIX, No. 3, 1967, 235-263.

1209   Wisser, Richard. "Jean-Paul Sartre y el 'Buon Dios'." Folia
       Humanistica (Barcelona), III, No. 31-32, July-August 1965,
       605-629.

1210   Wolff, Walter.   "Jean-Paul Sartre, Der Teufel und der liebe
       Gott." Die Kommenden (Freiburg), VI, No. 11, 1952, 6.

KEAN

STUDIES IN ENGLISH

1211   Bradby, David, ed. Kean, Jean-Paul Sartre. London: Oxford
       Univ. Pr., 1973.

1212   Brahms, Caryl. "Badel's Bright Sword." Guardian, 1 February
       1971, 8.

1213   David, Margaret Upchurch. "Sartre's Adaptation of Kean: The
       Role of the Actor in Society." South Atlantic Bulletin,
       XXXV, No. 1, January 1970, 25.

1214   Marcus, Frank. "The Actor Myth." Sunday Telegraph. No. 519,
       31 January 1971, 10.

1215   Mayne, Richard. "Good Kean Fun." The Listener, LXXXV, No.
       2186, 18 February 1971, 222.

1216   Maane, W. van. "Kean: From Dumas to Sartre." Neophilologus,
       LVI, 1972, 221-230.

1217   Nightingale, Benedict. "Fairly Kean." New Statesman, LXXXI,
       No. 2081, 5 February 1971, 191.

1218   Shadwick, Alan. "The Sartre Version of Edmund Kean." Church
       Times, No. 5636, 19 February 1971, 14.

       Upchurch, M. see 400.

       Walters, Jennifer   see 1235.

STUDIES IN FRENCH

1219   Ambrière, Francis. "Les pièces du mois: Kean ou Désordre et
       génie . . ." Les Annales-Conférencia, nouvelle série, LX,
       No. 38, décembre 1953, 34-37.

1220   Anonymous. "'Kean, c'est tout le drame de l'acteur de gé-
       nie'." Ciné-Club, numéro spécial, avril 1954. Interview.

1221 Carlier, Jean. "'Mon adaptation d'Alexandre Dumas ne sera pas
      une pièce de Jean-Paul Sartre'." Combat, 5 novembre 1953,
      7. Cf. Les Ecrits de Sartre, 270. Interview.

1222 Duché, Jean. "Quand Sartre 'rewrite' Dumas pour s'amuser
      et exaucer Brasseur." Figaro Littéraire. No. 7, 1953, 3.

1223 Maulnier, Thierry. "Kean." Revue de Paris, LXI, janvier
      1954, 147-150.

1224 Morelle, Paul. "Jean-Paul Sartre a coupé Kean (la pièce
      d'Alexandre Dumas) aux mesures de Pierre Brasseur." Libé-
      ration, 4 novembre 1953,. Cf. Les Ecrits de Sartre, 269.

1225 Saurel, René. "Une interview de Jean-Paul Sartre: 'La véri-
      table figure de Kean'." Lettres Françaises. No. 490,
      12-19 novembre 1953, 6.

1226 Ubersfeld, Annie. "Structures du théâtre d'Alexandre Dumas
      père." Linguistique et littérature. Colloque de Cluny,
      numéro spécial, de la Nouvelle Critique, 1968.

STUDIES IN OTHER LANGUAGES

1227 Fetscher, Irving. "Jean-Paul Sartres Kean." Antares, II,
      No. 6, 1954, 52-55.

1228 Veronisi, G. "Il Kean di Dumas nel rifacimento di Sartre."
      Il Nuovo Corriere, 27 décembre 1953.

NEKRASSOV

STUDIES IN ENGLISH

1229 Anonymous. "Nekrassov." New Statesman and Nation, LI, 14
      January 1956, 40.

1230 Gomm, Ted. "A Socialist at the Theater." Socialist Leader,
      XLIX, No. 40, 5 October 1957, 2.

1231 Magnan, Henri. "Nekrassov." Trans. from the French by Rima
      Drell Dreck. Yale French Studies. No. 16, 1955-1956, 3-7.

1232   Oxenhandler, Neal. "Nekrassov and the Critics." Yale French Studies. No. 16, Winter 1955-1956, 8-12.

1233   Salter, William, and Murrow, Thomas. "Jean-Paul Sartre." New Statesman and Nation, LII, 1 September 1956, 241-242.

1234   Trilling, O. "Nekrassov." London Magazine, IV, No. 7, 1957, 75-79.

1235   Walters, Jennifer. "The Absurd World in the Theater: Reflexions on Sartre and Camus." Revue de l'Université d'Ottawa, XLIV, June 1974, 218-233.

1236   Young, Wayland. "Sartre: The Red Robin Hood." Tribune, 27 September 1957, 15.

STUDIES IN FRENCH

1237   Anonymous. "La critique n'a pas été tendre pour Nekrassov." Combat, 14 juin 1955, 2.

1238   Barthes, Roland. "Nekrassov juge de sa critique." Théâtre Populaire, XIV, juillet 1955, 67-72.

1239   Bensimon, Marc. "Nekrassov ou l'anti-théâtre." French Review, XXXI, octobre 1957, 18-26.

1240   Bessé, Jean. "Nekrassov réhabilité." Lettres Françaises. No. 1259, 24 novembre-3 décembre 1968, 26-27.

1241   Carat, Jacques. "Nekrassov de Sartre." Preuves, No. 53, juillet 1955, 74-76.

1242   Chonez, Claudine. "Avec Jean-Paul Sartre à la vieille de Nekrassov." France-Observateur, 9 juin 1955, 8.

1243   Dort, Bernard. "Nekrassov, farce de Sartre, mise en scène par Jean Meyer, au Théâtre Antoine." Théâtre Populaire. No. 14, 1955, 102-104.

1244   Gautier, Jean-Jacques. "Au Théâtre Antoine. Nekrassov de Jean-Paul Sartre." Le Figaro, 13 juin 1955, 12.

1245   Gordeau, Paul "Au Théâtre Antoine: Nekrassov." France-Soir, 14 juin 1955, 9.

1246 Guignebert, Jean. "<u>Nekrassov</u>, une farce de Jean-Paul Sartre au Théâtre Antoine." <u>Libération</u>, 13 juin 1955, 2.

1247 Kemp, Robert. "<u>Nekrassov</u> au Théâtre Antoine." <u>Le Monde</u>, 14 juin 1955, 11.

1248 Leclerc, Guy. "'En dénonçant dans ma nouvelle pièce les procédés de la presse anticommuniste . . . je veux apporter une contribution d'écrivain à la lutte pour la paix." <u>L'Humanité</u>, 8 juin 1955. Cf. <u>Les Ecrits de Sartre</u>, 286.

1249 Leclerc, Guy. "<u>Nekrassov</u> de Jean-Paul Sartre fait rire les honnêtes gens, grimacer les crapules, et réfléchir tout le monde." <u>L'Humanité</u>, 13 juin 1955, 2.

1250 Leconte, Claude-Henri. "La dure bataille de <u>Nekrassov</u> laisse intact le moral de la troupe." <u>Combat</u>, 2 juin 1955, 2.

1251 Lemarchand, Jacques. "<u>Le Diable et le bon Dieu</u> au T.N.P. et <u>Nekrassov</u> au Théâtre National de Strasbourg." <u>Figaro Littéraire</u>. No. 1178, 2-8 décembre 1968, 37-38.

1252 Macaigne, Pierre. "M. Jean-Paul Sartre aime les farces . . . et les têtes de rechange." <u>Le Figaro</u>, 8 juin 1955, 1, 12.

1253 Magnan, Henri. "Avant la création de <u>Nekrassov</u> au Théâtre Antoine, Sartre nous dit . . ." <u>Le Monde</u>, 1 juin 1955. Cf. <u>Les Ecrits de Sartre</u>, 284.

1254 Magnan, Henri. "Hier au Théâtre Antoine, première de <u>Nekrassov</u>." <u>Combat</u>, 9 juin 1955, 1.

1255 Magnan, Henri. "<u>Nekrassov</u>." <u>Le Monde</u>, 1 juin 1955.

1256 Magnan, Henri. "<u>Nekrassov</u>, ô mon bel inconnu!" <u>Combat</u>, 1 15 juin 1955, 2.

1257 Magnan, Henri. "La première de <u>Nekrassov</u> au Théâtre Antoine." <u>Le Monde</u>, 10 juin 1955, 10.

1258 Marcabru, Pierre. "Au Théâtre Antoine: <u>Nekrassov</u>." <u>Arts</u>, No. 520, 15-21 juin 1955, 6.

1259 Marcel, Gabriel. "<u>Nekrassov</u> par Jean-Paul Sartre." <u>Nouvelles Littéraires</u>, 9 juin 1955, 6.

1260 Maulnier, Thierry. "<u>Nekrassov</u> au Théâtre Antoine." <u>Combat</u>, 13 juin 1955, 2.

1261   Montigny, Serge. "'Au train où vont les reactions je ne suis
       pas sûr que ma pièce trouve un public'." Combat, 7 juin
       1955. Cf. Les Ecrits de Sartre, 285. Interview.

1262   Morelle, Paul. "Nekrassov n'est pas une pièce à clef." Li-
       bération, 7 juin 1955.

1263   Naville, Pierre. "Les aventures de Nekrassov." Les Temps
       Modernes, XI, No. 123, mars-avril 1956, 1504-1509. Réponse
       de Sartre: "Réponse à Pierre Naville." Ibid., 1510-1525.

1264   Naville, Pierre. "Les mésaventures de Nekrassov." France-Ob-
       servateur, 8 mars 1956. Reimprimé L'Intellectuel commu-
       niste. Paris: Rivière, 1956.

1265   Naville, Pierre. "Les nouvelles mésaventures de Nekrassov."
       France-Observateur, 19 avril 1956. Reimprimé L'Intellectuel
       communiste. Paris: Rivière, 1956.

1266   Nimier, Roger. "Sartre." Arts. No. 520, 15-21 juin 1955, 1.

1267   Paninure. "Empressons-nous de rire de tout . . . par Jean-
       Paul Sartre ou . . . Figaro?" Combat, 1 juin 1955, 2.

1268   Poirot-Delpech, Bertrand. "Nekrassov de Jean-Paul Sartre."
       Le Monde. No. 7413, 13 novembre 1968, 25.

1269   Rolland, R.F. "'La pièce vise des institutions et non des in-
       dividus." L'Humanité, Dimanche. 19 juin 1955. Cf. Les
       Ecrits de Sartre, 286.

1270   Valensi, Raphael. "Il n'y a pas de méchants dans Nekrassov."
       L'Aurore, 7 juin 1955. Interview.

                    STUDIES IN OTHER LANGUAGES

1271   Chiaromonte, Nicolà. "Sarte e la farsa." Il Mondo, VII, No.
       29, 19 July 1955, 8.

1272   Forestier, Jerome. "Sartre-Premiere unter Polizei-Schutz."
       Weltwoche (Zürich), XXIII, No. 1126, 1955, 17.

1273   Lüthy, Herbert. "Jean-Paul Sartre und das Nichts." Der
       Monat, VII, No. 83, 1954-55, 407-414.

LES SEQUESTRES D'ALTONA

STUDIES IN ENGLISH

1274 Anonymous. "Altona Criticism." New Statesman and Nation,
      LXI, 28 April 1961, 680.

1275 Brustein, Robert. "Sartre, the Janus: The Condemned of Al-
      tona." Adapted by Justin O'Brien. Repertory Theater of
      Lincoln Center. The Third Theater. New York: Knopf, 1969,
      158-165.

1276 Dallas, Ian. "The New Sartre." Encore, VII, No. 1, January-
      February 1960, 28-34.

1277 Dallas, Ian. "The New Sartre." The Encore Reader: A Chron-
      icle of the New Drama. (A University Paperback, UP 329).
      Charles Marowitz, ed. London: Methuen and Co., 1970, 152-
      160.

1278 Galler, Dieter. "The Different Spheres of Sequestration in
      Sartre's Play Les Séquestrés d'Altona." South Central Bul-
      letin, XXIX, No. 3, October 1969, 102.

1279 Galler, Dieter. "The Phases of Schizophrenia in Jean-Paul
      Sartre's Les Séquestrés d'Altona." Language Quarterly, 11,
      No. 3-4, 1973, 5-10, 16.

1280 Galler, Dieter. "The Relationship Between Soma and Psyche in
      Sartre's Drama Les Séquestrés d'Altona." Language Quarter-
      ly, VI, No. 1-2, 1967, 35-38.

1281 Galler, Dieter. "Sterotyped Characters in Sartre's Play Les
      Séquestrés d'Altona." Kentucky Romance Quarterly, XV, No.
      1, 1968, 57-68.

1282 Gassner, John. "The Condemned of Altona." Dramatic Soun-
      dings. New York: Crown, 1968, 554-557.

1283 Goldthorpe, Rhiannon. "Sartre's Theory of Imagination and Les
      Séquestrés d'Altona." Journal of the British Society for
      Phenomenology, IV, No. 2, May 1973, 113-122.

1284 Jones, Mervyn. "Who are the Guilty?" Tribune, 5 May 1961,
      11.

1285   Ingham, Patricia. "The Renaissance of Hell." The Listener,
       LXII, NO. 1588, 3 September 1959, 349-351.

1286   Kanters, Robert. "The Theater." Evergreen Review, IV, No.
       11, January-February 1960, 143-152.

1287   Mackworth, Cecily. "Les Séquestrés d'Altona." Twentieth Cen-
       tury, CLXVI, 1959, 459-461.

1288   O'Brien, Justin. "Sartre: The Family Cell." The French Lit-
       erary Horizon. New Brunswick, New Jersey: Rutgers Univ.
       Pr., 1967, 389-392.

1289   Palmer, Jeremy J.N. "Les Séquestrés d'Altona: Sartre's Black
       Tragedy." French Studies, XXIV, April 1970, 150-162.

1290   Pucciani, Oreste F. "An Interview With Jean-Paul Sartre."
       Tulane Drama Review, V, No. 3, March 1961, 12-18.

1291   Pucciani, Oreste F. "Letter from Paris." The Nation,
       CLXXXIX, No. 22, 26 December 1959, 492-493.

1292   Pucciani, Oreste F. "Les Séquestrés d'Altona of Jean-Paul
       Sartre." Tulane Drama Review, V, No. 3, March 1961, 19-
       33. Reprinted Sartre: A Collection of Critical Essays.
       Edith Kern, ed. Englewood Cliffs, New Jersey: Prentice-
       Hall, 1962, 92-103.

1293   Rose, Marilyn Gaddis. "Sartre and the Ambiguous Thesis Play."
       Modern Drama, VIII, No. 1, May 1965, 12-19.

1294   Tembeck, R. "Dialectic and Time in The Condemned of Altona."
       Modern Drama, XII, No. 1, May 1969, 10-17.

1295   Thody, Philip. "Introduction." to Les Séquestrés d'Altona."
       (Coll. 'Textes français classiques et modernes.'). London:
       Univ. of London Pr., 1965.

1296   Trewin, J.C. "Talking It Out." Illustrated London News,
       CCXXXVIII, No. 6353, 6 May 1961, 768.

1297   Tynan, Kenneth. "Sartre Talks to Tynan." The Observer, 18
       June and 25 June 1961. Reprinted "An Interview with Jean-
       Paul Sartre." Tynan Right and Left. New York: Atheneum,
       1967, 302-312.

1298   Vial, Fernand.   "The Highlights of the Theatrical Season in
       France: Tête d'or and Les Séquestrés d'Altona."   American
       Society Legion of Honor Magazine, XXXI, No. 1, 1960, 15-32.

1299   Witt, Mary Ann.   "Confinement in Die Verwandlung and Les Sé-
       questrés d'Altona."   Comparative Literature, XXIII, No. 1,
       Winter 1971, 32-44.

1300   Wilbur, Richard.   "Les Séquestrés d'Altona."   Partisan Review,
       XXIX, No. 4, Fall 1962, 603-608.

1301   Williams, John S.   "Sartre's Dialectic of History: Les Séques-
       trés d'Altona."   Renascence, XXII, No. 2, Winter 1970, 59-
       68.

1302   Whiting, John.   "Les Séquestrés d'Altona."   On Theater.   Lon-
       don, 1966, 12-20.

STUDIES IN FRENCH

1303   Abirached, Robert.   "Les Séquestrés d'Altona."   Etudes, Tome
       CCCIII, 1959, 238-241.

1304   Anonymous.   "Avant-première: A la Renaissance, Rentrée de
       Jean-Paul Sartre, Les Séquestrés d'Altona."   Combat, 17
       septembre 1959, 2.

1305   Anonymous.   "Après huit ans d'absence, Serge Reggiani revient
       au théâtre dans la pièce de Jean-Paul Sartre."   France-
       Soir, 24 septembre 1959, 9.

1306   Anonymous.   "Jean-Paul Sartre: 'Voici l'histoire des Séques-
       trés d'Altona'."   Le Figaro, 11 septembre 1959, 14.

1307   Audry, Colette, Marcel, G., Richer, E., Poirot-Delpech, B.
       "Debat sur Les Séquestrés d'Altona."   Controverses.   (Coll.
       "Recherches et Débats du Centre catholique des intellectuels
       français.)   Paris: Librarie Arthème Fayard, No. 32, 1960.
       p. 42-66.

1308   Autrusseau, Jacqueline.   "Jean-Paul Sartre: Frantz non plus
       n'était pas nazi."   Lettres Françaises, 17-23 septembre
       1959.   Cf. Les Ecrits de Sartre, 329.

1309   Berger, Pierre. "Jean-Paul Sartre fait sa rentrée après
        quatre ans de retraite." Paris-Journal, 12 septembre 1959.
        Cf. Les Ecrits de Sartre, 326.

1310   Bernard, René. "La nouvelle pièce de Sartre: Les Séquestrés
        d'Altona; Sommes-nous coupables?" Arts, 26 août-1 septem-
        bre 1959, No. 737, 1-7.

1311   Bourget-Pailleron, Robert. "A propos des Séquestrés d'Al-
        tona." Revue des deux Mondes, septembre 1959, 726-727.

1312   Caprou, Marcelle. "Au Théâtre de la Renaissance: Les Séques-
        trés d'Altona." Combat, 26-27 septembre 1959, 2.

1313   Carat, Jacques. "Sartre le séquestré." Preuves. No. 105,
        novembre 1959, 66-69.

1314   Chapsal, Madeleine. "Entretien avec Sartre." L'Express, 10
        septembre 1959. Cf. Les Ecrits de Sartre, 325-326.

1315   Chonez, Claudine. "A la veille de la première des Séquestrés
        d'Altona, Sartre fait le point." Libération, 21 septembre
        1959. Cf. Les Ecrits de Sartre, 329.

1316   Contat, Michel. Explication des Séquestrés d'Altona de Sar-
        tre. Paris: Minard, 1968.

1317   Craipau, Maria. "Entretien avec Sartre." France-Observateur,
        10 septembre 1959, 6.

1318   Dort, Bernard. "Jean-Paul Sartre nous parle de théâtre."
        Théâtre Populaire. No. 15, septembre-octobre 1955, 1-9.

1319   Dort, Bernard. "Sartre prisonnier de son langage." Gazette
        de Lausanne, 3 octobre 1959.

1320   Dort, Bernard. "Les Séquestrés d'Altona nous concernent
        tous." Théâtre Populaire. No. 36, 1959, 1-13. Interview
        avec Sartre.

1321   Dort, Bernard. "Franz notre prochain." Théâtre public (1953-
        1966): Essais de critique. Paris: Editions du Seuil, 1967,
        129-135.

1322   Dutour, Jean. "Les Séquestrés d'Altona." Le Paradoxe du cri-
        tique suivi de Sept saisons: Impressions de théâtre. Paris:
        Flammarion, 1972, 145-146.

1323 Fabre, Jacqueline. "Sartre fait sa rentrée au théâtre (de la
      Renaissance) avec une pièce sur les séquelles de la défaite
      allemande." Libération, 14 septembre 1959.

1324 Fernandez, Dominique. "Les Séquestrés d'Altona." Nouvelle
      Revue Française. No. 83, novembre 1959, 893-897.

1325 Fields, Madeleine. "De la Critique de la raison dialectique
      aux Séquestrés d'Altona." PMLA, LXXVII, December 1963,
      622-630.

1326 Frank, Bernard. "Les Séquestrés d'Altona: S.O.S. Sartre ap-
      pelle Sartre." Arts. No. 742, 30 septembre-6 octobre,
      1959, 1, 8.

1327 Galler, Dieter. "Le portrait d'un schizophrène dans la pièce
      de Sartre, Les Séquestrés d'Altona." South Central Bulle-
      tin, XXIX, No. 4, Winter 1969, 136-138.

1328 Gautier, Jean-Jacques. "La Renaissance: Les Séquestrés d'Al-
      tona de Jean-Paul Sartre." Le Figaro, 27 septembre 1959,
      16.

1329 Gisselbrecht, André. "A propos des Séquestrés d'Altona." La
      Nouvelle Critique, XI, No. 111, decembre 1959, 119-129, and
      Ibid., No. 114, mars 1960, 101-119.

1330 Gordeaux, Paul. "Les Séquestrés d'Altona: Cinq actes de Jean-
      Paul Sartre, Huis (presque) clos." France-Soir, 26 septem-
      bre 1959, 10.

1331 Gouhier, Henri. "Le théâtre: Intrigue et action, de George
      Bernard Shaw à Jean-Paul Sartre." La Table Ronde. No. 143,
      1959, 173-178.

1332 Haroche, Charles. "Entretien avec Jean-Paul Sartre." France
      Nouvelle, 17 septembre, 1959. Cf. Les Ecrit de Sartre,
      328.

1333 Hughenin, Jean-René. "Une vedette de retour." Arts. No.
      740, 16-22 septembre, 1959, 1-2.

1334 Jamet, Claude. "Les Séquestrés d'Altona." Ecrits de Paris,
      novembre 1959, 83-89.

1335 Kanters, Robert. "Deux heures avec Sartre." L'Express, 17
      septembre 1959. Cf. Les Ecrits de Sartre, 327.

1336   Koehler, Alain. "Entretiens avec Jean-Paul Sartre." Perspec-
       tives du Théâtre. No. 3, mars 1960, 18-23, and Ibid., No.
       4, avril 1960, 5-9.

1337   Lacroix, Jean. "Les Séquestrés d'Altona et le tragizue mo-
       derne." Cahiers de l'ISEA, mars 1964, 115-126.

1338   Lacroix, Jean. "Le 'séquestré d'Altona' condamné à un deux-
       ième suicide." Paris-Presse, 29 avril 1966. Cf. Les Ecrits
       de Sartre, 333.

1339   Lalou, René. "Les Séquestrés d'Altona." Education Nationale,
       8 octobre 1959, No. 27, 18.

1340   Lebesque, Morvan. "Long peut-être, mais sublime." Carrefour.
       No. 785, 30 septembre 1959, 26.

1341   Leclerc, Guy. "Au Théâtre de la Renaissance: Les Séquestrés
       d'Altona de Jean-Paul Sartre, une oeuvre monumentale."
       L'Humanité, 29 septembre 1959, 2.

1342   Lemarchand, Jacques. "Pour ceux qui verront, dans dix ans,
       Les Séquestrés d'Altona et pour ceux que l'oeuvre de Sartre
       surprendrait aujourd'hui même." Figaro Littéraire. No.
       702, 3 octobre 1959, 12.

1343   Léon, Georges. "A propos des Séquestrés d'Altona, Jean-Paul
       Sartre nous dit: 'On ne peut émouvoir qu'avec de vrais prob-
       lèmes . . .'" L'Humanité, 16 septembre 1959, 7.

1344   Lorris, Robert. "Les Séquestrés d'Altona: Terme de la quête
       orestienne." French Review, XLIV, No. 1, octobre 1970, 4-
       14.

1345   Marcabru, Pierre. "Les Séquestrés d'Altona, drame bourgeois,
       analyse lucide d'une décomposition." Arts. No. 742, 30
       septembre-6 octobre 1959, 10.

1346   Marcel, Gabriel. L'Heure théâtrale: De Giraudoux à Jean-
       Paul Sartre. Paris: plon, 1959.

1347   Marcel, Gabriel. "Sartre nous tient enfermés quatre heures
       avec Les Séquestrés d'Altona." Nouvelles Littéraires, 1
       octobre 1959, 10.

1348   Marcel, Gabriel. "Les Séquestrés d'Altona de Sartre." Re-
        cherches et Débats. No. 32, 1960, 42-66.

1349   Maulnier, Thierry. "Les Séquestrés d'Altona." Revue de
        Paris, novembre 1959.

1350   Miller, Jacques-Alain. "De La Nausée aux Séquestrés."
        Cahiers Libres de la Jeunesse. No. 1, 1960, and L'Express,
        No. 455, 3 mars 1960, 29-30.

1351   Poirot-Delpch, Bertrand. "Les Séquestrés de Jean-Paul Sartre
        au Théâtre de la Renaissance." Le Monde, 26 septembre 1959,
        12.

1352   Poirot-Delpech, Bertrand. "Les Séquestrés d'Altona de Jean-
        Paul Sartre." Au Soir le Soir: Théâtre 1960-1970. Paris:
        Mercure de France, 1969, 17-22.

1353   Portal, Georges. "Un séquestré de temps qui passe: Jean-Paul
        Sartre." Ecrits de Paris. No. 181, avril 1960, 97-102.

1354   Poulet, Georges. "A propos de Jean-Paul Sartre: Rupture et
        création littéraire." Les chemins actuels de la critique.
        Paris: Plon, 1967, 393-411.

1355   Sarraute, Claude. "Les Séquestrés d'Altona: Jean-Paul Sartre,
        'Il ne s'agit ni d'une pièce politique . . . ni d'une pièce
        à thèse'." Le Monde, 17 septembre 1959. Cf. Les Ecrits de
        Sartre, 328-329.

1356   Sarrochi, Jean. "Sartre dramaturge: Les Mouches et Les Sé-
        questrés d'Altona." Travaux de linguistique et de litté-
        rature publiés par le Centre de Philologie et de Littéra-
        ture Romanes de l'Université de Strasbourg, VIII, 2: Etudes
        Littéraires. Strasbourg, Paris: Librairie C. Klincksieck,
        1970, 157-172.

1357   Sartre, Jean-Paul. "Voici l'histoire des Séquestrés d'Al-
        tona." Le Figaro, 11 septembre 1959.

1358   Schaeffer, Marlyse. "La mère de Sartre: 'Pauvre Poulou! dès
        qu'il touche au théâtre les ennuis arrivent." France-
        Soir, 24 septembre 1959, 9.

1359   Schaeffer, Marlyse. "De 20 h. à 0 h. 25: Le Séquestrés d'Al-
        tona ont été menés à un train d'enfer." France-Soir, 25
        septembre 1959, 9.

1360   Selz, Jean. "Les Séquestrés d'Altona." Lettres Nouvelles, 7 octobre 1959, 12-14.

1361   Simon, Alfred. "Un et un font un." Esprit, XXVII, No. 1, 1959, 547-551.

1362   Touchard, Pierre-Aimé. "Les Séquestrés d'Altona." La Nef, XVI, No. 31, 1959, 89-91.

1363   Zéraffa, Michel. "Les Séquestrés d'Altona." Europe. No. 367-368, novembre-décembre 1959, 272-274.

STUDIES IN OTHER LANGUAGES

1364   Bokenkamp, Werner. "Existentielle Autopsie." Frankfurter Allgemeine Zeitung, 14 October 1959, 14.

1365   Busse, Walter, und Steffen, Günther. "Wir alle sind Luthers Opfer." Der Spiegel. No. 20, 11 May 1960, 70-79. Cf. Les Ecrits de Sartre, 332.

1366   Codignola, Luciano. "Jean-Paul Sartre commediografo e martire." Tempo Presente, V, No. 2-3, February-March 1960, 171-173.

1367   Dietrich, Margeret. "Sartre und seine existentiellen Dramen: Von den Fliegen bis zu Den Eingeschlossenen." Universitas, XXIII, 1968, 795-799.

1368   Doglio, Mariangela. "Les Séquestrés d'Altona." Vita e Pensiero, XLIII, No. 3, March 1960, 206-208.

1369   LeGallois, Francis. "Sartre schockiert Bourgeoisie: Theaterbrief." Sonntag (Berlin), XV, No. 9, 1960, 16.

1370   Ofstad, Harald. "Ondska och frihet: Sartres Fangarna i Altona i belysning av hans filosofi." Bonniers Litterara Magasin, XXXII, No. 6, July-August 1963, 468-476.

1371   Riu, Federico. "Los Secuestrados de Altona." Revista Nacional de Cultura (Caracas), XXIX, No. 179, January-March 1967, 30-33.

1372   Sartre, Jean-Paul. "An der Elbchaussee." Der Spiegel, No. 41, 1959, 74-77.

1373 "(Jean-Paul) Sartre und sein Franz von Gerlach." Magnum
      (Köln). No. 27, 1959, 65.

1374 Sartre-Premiere: Vorm Krabben-Tribunal." Der Spiegel. No.
      20, 1960, 67-69.

1375 Schumann, Carl. "Sartres deutsches Nachkriegs-Panoptikum:
      Deutsche Erstaufführung von Die Eingeschlossenen in den
      Münchner Kammerspielen." Frankfurter Hefte, XV, 1960, 442-
      444.

1376 Smit, Gabriel. "Sartres grote spektakelstuk." Roeping, 36,
      1961, 586-589.

1377 Tynan, Kenneth. "Jean-Paul Sartre." Die Zeit, XXII, 8 July
      and 15 July 1961.

1378 Vossen, Frantz. "Sartre und sein Franz von Gerlach." Magnum
      (Koln). No. 27, 1959, 65-67.

1379 Werner, Herbert. "Eingeschlossenen." Kirche in der Zeit
      (Düsseldorf), XIX, No. 4, 1964, 153-155.

LES TROYENNES

STUDIES IN ENGLISH

1380 Anderson, Michael. "Translating Euripides." New Theater Mag-
      azine, VII, No. 1, Autumn 1966, 26-32.

1381 Genet (Janet Flanner). "Letter from Paris." New Yorker, 17
      April 1965, 183-184.

1382 Trewin, J.C. "Theater." Illustrated London Times, CCMLIX,
      No. 6632, 10 September 1966, 30.

STUDIES IN FRENCH

1383 Abirached, Robert. "L'Europe c'est l'enfer." Nouvel Observa-
      teur. No. 19, 25 mars 1965, 33.

1384 Gouhier, Henri. "Les Grecs à Paris-Présence de Pirandello."
      Table Ronde. No. 210-211, juillet-août 1965, 131-135.

1385 Kanters, Robert. "Sartre contre les dieux." L'Express. No.
      718, 22-28 mars 1965, 58-59.

1386 Laubreaux, Alain. "Euripide, Sartre et Cacoyannis." Nouvel
      Observateur, n.s., No. 16, 4 mars 1965, 26.

1387 Lemarchand, Jacques. "Les Troyennes au T.N.P." Figaro Litté-
      raire, XX, No. 988, 25-31 mars, 1965, 24.

1388 Pingaud, Bernard. "Les Troyennes: Jean-Paul Sartre s'expli-
      que." Bref (Journal du T.N.P.). No. 83, février 1965. Cf.
      Les Ecrits de Sartre, 410.

1389 Roy, Claude. "Quand deux 'traîtres' se rencontrent." Nouvel
      Observateur, 1 avril 1965, 25-26.

STUDIES IN OTHER LANGUAGES

1390 Domenech, Ricardo. "¿Porqué Las Troyanas?" Cuadernos Hispano-
      americanos. No. 185, mayo 1965, 402-406.

1391 Krauss, Henning. "Sartres Adaptation der euripideischen
      Troerinnen." Germanisch-Romanische Monatschrift, N.F.,
      XIX, No. 4, October 1969, 444-454.

1392 Pagano, Giacoma Maria. "Mito e modernità in Les Troyennes di
      Jean-Paul Sartre." Rivista di Studi Crociani, IV, No. 2,
      avril-juin 1967, 186-197.

GENERAL STUDIES OF SARTRE'S THEATER

STUDIES IN ENGLISH

1393 Allen, Marcus. "The Role of the 'Lâche' in the Theater of
      Sartre." College Language Association Journal (Morgan State
      College, Baltimore), IV, March 1961, 175-187.

1394 Aylen, Leo. "Tragedy and Philosophy," p. 169-185; "Poetry and
      Theater," p. 186-209; "Modern Tragic Writing: Introductory,"
      p. 213-228. Greek Tragedy and the Modern World. London:
      Methuen, 1964.

      Beard, Donald B. see 256.

1395 Bentley, Eric. "From Strindberg to Jean-Paul Sartre." The Playwright as Thinker. New York: Reynal and Hitchcock, 1946, Noonday Pr., 1956.

1396 Bentley, Eric. The Theater of Commitment and Other Essays on Drama in Our Society. London: Methuen, 1968.

1397 Bishop, Thomas. Pirandello and the French Theater. New York New York Univ. Pr., 1960, 122-127.

1398 Blau, Herbert. "Meanwhile, Follow the Bright Angels." Tulane Drama Review, V, Autumn, 1960, 80-101.

1399 Blau, Herbert. "The Popular, the Absurd and the 'Entente Cordiale'." Tulane Drama Review, V, No. 3, March 1961, 119-151.

1400 Bogard, Travis, and Olivers, William I., eds. Modern Drama: Essays in Criticism. New York: Oxford Univ. Pr., 1965.

1401 Bradby, David. "Sartre as Dramatist." Philosophical Journal. Reprinted Sartre: A Collection of Critical Essays. Mary Warnock ed. Garden City, New York: Doubleday, Anchor Books, 1971, 260-283.

1402 Brée, Germaine and Droff, A.Y., eds. Twentieth Century French Drama. New York: Macmillan, 1969.

1403 Brophy, Brigid. "Jean-Paul Sartre." Don't Ever Forget: Collected Views and Reviews. New York, Holt, 1967; London: Cape, 1966, 290-295.

1404 Bukala, C.R. "Sartre's Dramatic Philosophical Quest." Thought, XLVIII, No. 188, Spring 1973, 79-106.

1405 Burdick, Dolores Mann. "The Concept of Happiness in the Modern French Theater." Papers of the Michigan Academy of Science, Arts, and Letters, L, 1965, 609-620.

1406 Chiari, Joseph. "Jean-Paul Sartre." Contemporary French Theater. New York: Macmillan, 1959, 141-169.

1407 Cluzel, M.E. "Jean-Paul Sartre." Glimpses of the Theater and Dance. New York: Kamin, 1953, 38-44.

1408 Coe, Richard N. "Coming After the Gods." Stand, V, 1962, 48-51.

1409   Coe, Richard N. Review of Dorothy McCall, The Theater of
        Jean-Paul Sartre. Revue d'Histoire Littéraire de la France.
        No. 3, 1971, 531.

1410   Cohn, Ruby. Currents in Contemporary Drama. Bloomington, In-
        diana: Indiana Univ. Pr., 1969.

1411   Chiari, Joseph. Landmarks of Contemporary Drama. London:
        Herbert Jenkins, 1965, 53-59.

1412   Corrigan, Robert W., ed. Theater in the Twentieth Century.
        New York: Grove Pr., 1963.

1413   Curtis, Anthony. New Developments in the French Theater.
        London: Curtain Pr., 1948.

1414   Fowlie, Wallace. "Theater of Ideas." Dionysus in Paris. New
        York: Meridian, 1960, 166-183.

1415   Frank, Joseph. "Existentialist in the Underworld." Arts at
        Midcentury. R. Richman, ed. New York: Horizon Pr., 1954,
        109-144.

1416   Gascoigne, Bamber. "Jean-Paul Sartre." Twentieth Century
        Drama. London: Hutchinson University Library, 1972, 152-
        157.

1417   Gassner, John. Dramatic Soundings. New York: Crown, 1968,
        554-557.

1418   Gassner, John. "Forms of Modern Drama." Comparative Litera-
        ture, VII, No. 2, Spring 1955, 129-142.

1419   Gassner, John, ed. Ideas in the Drama. New York: Columbia
        Univ. Pr., 1964.

1420   Gassner, John. Masters of the Drama, third revised and en-
        larged edition. New York: Dover, 1954.

1421   Gassner, John. The Theater in Our Time. New York: Crown,
        1954.

1422   Fruchter, Norm. "Sartre and the Drama of Choice." Encore,
        IX, No. 4, July-August 1962, 35-42.

1423   Gaskell, Ronald. Drama and Reality: The European Theater
        Since Ibsen. London: Routledge and Kegan Paul, 1972.

1424   Geisman, Erwin W.   "Existentialist Theater."   Renascence,
       III, Spring 1951, 160-164.

1425   Goldmann, Lucien.   "The Theater of Sartre."   Drama Review,
       XV, No. 1, Fall 1970, 102-119.

1426   Gore, Keith O.   "The Theater of Sartre: 1940-1965."   Books
       Abroad, XLI, No. 2, Spring 1967, 133-147.

1427   Guicharnaud, Jacques, and Beckelman, June, eds.   "Jean-Paul
       Sartre."   Modern French Theater from Giraudoux to Beckett.
       New Haven: Yale Univ. Pr., 1961, 131-152. Reprinted "Man
       and His Acts: Sartre and Camus."   Sartre: A Collection of
       Critical Essays. Edith Kern, ed. Englewood Cliffs, New
       Jersey: Prentice-Hall, 1962, 62-72.

1428   Hethmon, Robert H.   "Total Theater and Yeats."   Colorado
       Quarterly, XV, No. 4, Spring 1967, 361-377.

1429   Hobson, Harold.   "Jean-Paul Sartre."   The French Theater of
       Today: An English View, 2nd ed. London: Harrap, 1953; New
       York: R. Blom, 1965, 75-127.

1430   Jackson, R.F.   "Sartre's Theater and the Morality of Being."
       Aspects of Drama and the Theater. Sydney: Sydney Univ. Pr.,
       1965, 33-70.

1431   Jarrett-Kerr, Martin.   "The Dramatic Philosophy of Sartre."
       Tulane Drama Review, I, No. 3, June 1957, 41-48.

1432   Jeanson, Francis.   "Hell and Bastardy."   Yale French Studies.
       No. 30, Winter 1962-1963, 5-22.

1433   Kerr, Walter.   Tragedy and Comedy. London: The Bodley Head,
       1968.

1434   Leavitt, Walter.   "Sartre's Theater."   Yale French Studies.
       No. 1, Spring-Summer 1948, 102-106.

1435   Levinson, A.   "The Playwright and the Skull."   Modern Lan-
       guage Review, XLII, December 1947, 4-7.

1436   Lumley, Frederick E.   "Existence in Theory: Jean-Paul Sartre."
       Trends in Twentieth Century Drama. 2nd ed. Fair Lawn, New
       Jersey: Essential Books, 1956, 146-163; New York: Oxford
       Univ. Pr., 1967, 139-158.

1437   Marcel, Gabriel.   "Sartre and Barrault: The Paris Spotlight."
       Theater Arts, February 1947.

1438   Matthews, H.J.   "The Hard Journey in the Plays of Eliot and
       Sartre."   The Hard Journey: The Myth of Man's Rebirth.   Lon-
       don, Chatto and Windus, 1968, 91-96.

1439   Matthews, H.J.   "Jean-Paul Sartre: The Existentialist Murder-
       er."   The Primal Curse: The Myth of Cain and Abel in the
       Theater.   London: Chatto and Windus, 1967, 137-147.

1440   Maurin, F.M.   "French Literature Since World War II: Criticism
       and Research, 2: The Theater."   Symposium, XI, Spring 1957,
       8-15.

1441   McCall, Dorothy K.   The Theater of Jean-Paul Sartre.   New
       York: Columbia Univ. Pr., 1969.

1442   Muller, H.J.   "Existentialist Tragedy: Sartre."   Spirit of
       Tragedy.   New York: Knopf, 1956, 302-311.

1443   Nelson, Robert J.   "Sartre: The Play as Lie."   The Play Within
       a Play: The Dramatist's Conception of his Art, Shakespeare
       to Anouilh.   New Haven: Yale Univ. Pr., 1958, 100-114.

1444   Nicoll, A.   "Theater in the Midst of War, and After."   World
       Drama.   New York: Harcourt, Brace, 1949, 897-919.

1445   Nielsen, M.L.   "Sartre Comes to Denmark."   Western Review, XI,
       No. 2, Winter 1947, 99-102.

1446   Peacock, Ronald.   The Art of Drama.   London: Routledge and
       Kegan Paul, 1957.

1447   Raphael, David Daiches.   The Paradox of Tragedy.   Bloomington,
       Indiana, Indiana Univ. Pr., 1960.

1448   Raymond, John.   "Paperback pick."   Punch, 5 February 1969,
       215.

1449   Reiss, Timothy J.   "Psychical Distance and Theatrical Distan-
       cing in Sartre's Drama."   Yale French Studies.   No. 46,
       1971, 5-16.

1450   Ridge, George R.   "Meaningful Choice in Sartre's Drama."
       French Review, XXX, No. 6, May 1957, 535-541.

1451   Rosenberg, Merril A.   "Vichy's Theatrical Venture."   Theater
       Survey, XI, No. 2, November 1970, 124-150.

1452   Sandor, Yvan.   "From Sartre to Coward."   New Hungarian Quar-
       terly, VII, No. 24, Winter 1966, 199-203.

1453   Schneider, Pierre.   "Play and Display."   The Listener, LI, No.
       1300, 28 January 1954, 174-177.

1454   Schnitzler, Henry.   "World Theater: A Mid-Century Appraisal."
       Educational Theater Journal, VI, December 1954, 289-302.

1455   Smith, H.A.   "Dipsychus Among the Shadows."   Contemporary
       Theater, XX, 1962, 139-163.

1456   Spanos, William V.   "Modern Drama and the Aristotelian Tra-
       dition: The Formal Imperatives of Absurd Time."   Contempor-
       ary Literature, XII, No. 3, Summer 1971, 345-372.

1457   Statford, Philip.   "Creativity and Commitment in Contemporary
       Theater."   Humanities Association of Canada Bulletin, XV,
       Autumn 1964, 35-39.

1458   Strozier, W.A.   "The Dramatic Heroes of Sartre."   South Atlan-
       tic Quarterly, XV, January 1950, 10 ff.

1459   Styan, J.L.   The Dramatic Experience.   Cambridge: Univ. Pr.,
       1965.   A guide to the reading of plays.

1460   Thody, Philip M.   "Jean-Paul Sartre."   Forces in Modern French
       Drama: Studies in Variations on the Permitted Lie.   John
       Fletcher, ed.   New York: Ungar, 1972; London: Univ. of Lon-
       don Pr., 110-128.

1461   Vial, Fernand.   "The Existentialist Drama."   American Society
       Legion of Honor Magazine, XX, No. 4, Winter 1949, 327-346.

1462   Vowles, Richard J.   "Existentialism and Dramatic Form."   Edu-
       cational Theater Journal, V, No. 3, October 1953, 215-219.

1463   Wardman, H.W.   "Sartre and the Theater of Catharsis."   Essays
       in French Literature (Univ. of Western Australia), I, No. 1,
       November 1964, 72-88.

       Welsbacher, R.C.   see 462.

       Williams, John S.   see 464.

1464   Williams, Raymond.   "Tragic Despair and Revolt."   Critical
       Quarterly, V, Summer 1963, 103-115.   Reprinted Modern Trag-
       edy.   Stanford Univ. Pr., 1966, 174-189.

1465   Williams, Raymond. Drama From Ibsen to Brecht. London: Chat-
       to and Windus, 1968.

1466   Worsley, T.C. "Sleepy Years: Some New Plays of 1948." Pen-
       guin New Writing. No. 35, 1948, 82-90.

1467   Wreszin, Michael. "Jean-Paul Sartre: Philosopher as Drama-
       tist." Tulane Drama Review, V, No. 3, March 1961, 34-57.

1468   Zivanovic, Judith K. "Sartre's Drama: The Key to Understand-
       ing His Concept of Freedom." Modern Drama, XIV, No. 2,
       September 1971, 144-154.

                        STUDIES IN FRENCH

1469   Adamov, Arthur. "Le théâtre peut-il aborder l'actualité poli-
       tique?" France-Observateur, 13 février 1958. Reimprimé Ici
       et Maintenant. Paris: Gallimard, 1964, 735-773. A round
       table discussion with Sartre, Butor, Vailland, Adamov, Le-
       besque.

1470   Ambrière, Francis. "Sartre au Théâtre Edouard VII." Opéra,
       VIII, No. 189, 12 janvier 1949.

1471   Anzias, Jean-Marie. "Un théâtre de complicité." Esprit. No.
       1, 1952, 125-127.

1472   Astruc, Alexandre. "Sartre, le théâtre, et la liberté."
       Verger. No. 2, juin 1947, 13-16.

1473   Audry, Colette. "La situation de l'héritier dans le théâtre
       de Sartre." Le Théâtre tragique. Jean Jacquot, ed. Paris:
       Edition du Centre National de la Recherche Scientifique,
       1962, 451-457.

1474   Barretier, Jacques. "'Pour un théâtre d'engagement, je ferai
       une pièce cette année et deux films' (Sartre)." Carrefour,
       No. 3, 9 septembre 1944.

1475   Beigbeder, Marc. "Théâtre philosophique: Sartre." Esprit,
       XVII, décembre 1949, 924-942.

1476   Belluc, Roger. "Propos sur le théâtre." Revue de la Méditer-
       ranée, VI, No. 6, novembre-décembre 1948, 735-752.

1477   Berckmans, J.P. et Garot, J.C.   "Mythe et réalité du théâtre."
       Le Point. No. 7, janvier 1967, 20-25; A La Page. No. 40,
       octobre 1967, 1476-1488. Cf. Les Ecrits de Sartre, 438-439.

1478   Berckmans, J.P. et Garot, J.C.   "Une structure du langage."
       Le Point. No. 8, février 1967.

1479   Boucher, Lucienne. "Le nouveau théâtre de Sartre." Amérique
       Française, VI, No. 2, février 1947, 43-46.

1480   Brisson, Pierre. "Le cas Sartre." Propos de théâtre.
       Paris: Gallimard, 1957, 21-53.

1481   Brochier, Jean-Jacques. "Le dossier Sartre." Magazine Litté-
       raire, mars 1967, 6-12.

1482   Charmel, André. "Le théâtre de Sartre." Europe, XXVIII, No.
       50, février 1950, 43-53.

1483   Chazel, Pierre. "Le tragique de la connaissance dans le thé-
       âtre de Sartre et de G. Marcel." Revue d'Histoire et de
       Philosophie Religieuses, XXX, 1950, 81-92.

1484   Contat, Michel, et Rybalka, Michel, eds. Jean-Paul Sartre:
       Un théâtre de situations (Coll. "Idées"). Paris: Gallimard,
       1973.

1485   Cormeau, Nelly. Littérature existentialiste: Le roman et le
       théâtre de Sartre. Liège: Thone, 1950.

1486   Dellevaux, R. L'Existentialisme et le théâtre de Sartre.
       Bruxelles: Editions La Lecture au Foyer, 1953.

1487   Denat, Antoine. "Dialogue et dialectique." Vu des antipodes:
       Synthèses critiques. Paris: Didier, 1969, 18-27.

1488   Dort, Bernard. "Le jeu du théâtre et de la réalité." Les
       Temps Modernes. No. 263, avril 1968, 1847-1877.

1489   Dussane, B. J'Etais dans la salle. Paris: Mercure de France,
       1963.

1490   Dussane, B. Notes de théâtre, 1940-1950. Paris: Lardouchet,
       1951.

1491   Duvignaud, Jean. Le Théâtre et après. Paris: Castermann,
       1971.

1492 Gandillac, Maurice de. "Le théâtre de Sartre." Cahiers de la
      Nouvelle Epoque. No. 1, 1946.

1493 Gautier, Joseph Delphis, ed. Douze Voix françaises, 1900-
      1960. Englewood Cliffs, New Jersey: Prentice-Hall, 1969.

1494 Gautier, Jean-Jacques. Théâtre d'aujourd'hui: Dix ans de cri-
      tique dramatique et des entretiens avec M. Abadi sur le thé-
      âtre et la critique. Paris: Julliard, 1972.

1495 Goldmann, Lucien. "Problèmes philosphiques et politiques dans
      le théâtre de Sartre-Itinéraire d'un penseur." L'Homme et
      la Société. No. 17, juillet-septembre 1970, 5-34. Reimpri-
      mé Structures mentales et création culturelle. Paris: Edi-
      tions Anthropos, 1970, 209-264.

1496 Jacquot, Jean, ed. Le Théâtre tragique. Etudes de G. An-
      toine, et al. Paris: Edition du Centre National de la Re-
      cherche Scientifique, 1962.

1497 Jeanson, Francis. Sartre par lui-même. 2e éd. Paris: Edi-
      tions du Seuil, 1967.

1498 Jeanson, Francis. "Le théâtre de la bâtardise." Spécial
      Sartre: L'Avant-Scène. No. 402-403, 1-15 mai 1968.

1499 Jeanson, Francis. "Le théâtre de Sartre." Magazine Litté-
      raire. No. 55-56, septembre 1971, 16-19.

1500 Jeanson, Francis. "Le théâtre de Sartre ou les hommes en
      proie à l'homme." Biblio, Livres de France, XVII, janvier
      1966, 8-13.

1501 Kanters, Robert. "Le théâtre et son public en 1949." La
      Table Ronde,. No. 20-21, août-septembre 1949, 1424-1429.

1502 Lemarchand, Jacques. "Un auteur dramatique en situation
      (fausse)." Figaro Littéraire. No. 966, 29 octobre 1964, 7.

1503 Marcel, Gabriel. "Le débat de la saison théâtrale." Etudes,
      janvier 1946.

1504 Marcel, Gabriel. "Le phénomène Sartre." Temps Présent. No.
      9, 1945, 5.

1505 Marcel, Gabriel. "Responsabilités." Eaux Vives, septembre
      1945.

1506   Marcel, Gabriel. "Théâtre par Jean-Paul Sartre." J'ai Lu,
        juillet 1947.

1507   Maulnier, Thierry. "Le théâtre: Marcel Aymé, Sartre,
        Anouilh." Revue de Pari , LXVI, No. 11, novembre 1959,
        147-150.

1508   Mignon, Paul-Louis. "Le théâtre de A jusqu'à Z: Jean-Paul
        Sartre." Spécial Sartre: L'Avant Scène. No. 402-403,
        1-15 mai 1968. Cf. Les Ecrits de Sartre, 461.

1509   Miller, Jacques-Alain. "Sartre 1960-Entretien avec Jean-Paul
        Sartre." Les Cahiers Libres de la Jeunesse. No. 1, 15 fé-
        vrier, 1960, 2-4. Cf. Les Ecrits de Sartre, 353-354.

1510   Nimier, Roger. "Jean-Paul Sartre." Journées de lectures.
        Paris: Gallimard, 1965, 251-259.

        Ponasse, Lorris Robert. see 366.

1511   Rabi. "Les thèmes majeurs du théâtre de Sartre." Esprit,
        XVIII, 1950, 433-456.

1512   Sandier, Gilles. "Socrate dramaturge." L'Arc: Sartre au-
        jourd'hui. No. 30, décembre 1966, 77-86.

1513   Sandier, Gilles. Théâtre et combat: Regards sur le théâtre
        actuel. Paris: Stock, 1970.

1514   Simon, Pierre-Henri. Théâtre et destin: La signification de
        la renaissance dramatique en France au XXe siècle. Paris:
        A. Colin, 1954.

1515   Surer, Paul. Cinquante an de théâtre. Paris: Société d'Edi-
        tion et d'Enseignement Supérieur, 1964.

1516   Surer, Paul. "Etudes sur le théâtre français contemporain:
        XI, Le théâtre depuis la Libération, Jean-Paul Sartre et
        Albert Camus." L'Information Littéraire, XIII, No. 4,
        septembre-octobre 1961, 145-153.

1517   Surer, Paul. Le Théâtre français contemporain. Paris: Soci-
        été d'Edition et d'Enseignement Supérieur, 1964.

1518   Versini, Georges. "Jean-Paul Sartre." Le Théâtre français
        depuis 1900 (Coll. 'Que sais-je?' No. 461, 1970). Paris:
        Presses Univ. de France, 92-102.

STUDIES IN OTHER LANGUAGES

1519 Amoco, Silvio d'. Palconscenico del dopoguerra, Vol. I: 1948;
      Vol. II: 1949-1952. Torino: Edizioni Radio Italiana, 1953.

1520 Aragones, Juan Emilio. "Jean-Paul Sartre, dramaturgo." Este-
      feta Literaria. No. 392, 23 March 1968, 33.

1521 Astruc, Alexandre. "Freiheit und Schicksal in Sartres Dram-
      en." Quelle (Urach), I, No. 2, 1947, 4-8.

1522 Benitez Claros, Rafael. "Teatro europeo del existencialismo
      al antiteatro." Revista de la Universidad de Madrid, IX,
      No. 33, 1960, 235-254.

1523 Chentrens, Roberto C. "Ricercà dei valori nel teatro di Sar-
      tre." Il Pensiero Critico. No. 4, October-December 1959,
      30-62.

1524 Coenen-Mennemeier, Brigitta. Einsamkeit und Revolte: Franz-
      ösische Dramen de 20. Jahrhunderts. Dortmund: Lensing,
      1966.

1525 Corrales, Egea José. "Carta de Paris: dos estrenos y un pri-
      mio." Insula, XIII, No. 157, December 1959, 7.

1526 Dietrich, Margret. Das moderne Drama: Strömungen, Gestalten,
      Motive. Stuttgart: Alfred Kröner, 1963, 284-298, 472-475.

1527 Elizalde, Ignacio. "Teatro comprometido." Razón y Fé. No.
      844, May 1968, 535-541.

1528 Fechter, Paul. Das europaïsche Drama: Geist und Kultur im
      Spiegel des Theaters, Vol. III: Vom Expressionismus zur
      Gegenwart. Mannheim: Bibliographisches Institut, 1958.

1529 Ferrieri, Enzo. Novità di teatro: Vol. II. Torino: Edizione
      Radio Italiana, 1952.

1530 Ferro, Helen. "El teatro de Sartre en Buenos Aires." Fic-
      ción. No. 6, March-April 1957, 89-92.

1531 Frank, Helmar. "Jean-Paul Sartre: Theater." Philosophischer
      Literaturanzeiger, II, No. 4, 1950, 145-149.

1532 Franzen, Erich. Formen des modernen Dramas: Von der Illu-
      sionsbühne zum antitheater. München: Beck, 1961.

1533 Guerrero Zamorra, Juan. "Jean-Paul Sartre." Historia del
      teatro contemporaneo, Vol. III. Barcelona: Juan Flors,
      1962, 407-449.

1534 Gozzi, Luigi. "Notà per una utilizzazione del teatro sar-
      triano." Il Verri, V, No. 6, December 1961, 99-106.

1535 Heering, J.H. Tragiek: Van Aeschylus tot Sartre. S'Graven-
      hage: L.J.C. Boucher, 1961.

1536 Jeanson, Francis. "Das Thema der Freiheit in Sartres drama-
      tischen Werk." Antares, II, No. 7, 1954, 67-75.

1537 Kummer, Bernhard. Fehlentscheidung des deutschen Theaters:
      Jean-Paul Sartre, Kritik und Warnung. Zeven, 1960.
      Forschungsfragen unserer Zeit.

1538 Mennemeier, F.N. "Jean-Paul Sartre." Das moderne Theater
      des Auslandes. Düsseldorf, 1961, 172-192.

1539 Miserocchi, Mario. "Teatro francese." Nuova Antologia,
      LXLV, No. 3, Facsimile 1918, October 1960, 209-222.

1540 Mittwenzwei, Werner. "Der Dramatiker Jean-Paul Sartre."
      Sinn und Form, XVIII, No. 4, 1966, 1153-1178.

1541 Müller, Horst. Moderne Dramaturgie. Frankfurt am Main-Ber-
      lin-München: Moritz Diesterweg, 1967.

1542 Pabst, Walter. Das moderne französische Drama: Interpreta-
      tionen. Unter Mitwirkung zahlreicher Fachgelehrter heraus-
      gegeben von Walter Pabst. Berlin: Erich Schmidt, 1971.

1543 Paci, Enzo. "Filosofia e teatro." Questioni. No. 5-6, Octo-
      ber-December 1954, 308-318.

1544 Paci, Enzo. "Sartre e il problema del teatro." Ancora
      sull'esistenzialismo. Torino: RAI, 1956.

1545 Pandolfi, Vito. Spettaccolo del secolo: Il teatro dram-
      matico. Pisa: Nistri-Lischi, 1953.

1546 Perroud, Robert. "Jean-Paul Sartre: Narratoree dramaturgo."
      Vita e Pensiero, XLII, No. 2, 1959, 99-105.

1547 Ponce, Fernando. Introduccion al teatro contemporaneo. Ma-
      drid: Editora Nacional, 1969.

1548   Putz, Peter. Die Zeit im Drama: Zur Technik, dramatischer
       Spannung. Göttingen: Vandenhoeck and Ruprecht, 1970.

1549   Quinto, José Maria de. "Dos dramas de Sartre." Insula,
       XXIII, No. 257, April 1968, 15-16.

1550   Schoell, Konrad. Das französische Drama seit dem Zweiten
       Weltkrieg: Erster Teil, Konventionelle Formen von Sartre
       bis Sagan. Göttingen: Vanderhoeck and Ruprecht, 1970.

1551   Spadaro, Giuseppe. "Il teatro di prosa." Studi Romani,
       VIII, No. 3, May-June 1960, 362-365.

1552   Stern, Alfred. "El teatro filosófico de Jean-Paul Sartre."
       Torre, XIX, No. 72, April-June 1971, 11-28.

1553   Toschi, Gastone. "Jean-Paul Sartre." Angoscia e solitudine
       nel teatro contemporaneo. Fossano (Cunco): Editrice Esper-
       ienze, 1970, 53-67.

1554   Walker Linares, Francisco. "Il teatro de Sartre." Atenea,
       XXIV, Tomo LXXXVIII, No. 269-270, November-December 1947,
       352-364.

1555   Weidner, Walther. "Sartre und das Theater." Besinning (Nürn-
       berg), II, 1947, 211-212.

1556   Werrie, J. "Jean-Paul Sartre y su teatro existencialisto."
       Arbor, XXVIII, 1948, 589-596.

1557   Zehm, Günter Albrecht. Jean-Paul Sartre (Friedrichs Dram-
       atiker des Welttheater, 8). Velber b. Hannover: Friedrich,
       1965.

QU'EST-CE QUE LA LITTERATURE?

STUDIES IN ENGLISH

1558   Abel, Lionel. "What is Literature?-An Open Letter to Jean-
       Paul Sartre." Dissent, XII, No. 3, Summer 1965, 334-347.

1559   Barrett, William. "End of Modern Literature: Existentialism
       and Crisis." Partisan Review, XVI, September 1946, 942-
       950. Reprinted Literary Opinion in America. M.D. Zabel,
       ed. New York: Harper, 1961, 749-756.

1560 Duthuit, Georges. "Sartre's Last Class." Transition Forty-
      Eight, I, No. 1, January 1948, 7-20; Ibid., No. 2, 98-116;
      Ibid., No. 3, 47-61; Ibid., No. 4, 96-104; Ibid., No. 6.

1561 Filler, Louis. "Book Notes." Antioch Review, XI, No. 2,
      Summer 1949, 252-254.

1562 Grover, R.R. "The Relevance of Sartre's Qu'est-ce que la lit-
      térature?" Critical Survey, III, No. 1, Winter 1966, 42-51.

1563 Levi, Peter, S.J. "What is Literature by Jean-Paul Sartre."
      Notes and Queries, XV, No. 9, September 1968, 358.

1564 Pucciani, Oreste F. "The Universal Language of Symbolism."
      Yale French Studies. No. 9, Spring 1952, 27-35.

1565 Savage, D.S. "Jean-Paul Sartre and 'Committed Literature'."
      The European. No. 5, July 1953, 17-32.

1566 Seznec, Jean. On Two Definitions of Literature. Oxford:
      Clarendon Pr., 1952.

1567 Whiting, Charles G. "The Case for 'Engaged' Literature."
      Yale French Studies. No. 1, Spring-Summer 1948, 84-89.

                    STUDIES IN FRENCH

1568 Beau de Lomenie, E. "Les doctrines littéraires et politiques
      de Jean-Paul Sartre." Chroniques de quatrième. Paris:
      Denöel, 1956, 151-169.

1569 Benda, Julien. "Qu'est-ce que la littérature?" Revue de
      Paris, LVII, January 1950, 87-98.

1570 Bespaloff, Rachel. "A propos de Qu'est-ce que la littérature?
      Réflexions sur une exégèse." Fontaine. No. 63, novembre
      1947, 704-719.

1571 Cuénot, Claude. "Littérature et philosophie chez Sartre."
      Renaissance. No. 21, mai 1946, 49-61.

1572 Curtis, Jean-Louis. Questions à la littérature. Paris:
      Stock, 1973.

1573 Etiemble, René. "Heureux les écrivains qui meurent pour quel-
      que chose." Combat, 24 janvier 1947, 2.

1574   Gaillard, Pol. "Pour qui écrit Sartre?" Pensée. No. 15, novembre-décembre 1947, 110-112.

1575   Magny, Claude-Edmonde. "Le temps de la réflexion: Jean-Paul Sartre et la littérature." Esprit, XVI, No. 144, 1948, 686-703. Reimprimé Littérature et critique. Paris: Payot, 1971, 167-184.

1576   Maulnier, Thierry. "Feuilleton littéraire: Littérature et liberté." Hommes et Mondes. No. 11, juin 1947, 316-323. Reimprimé Esquisse littéraires, Paris: Robert Cayla, 1948, 129-168.

1577   Maulnier, Thierry. "Sartre et le suicide de la littérature." Table Ronde, I, No. 2, février 1948, 195-210.

Maulnier, Thierry. see 1613.

1578   Monsour, Bernard. "Le prix du jeu." Arche, 13, février 1946, 149-155.

1579   Patri, Aimé. "Commentaire sur 'Ecrire pour son époque'." Paru. No. 30, mai 1946.

1580   Patri, Aimé. "A propos de Qu'est-ce que la littérature?" Paru. No. 46, septembre 1948, 7-12.

1581   Perruchot, Henri. "La littérature gengagée." Larousse Mensuel, XIV, 1956-1957, 232-234.

1582   Rousseaux, André. "La littérature selon Jean-Paul Sartre." Figaro Littéraire. No. 72, 1947, 2.

1583   Sigaux, Gilbert. "Engagement et solitude de l'écrivain." Gazette des Lettres, 20 septembre 1947.

1584   Skreb, Zdenko. "Littérature engagée." Joseph P. Strelka, ed., Literary Criticism and Sociology (Yearbook of Comparative Criticism, 5). University Park: Penn State Univ. Pr., 1973, 195-205.

1585   Thiébault, Marcel. "Qu'est-ce que la littérature?" Revue de Paris, LVI, avril 1949, 155-163.

1586   Thoroval, Jean et Leo, Maurice. "Jean-Paul Sartre: Qu'est-ce que la littérature?" Le Commentaire des textes littéraires. Paris: Bordas; La Hague: Mouton, 1971, 196-200.

1587   Vendome, André. "Jean-Paul Sartre et la littérature."
       Etudes, Tome 259, No. 8, octobre 1948, 39-54.

1588   Viatte, Auguste. "Les idées littéraires de Jean-Paul Sartre."
       Revue de l'Université Laval, III, No. 4, décembre 1948, 320-
       325.

STUDIES IN OTHER LANGUAGES

1589   Addamo, Sebastiano. "Jean-Paul Sartre: Che cos'è la lettera-
       tura?" Il Ponte, XVI, No. 8-9, août-septembre 1960, 1331-
       1332.

1590   Adorno, Theodor W. Noten zur Literatur III. Frankfurt:
       Suhrkamp, 1965.

1591   Anonymous. "Man schreibt für seine Zeit." Der Monat, I, No.
       1, 1948-1949, 47-51.

1592   Kohut, Karl. "Was ist Literatur?" Die Theorie der 'littéra-
       ture engagée' bei Sartre. Marburg: Kohut, 1965.

1593   Mayer, Hans. "Was ist Literatur?" Anmerkungen zu Sartre.
       Pfüllingen: Günther Neske, 1972, 25-30.

1594   Mennemeier, F.N. "Jean-Paul Sartre und die Literatur."
       Rheinischer Merkur (Koblenz), VI, No. 8, 1951, 10-11.

1595   Nerlich, Michael. "Review of Karl Kohut, Was ist Literatur?,
       Die Theorie der 'littérature engagée'." Romanische For-
       schungen, LXXX, No. 2-3, 1968, 510-511.

1596   Passeyro, R. "Para qué sirve la literatúra?" Indice. No.
       193, 1964, 10.

1597   Rodriguez Bustamante, Norberto. "Jean-Paul Sartre: Qué es la
       literatura?" Sur. No. 202, August 1951, 63-67.

1598   Saporta, Marcelo. "Entrevista Jean-Paul Sartre." Insula.
       No. 32, 15 August 1948. Cf. Les Ecrits de Sartre, 192-193.

1599   Torre, Guillermo de. Doctrina y estetica literaria. Madrid:
       Editorial Guadarrama, 1970, 90-125 and passim.

ENTRETIENS SUR LA POLITIQUE

1600   Aron, Raymond. "Lettre à Jean-Paul Sartre." Temps Modernes.
       No. 38, novembre 1948, 957. Cf. Les Ecrits de Sartre, 202.

1601   Aron, Raymond. "Réponse à Jean-Paul Sartre." Liberté de
       l'Esprit, juin 1949.

1602   Mauriac, François. "Entretiens sur la politique." Le Figaro,
       4 mai 1949.

1603   Mouillaud, Maurice. "Quand MM. Sartre, Rousset et Rosenthal
       parlent politique." La Nouvelle Critique, I, No. 10, novem-
       bre 1949, 15-24.

SITUATIONS

I.

1604   Brissaud, André. "Situation de Jean-Paul Sartre." Synthèses,
       II, No. 11, 1947, 215-228; Ibid., No. 12, 1947, 332-347.

1605   Bruch, Jean-Louis. "Jean-Paul Sartre: Situations." Revue du
       Caire, XII, No. 124, novembre 1949, 80-84.

1606   Davy, M.M. "Les 'Situations' de Sartre." Adam International
       Review, XVI, No. 179, February 1948, 15-16.

1607   Davy, M.M. "Situations." La Nef. No. 40, mars 1948, 154-
       156; Also Présence Africaine, mars 1949, 513.

1608   Derycke, Gaston. "Jean-Paul Sartre: l'existence et le roman."
       Cahiers du Sud, XXVII, No. 225, juin 1940, 387-392. On the
       articles later included in Situations I.

1609   Kanapa, Jean. "Situations I." Lettres Françaises. No. 199,
       1948.

1610   Lalou, René. "Situations I, par Jean-Paul Sartre." Nouvelles
       Littéraires. No. 1065, 1948, 3.

1611   Maulnier, Thierry. "Feuilleton littéraire: Situations et sit-
       uation de Sartre." Hommes et Mondes. No. 29, décembre 1948,
       1948, 712-716.

II.

see Qu'est-ce que la littérature?

1612 Etiemble, René. "Heureux les écrivains qui meurent pour quelque chose." Combat, 24 janvier 1947, 2.

1613 Maulnier, Thierry. "Situations II." Hommes et Mondes, VII, No. 29, décembre 1948, 686-691.

III.

1614 Boutang, Pierre. "Situation et contradiction de Sartre." Aspects de la France et du Monde. No. 55, 28 juillet 1949, 3; Ibid., No. 56, 4 août 1949, 3.

1615 Catesson, Jean. "La prétendue contradiction de Sartre." Critique. No. 46, 1951, 291-301.

1616 Daix, Pierre. "Situation et intention de Monsieur Sartre." Lettres Françaises. No. 277, 1949, 3.

1617 Kemp, Robert. "Evadés de l'existentialisme." Nouvelles Littéraires. No. 1144, 1949, 2.

1618 Lentin, André. "Sartre, le marxisme et la science." La Pensée. No. 9, octobre-décembre 1946, 112-115.

1619 Mascolo, Dionys. "Matérialisme et révolution." Le Communisme: Révolution et communication ou la dialectique des valeurs et des besoins. Paris: Gallimard, 1953, 375-405.

1620 Mounier, Emmanuel. "Récents critiques du communisme." Esprit, XIV, No. 10, octobre 1946, 482-484.

1621 Riefstahl, Hermann. "Jean-Paul Sartre: Materialismus und Revolution." Philosophischer Literaturanzeiger, III, No. 1, 1951, 12-13.

IV.

1622 Abel, Lionel. "Arguments: Situating Sartre, With a Reply by Stuart Hampshire." Partisan Review, XXXIII, Winter 1966, 152-161.

1623   Alicata, Mario. "Preface." Il Filosofo e la politica. Roma:
       Editori Riuniti, 1964. Italian translation of articles from
       Situations IV, V, and VI.

1624   Anonymous. "The Sartrian Phrase." Times Literary Supplement,
       4 June 1964, 470.

1625   Blanchet, André. "Situations IV." Etudes, Tome CCCXXI, sep-
       tembre 1964, 151.

1626   Bondy, François. "Jean-Paul Sartre et la révolution."
       Preuves. No. 202, décembre 1967, 57-69. Also concerns
       Situation VII.

1627   O'Neill, John. "Situation and Temporality." Philosophy and
       Phenomenological Research, XXVIII, March 1968, 413-422.

1628   Pingaud, Bernard. "Pour et contre Sartre." L'Express. No.
       682, 9 juillet 1964, 27-28.

1629   Weightman, John. "The Unmarried Wife's Tale." The Observer.
       No. 9090, 19 September 1965, 28.

                          V. to IX.

1630   Albérès, René-Marill. "Reste le polémiste." Nouvelles Litté-
       raires, XLII, No. 1923, 9 juillet 1964, 5. Situations IV
       and V.

1631   Anonymous. "L'itnéraire mouvementé de Sartre: deux livres,
       Situations VIII et Situations IX." Le Figaro, 18 mars 1972,
       15.

1632   Cismaru, Alfred. "French Fiction in 1964." Books Abroad,
       XXXIX, Summer 1965, 278-280. Situations V and VI.

1633   C.,J. "Situations VIII et IX par Jean-Paul Sartre." Maga-
       zine Littéraire. No. 67-68, septembre 1972, 48.

1634   "Choose and Accept the Consequences." Times Literary Supple-
       ment. No. 3656, 24 March 1972, 330. Situations VIII and
       IX.

1635   Mauriac, Claude. "L'itinéraire mouvementé de Sartre." Fi-
       garo Littéraire. No. 1348, 18 mars 1972, 15. Situations
       VIII and IX.

1636 Mayer, Hans. "Sartre uber Sartre: Situationen VIII und IX."
      Anmerkungen zu Sartre. Pfüllingen: Gunther Neske, 1972,
      72-80.

1637 "Sub-Sartre." Times Literary Supplement. No. 3713, 4 May
      1973, 502.

1638 Wahl, François. "Sartre et les fantômes." L'Express. No.
      714, 22-28 février, 1965, 58-59.

                          BAUDELAIRE

                      STUDIES IN ENGLISH

1639 Anglès, Auguste. "Sartre Versus Baudelaire." Yale French
      Studies, I, No. 2, Fall-Winter 1948, 119-124.

1640 Hamburger, Michael. "Sartre and Baudelaire." World Review,
      n.s., No. 15, May 1950, 52-57.

1641 MacCarthy, Desmond. "Baudelaire." Sunday Times. No. 6620,
      5 March 1950, 3.

1642 McEwen, J.H.F. "Baudelaire Under the Microscope." The Tab-
      let, CLXXXV, No. 5728, 4 March 1950, 170.

      McKenna, Andrew J. see 347.

1643 Meyerhoff, Hans. "Existential Analysis." Partisan Review,
      XVII, No. 7, September-October 1950, 752-755.

1644 Picard, Raymond. "Critical Trends in France." Times Literary
      Supplement, 27 September 1963, 719-720.

1645 Tremblay, N.J. "Baudelaire by Jean-Paul Sartre." Arizona
      Quarterly, VII, No. 1, Spring 1951, 94-96.

1646 Turnell, Martin. "Mr. Sartre's Baudelaire." Changing World,
      I, No. 4, May-July 1948, 88-93.

1647 White, Martin L. "Baudelaire, by Jean-Paul Sartre." Chicago
      Review, V, No. 1, Winter 1954, 46-47.

STUDIES IN FRENCH

1648 Audry, Colette. "Sur une introduction à Baudelaire." Cahiers
du Sud, XXVI, No. 284, 1947, 621-629.

1649 Bataille, Georges. "Baudelaire 'mis a nu', l'analyse de Sartre et l'essence de la poésie." Critique, II, No. 8-9, janvier-février 1947, 3-27. Reimprimé La Littérature et le
mal. Paris: Gallimard, 1957, 33-63.

1650 Blanchot, Maurice. "L'échec de Baudelaire." L'Arche, III,
No. 24, février 1948, 80-91; Ibid., III, No. 25, mars 1947.
Texte complet reimprimé La Part du feu. Paris: Gallimard,
1949, 137-156.

1651 Blin, Georges. "Jean-Paul Sartre et Baudelaire." Fontaine,
avril 1947, No. 59, 3-17; Ibid., No. 60, mai 1947, 200-216.

1652 Blin, Georges. "Jean-Paul Sartre et Baudelaire." Le Sadisme
de Baudelaire. Paris: Corti, 1948, 101-140.

1653 Bolle, Louis. "Sartre et Baudelaire." Les Lettres et l'absolu: Valéry, Proust, Sartre. Genève: Perret Gentil, 1960,
85-106.

1654 Davy, N.M. "Baudelaire et Sartre." La Nef, V, No. 39, février 1948, 146-148.

1655 Doneux, Guy. "Regard su Sartre à travers Baudelaire." Mar-
ginales, XXV, No. 130, février 1970, 15-18.

1656 Fouchet, Max-Pol. "Baudelaire en question." Europe, No. 456-
457, 1967, 3-15.

1657 Fumet, Stanilas. "Face à face: Baudelaire-Sartre." La Table
Ronde. No. 232, mai 1967, 6-19.

1658 Jourdain, Louis. "Sartre devant Baudelaire." Tel Quel. No.
19, Fall 1964, 70-85; Ibid., No. 21, Spring 1965, 79-95.

1659 Kushner, Eva. "Sartre et Baudelaire." Baudelaire, Actes du
Colloque de Nice (25-27 mai 1967). Paris, Minard, 113-124,
1968, Annales de la Faculté des Lettres et Sciences Humaines
de Nice, No. 4-5, 1968.

1660 Levy, Yves. "Baudelaire vu par Sartre." Paru. No. 27, février 1947, 72-77.

1661   Loisy, Jean. "Sartre et Baudelaire." Points et Contrepoints.
       No. 75, décembre 1965, 4-10.

1662   Madaule, Jacques. "Jean-Paul Sartre: Baudelaire." Cahiers du
       Monde Nouveau, IV, No. 4, avril 1948, 115-116.

1663   Neveux, Georges. "Sartre, Baudelaire et la liberté." La Nef,
       IV, No. 22, avril 1947, 138-141.

1664   Patri, Aimé. "Sur le 'cas' Baudelaire." Paru. No. 42, mai
       1948, 5-9.

1665   Picon, Gaëtan. "Sartre juge de Baudelaire." Gazette des
       Lettres, III, No. 22, 22 mars 1947, 8-9.

1666   Rousseaux, André. "Le Baudelaire de Sartre." Figaro Litté-
       raire. No. 58, 1947, 2.

1667   Rybalka, Michel. "Le Baudelaire de Sartre." Adam Internation-
       al Review, XXXIV, No. 331-333, 1969, 31-32.

1668   Saget, Justin. "Baudlelaire vu par Jean-Paul Sartre."
       Combat, 22 novembre 1946, 2.

1669   Saillet, Maurice. "Baudelaire et Sartre." Billets doux de
       Justin Saget. Paris: Mercure de France, 1952, 16-20.

1670   Salel, Jean-Claude. "A propos du Baudelaire de Sartre." La
       Table Ronde, I, No. 3, mars 1948, 470-475.

STUDIES IN OTHER LANGUAGES

1671   Chacal, Rosa. "Baudelaire y el Baudelaire de Sartre." Sur,
       No. 171, January 1949, 17-34.

1672   Grangier, E. "Sartre als Richter über Baudelaire." Frank
       reichs zeitgenössische Literatur: Geist und Geltalt. Her-
       ausgegeben unter der Leitung von Emile Callot. Stuttgart:
       Dr. Roland Schmiedel, 1949, 148-178.

1673   Laaban, Ilmar. "Sartre frihet och Baudelaire." Prisma. No.
       4, 1949, 70-80.

1674   Lupo, Valeria. "Un affronto a Baudelaire." Humanitas, IV,
       1949, 404-419.

1675   Morando, L. "Il Baudelaire di Jean-Paul Sartre." Rivista
       Rosminiana, XLII, 1948, 117-124.

1676   Perroud, Robert. Tra Baudelaire e Sartre. Milano: Vita e
       Pensiero, 1952.

1677   Viatte, Auguste. "Tra Baudelaire e Sartre." Erasmus, VIII,
       1955, 486-487.

1678   Whitaker, Marie. "Sartre und Baudelaire." Standpunkte, 79,
       1968, 35-40; Ibid., No. 80, 1968, 27-35.

SAINT GENET: COMEDIEN ET MARTYR

STUDIES IN ENGLISH

1679   Barish, Jonas A. "The Veritable Saint Genet." Wisconsin
       Studies in Contemporary Literature, VI, Autumn 1965, 267-
       285.

1680   Coe, Richard J. The Vision of Jean Genet. London: Peter
       Owen, 1968.

1681   Cooper, David. "Sartre on Genet." New Left Review. No. 25,
       May-June 1964, 69-73.

1682   Curtis, Jerry L. "The World as a Stage: Sartre Versus Genet."
       Modern Drama, XVII, No. 1, March 1974, 33-42.

1683   Elevitch, Bernard. "Sartre and Genet." Massachusetts Review,
       V, Winter 1964, 408-413.

1684   Fowlie, Wallace. "Saint Genet." Sewanee Review, LXXII,
       Spring 1964, 342-348.

1685   Girard, René. "Existentialism and Criticism." Yale French
       Studies. No. 16, Winter 1955-1956, 45-52. Reprinted
       Sartre: A Collection of Critical Essays. Edith Kern, ed.
       Englewood Cliffs, New Jersey: Prentice-Hall, 1962, 121-128.

1686   Gold, Herbert. "Saint Genet: The Spaces Between the Words."
       Hudson Review, XVII, No. 4, Winter 1964-1965, 580-586.

1687   Guicharnaud, Jacques. "Saint Genet." Yale Review, LIII,
       Spring 1964, 435-440.

1688 Heinemann, F.H. "Theologia Diaboli." Hibbert Journal, LII,
      October 1953, 65-72.

1689 Littlejohn, D. "Sartre's Genet." Interruptions. New York:
      Grossman, 1970, 116-130.

      Lovitt, C.W. see 338.

1690 Nelson, Benjamin. "Sartre, Genet, Freud." Psychoanalytic
      Review, L, Fall 1963, 155-171.

      Nordstrom, Louis D. see 357.

1691 Royce, Barbara C. "La Chute and Saint Genet: The Question of
      Guilt." French Review, XXXIX, April 1966, 709-716.

1692 Sontag, Susan. "Sartre's Saint Genet." Against Interpreta-
      tion and Other Essays. New York: Farrar and Strauss, 1966,
      83-99.

1693 St. Aubyn. F.C. "Sartre and the Essential Genet." Symposium,
      VIII, Summer 1954, 82-101.

1694 Stewart, Harry E. "Jean Genet's Saintly Preoccupation in Le
      Balcon." Drama Study, VI, Spring-Summer 1967, 24-30.

STUDIES IN FRENCH

1695 Bataille, Georges. "Jean-Paul Sartre et l'impossible révolte
      de Jean Genet." Critique. No. 65, octobre 1952, 819-832;
      Ibid., No. 66, novembre 1952, 946-961.

1696 Bataille, Georges. "Genet et Sartre." La Littérature et le
      mal. Paris: Gallimard, 1957, 183-225.

1697 Kemp, Robert. "Répugnances." Nouvelles Littéraires, 14 août
      1952, 3.

1698 Nadeau, Maurice. "Jean-Paul Sartre et Jean Genet." Mercure
      de France, Tome CCCXVI, octobre 1952, 300-306.

1699 Sempe, Dr. J.C. "Méditation sur Saint Genet: Comédien et mar-
      tyr." Entretiens psychologiques. No. 9. Toulouse: Privat,
      1963.

STUDIES IN OTHER LANGUAGES

1700   Astaldi, Maria Luisa. "Genet e Sartre." Studi di lettera-
        tura francese, I. Firenze: Leo S. Olschki Editore, 1967,
        1-7.

1701   Gibelli, Dario. "Saint Genet mondato." Belfagor, XXVIII,
        No. 4, July 1973, 488-492.

1702   Heinemann, F.H. "Theologia diaboli." Rivista di Filosofia,
        XLV, No. 1, 1954, 3-13.

1703   Heinemann, F.H. "Theologia diaboli." La Torre, V, No. 17,
        February-March 1957, 11-22.

1704   Heist, Walter. Genet und Andere: Exkurse uber eine faschis-
        tische Literatur von Rang. Hamburg: Claassen, 1965.

1705   Rosa, Nicolas. "Sexo y creacion: Sartre y Genet." Critica y
        significacion. Buenos Aires: Editorial Galerna, 1970, 101-
        143.

1706   Vigevani, Roberto. "Sartre, Genet e una psicologia marxista."
        Il Ponte, XXXV, No. 10, 31 October 1969, 1355-1359.

1707   Walther, Elisabeth, und Bense, Max. "Sartre und Genet." Au-
        genblick, III, No. 4, 1958, 13-18.

REFLEXIONS SUR LA QUESTION JUIVE

STUDIES IN ENGLISH

1708   Abel, Lionel. "The Existence of Jews and Existentialism."
        Politics, I, No. 42, Winter 1949, 37-40.

1709   Aranson, J. "Sartre on Anti-Semitism." Phylon, X, No. 3,
        1949, 231-232.

1710   Ayer, A.J. "Sartre on the Jews." The Spectator, CCXXI, No.
        7317, 20 September 1968, 394-395.

1711   Cohen, A.D. "Anti-Semitism in France." Literary Guide, LXX,
        No. 4, April 1955, 14-16.

1712   Gendzier, Irene L.   "Reflections on Fanon and the Jewish Ques-
       tion." New Outlook, XII, No. 1, January 1969, 13-20.

1713   Hannush, Mufid J.   "Adorno and Sartre: A Convergence of Two
       Methodological Approaches." Journal of Phenomenological
       Psychology, IV, No. 1, Fall 1973, 297-314.

1714   Hook, Sydney. "Reflections on the Jewish Question." Partisan
       Review, XVI, No. 5, May 1949, 463-482.

1715   Marks, Elaine. "The Limits of Ideology and Sensibility: Jean-
       Paul Sartre's Réflexions sur la question juive and E.M.
       Cioran's Un Peuple de solitaires." French Review, XLV,
       1972, 779-788.

1716   Orwell, George. "Portrait of the Antisemite." The Collected
       Essays, Journalism and Letters of George Orwell, Vol. IV: In
       Front of Your Nose, 1945-1950. Sonia Orwell and Ian Angus,
       eds. London: Secker and Warburg, 1968, 452-453.

1717   Rosenberg, Harold. "Does the Jew Exist? Sartre's Morality
       Play About Anti-Semitism." Commentary, VII, No. 1, January
       1949, 8-18.

1718   Sunglowsky, Joseph. "Criticism of Anti-Semite and Jew." Yale
       French Studies, No. 30, Fall-Winter 1962-1963, 68-72.

STUDIES IN FRENCH

1719   Bataille, Georges. "Jean-Paul Sartre, Réflexions sur la ques-
       tion juive." Critique, II, No. 12, 1947, 471-473.

1720   Bonaparte, Marie. "Des causes psychologiques de l'antisémitis-
       me." Revue Française de Psychanalyse, XV, No. 4, octobre-
       décembre 1951, 478-491.

1721   Jehouda, Josué. L'Antisémitisme, miroir du monde. Genève,
       1958, 261-264.

1722   Kronengold, Tobie. "Sartre envisage la question juive."
       Flambeau, 1949, 5-8.

1723   Mandel, Arnold. "La conscience juive en France." European
       Judaism, IV, No. 1, Summer 1969, 34-40.

1724   Mandel, Arnold. "Réflexions sur la question juive." L'Arche, février 1962.

1725   Mauriac, François. "Sartre et la question juive." Le Figaro. No. 2578, 23 décembre 1953, 1.

1726   Memmi, Albert. Portrait d'un Juif. Paris: Gallimard, 1962.

1727   Patri, Aimé. "Sur la question juive." La Table Ronde. No. 11, novembre 1948, 1894-1902.

1728   Payet-Burin, Roger. "La question juive vue par Jean-Paul Sartre." Revue Internationale, III, No. 16, juin 1947, 452-458.

1729   Rabi. "Sartre, portrait d'un philosémite." Esprit, XV, No. 138, octobre 1947, 532-546.

1730   Roy, Claude. "Réflexions sur la question juive." Europe, XXVI, No. 31, juillet 1948, 104-105.

1731   Sartre, Jean-Paul. "Il n'y a plus de doctrine antisémite." Evidences. No. 23, janvier 1952, 7-8. Cf. Les Ecrits de Sartre, 245-246.

1732   Watteau, Maurice. "Situations raciales et condition de l'homme dans l'oeuvre de Sartre." Présence Africaine. No. 2, janvier 1948, 209-229; Ibid., No. 3, 1948, 405-417.

1733   Yéfine. "Réflexions sur la question juive." Esprit, XV, No. 135, juillet 1947, 168-170.

STUDIES IN OTHER LANGUAGES

1734   Baruch, J.Z. "Sartre en het anti-semitisme." Critisch Bulletin, XV, June 1948, 266-271.

1735   Friedrich, O. Christopher. "Der antisemitische Anti-Anti-Semit." Prisma (München), No. 19-20, 1948, 30-31.

1736   Jacob, Armand. "Sartres Betrachtungen zur Judenfrage." Geistiges Frankreich (Wien), V, No. 231, 1952, 1-6.

1737   Strasser, Jadja. "Jean-Paul Sartre und seine Stellung zum Judentum." Weg (Berlin), III, No. 13-14, 1948, 5-6.

1738   Weghe, Jan van den. "Psychologische aspecten van het anti-
semitisme." Nieuw Vlaams Tijdschrift, XVI, 1963, 108-116.

LA TRANSCENDENCE DE L'EGO

1739   Berger, Gaston. Le Cogito dans la pensée de Husserl. Paris:
Gallimard, 1941. Trans. by Kathleen McLaughlin: The Cogito
in Husserl's Philosophy. Evanston, Illinois: Northwestern
Univ. Pr., 1972, 125-127.

1740   Bjelke, Johann F. "Noen refleksjoner over Sartres Transcendence de l'ego." Exil, III, 1968-1969, 78-83.

1741   Carrolo, C.A. "La Transcendence de l'ego." Revista Portuguesa de Filosofia, XXIV, 1968, 248-251.

1742   Doran, Robert M. "Sartre's Critique of the Husserlian Ego."
Modern Schoolman, XLIV, May 1967, 307-318.

1743   Gurwirsch, Aron. "A Non-Egological Conception of Consciousness." Philosophy and Phenomenological Research, I, March
1941, 325-338.

1744   Lapointe, François H. "Psicología fenomenólogica de Husserl
y Sartre." Revista Latinoamericana de Psicología, II, No.
3, 1970, 377-385.

1745   Lebon, Sylvie. "Introduction, notes et appendices." La
Transcendence de l'ego. Paris: J. Vrin, 1965.

1746   McGill, J.V. "The Transcendence of the Ego: An Existentialist
Theory of Consciousness." Journal of Philosophy, LV, 1958,
966-968.

1747   Natanson, Maurice. "The Empirical and Transcendental Ego."
For Roman Ingarden: Nine Essays in Phenomenology. The
Hague: Nijhoff, 1959. Reprinted Literature, Philosophy and
the Social Sciences. The Hague: Nijoff, 1962, 44-54.

1748   Natanson, Maurice. "Husserl and Sartre on Intentionality."
Literature, Philosophy and the Social Sciences. The Hague:
Nijhoff, 1962, 26-33.

1749   Natanson, Maurice. "Phenomenology and Existentialism: Husserl
and Sartre on Intentionality." Modern Schoolman, XLVII,
November 1959, 1-10. Reprinted Philosophy Today, Jerry H.
Hill, ed. New York: Macmillan, 1970, 67-71.

1750   Scanlon, John D.   "Consciousness, the Streetcar, and the Ego: Pro Husserl, Contra Sartre." Philosophical Forum (Boston), II, Spring 1971, 332-354.

1751   Williams, Forest, and Kirkpatrick, Robert, trans. The Transcendence of the Ego: An Existential Theory of Consciousness. New York: Octagon Books, 1972.

L'IMAGINATION et L'IMAGINAIRE

STUDIES IN ENGLISH

1752   Abenheimer, M.M.   "Psychology of the Imagination." British Journal of Medical Psychology, XXIV, 1951, 215-218.

1753   Alamshah, William H.   "L'Imagination." The Personalist, XLIII, Autumn 1962, 562-564.

1754   Anonymous.   "Aesthetic Discussion." Times Literary Supplement. No. 2570, 4 May 1951, 281.

1755   Blair, R.G.   "Imagination and Freedom in Spinoza and Sartre." Journal of the British Society for Phenomenology, I, No. 2, May 1970, 13-16.

1756   Bunting, I.A.   "Sartre on imagination." Philosophical Studies (Ireland), XIX, 1970, 236-253.

1757   Casey, Edward S.   "Toward a Phenomenology of Imagination." The Journal of the British Society for Phenomenology, 5, No. 1, January 1974, 3-19.

1758   Courtney, Richard.   "Imagination and the Dramatic Act: Comments on Sartre, Ryle and Furlong." Journal of Aesthetics and Art Criticism, XXX, Winter 1971, 163-170.

1759   Fulton, James S.   "L'Imaginaire." Philosophical Review, LXVIII, No. 2, March 1949, 182-184.

1760   Furlong, E.J.   Imagination. London: George Allen and Unwin; New York: Macmillan, 1961.

1761   Goldthorpe, Rhiannon.   "Sartre's Theory of Imagination and Les Séquestrés d'Altona." Journal of the British Society for Phenomenology, IV, No. 2, May 1973, 113-122.

1762 Grimsley, Ronald. "Sartre and the Phenomenology of Imagina-
      tion." Journal of the British Society for Phenomenology,
      III, No. 1, January 1972, 58-62.

1763 Hannay, Alastair. Mental Images. London: G. Allen and Unwin;
      New York: Humanities Pr., 1971.

1764 Hering, Jean. "Concerning Image, Idea and Dream." Philosophy
      and Phenomenological Research, VIII, No. 2, December 1947,
      188-205.

1765 Ishiguro, Hide. "Imagination." British Analytic Philosophy.
      Bernard Williams and Alan Montefiore, eds. London: Rout-
      ledge and Kegan Paul, 1966. Reprinted Sartre: A Collection
      of Critical Essays. Mary Warnock, ed. Garden City, New
      York: Doubleday, Anchor Books, 1971.

1766 Kracauer, Siegfried. "Consciousness, Free and Spontaneous."
      Saturday Review of Literature, XXXI, No. 26, 1948, 22-23.

1767 Kvehl, James. "Perceiving and Imagining." Philosophy and
      Phenomenological Research, XXXI, No. 2, December 1970,
      212-224.

1768 Lycos, Kimon. "Images and the Imaginary." Australian Journal
      of Philosophy, XLIII, No. 3, December 1965, 321-328.

1769 Mace, C.A. "The Psychology of Imagination." Hibbert Journal,
      XLVII, 1948, 99-100.

1770 Manser, A.R. "The Imagination." Durham University Journal,
      LVIII, No. 1, December 1965, 12-22.

1771 McKenna, Ross. "The Imagination: A Central Sartrean Theme."
      Journal of the British Society for Phenomenology, V, No. 1,
      January 1974, 63-70.

1772 Morgan, Kathryn Pauly. "A Critical Analysis of Sartre's
      Theory of Imagination." Journal of the British Society for
      Phenomenology, V, No. 1, January 1974, 20-33.

1773 Nuttall, A.D. The Common Sky: Philosophy and the Literary Im-
      agination. London: Chatto and Windus for the Sussex Univ.
      Pr., 1974.

1774 Theobald, David W. "The Imagination and What Philosophers
      Have to Say." Diogenes. No. 57, Spring 1967, 47-63.

1775   Vassilieff, Elizabeth. "Sartre on Imagination." Meanjin
        Quarterly, X, No. 46, Spring 1951, 267-286.

1776   Warnock, Mary. "The Concrete Imagination." Journal of the
        British Society for Phenomenology, I, No. 2, May 1970, 6-
        12.

1777   Warnock, Mary. "Imagination in Sartre." British Journal of
        Aesthetics, X, October 1970, 323-336.

1778   Warnock, Mary. "Introduction" to Sartre, The Psychology of
        Imagination. London: Methuen, 1972.

STUDIES IN FRENCH

1779   Anonymous. "L'Imaginaire." Revue de Métaphysique et de Mor-
        ale, XLI, 1940, 417-418.

1780   Baladie, Naguib. "La structure de l'image d'après Jean-Paul
        Sartre." Valeurs (Alexandrie), No. 1, avril 1945, 45-64.

1781   DePetter, D.M. "L'Imagination." Revue des Sciences Philoso-
        phiques et Théologiques, XXVII, janvier 1938, 88-91.

1782   Durand, Gilbert. Les Structures anthropologiques de l'imagi-
        naire. Paris: Presses Universitaires de France, 1963.

1783   Etiemble René. "L'Imaginaire par Jean-Paul Sartre." Fon-
        taine, VI, No. 36, 1944, 115-117. Aussi Lettres Françaises
        (Buenos Aires), IV, No. 15, janvier 1945, 79-84.

1784   Faure, Henri. Hallucinations et réalité perceptive. Paris:
        Presses Universitaires de France, 1965.

1785   Gagey, Jacques. Gaston Bachelard ou la conversion à l'imagi-
        naire. Paris: Éditions Marcel Rivière et Cie., 1969.

1786   Feldmann-Comti, Yanne. "Structure intentionelle: Introduction
        à l'étude phénoménologique de l'image à propos d'un ouvrage
        récent." Revue de Métaphysique et de Morale, XLIV, 1937,
        767-770.

1787   Lagache, Daniel. "L'imagination de Sartre." Bulletin de la
        Faculté des Lettres de Strasbourg, XIX, No. 8, juin 1941,
        309-325.

1788   Lefebvre, Maurice-Jean.   L'Image fascinante et le surréel.
       Paris: Plon, 1965.

1789   Merleau-Ponty, Maurice.   "L'Imagination."   Journal de Psy-
       chologie Normale et Pathologique, XXXIII, No. 9-10, novem-
       bre-décembre 1936, 756-761.

1790   Michelis, R.A.   "De l'imagination abstractive."   Revue Inter-
       nationale de Philosophie, No. 68-69, 1964, 229-249.

1791   Schiff, Paul.   "L'Imaginaire de Sartre."   Evolution Psychia-
       trique, Fascicule 1, 1947, 325-331.

STUDIES IN OTHER LANGUAGES

1792   Borrello, Oreste.   "Sartre e la psicologia fenomenologica
       dell'immaginazione."   Rassegna di Scienze Filosofiche, XV,
       1962, 169-199, 319-339.

1793   Casares, A.J.   "Lo imaginario en Sartre."   Universidad (Sante
       Fé), No. 40, 1959, 39-90.

1794   Gordón, Sigfredo.   "Filosofía pura."   Hispano Americano, LII,
       No. 1339, 45.

1795   Pignagnoli, Sante.   "Jean-Paul Sartre: L'immaginazione-idee
       per una teoria delle emozioni."   Humanitas, XVII, No. 11,
       November 1962, 968-969.

1796   Schneemann, R.T.   "Eine psychologische Exploration der Sen-
       sation unter Bezügnahme von Sartres Abhandlung über die Ein-
       gildung."   Folia Psychiatrica, LXI, No. 2, 1958, 167-173.

1797   Schultz, Uwe.   "Freiheit der Phantasie-Sartres Kunsthistorie."
       Deutsche Zeitung/Christ und Welt, 28 January 1972, No. 4,
       13.

1798   Vaccari, G.   Filosofia dell'immaginario ed existenzialismo.
       Pavia, 1952.

LES EMOTIONS: ESQUISSE D'UNE THEORIE

1799   Anders-Stern, Gunther.   "Emotion and Reality."   Philosophy
       and Phenomenological Research, X, 1950, 553-562.

1800   Dilman, I. "An Examination of Sartre's Theory of Emotions."
       Ratio, V, December 1963, 190-212.

       Fell, Joseph J. see 297.

1801   Fell, Joseph J. Emotion in the Thought of Sartre. New York:
       Columbia Univ. Pr., 1965.

1802   Garcia de Onrubia, Luis Felipe. "Fenomenología de la emo-
       ción: Notas críticas sobre la teoría de Sartre." Humanitas,
       I, 1954, 213-217.

1803   Gotlind, Erik. Three Theories of Emotion: Some Views on Phil-
       osophic Method. Copenhagen: Ejnar Munksgaard, 1958.

1804   Grene, Marjorie. "Sartre's Theory of Emotions." Yale French
       Studies, I, No. 1, Spring-Summer 1948, 97-102.

1805   Hillman, James. Emotion: A Comprehensive Phenomenology of
       Theories and Their Meanings for Therapy. Evanston, Illin-
       ois: Northwestern Univ. Pr., 1961.

1806   MacGregor, Joaquim. "Las emociones según Jean-Paul Sartre."
       Filosofía y Letras. No. 34, April 1949, 251-265.

1807   Moloney, Robert. "Sketch For a Theory of the Emotions." Hey-
       throp Journal, XIV, October 1973, 453-460.

1808   Murdoch, Iris. "The Emotions: Outline of a Theory." Mind,
       LIX, 1950, 268-271.

1809   Naidu, P.S., and Thygarajn, A.F. "Existentialism, II-III."
       Aryan Path, XX, No. 5, May 1949, 223-224.

1810   Pignagnoli, Sante. "Jean-Paul Sartre: L'immaginazione-idee
       per una teoria della emozioni." Humanitas, XVII, No. 11,
       November 1962, 968-969.

1811   Pleydell-Pearce, A.G. "Freedom, Emotion and Choice in the
       Philosophy of Sartre." Journal of the British Society for
       Phenomenology, I, No. 2, May 1970, 35-46.

1812   Ritchie, A.M. "Sartre: The Emotions: Outlines of a Theory."
       Australasian Journal of Philosophy, XXVII, December 1949,
       217-222.

1813 Rodie, C. Christopher. "Emotion, Reflection and Action in Sartre's Ontology." Man and World, VII, No. 4, November 1974, 379-393.

1814 William, Daniel D. "Insights of an Existentialist." Christian Century, LXV, 1948, 1304-1305.

1815 Williams, Bernard. "World as It Seems." The Spectator, No. 6997, 3 August 1962, 162-163.

L'ETRE ET LE NEANT

STUDIES IN ENGLISH

1816 Ames, Van Meter. "Fetichism in the Existentialism of Sartre." Journal of Philosophy, XLVII, 6 July 1950, 407-411.

1817 Ames, Van Meter. "Reply to Mr. Natanson." Journal of Philosophy, XLVIII, 4 January 1951, 99-102.

1818 Ayer, A.J. "Novelist-Philosophers, V: Jean-Paul Sartre." Horizon, XII, No. 67, July 1945, 12-26; Ibid., No. 68, August 1945, 101-110.

1819 Barnes, Hazel E. "Jean-Paul Sartre and the Haunted Self." Western Humanities Review, X, Spring 1956, 119-128.

1820 Barnes, Hazel E. "Translator's Introduction." Being and Nothingness. New York: Philosophical Library, 1956.

1821 Barrett, William. "Sartre." Irrational Man: A Study of Existential Philosophy. Garden City, New York: Doubleday, 1958, 213-234. Reprinted On Contemporary Literature. R. Kostelanetz, ed. New York: Avon, 1964, 555-578.

1822 Barrett, William. "The Talent and Career of Jean-Paul Sartre." Partisan Review, XIII, No. 2, Spring 1946, 237-246.

1823 Barrett, William. What is Existentialism? New York: Partisan Review, 1947.

1824 Blackham, Harold J. "Sartre." Six Existential Thinkers. New York: Macmillan, 1952, 110-148.

1825 Blondel, Maurice. "The Inconsistency of Jean-Paul Sartre's Logic." The Thomist, X, No. 4, October 1947, 393-397.

1826   Bochenski, I.M. Contemporary European Philosophy. Berkeley: Univ. of California Pr., 1956.

Brantl, George E. see 266.

1827   Butts, R.E. "Does Intentionality Imply Being? A Paralogism in Sartre's Ontology." Kant-Studien, LII, 1960-1961, 426-432. Abstract appears in Journal of Philosophy, LV, 1958, 911-912.

1828   Champigny, Robert. Stages on Sartre's Way: 1938-1952. Bloomington, Indiana: Indiana Univ. Pr., 1959.

1829   Collins, James. "The Existentialism of Sartre." Thought, XXIII, No. 88, March 1948, 59-100.

1830   Collins, James. "Sartre's Postulatory Atheism." The Existentialists: A Critical Study. Chicago: Henry Regnery, 1952, 38-79.

1831   Copleston, Frederick C. Contemporary Philosophy: Studies in Logical Positivism and Existentialism. Westminster, Maryland, Newman Pr.; London: Burns and Oates, 1956.

1832   Cranston, Maurice. "Sartre as a Thinker." Sunday Times, No. 6987, 14 April 1957, 6.

1833   Desan, Wilfrid. The Tragic Finale: An Essay on the Philosophy of Sartre. Cambridge, Massachusetts: Harvard Univ. Pr., 1954; New York: Harper Torchbooks, 1960.

1834   Dina, Stephan A. "Intentionality in the Introduction to Being and Nothingness." Research in Phenomenology, I, 1971, 91-118.

1835   Douglas, Kenneth N. "The Nature of Sartre's Existentialism." Virginia Quarterly Review, XXIII, Spring 1947, 244-260.

1836   Fink, Paul F. "Jean-Paul Sartre: An Existentialist Approach to Metaphysics." The Challenge of Philosophy. San Francisco: Chandler, n.d., 415-426.

1837   Foulquié, Paul. Existentialism. Trans. from the French by Kathleen Raine. London: Dennis Dobson, 1948.

1838   Grene, Marjorie. "L'homme est une passion inutile: Sartre and Heidegger." Kenyon Review, IX, No. 2, Spring 1947, 167-185.

1839 Grene, Marjorie. "Sartre and Heidegger: The Free Resolve."
      and "Sartre and Heidegger: The Self and Other Selves."
      Dreadful Freedom. 2nd ed., Chicago: Chicago Univ. Pr.,
      1960, 41-66, 67-94.

1840 Gregory, J.C. "Sartre's Existentialism." Contemporary Re-
      view, CLXXVI, September 1949, 163-168.

1841 Grimsley, Ronald. "Jean-Paul Sartre." Existentialist
      Thought. Cardiff: Univ. of Wales Pr., 1960, 90-148.

1842 Hampshire, Stuart. "Sartre the Philosopher." Sartre: A Col-
      lection of Critical Essays. Mary Warnock, ed. Garden City,
      New York: Doubleday, Anchor Books, 1971, 59-62.

1843 Hartmann, Klaus. Sartre's Ontology: A Study of Being and
      Nothingness in the Light of Hegel's Logic. Evanston, Ill-
      inois: Northwestern Univ. Pr., 1966.

1844 Heinemann, F.H. "Sartre." Existentialism and the Modern Pre-
      dicament. New York: Harper and Row, 1958, 109-133.

1845 Javet, Pierre. "From Being and Nothingness to Critique of
      Dialectic Reason." Philosophy Today, IX, Fall 1965, 176-
      183.

1846 Jolivet, Régis. Sartre or the Theology of the Absurd. Trans.
      from the French by Wesley C. Piersol. New York: Newmann
      Pr., 1968.

1847 Kersten, Fred. "Can Sartre Count?" Philosophy and Phenomeno-
      logical Research, XXXIV, No. 3, March 1974, 339-354.

1848 Kuhn, Helmut. Encounter With Nothingness: An Essay on Exis-
      tentialism. Chicago: Henry Regnery, 1949.

1849 Lafarge, René. Jean-Paul Sartre: His Philosophy. Trans. from
      the French by Marina Smyth Kok. Notre Dame, Indiana: Univ.
      of Notre Dame Pr., 1970.

1850 Larson, Gerald J. "Classical Samkhya and the Phenomenologi-
      cal Ontology of Sartre." Philosophy East and West, XIX,
      January 1969, 45-58.

1851 Lynch, L.E. "Past and Being in Jean-Paul Sartre." American
      Catholic Philosophical Association Proceedings, XXII, 1947,
      212-220.

1852   MacIntyre, Alasdair C. "Sartrian Ontology." A Critical His-
       tory of Western Philosophy. D.J. O'Connor, ed. New York:
       Collier-Macmillan, 1960, 518-522.

1853   Manser, A.R. "Sartre and 'le néant'." Philosophy, XXXVI,
       No. 137, Spring 1961, 177-187.

1854   Marcel, Gabriel. "Being and Nothingness." Homo Viator: An
       Introduction to a Metaphysic of Hope. Trans. from the
       French by Emma Crawford. New York: Harper and Row, 1962,
       66-184.

1855   Marcuse, Herbert. "Existentialism: Remarks on Jean-Paul Sar-
       tre's L'Etre et le néant." Philosophy and Phenomenological
       Research, VIII, No. 3, March 1948, 309-326.

1856   McBride, William L. "Sartre: Man, Freedom and Praxis." Exis-
       tential Philosophers: Kierkegaard to Merleau-Ponty. George
       Schrader, ed. New York: McGraw-Hill, 1967, 261-330.

1857   Merleau-Ponty, Maurice. The Visible and the Invisible.
       Trans. from the French by Alphonse Lingis. Evanston, Illin-
       ois: Northwestern Univ. Pr., 1970, 50-104.

1858   Moreland, John M. "For-Itself and In-Itself in Sartre and
       Merleau-Ponty." Philosophy Today, XVII, Winter 1973, 311-
       318.

1859   Naess, A. Four Modern Philosophers (Carnap, Wittgenstein,
       Heidegger, Sartre). Chicago: Univ. of Chicago Pr., 1968.

1860   Natanson, Maurice. A Critique of Jean-Paul Sartre's Ontol-
       ogy. Lincoln, Nebraska: Univ. of Nebraska Pr., 1951; The
       Hague: Nijhoff, 1972.

1861   Netzky, Ralph. "Sartre's Ontology Re-Appraised: Playful Free-
       dom." Philosophy Today, XVIII, No. 2, Summer 1974, 125-136.

1862   Owens, Thomas. "Absolute Aloneness as Man's Existential
       Structure: A Study of Sartrean Ontology." New Scholasti-
       cism, XL, 1966, 341-360.

1863   Ramsey, Paul. "Jean-Paul Sartre: Sex in Being." Nine Modern
       Moralists. Englewood Cliffs, New Jersey: Prentice-Hall,
       1964, 71-109.

1864   Reinhardt, Kurt F. Existentialist Revolt: The Main Themes and
       Phases of Existentialism. 2nd revised ed. New York: Un-
       gar, 1960.

1865   Rice, P.   "Existentialism and the Self."   Kenyon Review, XII,
       No. 2, Spring 1950, 304-320.

1866   Ricoeur, Paul.   "Negativity and Primary Affirmation."   History
       and Truth.   Trans. from the French by Charles E. Kelbley.
       Evanston, Illinois: Northwestern Univ. Pr., 1965, 305-328.

1867   Royle, Peter.   "Weltanschauung and Ontology in Sartre's Work
       and Thought."   Theoria, XXXVI, 1971, 59-66.

1868   Santoni, Ronald E.   "Sartre's Ontology, by Klaus Hartmann."
       International Philosophical Quarterly, VIII, No. 2, June
       1968, 303-306.

1869   Schaldenbrand, Sister Mary A.   "Freedom and the 'I': An Exis-
       tential Inquiry."   International Philosophical Quarterly,
       III, December 1963, 571-599.

1870   Schaldenbrand, Sister Mary A.   Phenomenologies of Freedom:
       An Essay on the Philosophies of Sartre and G. Marcel.
       Washington, D.C.: Catholic Univ. of America Pr., Philosoph-
       ical Study No. 91, 1960.

1871   Shalom, Albert, and Yolton, John.   "Sartre's Ontology."   Dia-
       logue (Canada), VI, December 1967, 383-398.

1872   Sheridan, James F.   "On Ontology and Politics: A Polemic."
       Dialogue (Canada), VII, December 1968, 449-460.

1873   Shouery, Imad T.   "Reduction in Sartre's Ontology."   South-
       western Journal of Philosophy, II, No. 1-2, Spring-Summer
       1971, 47-53.

1874   Shouery, Imad T.   "The Phenomena of the 'Look', 'Shame', and
       the 'Other' in Sartre."   Darshana International, XI, April
       1971, 43-57.

1875   Smith, Vincent E.   "Existentialism and Existence."   The Tho-
       mist, XI, No. 2, April 1948, 141-196; Ibid., No. 3, July
       1948, 297-329.

1876   Smith, Vincent E.   "The Existentialism of Sartre."   Catholic
       Mind, XLV, April 1947, 202-207.

1877   Spiegelberg, Herbert.   "The Phenomenology of Jean-Paul Sar-
       tre."   The Phenomenological Movement: A Historical Introduc-
       tion, Vol. II.   The Hague: Nijhoff, 1960, 445-515.

1878   Stern, Alfred. Sartre, His Philosophy and Psychoanalysis.
       2nd revised ed. New York: Delacorte, 1967.

1879   Streller-Justus, J. Jean-Paul Sartre: To Freedom Condemned.
       Trans. from the German by Wade Baskin. New York: Philoso-
       phical Library, 1960.

1880   Thévenaz, Pierre. What Is Phenomenology? Trans. from the
       French by James Edie. Chicago: Quadrangle Paperback Orig-
       inal, 1962.

1881   Ussher, Arland. Journey Through Dread: A Study of Kierke-
       gaard, Heidegger and Sartre. London: Darwen-Finlayson,
       1955; New York, Devin-Adair, 1959.

1882   Van de Pitte, M.M. "On Bracketing the Epoche." Dialogue
       (Canada), XI, No. 4, December 1972, 535-545.

1883   Van de Pitte, M.M. "Sartre as Transcendental Realist." Jour-
       nal of the British Society for Phenomenology, I, No. 2, May
       1970, 22-26.

1884   Warnock, Mary. "The Philosophy of Sartre." New York: Hillary
       House; London: Hutchinson, 1965.

1885   Warnock, Mary, ed. Sartre: A Collection of Critical Essays.
       Garden City, New York: Doubleday, Anchor Books, 1971.

1886   White, Morton G. "Existentialism: Jean-Paul Sartre." The Age
       of Analysis: Twentieth Century Philosophy. Boston: Houghton
       Mifflin, 1955, 116-135. With introduction and interpreta-
       tive commentary.

1887   Whittemore, Robert C. "Metaphysical Foundations of Sartre's
       Ontology." Tulane Studies in Philosophy, VIII, 1959, 111-
       121.

1888   Wieczynski, Joseph. "A Note on Jean-Paul Sartre: Monist or
       Dualist?" Philosophy Today, XII, 1968, 184-189.

1889   Wild, John. The Challenge of Existentialism. Bloomington,
       Indiana: Indiana Univ. Pr., 1955.

1890   Wild, John. "Existentialism as a Philosophy." Journal of
       Philosophy, LVII, January 1960, 45-62. Reprinted Sartre:
       A Collection of Critical Essays. Edith Kern, ed. Engle-
       wood Cliffs, New Jersey: Prentice-Hall, 1962, 142-149.

1891 Yolton, John W. "The Metaphysics of En-Soi and Pour-Soi."
      Journal of Philosophy, XLVIII, 1951, 548-556.

1892 Yolton, John W., and Shalom, Albert. "Sartre's Ontology."
      Dialogue (Canada), VI, December 1967, 383-398.

1893 Zaner, Richard M. "Sartre's Ontology of the Body." The Prob-
      lem of Embodiment: Some Contributions to a Phenomenology of
      the Body. The Hague: Nijhoff, 1964, 57-125.

1894 Zuidema, Sytse Ulbe. Jean-Paul Sartre. Trans. from the
      Dutch by Dirk Jellema. Philadelphia: Presbyterian and Re-
      formed, 1960.

STUDIES IN FRENCH

1895 Albérès, René-Marill. Essais et études universitaires, I,
      Paris: Etudes Universitaires, 1943, 129-132.

1896 Alquié, Ferdinand. "L'Etre et le néant." Cahiers du Sud,
      XXIII, No. 273, 648-662; Ibid., No. 274, 807-816.

1897 Anonymous. "L'Etre et le néant." Revue Métaphysique et de
      Morale, XLIV, 1944, 183-185.

1898 Astruc, Alexandre. "L'Etre et le néant." Poésie 44. No. 17,
      janvier-février 1944, 87-92.

1899 Ayraud, Pierre. "Réflexions sur L'Etre et le néant. Témoig-
      nages, X, août 1946, 213-229.

1900 Bénèze, G., and Cuénot, Claude. Qu'est-ce que l'existentialisme?
      Paris: Vrin, 1947.

1901 Bertrand, R. "Notes sur l'essence et l'existence." Revue
      de Métaphysique et de Morale, LI, 1946, 193-199.

1902 Birault, Henri. "Pour ou contre l'ontologie: Réflexions sur
      l'histoire de la pensée existentielle." Critique, XVI, No.
      153, février 1960, 139-157.

1903 Bucio, Francisco P. "De l'ontologie phénoménologique à la
      psychanalyse existentielle chez Sartre." Revista Mexicana
      de Filosofía, IV, No. 4, 1961, 55-85.

1904   Caes, P. "De Descartes à Sartre." Synthèses, VII, No. 78, novembre 1952, 33-42.

1905   Caillois, Roger. "Analyse réflexive et réflexion." Deucalion, I, 1946, 127-136.

1906   Caillois, Roland. "Sartre, l'existence et la réflexion." Critique, Tome 5, IV, No. 37, June 1949, 561-563. Varet, L'Ontologie de Sartre.

1907   Campbell, Robert. Jean-Paul Sartre ou une littérature philosophique. 2e éd. révisée et augmentée. Paris: Pierre Ardent, 1965.

1908   Carette, R. Sartre et la philosophie du possible. Gand: J.D.S., 1953.

1909   Champaux, A.R. "L'intelligible et le réel." Proust et Ruskin: Essai de Henri Lemaitre. Toulouse: Privat Didier, 1944, 421-426.

1910   Champigny, Robert. "L'expression élémentaire dans l'Etre et le néant." PMLA, LXVIII, 1953, 56-64.

1911   Champigny, Robert. "Le mot 'être' dans L'Etre et le néant." Revue de Métaphysique et de Morale, LXI, 1956, 155-165.

1912   Chenu, Joseph. "Jean-Paul Sartre et l'existentialisme." Le Monde Français, II, No. 16, mars 1946, 431-439.

1913   Colin, Pierre. "La phénoménologie du corps dans L'Etre et le néant de Sartre." L'Ame et le corps. Recherches et Débats du Centre Catholique des Intellectuels Français, Cahier No. 35, juin 1961, 174-180.

1914   Corvez, Maurice. "Etre-en-soi dans la philosophie de Sartre." Revue Thomiste, L, No. 3, 1950, 360-372.

1915   Corvez, Maurice. "L'être de la conscience dans la philosophie de Sartre." Revue Thomiste, LI, 1951, 563-574.

1916   Corvez, Maurice. "Existence et essence." Revue Thomiste, LI, No. 2, 1951, 305-330.

1917   Croteau, Jacques. "Notes sur l'ontologie phénoménologique de Sartre." Revue de l'Université d'Ottowa, XXIV, 1954, 53-60.

1918 Dreyfus, Dina. "Jean-Paul Sartre et le mal radical: De L'Etre
      et le néant à la Critique de la raison dialectique." Mer-
      cure de France, Tome CCCXXXVIII, No. 1169, janvier 1961,
      154-167.

1919 Dubarle, D. "L'ontologie phénoménologique de Sartre." Revue
      de Philosophie, No. 2, 1946, 90-123. Aussi L'Existentialis-
      me. Paris: Tequi, 1947, 90-123.

1920 Duméry, Henry. "La méthode complexe de Sartre." Vie Intel-
      lectuelle, XVI, No. 7, juillet 1948, 102-121.

1921 Ecole, Jean. "La création du moi par lui-même et l'optimisme
      sartrien." Etudes Philosophiques, XII, No. 3, 1957, 469-
      483.

1922 Ecole, Jean. "Essence et existence chez Sartre." Etudes
      Philosophiques, VI, No. 2-3, 1951, 161-174.

1923 Ecole, Jean. "Les pièces maîtresses de l'univers de l'être et
      l'échec de la théorie générale de l'être dans l'ontologie
      sartrienne." Giornale di Metafisica, XV, 1960, 52-112.

1924 Emmanuel, Pierre. "Réflexions sur une mise au point." Fon-
      taine, VIII, No. 41, avril 1945, 107-117.

1925 Fabre, Lucien. "Essentialisme et Existentialisme: Le néant et
      M. Sartre." Revue de Paris, LIV, No. 4, avril 1947, 91-112.

1926 Féraud, Henri. "Une philosophie de naufrage: L'existentialis-
      me." Cahiers du Sud, XXVI, No. 281, 1947, 96-103.

1927 Finance, Joseph de. "L'horizon du désir." Doctor Communis,
      XIV, 1961, 128-201.

1928 Finance, Joseph de. "La négation de la puissance chez Sar-
      tre." Sapientia Aquinatis, I, 1947, 473-481.

1929 Forest, Aimé. "L'essence et l'existence." Témoignages.
      Paris: Cahiers de la Pierre-qui-vit, 1947, 212-225.

1930 Foulquié, Paul. L'Existentialisme. Paris: Presses Univer-
      sitaires de France, 1947.

1931 Gandillac, Maurice de. "Apories de l'action et de la liberté
      dans la philosophie de Sartre." Cahiers de la Nouvelle
      Epoque. No. 1, 1945, 81-103.

1932   Georges, André, et al. Les Grands appels de l'homme contempo-
       rain. Paris: Edition du Temps Présent, 1946.

1933   Gilson, Etienne. "Le thomisme et les philosophies existen-
       tielles." Vie Intellectuelle, XIII, No. 5, juin 1945, 144-
       155.

1934   Godet, P. "Note sur L'Etre et le néant de Sartre." Jahrbuch
       Schweizer Philosophische Gesellschaft, V, 1945, 144-155.

1935   Grevillot, Jean-Marie. "L'existentialisme de M. Sartre."
       Les Grands courants de la pensée contemporaine: Existen-
       tialisme, marxisme, personnalisme chrétien. Paris: Edi-
       tion du Vitrail, 1948, 1-64.

1936   Javet, Pierre. "De L'Etre et le néant à la Critique de la
       raison dialectique." Revue de Théologie et Philosophie,
       XI, No. 1, 1961, 51-60.

1937   Jeanson, Francis. Le Problème moral et la pensée de Sartre.
       2e éd. avec un nouveau chapitre, "Un quidam nommé Sartre".
       Paris: Editions du Seuil, 1965.

1938   Jeanson, Francis. Sartre par lui-même. 2e éd. (Coll. Micro-
       cosme). Paris: Editions du Seuil, 1967.

1939   Jolivet, Régis. "Jean-Paul Sartre." Les Doctrines existen-
       tialistes de Kierkegaard à Sartre. Abbaye de Saint Wan-
       drille: Edition de Fontenelle, 1948, 144-230.

1940   Jolivet, Régis. "Jean-Paul Sartre et le matérialisme."
       Giornale di Metafisica, IV, 1949, 510-518.

1941   Jolivet, Régis. Sartre ou la théologie de l'absurde. Paris:
       Arthème Fayard, 1965.

1942   Juin, Hubert. Jean-Paul Sartre ou la condition humaine. Bru-
       xelles: Editions de la Boetie, 1946.

1943   Kemp, Peter. "Le non de Sartre à la logique de Hegel: L'in-
       terprétation et la critique de La Science de la logique
       dans L'Etre et le néant de Sartre." Revue de Théologie et
       Philosophie. No. 5, 1970, 289-300.

1944   Lafarge, René. La Philosophie de Sartre. Toulouse: Privat,
       1967.

1945   Langlois, Jean. "Introduction à l'univers philosophique de
       Sartre." Sciences Ecclésiastiques, IX, 1959, 383-407.

1946 Lapointe, Roger. "Revue du transphénomène sartrien vu par
      A. Shalom." Dialogue (Canada), VI, 1967, 576-582.

1947 Lavelle, Louis. "Dissociation de l'essence et de l'exis-
      tence." Revue de Métaphysique et de Morale, LII, 1947,
      201-227.

1948 Marcel, Gabriel. "L'Etre et le néant." Homo Viator. Paris:
      Aubier, 1945, 233-256.

1949 Marcel, Gabriel. "L'homme selon Sartre." Les Grands appels
      de l'homme contemporain. André Georges, ed. Paris: Edi-
      tion du Temps Présent, 1946.

1950 Mercier, Jeanne. "L'homme, ce magicien du néant: L'existen-
      tialisme sartrien." Hommes et Mondes, XI, No. 43, février
      1950, 268-277.

1951 Mercier, Jeanne. "Le ver dans le fruit: A propos de l'oeuvre
      de Sartre." Etudes, Tome CCXLIV, février 1945, 232-249.

1952 Merleau-Ponty, Maurice. Le Visible et l'invisible. Paris:
      Gallimard, 1964.

1953 **Polin, Raymond.** "Introduction à la philosophie de. Sartre."
      Revue de Paris, LIII, No. 4, avril 1946, 91-97.

1954 Pouillon, Jean. "Une philosophie de la liberté." Pour et
      contre l'existentialisme, grand débat. Colette Audry, ed.
      Paris: Editions Atlas, 1948.

1955 Presseault, Jacques. "L'être-pour-autrui: Problème de struc-
      ture ontologique dans la philosophie de Sartre." Revue de
      l'Université d'Ottawa, XXXVI, No. 1, janvier-mars 1966, 132-
      146; Ibid., avril-juin 1966, 272-294.

1956 Presseault, Jacques. L'Etre-pour-autrui dans la philosophie
      de Sartre. Bruxelles-Paris: Desclée de Brouwer; Montréal:
      Les Editions Bellarmin, 1970.

1957 Pruche, Benoît. Existentialisme et acte d'être. Paris: Ar-
      thaud, 1947.

1958 Pruche, Benoît. L'Homme de Sartre. Paris: Arthaud, 1949.

1959 Shalom, Albert. "Remarques sur l'ontologie de Sartre." Dia-
      logue (Canada), V, mars 1967, 541-554.

1960 Thévenaz, Pierre. "La phénoménologie de Sartre." De Husserl
      à Merleau-Ponty: Qu'est-ce que la phénoménologie? Neu-
      châtel: Editions de la Baconnière, 1956, 79-102.

1961 Tordai, Zador. "Existence et réalité: Polémique avec cer-
      taines thèses fondamentales de L'Etre et le néant de Sar-
      tre." Studia Philosophica (Budapest), XII, Akademiai Mi-
      ado, 1967.

1962 Troisfontaines, Roger. Le Choix de Jean-Paul Sartre: Exposé
      et critique de 'l'Etre et le néant'. Paris: Aubier, 1945.

1963 Truc, Gonzague. De Jean-Paul Sartre à Louis Lavelle, ou dé-
      sagrégation et réintégration. Paris: Tissot, 1946.

1964 Varet, Gilbert. L'Ontologie de Sartre. Paris: Presses Uni-
      versitaires de France, 1948.

1965 Verneaux, R. "De l'absurde." Revue de Philosophie, No. 2,
      1946, 165-197.

1966 Verneaux, R. "Esquisse d'une ontologie du créé." Revue des
      Sciences Religieuses, XXIV, No. 3-4, 1950, 301-314.

1967 Vuillemin, Jules. "La dialectique négative dans la connais-
      sance et l'existence." Dialectica, IV, 1950, 21-42.

1968 Waelhens, Alphonse de. "Jean-Paul Sartre, L'Etre et le né-
      ant." Erasmus, I, No. 9-10, mai 1947, Colonnes 522-539.

1969 Waelhens, Alphonse de. "De la phénoménologie à l'existenti-
      alisme." Le Choix, le monde, l'existence. Paris: Cahiers
      du Collège Philosophique, 1948, 37-82.

1970 Wahl, Jean. "Essai sur le néant d'un problème, sur les pages
      37-84 de L'Etre et le néant de Jean-Paul Sartre." Deuca-
      lion, I, 1946, 40-72.

1971 Wahl, Jean. La Pensée de l'existence. Paris: Flammarion,
      1951.

1972 Wahl, Jean. "Sur l'introduction à L'Etre et le néant." Deu-
      calion, III, 1950, 143-166.

1973 Wahl, Jean. "Sur les philosophies de l'existence." Glanes
      (Amsterdam), No. 15-16, novembre 1950-février 1951, 10-32.

1974   Woelffel, J.   "Notes pour une introduction à l'existentialisme de Sartre."   Bulletin d la Société des Bibliolâtres de
France.   No. 31, octobre 1946, 431-436.

STUDIES IN OTHER LANGUAGES

1975   Arntz, Joseph T.   De liefde in de ontologie van Jean-Paul Sartre.   Nijmegen: Drukkerij Gebr. Janssen, 1960.

1976   Arntz, Joseph T.   "De verhouding tot de ander in het oeuvre
van Jean-Paul Sartre."   Tijdschrift voor Philosophie, XXIII,
1961, 237-274.

1977   Bochenski, I.M.   Europaïsche Philosophie der Gegenwart.   Bern:
Francke, 1948, 173-181.

1978   Bochenski, I.M.   "Jean-Paul Sartre."   Philosophisches Jahrbuch, LVIII, 1948, 282-283.

1979   Braido, R.S.D.B.   "L'umanesimo 'ontologico' di M. Heidegger
contro l'umanesimo 'esistenzialistico' di Jean-Paul Sartre."
Salesianum (Torino), XIV, 1952, 1-25.

1980   Brecht, Franz J.   Einfuhrung in die Philosophie der Existenz.
Heidelberg (Heidelberger Schriften), 1948.

1981   Brock, Erich.   "Sartre, L'Etre et le néant."   Trivium (Zürich), III, No. 3, 1945, 236-242.

1982   Brufau-Prats, Jaimé.   Lineas fundamentales de la ontología y
antropología de Sartre en L'Etre et le néant.   Salamanca:
Universidad de Salamanca, 1971.

1983   Brunner, August.   "Zur Freiheit verurteilt: Jean-Paul Sartres
Existenzphilosophie."   Stimmen der Zeit, CXL, 1947, 178-
190.

1984   Carlini, Armando.   "Sartre, L'Etre et le néant."   Giornale
Critico della Filosofia Italiana, XXVI, Facscilolo 3-4,
July-December 1947, 401-409.

1985   Caruso, Paolo.   "L'ontologia fenomenologica di Sartre."   Aut
Aut.   No. 51, May 1959, 138-156.

1986 Cavaciuti, Santino. L'Ontologia di Jean-Paul Sartre. (Pub-
      blicazione dell'Istituto di Filosofia, Facoltà di Magistero
      dell'Università di Genova, 7). Milano: Marzorati, 1969.

1987 Cera, Giovanni. "Esistenza e realta." Giornale Critico della
      Filosofia Italiana, XXIII, October-December 1969, 548-560.

1988 De Brie, G.A. "Ontologie en ethiek bij Sartre." Tijdschrift
      voor Philosophie, XXIV, 1962, 180-188.

1989 Delfgaauw, B.M.I. "Het existentialisme van Jean-Paul Sartre."
      Studiën, 1944, 63-88.

1990 Derisi, Octavio. "El ser en el existencialismo materialista
      de Sartre." Temas de Filosofía contemporanea. Emilio Sosa
      Lopez and Alberto Caturelli, eds. (2nd Congreso Nacional de
      Filosofía). Buenos Aires: Editorial Sud-America, 1971.

1991 Fabro, Cornelio. "Ontologia esistenzialistica e metafisica
      tradizione." Rivista di Filosofía Neoscolastica, XLV, No.
      6, 1953, 581-618.

1992 Fantone, Vicente. El Existencialismo y la libertad creadora:
      Una critica al existencialismo de Sartre. Buenos Aires:
      Argos, 1948.

1993 Faucitano, Filiberto. L'Essere e il nulla di Jean-Paul Sar-
      tre. Napoli: S. Iodice, 1959.

1994 Flam, Leopold. De Walg van Jean-Paul Sartre. Vilvoorde:
      Dethier, 1960.

1995 Gabriel, Leo. "Sartre." Existenzphilosophie von Kierkegaard
      bis Sartre. Wien: Herold, 1968.

1996 Garcia Baca, J.D. "La ontología fenomenológica de Sartre."
      Filosofía y Letras, XXX, April-June 1948, 185-218.

1997 Gemmer, Anders. Jean-Paul Sartre Ecksistentialism en kritisk
      Verdering. Copenhagen: Munsgaard, 1947.

1998 Giordani, Mario C. "Sartre, o filosofo de ser o do nada."
      Vozes (Petropolis), LVI, No. 7, September 1962, 641-661.

1999 Hartmann, Klaus. Grundzüge der Ontologie Sartres in ihrem
      Verhältnis zu l'Etre et le néant. Berlin: de Gruyter, 1963.

2000 Haug, Wolfgang, F. Jean-Paul Sartre und die Konstruktion des
      Absurden. Frankfurt am Main: Suhrkamp, 1966.

2001 Heinemann, F.H. "Sartre." Existenzphilosophie: Lebendig oder
      tot? Stuttgart, 1954, 112-145.

2002 Holz, Hans Heinz. Jean-Paul Sartre: Darstellung und Kritik
      seiner Philosophie. Meiseneim am Glan: Westkulturverlag,
      Anton Hain, 1951.

2003 Iriarte, Joaquin. "Sartre o la filosofía del absurdo."
      Razón y Fé, XLVIV, No. 140, July-December 1949, 149-161.
      Reprinted "Sartre oder die Philosophie des Absurden."
      Schweizer Rundschau, L, 1950, 534-544.

2004 Jimenez, V. Marta. "El concepto de substancia en la filoso-
      fía de Jean-Paul Sartre." Revista de Filosofía de la Uni-
      versidad de Costa Rica, IV, No. 15-16, 1965, 295-301.

2005 Kemp, Peter. "Die göttliche Krankheit im Sein: Anmerkungen
      zum Verstandnis von Sartres Buch Das Sein und das Nichts."
      Neue Zeitschrift für Syst: Theologie und Rel.-Philosophie,
      VI, No. 3, 1964, 360-375.

2006 Kerkfoff, Manfred. "La controversia de los universales en la
      filosofía de Sartre." Dialogos, II, No. 4, 1965, 145-165.

2007 Kobayaski, Toshihro. Sartre teisugaku kenkuy. Tokoyo: San-
      serva-Shobo, 1957. Studies on the philosophy of Sartre.

2008 Marcuse, Herbert. "Existentialismus: Bemerkungen zu Jean-Paul
      Sartres L'Etre et le néant." Sinn und Form, II, No. 1,
      1950, 50-82.

2009 Moeller, Joseph. Absurdes Sein? Eine Auseinandersetzung mit
      der Ontologie Sartres. Stuttgart: Kohlhammer, 1959.

2010 Napoli, Giovanni di. La Concezione dell'essere nella filoso-
      fia contemporanea. Roma: Studium, 1953.

2011 Natoli, Salvatore. "L'ontologia fenomenologica di L'Essere
      e il nulla." Contributi dell'Instituto di Filosofia (Pub-
      blicazione dell'Università dattólica del Sacro Cuore. Sci-
      enze filosofiche, 14). Milano: Vita e Pensiero, 1969, 191-
      221.

2012 Nuño, Juan A. "La prueba ontológica como determinante de la
      concepción antropológica sartriana." Memoirs, Thirteenth
      International Congress of Philosophy, Vol. III. Also Epis-
      témé (Caracas), 1961-1962, 323-335.

2013   Papone, Annagrazia. Esistenza e corporeità in Sartre: Dalle prime opera all'Essere e il nulla. (Instituto de Filosofia della Facolt' de Lettere e Filosofia dell'Università de Genova). Firenze: F. Le Monnier, 1969.

2014   Pires, Celestino. "Ontologia e metafisica." Revista Portuguesa di Filosofia, XX, 1964, 31-61.

2015   Porcarelli, Vanio. "La metafisica di Sartre." Rivista Filosofia Neoscolastica, XL, 1948, 249-258.

2016   Rainho, A.A. Leite. "Jean-Paul Sartre e o existencialismo ateu." Filosofias do concrete. Lisboa: Uniao Grafica, 1957, 173-488.

2017   Ramos, O.G. "La ontologia fenomenológica de Sartre." Revista Universidad de Antioquia, XL, 1963, 624-646.

2018   Reding, Marcel. Die Existenzphilosophie: Heidegger, Sartre, G. Marcel und Jaspers in kritisch-systematischer Sicht. Dusseldorf: L. Schwann, 1949.

2019   Sanchez Villaseñor, José. Introducción al pensamiento de Jean-Paul Sartre. Mexico: Editorial Jus, 1950.

       Schlisske, Gunther. see 381.

2020   Schwappach, Gerlinde. "Systematische Kritik der Grundlagen von Sartres L'Etre et le néant." Zeitschrift für Philosophische Forschung, XXIV, April-June 1970, 269-294.

2021   Seel, Gerhard. Sartres Dialektik: Zur Methode und Begründung seiner Philosophie unter besonderer Berücksichtigung der Subjekts, Zeit-und Werttheorie. Bonn: Bouvier Verlag H. Grundmann, 1971.

2022   Streller-Justus, J. Zur Freiheit verurteilt: Ein Gründriss des Philosophie Sartres. Hamburg, 1952.

2023   Struyker Boudier, C.E.M. Jean-Paul Sartre: Een inleiding tot zijn denken. Tielt-Den Haag: Lannoo, 1967.

2024   Thyssen, Johannes. "Vom Gegebenen zum Realen: Mit Blick auf die Erkenntniss-Metaphysik von Sartre." Kant Studien, XLVI, No. 1, 1954-1955, 68-87; Ibid., No. 2, 157-171. Reprinted Realismus und moderne Philosophie. Bonn: Bouvier, 1959, 92-138.

2025   Vanni-Rovighi, Sofia. "L'Essere e il nulla di Jean-Paul Sar-
       tre." Rivista di Filosofia Neoscolastica, XL, 1948, 73-90.

2026   Virasoro, Miguel A. "La filosofía de Jean-Paul Sartre."
       Realidad, I, No. 3, May-June 1947, 368-381.

2027   Vircillo, Domenico. "Presupposti e limiti della ricerca meta-
       fisica nell'esistenzialismo di Sartre." Giornale di Meta-
       fisica, XXV, No. 2-3, March-June 1970, 185-214.

2028   Waelhens, Alphonse de. "Zinj en niet-zijn over de philosophie
       van Jean-Paul Sartre." Tijdschrift voor Filosofie, VII,
       1945, 35-116.

2029   Weizsäcker, Viktor von. "Jean-Paul Sartres Sein und Nichts."
       Die Umschau, 1947, 666-675.

2030   Zuidema, Sytse Ulbe. Nacht zonder dageraad naar aanleiding
       van het atheistisch en nihilistisch existentialisme van
       Jean-Paul Sartre. Franeker: Wever, 1948.

L'EXISTENTIALISME EST UN HUMANISME

STUDIES IN ENGLISH

2031   Hart, Samuel L. "L'Existentialisme est un humanisme." Phi-
       losophy and Phenomenological Research, IX, No. 4, June 1949,
       768-771.

2032   Hinshaw, J. Virgil. "Cogito ergo sum." Cronos, I, No. 3,
       1947, 48-50.

2033   Keefe, T. "Sartre's L'Existentialisme est un humanisme."
       Philosophical Journal, IX, 1972, 43-60.

2034   Larrabee, Harold A. "Existentialism is not Humanism." The
       Humanist, VIII, No. 1, 1948, 7-11.

2035   Thompson, J.M. "Existentialism and Humanism." Hibbert Jour-
       nal, XLVII, No. 2, 1949, 170-174.

2036   Todd, Oliver. "Existentialism and Humanism." Horizon, XVIII,
       No. 105, September 1948, 221-224.

2037   Vial, Fernand. "Existentialism and Humanism." Thought,
       XXIII, No. 88, March 1948, 17-20.

STUDIES IN FRENCH

2038   Berne-Jouffroy, L. "Le triomphe de Sartre." Terre des
        Hommes, I, 3 novembre 1945, 1-2.

2039   Bisson, L.A. "L'Existentialisme est un humanisme par Jean-
        Paul Sartre." French Review, I, No. 1, janvier 1947, 70-76.

2040   Bodart, Roger. "L'humanisme de Jean-Paul Sartre ou la vie
        avortée." Empreinte. No. 2, 1947, 29-37. Reimprimé
        Dialogues européens (de Montaigne à Sartre). Bruxelles:
        Edition des Artistes, 1950.

2041   Delhomme, Jeanne. "Jean-Paul Sartre: L'Existentialisme est
        un humanisme." Vie Intellectuelle, XIV, No. 6, juin 1946,
        130-134.

2042   Kanapa, Jean. L'Existentialisme n'est pas un humanisme.
        Paris: Editions Sociales, 1947.

2043   Lecomte, Marcel. "L'Existentialisme est un humanisme." La
        Pensée, XVI, 1948, 105-106.

2044   Marcel, Gabriel. "Existentialisme et humanisme." J'ai Lu,
        mars 1946.

2045   Maulet, Pierre. "Après la conférence de Sartre." Arts. No.
        41, 10 novembre 1945, 3.

2046   Mounin, Georges. "L'existentialisme est-il un humanisme?"
        Action. No. 82, 29 mars 1947, 12-13.

2047   Mounin, Georges. "Philosophie du septième jour." Conflu-
        ences. No. 9, 1947.

2048   Mounin, Georges. "Position de l'existentialisme." Cahiers
        d'Action, mai 1946.

2049   Patri, Aimé. "L'Existentialisme est un humanisme par Jean-
        Paul Sartre." Arche, III, No. 18-19, 1946, 198-199.

2050   Waelhens, Alphonse de. "L'existentialisme de Sartre est-il un
        humanisme?" Revue Philosophique de Louvain, XLIV, No. 2,
        1946, 291-300.

STUDIES IN SPANISH

2051   Marcel, Gabriel. "¿Humanismos?" Mecurio Peruano, XXVI, No.
       291, June 1951, 301-304.

2052   Viana, Felix Fernandez de. "L'Existentialisme est un human-
       isme." Revista de Filosofiá (Madrid), No. 22, 1947, 552-
       557.

CRITIQUE DE LA RAISON DIALECTIQUE et QUESTIONS DE METHODE

STUDIES IN ENGLISH

2053   Abel, Lionel. "Metaphysical Stalinism." Dissent, Spring
       1961, 137-152.

2054   Abel, Lionel. "Sartre vs. Lévi-Strauss: Who Are the Radicals
       Today?" The Commonweal, LXXXIV, No. 13, 17 June 1966, 364-
       368. Reprinted Claude Lévi-Strauss: The Anthropologist as
       Hero. E.N. and T. Hayes, ed. Cambridge, Massachusetts:
       M.I.T. Pr., 1970

2055   Albérès, René-Marill. "Neo-Marxism and Criticism of Dialec-
       tal Reasoning." Sartre: A Collection of Critical Essays.
       Edith Kern, ed. Englewood Cliffs, New Jersey: Prentice-
       Hall, 1962, 161-165.

2056   Anderson, Perry, et al. "Itinerary of a Thought: An Inter-
       view with Jean-Paul Sartre." New Left Review. No. 58,
       November-December 1969, 43-66. Reprinted New York Review
       of Books, XIV, No. 6, 26 March 1970, 22-31.

2057   Aron, Raymond. "The Impact of Marxism in the Twentieth Cen-
       tury." Marxism in the Modern World. Milorad K. Drachko-
       vitch, ed. Stanford, California: Stanford Univ. Pr., 1965,
       1-46. Reprinted Marxism and the Existentialists, 111-163.

2058   Aron, Raymond. "Of Passions and Polemics." Encounter,
       XXXIV, No. 5, May 1970, 49-55.

2059   Aron, Raymond. "Sartre and the Marxist-Leninists." Marxism
       and the Existentialists. New York: Harper and Row, 1969,
       19-41.

2060   Aron, Raymond, "Sartre's Marxism." Encounter, XXIV, June
       1965, 34-39. Reprinted Marxism and the Existentialists.
       New York: Harper and Row, 1969, 164-176.

2061   Aronson, Ronald. "Sartre's Individualist Social Theory."
       Telos. No. 16, Summer 1973, 68-91.

2062   Barnes, Hazel E. "Introduction" to her translation of Search
       for a Method. New York: Knopf, 1967.

2063   Barnes, Hazel E. "Jean-Paul Sartre and the Outside World."
       Chicago Review, XV, No. 1, Summer 1961, 107-112.

2064   Bell, David R. "Marx, Sartre and Marxism." The Listener,
       LXIX, 23 May 1963, 867-868.

2065   Bell, David R. "Marx, Sartre and Marxism." Manchester Lite-
       rary and Philosophical Society Publications CIV, 1961-1962,
       47-64.

2066   Blakely, Thomas J. "Sartre's Critique de la Raison Dialec-
       tique and the Opacity of Marxism-Leninism." Studies in
       Soviet Thought, VIII, June-September 1968, 122-135.

2067   Bondy, François. "Jean-Paul Sartre." The New Left. Maurice
       W. Cranston, ed. New York: Liberal Pr., 1971, 51-82.

2068   Burkle, Howard R. "Jean-Paul Sartre: Social Freedom in the
       Critique de la raison dialectique." Review of Metaphysics,
       XIX, June 1966, 742-757.

2069   Burkle, Howard R. "Sartre's 'Ideal' of Social Unity." Sar-
       tre: A Collection of Critical Essays. Mary Warnock, ed.
       Garden City, New York: Doubleday, Anchor Books, 1971, 315-
       336.

2070   Burkle, Howard R. "Schaff and Sartre on the Grounds of Indi-
       vidual Freedom." International Philosophical Quarterly, V,
       December 1965, 647-665.

2071   Busch, Thomas W. "Sartre: From Phenomenology to Marxism."
       Research in Phenomenology, II, 1972, 111-120.

2072   Cranston, Maurice W. "The Later Thought of Jean-Paul Sartre."
       Modern Occasions. Philip Rahv, ed. New York: Farrar,
       Strauss and Giroux, 1966.

2073   Cranston, Maurice W. "More Marxist than Marx?" Sunday Times.
       No. 7361, 14 June 1964, 38.

2074 Cranston, Maurice W., ed. The New Left: Six Critical Essays
      on Che Guevera, Sartre, Marcuse, Fanon, Black Power. New
      York: The Liberal Pr., 1971.

2075 Cunningham, Frank. "Practice and Some Muddles About the Meth-
      odology of Historical Materialism." Canadian Journal of
      Philosophy, December 1973, 235-248.

      Delue, Steven M. see 284.

2076 Desan, Wilfrid. "The Anti-Cartesian Man or Man in the Collec-
      tive." American Catholic Philosophical Association Proceed-
      ings, XXXVIII, 1964, 119-128.

2077 Desan, Wilfrid. The Marxism of Sartre. Garden City, New
      York: Doubleday, Anchor Books, 1965.

2078 Desan, Wilfrid. "Sartre the Individualist." Patterns of the
      Life-World: Essays in Honor of John Wild. James M. Edie et
      al, ed. Evanston, Illinois: Northwestern Univ. Pr., 1970,
      228-247.

2079 Dreyfus, Hubert L. "Search for a Method, by Jean-Paul Sartre."
      Philosophical Review, LXV, No. 416, October 1966, 537-540.

2080 Fell, Joseph J. "Sartre as Existentialist and Marxist."
      Bucknell Review, XIII, No. 3, December 1965, 63-74.

2081 Finklestein, Sydney. "Marxism and Existentialism." Science
      and Society, XXXI, Winter 1967, 58-66.

2082 Finkelstein, Sydney. "Sartre, Existentialism and Marxism."
      Political Affairs, XLIV, No. 10, October 1965, 52-64.

      Flynn, Bernard C. see 300.

2083 Garaudy, Roger. Marxism in the Twentieth Century. Trans.
      from the French by René Hague. New York: Scribner's; Lon-
      don: Williams Collins and Sons, 1970.

2084 Gorz, André. "Sartre and Marx." New Left Review. No. 37,
      May-June 1966, 33-52.

2085 Green, Martin. "British Marxists and American Freudians."
      Innovations: Essays on Art and Ideas. Bernard Bergonzi, ed.
      London: Macmillan, 1968, 158-184.

2086   Hartmann, Klaus. "Lévi-Strauss and Sartre." Journal of the British Society for Phenomenology, II, No. 3, October 1971, 37-45.

2087   Hartman, Klaus. "Praxis: A Ground for Social Theory?" Journal of the British Society for Phenomenology, I, No. 2, May 1970, 47-58.

2088   Hook, Sydney. "Marxism in the Western World: From 'Scientific Socialism' to Mythology." Marxist Ideology in the Contemporary World-Its Appeals and Paradoxes. M.K. Drachkovitch, ed. New York: Praeger, 1966.

2089   Howard, Dick. "A Marxist Ontology? On Sartre's Critique of Dialectic Reason." Cultural Hermeneutics, I, 1973, 251-283.

2090   Jameson, Fredric. "Sartre and History." Marxism and Form: Twentieth Century Dialectical Theories of Literature. Princeton: Princeton Univ. Pr., 1971, 206-305.

        Javet, Pierre. see 1845.

        Jones, William A. see 320.

2091   Laing, R.D. "Series and Nexus in the Family." New Left Review. No. 15, May-June 1962, 7-14.

2092   Laing, R.D., and Cooper, D.G. Reason and Violence: A Decade, of Sartre's Philosophy, 1950-1960. Rev. ed. with foreword by Jean-Paul Sartre. London: Tavistock, 1971.

2093   Larson, Gerald J. "Revolutionary Praxis and Comparative Philosophy." Philosophy East and West, XXIII, July 1973, 333-341.

        Lessing, Arthur. see 335.

2094   Lessing, Arthur. "Marxist Existentialism." Review of Metaphysics, XX, March 1967, 461-482.

2094a   Lévi-Strauss, Claude. "History and Dialectics." The Savage Mind. Chicago: Univ. of Chicago Pr., 1969.

2095   Lewis, John. "Sartre and Marxism." Marxism Today, V, No. 4, April 1961, 120-122.

2096   Lichtheim, George. "Philosopher in Revolt." The Concept of Ideology and Other Essays. New York: Random House, 1967, 282-288.

2097 Lichtheim, George. "Rebel." New York Review of Books, 28
      January 1965, 8-9. On Desan's The Marxism of Sartre.

2098 Lichtheim, George. "Sartre, Marxism and History." History
      and Theory, III, No. 2, 1963-1964, 222-246. Reprinted The
      Concept of Ideology and Other Essays. New York: Random
      House, 1967, 289-315.

2099 MacIntyre, Alasdair C. "Sartre as a Social Theorist." The
      Listener, LXVII, No. 1721, 22 March 1962, 512-513.

2100 MacLeod, Norman. "Existential Freedom in the Marxism of Sar-
      tre." Dialogue (Canada), VII, June 1968, 26-44.

2101 Manser, Anthony. "Praxis and Dialectic in Sartre's Critique."
      Sartre: A Collection of Critical Essays. Mary Warnock, ed.
      Garden City, New York: Doubleday, Anchor Books, 1971, 337-
      365.

      McClusky, John Evans. see 344.

2102 Molnar, Thomas. "The Manichean Marxist." Modern Age, IX, No.
      3, Summer 1965, 319-322.

2103 Morot-Sir, Edouard. "Sartre's Critique of Dialectical Reason-
      ing." Journal of History of Ideas, XXII, No. 4, October-
      December 1961, 573-581.

2104 Novack, George. Existentialism versus Marxism. New York:
      Dell, 1966, 69-109, 175-206.

2105 Odajnyk, Walter. "The Individual and Marxism." Darshana In-
      ternational, III, No. 3, August 1963, 46-56.

2106 Odajnyk, Walter. Marxism and Existentialism. Garden City,
      New York: Doubleday, Anchor Books, 1965.

      Odini, Eleni Mahousa. see 359.

2107 Paci, Enzo. "Practico-Inert Praxis and Irreversibility." The
      Function of the Sciences and the Meaning of Man. Trans.
      with an introduction by Paul Piccone and James E. Hansen.
      Evanston, Illinois: Northwestern Univ. Pr., 1972, 347-370.

2108 Pierce, Roy. "Biography of a Generation." and "Jean-Paul Sar-
      tre: Existentialist Marxist." Contemporary French Political
      Thought. New York: Columbia Univ. Pr., 1966, 24-48, 148-
      184.

2109 Parsons, Howard L. "Existentialism and Marxism in Dialogue."
      Marxism and Alienation. Herbert Aptheker, ed. New York:
      Humanities, 1965, 90-124.

2110 Parsons, Howard L. "Marx's Humanism vs. Sartre's Existential-
      ism." Humanism and Marx's Thought. Springfield, Illinois:
      Charles C. Thomas, 1971, 190-217.

      Quinn, Bernard J. see 371.

2111 Rosen, Lawrence. "Language, History and the Logic of Inquiry
      in Lévi-Strauss and Sartre." History and Theory, X, 1971,
      269-294.

2112 Schaff, Adam. "Marxism and the Philosophy of Man." in So-
      cialist Humanism. Erich Fromm, ed. Garden City, New York:
      Doubleday, 1965.

2113 Schneider, Werner. "Sartre's Social Theory." Dialogue (Cana-
      da), VII, June 1968, 16-25.

2114 Sheridan, James F. "On Ontology and Politics: A Polemic."
      Dialogue (Canada), VII, December 1968, 449-460.

2115 Sheridan, James F. Sartre: The Radical Conversion. Athens,
      Ohio: Ohio Univ. Pr., 1969.

2116 Stack, George. "The Background of Sartre's Social Dialectic."
      Journal of Social Philosophy, IV, Summer 1973, 4-8.

2117 Stack, George. "Necessity Versus Freedom in Social Proces-
      ses." Philosophische Rundschau, XVII, 1970, 94-107.

2118 Stack, George. "Sartre's Dialectic of Social Relations."
      Philosophy and Phenomenological Research, XXXI, No. 3,
      March 1971, 393-408.

2119 Stack, George. "Sartre's Hyperempirical Dialectic." Journal
      of Thought, VIII, July 1973, 196-205.

2120 Stack, George. "Sartre's Social Phenomenology." Studium
      Generale, XXII, October 1969, 985-1015.

2121 Tint, Herbert. "Jean-Paul Sartre, Critique de la raison di-
      alectique." French Studies, XIX, No. 2, 1965, 204-206.

2122 Tordai, Zador. "Sartre and Marxism." New Hungarian Quarter-
      ly, X, No. 34, Summer 1969, 128-131.

2123   Wein, Hermann.   "The Concept of Ideology in Sartre: 'Situated-
       ness' as an Epistemological and Anthropological Concept."
       Dialogue (Canada), VII, 1968-1969, 1-15.

STUDIES IN FRENCH

2124   Anzieu, Didier.   "Sur la méthode dialectique dans l'étude des
       groupes restreints."   Etudes Philosophiques, XVII, 1962,
       501-509.

2125   Aron, Raymond.   "Sartre et le marxisme."   Figaro Littéraire,
       29 octobre-4 novembre 1964, 1, 6.

2126   Aron, Raymond.   "Le serment et le contrat."   Contrepoint.
       No. 5, hiver 1971, 51-59.

2127   Balliu, Julien.   "L'aliénation et les avatars de l'ontologie."
       Revue de l'Université de Bruxelles, XX, No. 5, août-septem-
       bre 1968, 403-419.

2128   Clavel, Maurice.   "A propos de Sartre."   La Nef, XXVI, nouveau
       série, Cahier No. 37, avril-août 1969, 214-218.

2129   Colombel, Jeannette.   "Jean-Paul Sartre: Approches metholo-
       giques."   Sartre est-il marxiste? Numéro spécial de La Nou-
       velle Critique.   No. 173-174, mars 1966, 129-156.

2130   Colombel, Jeannette.   "Y a-t-il une morale marxiste?"   La Nou-
       velle Critique.   No. 160, novembre 1964, 22-54.

2131   Cranston, Maurice W.   "Le marxisme et l'existentialisme: Quel-
       ques réflexions sur la philosophie politique de Sartre."
       Studi Internazionali di Filosofia, V, Autumn 1973, 183-198.

2132   Domarchi, Jean.   "Lettre ouverte à Jean-Paul Sartre: Le marx-
       isme reste inachevé, l'existentialisme ne lui apporte rien."
       Arts.   No. 792, 19-25 octobre 1960, 1-2.

2133   Doubrovsky, Serge.   "Sartre et le mythe de la raison dialec-
       tique."   Nouvelle Revue Française, IX, No. 105-106-107, sep-
       tembre-novembre 1961.

2134   Dreyfus, Dina.   "Jean-Paul Sartre et le mal radical: de L'Etre
       et le néant à la Critique de la raison dialectique."   Mercure
       de France, Tome CCCXXXVIII, No. 1169, janvier 1961, 154-167.

2135 Dufrenne, Mikel. "La Critique de la raison dialectique."
      Esprit, avril 1961, 675-692. Reimprimé Jalons. The Hague:
      Nijhoff, 1966, 150-168.

2136 Garaudy, Roger. Marxisme du vingtième siècle. Paris: Edition
      La Palatine, 1966.

2137 Garaudy, Roger. "A propos du dernier ouvrage de Sartre: Cri-
      tique de la raison dialectique." Lettres Françaises. No.
      833, 14-20 juillet 1960, 1, 8.

2138 Garaudy, Roger, et al. Marxisme et existentialisme: Contro-
      verses sur la dialectique. Paris: Plon, 1962.

2139 Fields, Madeleine. "De la Critique de la raison dialectique
      aux Séquestrés d'Altona." PMLA, LXXVIII, décembre 1963,
      622-630.

2140 Fieschi, Pascal. "Sartre a enfin célébré les noces du marx-
      isme et de l'existentialisme." Arts. No. 772, 27 avril-3
      mai 1960, 16.

2141 Gervais, Charles. "Le marxisme de Sartre: Mystification ou
      réalité?" Dialogue, X, No. 4, décembre 1971, 727-742.

2142 Gervais, Charles. "Le marxisme de Sartre: Signification et
      projet." Dialogue, VIII, septembre 1969, 272-292.

2143 Gervais, Charles. "Y a-t-il un deuxième Sartre? A propos de
      la Critique de la raison dialectique." Revue Philosophique
      de Louvain, LXVII, février 1969, 74-103.

2144 Girardin, Jean-Claude. "Sartre et le marxisme." Magazine
      Littéraire. No. 55-56, septembre 1971, 20-23.

2145 Gisselbrecht, André. "Présentation." Sartre est-il marxiste
      Numéro spécial de La Nouvelle Critique. No. 173-174, mars
      1966, 92-99.

2146 Goldmann, Lucien. "Jean-Paul Sartre: 'Question de méthode',"
      Marxisme et sciences humaines. Gallimard, 1970, 242-258.

2147 Gorz, André. "Jean-Paul Sartre: De la conscience à la prax-
      is." Livres de France, XVII, No. 1, janvier 1966, 3-7.

2148 Gorz, André. "Sartre et le marxisme." Le Socialisme diffi-
      cile. Paris: Editions du Seuil, 1967, 215-244.

2149 Guérin, Daniel. "Sartre, Lukacs et . . . la Gironde." Les
      Temps Modernes, XIII, 1957, 1132-1137. Réponse de Sartre,
      Ibid., 1137.

2150 Gurvitch, Georges. "Dialectique et sociologie selon Jean-
      Paul Sartre." Cahiers Internationaux de Sociologie, XXXI,
      1961, 113-128.

2151 Gurvitch, Georges. "La dialectique chez Jean-Paul Sartre."
      Dialectique et socialogie. Paris: Gallimard, 1962.

2152 Hyppolite, Jean. "Il faut lire le polonais pour savoir où
      en est Sartre." L'Express, 21 juin 1957, 24-25.

2153 Lagueux, Maurice. "Sartre et la praxis économique." Dialogue
      (Canada), XI, No. 1, mars 1972, 35-47.

2154 Lapassade, Georges. "Sartre et Rousseau." Etudes Philosophi-
      ques, XVII, octobre-décembre 1962, 511-517.

2155 Lefebvre, Henri. "Critique de la critique non-critique."
      Nouvelle Revue Marxiste, juillet 1961.

2156 Lefebvre, Henri. "Les dilemmes de la dialectique." Médita-
      tions. No. 2, 1961, 79-105.

2157 Lévi-Strauss, Claude. "Histoire et dialectique." La Pensée
      Sauvage. Paris: Gallimard, 1962, 324-338.

2158 Maurois, André. "Existentialisme et marxisme." Nouvelles
      Littéraires. No. 1711, 16 juin 1960, 1, 6.

2159 Morot-Sir, Edouard. "De l'angoisse existentielle à la parti-
      cipation sociale: La Critique de la raison dialectique de
      Sartre." Bulletin de la Société des Professeurs Français
      en Amérique, 1960, 5-10.

2160 Morot-Sir, Edouard. "La critique existentialiste: 2, Jean-
      Paul Sartre. La Pensée française d'aujourd'hui. Paris:
      Presses Universitaires de France, 1971.

2161 Nouvelle Critique (La). Sartre est-il marxiste? Numéro spé-
      cial, No. 173-174, mars 1966.

2162 Parain-Vial, Jeanne. "Intérêt et limites de la Critique de
      la raison dialectique." Etudes Philosophique,
      493-499.

2163   Poulantzas, N.   "La Critique de la raison dialectique de Jean-
       Paul Sartre et le droit."   Archives de Philosophie du Droit,
       X, 1965, 83-106.

2164   Pouillon, Jean.   "Sartre et Lévi-Strauss: Analyse dialectique
       d'une dialectique analytique."   L'Arc.   No. 26, 1965, 55-60.

2165   Reynaud, Jean-Daniel.   "Sociologie et 'raison dialectique'."
       Revue Française de Sociologie, II, No. 1, janvier-mars 1961,
       50-66.

2166   Robberechts, L.   "Critique de la raison dialectique."   Revue
       Nouvelle, XXXV, 1962, 307-314.

2167   Schaff, Adam.   "Sur le marxisme et l'existentialisme."   Les
       Temps Modernes.   No. 173-174, août-septembre 1960, 394-417.

2168   Waelhens, Alphonse de.   "Sartre et la raison dialectique."
       Revue Philosophique de Louvain, LX, février 1962, 79-99.

2169   Warnock, Mary.   "L'individu dans la philosophie de Sartre."
       Philosophie et littérature.   Deuxième Colloque de la Soci-
       été britannique de philosophie de langue française.   Hull:
       Fretwells, 1963, 31-38.

                      STUDIES IN OTHER LANGUAGES

2170   Adorno, Theodor W.   "Zur Dialektik des Engagements."   Die Neue
       Rundschau, LXXIII, No. 1, 1962, 93-110.

2171   Amoros, Celia.   "El concepto de razón dialectica en Jean-Paul
       Sartre."   Teorema, I, No. 2, June 1971, 103-116.

2172   Antunes, M.   "Sartre e o marxismo."   Broteria, LXXV, 1962,
       540-550.

2173   Bitschko, I.W.   "Friedrich Engels und die Begruendung des
       marxistischen Humanismus."   Deutsche Zeitschrift für Philos-
       ophie, XVIII, 1970, 1184-1192.

2174   Brufau-Prats, Jaimé.   Moral, vida social y derecho en Jean-
       Paul Sartre.   (Col. Acta Salmanlicensis, Derecho, 20).   Sal-
       amanca, Universidad, 1967.

2175   Beese, Henriette.   "Jean-Paul Sartre: Kritik der dialektischen
       Vernunft."   Neue Deutsche Hefte.   No. 119, 1968, 211-212,
       214-215.

2176 Buehl, Walter. "Dialektische Soziologie und soziologische Dialektik." Köelner Zeitschrift Soziologie, XXI, 1969, 717-751.

2177 Buonajuto, Maria. "Libertà e storia." Giornale Critica della Filosofia Italiana, XXIII, July-September 1969, 400-445.

2178 Compagnolo, Umberto. "L'innesto dell'esistenzialismo sul marxismo: Appunti di una lettura della Question de méthode di Jean-Paul Sartre." Annali della Facoltà di Lingue e Letterature Straniere di Ca'Foscari, I, 1962. Milano: Ugo Mursia, 1962, 41-49.

2179 Daghiri, Giairo. "Materialismo objettivato ed esistenzialismo dialettico." Aut Aut. No. 82, 1965, 18-39.

2180 Chiodi, Pietro. Sartre e il marxismo. Milano: Feltrinelli, 1965.

2181 Chiodi, Pietro. "Sartre e il marxismo." Rivista di Filosofia, LVI, No. 1, 1965, 47-55.

2182 Cotroneo, Girolamo. "Il marxismo fra storia e struttura." Rivista Studi Crociani, X, April-June 1973, 184-191.

2183 Diaz, Carlos. "Marxismos, hoy." Pensamiento, XXIX, April 1973, 195-207.

2184 Duvignaud, Jean. "Der marxistisch-existentialistische Disput." Französische Kultur 1962. Köln: Verlag der Dokumente, 1962, 39-46.

2185 Espiau de la Maestre, André. "Jean-Paul Sartre Auseinandersetzung mit dem Marxismus." Stimmen der Zeit, June 1965, 161-170.

2186 Espiau de la Maestre, André. "Jean-Paul Sartre." Der Sinn und das Absurde. Salzburg: Müller, 1961, 87-133.

2187 Fergnani, Franco. "La Critique de la raison dialectique nell'itinerario filosofico di Jean-Paul Sartre." Il Pensiero Critico, III, No. 4, October-December 1961, 44-94.

2188 Fergnani, Franco. "Marxismo ed esistenzialismo nell'ultimo Sartre." Il Pensiero Critico, January-March 1959, 46-78.

2189 Fetscher, Irving. Der Marxismus im Spiegel der französischen Philosophie. Schriften der Studiengemeinschaft der Evangelischen Akademien. Tübingen, 1961.

2190 Flam, Leopold. "Sartre tussen Kierkegaard en Marx." Tijd-
      schrift van de Vrije Universiteit van Brussel, IV, 1961-
      1962, 1-29.

2191 Fossdal, Alf. "Eksistensialisme og marxisme." Samtiden,
      LXVIII, No. 4, 1959, 226-240.

2192 Hartmann, Klaus. Sartres Sozialphilosophie: Eine Untersuchung
      zu Critique de la raison dialectique. Berlin: de Gruyter,
      1966.

2193 Hartmann, Klaus. "Sartres Stellung zum Marxismus." Archiv
      für das Studium der Neueren Sprachen, CXCLX, December 1962,
      298-312.

2194 Hermann, Friedrich-Wilhelm von. "Die Grenze des Coexistenz-
      Verständnisses in der Philosophie Sartres." Philosophische
      Perspektiven, II, 1970, 134-157.

2195 Holz, Hans Heinz. "Sartres Kritik der dialektischen Ver-
      nunft." Merkur. No. 6, 1961, 969-976.

2196 Kopper, Joachim. "Sartres Kritik der dialektischen Vernunft."
      Kant Studien, LIII, 1961-1962, 351-375.

2197 Krosigk, Frederich von. Philosophie und politische Aktion bei
      Sartre. München: Beck, 1969.

2198 Kruithof, J. "Sartre en het marxisme." Dialoog, I, 1960-
      1961, 41-60.

2199 Kwant, Remy C. "Het marxisme van Sartre." Tijdschrift voor
      Filosofie, XXII, 1960, 617-676.

2200 Kwant, Remy C. "De maatschappijkritiek van Sartre's Critique
      de la raison dialectique." Wijsg. Persp. op Maatsch en
      Wet., X, 1969-70, 22-35.

2201 Kwant, Remy C. "Il marxismo di Sartre." Augustianum, I,
      1961, 94-119.

2202 Kwant, Remy C. "De verhouding tussen existentialisme en marx-
      isme volgens de leer van Jean-Paul Sartre." Alg. Nederl.
      Tijdschrift voor Wijsb. en Psychologie, LIV, 1961-1962, 87-
      100.

2203 Lévi-Strauss, Claude. Il pensiero selvaggio. Milano: Il Sag-
      giatore, 1964, 267-290.

2204 Maccio, Marco. "La dialettica sartriana e la critica della
      dialettica oggettivistica." Aut Aut, July 1964, 58-92.

2205 Maccio, Marco. "Questioni di metodo come introduzione all
      'critica' sartriana." Aut Aut. No. 101, September 1967,
      48-67.

2206 Mauro, Walter. "La ragione dialettica di Sartre: Un dialogo
      con l'uomo." La Fiera Letteraria, XIX, No. 15, 12 April
      1964.

2207 Mayer, Hans. "Philosophische Zwischenbiland 1960: Kritik der
      dialektischen Vernunft." Anmerkungen zu Sartre. Pfüllin-
      gen: Günther Neske, 1972, 16-24.

2208 Ogiermann, Helmut. "Sartre und der dialektische Materialis-
      mus." Theologie und Philosophie, XLIII, No. 3, 1968, 384-
      391.

2209 Oisermann, T.I. "Das Problem der Entfremdung im Zerrspiegel
      der bürgerlichen und revisionistischen 'Kritik' des Marxis-
      mus." Deutsche Zeitschrift für Philosophie, VI, 1962.

2210 Olaso, Ezequiel de. "Sartre ideólogo." Cuadernos. No. 73,
      June 1963, 57-61.

2211 Pagano, Giacoma Maria. Sartre e la dialettica (I principii,
      I). Napoli: Giannini, 1970.

2212 Pagano, Giacoma Maria. "Sartre e l'insuperabile filosofia del
      nostro tempo." Rivista di Studi Crociani, VI, October-De-
      cember 1969, 435-446.

2213 Panou, S. Dialektisches Denken: Sartre, Bloch, Garundy. Mün-
      chen: Uni-Druck, 1973.

2214 Petruzzellis, Nicolà. "L'autocritica di Sartre." Rassegna
      Scienze Filosofici, XVIII, 1965, 64-67.

2215 Petruzzellis, Nicolà. "Dal gruppo alla storia, secondo Sar-
      tre." Rassenga Scienze Filosofici, XVI, 1963, 612-620.

2216 Petruzzellis, Nicolà. "Jean-Paul Sartre tra filosofia e
      ideologia." Rassegna Scienze Filosofici, XV, 1962, 1-27.

2217 Petruzzellis, Nicolà. "La materia e la prassi nell Critica
      della ragione dialettica di Sartre." Rassegna Scienze Filo-
      sofici, XV, 1962, 269-285.

2218   Piersanti, Umberto. "Umanesimo e marxismo: Riflessioni su
       La Critique de la raison dialectique e su Adam Schaff."
       Studi Urb., n.s. B, XLVI, 1972, 222-258.

2219   Rivera, de Ventosa F. "Sartre: Les Mains sales y la Critique
       de la raison dialectique." Punta Europa. No. 102, 1964,
       62-66.

2220   Ruig, Rainaldo. "El existencialismo filo-marxista de Jean-
       Paul Sartre." Convivium. No. 11-12, 1961, 181-186.

2221   Sabetti, A. "L'esistenzialismo marxista di Jean-Paul Sartre."
       Società, XV, 1959, 1199-1224.

2222   Schaff, Adam. Marx oder Sartre? Versuch eine Philosophie der
       Menschen. Berlin: Deutscher, 1965.

2223   Schaff, Adam. "Sartre und Marx oder Moral und Politik."
       Forum (Wien), XI, No. 123, March 1964, 135-139.

2224   Schwarz, Theodor. Jean-Paul Sartres Kritik der dialektis-
       chen Vernunft. Berlin: Deutscher Verlag der Wissenschaften,
       1967.

2225   Schwarz, Theodor. "Uber einige Grundtheses in Jean-Paul Sar-
       tres 'Kritik der dialektischen Vernunft'." Zbornik Filo-
       zofiskej Fakulty Univerzity Komenskeho. Philosophica (Bra-
       tislava), XVI, No. 7, 1966, 121-140.

2226   Schwarz, Theodor. "Zu Jean-Paul Sartres Soziologie in der
       Kritik der dialektischen Vernunft." Zbornik Filozofiskej
       Fakulty Komenskeho. Philosophica, XVII, No. 8-9, 1967-
       1968, 351-376.

2227   Segre, Umberto. "Nota sulle Questions de méthode." Aut Aut.
       No. 51, May 1959, 180-187.

2228   Sotelo, Ignacio. "Sartre y el marxismo." Boletín Informativo
       del Seminario de Derecho Politico (Universidad de Salaman-
       ca), October 1964, 203-217.

2229   Sotelo, Ignacio. Sartre y la razon dialectica. Madrid: Tec-
       nos, 1967.

2230   Stack, George. "Sartre: De la libertad abstracta a la con-
       creta." Folia Humanistica, XI, No. 121, January 1973,
       19-35.

2231   Stack, George. Sartre: Dialéctica y realidad social." Folia
       Humanistica, XI, 1973, 621-646.

2232   Svitsov, V.I. "Kritika Eksistentsialisskish." Voprosy Filo-
        sofi, XVII, No. 1, 1963, 167-172.

2233   Torrevejano, Mercedes. "Sartre, del existencialismo al marx-
        ismo: Un filosofo premio Nobel." Eidos, July-December 1964,
        9-24.

2234   Valenti, G. "Questions de méthode di Jean-Paul Sartre." Ri-
        cerche Filosofiche, XXVI, 1958, 43-70.

2235   Valentini, Francesco. "Sartre e il marxismo." Aut Aut. No.
        51, May 1959, 189-194.

2236   Vircillo, Domenico. "Esistenzialismo ateo e umanesimo total-
        itario in Sartre." Sapienza: Rivista Internazionale di
        Filosofia e Teologia, XXIX, 1971, 276-341.

2237   Vigorelli, Amedeo. "Bosogno e 'rareté': Sartre tra l'ideo-
        logia e la critica." Aut Aut. No. 136-137, July-October
        1973, 117-131.

2238   Wein, Hermann. "Sartre und philosophische Anthropologie."
        Zeitschrift Philosophische Forschung, XXII, October-December
        1968, 569-574.

2239   Wein, Hermann. "Sartre und das Verhältnis von Geschichte und
        Wahrheit: Glossen zu Sartres Kritik der Dialektischen Ver-
        nunft." Verstehen und Vertrauen: Otto Friedrich Bollnow zum
        65. Geburtstag. Johannes Schwartlander, et al, ed. Stutt-
        gart: Kohlhammer, 1968, 245-255.

2240   Wroblewski, Vincent von. "Sartres Existenzialistiche Hegeldeu-
        tung und Revision des Marxismus." Deutsche Zeitschrift Phi-
        losophie, XVIII, 1970, 869-878.

2241   Zbinden, Louis-Albert. "Lettera da Parigi: Critica della rag-
        ione dialettica di Sartre." L'Osservatore Politico Lettera-
        rio, VI, No. 7, July 1960, 119-120.

2242   Zehm, Günter Albrecht. Historische Vernunft und direkte Ak-
        tion: Zur Politik und Philosophie Sartres. Stuttgart:
        Klett, 1964.

LES MOTS

STUDIES IN ENGLISH

2243 Abel, Lionel. "The Retroactive 'I'." Partisan Review, XXXII,
      No. 2, Spring 1965, 255-261.

2244 Alvarez, A. "Jean-Paul Sartre." Beyond All This Fiddle:
      Essays 1955-1967. London: Allan Lane, Penguin Pr., 1968,
      128-132.

2245 Barron, J.D. "Word Upon the Page." The Tablet, CCXVIII, No.
      6493, 31 October 1964, 1230-1231.

2246 Beattie, Arthur H. "The Words." Arizona Quarterly, XXI, Sum-
      mer 1965, 177-179.

2247 Behard, Jack. "Jean-Paul Sartre: The Great Awakening."
      Centennial Review, XIV, No. 4, Fall 1967, 549-564.

2248 Cismaru, Alfred. "French Fiction in 1964." Books Abroad,
      XXXIX, Summer 1965, 278-280.

2249 Cranston, Maurice W. "The Formation of an Intellectual." The
      Listener, LXXI, No. 1833, 14 May 1964, 793-795.

      Culbertson, Diana. see 283.

2250 Daniel, Jean. "Sartre: Fragments of an Autobiography." New
      Republic, 10 October 1964, 19-21.

2251 Elevitch, Bernard. "Jean-Paul Sartre: From the Roof of the
      World." Massachusetts Review, VI, Winter 1965, 367-378.

2252 Elliott, George. "Childhood of a Leader." The Nation, CXCIX,
      No. 6, 14 September 1964, 118-119.

2253 Fell, Joseph J. "Sartre's Words: An Existential Self-Analy-
      sis." Psychoanalytic Review, LV, No. 3, 1968, 426-441.

2254 Flanner, Janet (Genet). "Letter from Paris." New Yorker, 16
      November 1963, 142 ff.

2255 Gold, Herbert. "Saint Sartre." Books and Bookmen, X, No. 11,
      August 1965, 44-47.

2256 Huertas-Jourda, D. "The Place of Les Mots in Sartre's Philos-
      ophy." Review of Metaphysics, XXI, June 1968, 724-744.

2257   Kauffmann, Walter. "Words to Describe His Feelings." New
       York Times Book Reviews, 2 May 1965, 22-23.

2258   Man, Paul de. "Sartre's Confession." New York Review of
       Books. No. 7, 5 November 1964, 10-13.

2259   Mehlman, Jeffrey. A Structural Study of Autobiography:
       Proust, Leiris, Sartre, Lévi-Strauss. Ithaca, New York:
       Cornell Univ. Pr., 1974.

       Mehlman, Jeffrey. see 348.

2260   Moravcevich, June. "La Nausée and Les Mots: Vision and Revis-
       ion." Studies in Philology, LXX, No. 2, April 1973, 222-
       232.

2261   Nott, Kathleen. "The Words." Commentary, XXXIX, February
       1965, 82-86.

2262   O'Brien, Conor Cruise. "A Vocation." New Statesman, LXVIII,
       9 October 1964, 538. Reprinted Writers and Politics, New
       York: Pantheon Books, 1965, 76-80.

2263   O'Brien, Justin. "Sartre Resartus." The French Literary Hor-
       izon. New Brunswick, New Jersey: Rutgers Univ. Pr., 1967,
       317-319.

2264   Peyre, Henri. "On Sartre." Yale Review, LIV, No. 2, December
       1964, 241-248.

2265   Prentice, Robert P. O.F.M. "On Sartre's Les Mots." Autoni-
       anum, XLV, Facsimile 3-4, July-December 1970, 474-504.

2266   Rosenberg, Harold. "From Play-Acting to Self." New Yorker,
       6 February 1965, 131-136. Reprinted Art and the Actor:
       Making of the self. Cleveland: World Pub., 1970, 126-133.

2267   Rycroft, Charles. "Look Back in Loathing." New Society, IV,
       No. 114, 3 December 1964.

2268   Shapiro, Stephen A. "The Dark Continent of Literature: Auto-
       biography." Comparative Literature Studies, V, No. 4, De-
       cember 1968, 421-452.

2269   Thody, Philip. "Existential Psychonalysis." Journal of the
       British Society for Phenomenology, I, No. 2, May 1970, 83-
       92.

2270 Thody, Philip. "Sartre's Autobiography: Existential Psycho-
      analysis or Self-Denial?" Southern Review (Louisiana State
      Univ.), V, No. 4, Autumn 1969, 1030-1044.

2271 Todd, Oliver. "Jean-Paul Sartre on His Autobiography: An
      Interview." The Listener, LVII, No. 1471, 6 June 1957,
      915-916. Cf. Les Ecrits de Sartre, 310.

2272 Toynbee, Philip. "The Little Sartre Monster." The Observer.
      No. 9040, 4 October 1964, 26.

2273 Weightman, John. "Explorations and Explanations." New York
      Times Book Reviews, 11 October 1964, 1, 50.

2274 Weightman, John. "Sartre on Sartre." The Observer. No.
      9009, 1 March 1964, 28.

2275 Zimmermann, Eugenia N. "Jean-Paul Sartre's Les Mots: Problems
      In Criticism." Criticism, VI, Fall 1964, 313-323.

                        STUDIES IN FRENCH

2276 Albérès, René-Marill. "Ce Sartre qui deteste Jean-Paul."
      Nouvelles Littéraires, XLII, No. 1898, 16 janvier, 1, 7.

2277 Anonymous. "L'enfance de Sartre." L'Express. No. 650, 28
      novembre 1963, 42-43.

2278 Anonymous. "Jean-Paul Sartre s'explique sur Les Mots: 'Je ne
      suis pas désespéré et je ne renie pas mon oeuvre antéri-
      eure'." Le Monde. No. 5990, 18 avril 1964, 13.

2279 Arnold, James A. et Piriou, Jean-Pierre. Les Mots de Jean-
      Paul Sartre: Genèse et critique d'une autobiographie. (Ar-
      chives des Lettres Modernes, No. 144). Paris: Minard, 1973.

2280 Bède, Jean-Albert. "Madame de Staël et Les Mots." Mme de
      Staël et l'Europe. Colloque de Coppet, 18-24 juillet 1966.
      Paris: Klincksieck, 1970.

2281 Bensimon, Marc. "D'un mythe à l'autre: Essai sur Les Mots de
      Jean-Paul Sartre." Revue des Sciences Humaines, XXX, No.
      119, 1966, 415-430.

2282 Berkvam, Michael. "Les pouvoirs du mot." Revue des Sciences
      Humaines, XXXVII, 1973.

2283 Besnier, Charles. "Jean-Paul Sartre et 'Les Mots'." Nouvelle
      Revue Pédagogique, 15 décembre 1964, 1-3.

2284 Blanchet, André. "Les Mots de Jean-Paul Sartre." Etudes,
      Tome CCCXX, août 1964, 388-390.

2285 Brincourt, André. "L'abus du pouvoir des mots." Le Figaro,
      11 juin 1971, 27.

2286 Brombert, Victor. "Sartre et la biographie impossible." Ca-
      hiers de l'Association des Etudes Françaises, VII, 1967,
      155-166.

2287 Campoux, Charles. "La langue et le style de Jean-Paul Sar-
      tre." Lettres Françaises. No. 1050, 15-21 octobre 1964, 4.

2288 Clémot, Michel. "Existentialisme et Humanisme: Les Mots de
      Sartre." Moderna Sprak, LVIV, No. 4, 1965, 427-439.

2289 C., M. "Jean-Paul Sartre: Les Mots." Revue Thomiste, LXIV,
      No. 4, octobre-décembre 1964, 659-663.

2290 Deguise, Pierre. "Stendhal et Sartre: Du Naturel à l'Authen-
      ticité." French Review, XLII, mars 1969, 540-547.

2291 Dumur, Guy. "Fils de personne." France-Observateur, XV, No.
      738, 25 juin 1964, 15.

2292 Dutour, Jean. "Le petit Jean-Paul." Nouvelle Revue Fran-
      çaise, XII, No. 135, mars 1964, 563-565.

2293 Ellenberger, Henri. "Les Mots de Sartre." Dialogue (Canada),
      III, No. 4, mars 1965, 433-437.

2294 Frank, Bernard. "Allez donc vous y reconnaître!" France-Ob-
      servateur, No. 720, 20 février 1964, 20.

2295 Frank, Jacques. "Jean-Paul Sartre destructeur de son en-
      fance." Revue Générale Belge, C, No. 2, février 1964, 133-
      138.

2296 Hyppolite, Jean. "Sur Les Mots de Sartre." Figures de la
      pensée philosophique: Ecrits 1931-1968, Vol. II. Paris:
      Presses Universitaires de France, 1971, 807-813.

2297 Ibert, Jean-Claude. "Jean-Paul Sartre et les secrets d'une
      enfance." Revue Nationale. No. 367, September 1964, 235-
      236.

2298   Josa, Solange Claude, et Deplégou, Jacques. "Les Mots." Esprit, XXXII, No. 327, No. 4, avril 1964, 654-659.

2299   Kanters, Robert. "Moi, dis-je, et c'est assez." Revue de Paris, LXXI, février 1964, 115-123.

2300   Kanters, Robert. "De Sartre à Beauvoir." Figaro Littéraire. No. 927, 23-29 janvier 1964, 4.

2301   Lejeune, Philippe. L'Autobiographie en France. Paris: Armand Colin, 1971.

2302   Lena, Marguerite. "Le piège des mots." Cahiers du Neuilly, juillet 1965, 18-23.

2303   Matignon, Renaud. "Jeunesse de Sartre." Mercure de France, Tome CCCLII, No. 1212, octobre 1964, 317-320.

2304   Patri, Aimé. "Les années d'apprentissage de Sartre." Preuves. No. 122, 1961, 70-75.

2305   Patri, Aimé. "Sartre avant les maux." Preuves. No. 159, 1964, 72-77.

2306   Piatier, Jacqueline. "Jean-Paul Sartre s'explique sur Les Mots." Le Monde, 18 avril 1964. Cf. Les Ecrits de Sartre, 398.

2307   Picon, Gaëtan. "Les Mots." Mercure de France. No. 1212, octobre 1964, 313-316.

2308   Recherches et Débats du Centre Catholique des Intellectuels Français, mars 1965, No. 50, 143-168.

2309   Ritzen, Quentin. "Sartre et la délinquance de l'esprit." Nouvelles Littéraires, XLII, No. 1901, 6 février 1964, 1, 10.

2310   Roy, Claude. "Sartre ou le prix des mots." France-Observateur, XV, No. 756, 29 octobre 1964, 17-18.

2311   Sénart, Philippe. "Jean-Paul Sartre ou l'enfant du miracle." La Table Ronde. No. 195, avril 1964, 7-16.

2312   Simon, Pierre-Henri. "Les écrivains contre Sartre." Le Monde. No. 817, 11-17 juin 1964, 10.

2313   Simon, Pierre-Henri. "Les écrivains contre Sartre." Le Monde. No. 6034, 10 juin 1964, 12-13.

2314 Simon, Pierre-Henri. "De Jean-Paul Sartre: Les Mots." Diag-
      nostic des lettres françaises contemporaines. Bruxelles: La
      Renaissance du Livre, 1966, 151-157.

2315 Simon, Pierre-Henri. "Sartre après Les Mots." Diagnostic des
      lettres françaises contemporaines. Bruxelles: La Renais-
      sance du Livre, 1966, 158-165.

2316 Talbot, Serge. "Jean-Paul Sartre a-t-il imité Paul Bourget?"
      Arcadie. No. 125, mai 1964, 251-257.

2317 Thérive, André. "Jean-Paul Sartre: Les Mots." Revue des Deux
      Mondes, 1 avril 1964, 441-443.

2318 Viatte, Auguste. "L'enfance de Jean-Paul Sartre." Revue de
      l'Université Laval, XIX, No. 1, septembre 1964, 27-32.

2319 Vier, Jacques. "Les Mots de Jean-Paul Sartre." L'Homme Nou-
      veau, 1 mars 1964, 14.

2320 Villeneuve, Suzanne, et al. "Les Mots de Jean-Paul Sartre."
      Recherches et Débats, mars 1965, 143-168.

                 STUDIES IN OTHER LANGUAGES

2321 Agamben, Giorgio. "L'infanzia e le parole." Il Mondo, 21
      April 1964, 10.

2322 Alfaro, M. "Les Mots." Indice. No. 191, 1964, 29.

2323 Alopaeus, Marianne. "Sartre om Jean-Paul." Nya Argus, LVII,
      No. 20, 1 December 1964, 297-300.

2324 Andersch, Alfred. "Sartres Kritik an einem Kinde." Die
      Blindheit des Kunstwerks und andere Aufsätze. Frankfurt am
      Main: Suhrkamp, 1965, 139-145.

2325 Bein, Siegfried. "Selbstverwirklichung im Wort: Zu Jean-Paul
      Sartres Memoiren." Welt und Wort, XX, No. 9, September
      1965, 296-297.

2326 Blümel, Adolf. "Selbstporträt und Antriebserlebnis: Zum Motiv
      des Zuges in der Autobiographie bei R. Rolland und Jean-Paul
      Sartre." Die Neuereren Sprachen. No. 2, February 1970,
      59-79.

2327   Bokenkamp, Werner. "Die Illusion zerbricht." Frankfurter
        Allgemeine Zeitung, 12 February 1964, 12.

2328   Colomer, Eusebio. "Les Mots." Selección de Libros, II, 1964,
        326-336.

2329   Colomer, Eusebio. "Lecturas commentadas: El último libro del
        'Nobel' Jean-Paul Sartre." Razón y Fé. No. 170, December
        1964, 485-489.

2330   Daniels, J. "Jean-Paul Sartre buigt zich over zijn kinder-
        jaren." Streven, XVII, No. 8, May 1964, 782-785.

2331   De Groot, C. "Sartres litteraire zelfkastijding." Raam. No.
        9, 1964, 57-64.

2332   Derisi, Octavio. "El último libro de Sartre." Sapientia, XX,
        1965, 210-214.

2333   Gabinizza, Clara. "Le parole di Sartre." L'Italia Che
        Scrive, XLVIII, No. 1-2, 1965, 217-218.

2334   Hagen, Rainer. "Jean-Paul Sartre: Kritik einer Kindheit."
        Sonntagsblatt, 23 November 1964, 28.

2335   Horst, Karl A. "Einige Befriedigung und noch mehr Beunruhi-
        gung: Anmerkungen zu Jean-Paul Sartre Les Mots." Merkur,
        XVIII, No. 197, July 1964, 671-678.

2336   Kaiser, Joachim. "Jean-Paul Sartres Autobiographie." Uni-
        versitas, XX, April 1965, 261-265.

2337   Kopper, Joachim. "Die Ubereignung des Lebens an das Selb-
        stbewusstein: Zur Selbstbiographie Jean-Paul Sartres."
        Kant Studien, LV, 1963-1964, 466-487.

2338   Luzuriaga, Jorge. "Jean-Paul Sartre: Las palabras." Revista
        de Occidente, XX, 1965, 253-259.

2339   Mayer, Hans. "Sartre erzählt seine Kindheit: Die Wörter."
        Anmerkungen zu Sartre. Pfüllingen: Günther, Neske, 1972,
        45-52.

2340   Mendes, Joao. "Les Mots de Sartre: Marginalia." Brotéria,
        79, July 1964, 56-61.

2341   Paci, Enzo. "Le parole." Aut Aut. No. 82, 1965, 7-17.

2342   Petruzzelis, Nicolà. "L'autocriticà di Sartre." Rassegna Scienze Filosofici, XVIII, 1965, 64-67.

2343   Picchi, Mario. "L'infanzia di Sartre." La Fiera Letteraria, n.s., XIX, No. 36, 8 November 1964, 4.

2344   Polanscak, Antun. "Sartreove Rijeci." Od povjerena do sumnje. Zagreb: Naprijed, 1966, 125-132.

2345   Risi, Nelo. "Sartre: in principio erano 'le parole'." Europa Letteraria, V, No. 26, February 1964, 65-69.

2346   Roig, R. "Sartre, Les Mots." El Ciervo. No. 130, 1964, 13.

2347   Soll, Ludwig. "Der Doppelpunkt als Stilphänomen und Ubersetzungsproblem: Bemerkungen zu Les Mots von Sartre." Germanisch-Romanische Monatschrift, N.F., XVIII, 1968, 422-431.

2348   Süssmuth, R. "Sartres autobiographischer Beitrag zur Anthropologie des Kindes." Pädagogische Rundschau, XXIII, No. 9-10, 1969, 690-702.

2349   Tiempo, Cesar. "Sartre, entre Dios y su mama." La Estafeta Literaria. No. 331, 20 November 1965, 8-9.

2350   Trabazo, Luis. "Contestando a Sartre." Indice, XVII, No. 190, November 1964, 4-6.

2351   Verga, Leonardo. "L'ultimo libro di Sartre: Les Mots." Rivista Filosofia Neoscolastica, LVI, May-August 1964, 409-416.

2352   Weber, Werner. "Abschliessend eine Untersuchung über Jean-Paul Sartres Les Mots." Tagebuch eines Lesers: Bemerkungen und Aufsätze zur Literatur. Olten U. Freiburg: Walter, 1965.

L'IDIOT DE LA FAMILLE

STUDIES IN ENGLISH

2353   Adamowski, T.H. "The Condemned of Rouen: Sartre's Flaubert." Novel, VI, No. 1, Fall 1972, 79-83. Vol. I and II.

2354   Anonymous. "Flaubert, c'est moi." Times Literary Supplement. No. 3682, 29 September 1972, 1155-1156. Vol. III.

2355 Anonymous. "The Son as Father of the Man." Times Literary
      Supplement. No. 3630, 24 September 1971, 1133-1135.

2356 Aronson, Ronald. "L'Idiot de la famille: The Ultimate Sar-
      tre." Telos. No. 20, Summer 1974, 90-107.

2357 Bondy, François. "The Idiot, or Sartre's Flaubert." En-
      counter, XXXVII, No. 6, December 1971, 37-41.

2358 Caute, David. "The Refusal to be Good." Modern Occasions,
      Winter 1972, 308 ff.

2359 Champigny, Robert. "Trying to Understand l'Idiot." Diacrit-
      ics, II, No. 2, Summer 1972, 2-6.

2360 Culler, Jonathan. "Genius on Genius." World, I, No. 10, 7
      November 1972, 62, 64.

2361 Flanner, Janet (Genet). "Letter from Paris." New Yorker, 12
      June 1971, 106 ff.

2362 Gore, Keith. "Sartre and Flaubert: From Antipathy to Empa-
      thy." Journal of the British Society for Phenomenology, IV,
      No. 2, May 1973, 104-112.

      Halpern, Joseph. see 310.

2363 Halpern, Joseph. "From Flaubert to Mallarmé: The Knights of
      Nothingness." Diacritics, III, No. 3, Fall 1973, 14-17.
      Vol. III.

2364 Halpern, Joseph. "Trying to Understand l'Idiot." Diacritics,
      II, No. 4, Winter 1972, 60-64.

2365 Hertz, Neil. "Flaubert's Conversions." Diacritics, II, No.
      2, Summer 1972, 7-12.

2366 Levin, Harry. "Literary Enormity: Sartre on Flaubert." Jour-
      nal of the History of Ideas, XXXIII, October 1972, 643-649.

2367 Weightman, John. "Battle of the Century-Sartre versus Flau-
      bert." New York Review of Books, XVIII, No. 6, 6 April
      1972, 10-12.

2368 Weightman, John. "Idiot-Genius: Sartre on Flaubert." Cam-
      bridge Review, XCIII, No. 2205, 19 November 1971.

STUDIES IN FRENCH

2369 Anonymous. "Flaubert au microscope." Les Amis de Flaubert.
      No. 26, mai 1965, 44.

2370 Barberis, Pierre. "Flaubert pour quoi faire?" Le Monde des
      Livres. No. 8231, 2 juillet 1971, 17.

2371 Bersani, Jacques. "L'idiot et sa famille." Combat, 3 juin
      1971.

2372 Bersani, Jacques. "L'idiot de la famille (Tome III) de Jean-
      Paul Sartre." Le Monde des Livres. No. 8570, 4 août 1972,
      9. Hebdomadaire: No. 1242, 10-16 août 1972, 12.

2373 Boisdeffre, Pierre de. "L'élève Flaubert devant le professeur
      Sartre." Nouvelles Littéraires, 50e année, No. 2342, 14-20
      août 1972, 3-4. Tome III.

2374 Boisdeffre, Pierre de. "La revue littéraire . . . L'Idiot de
      la famille." Revue des Deux Mondes, juillet 1971, 179-187.

2375 Brochier, Jean-Jacques. "Sartre critique littéraire." Maga-
      zine Littéraire. No. 55-56, septembre 1971, 24-26.

2376 Burgelin, Claude. "Lire L'Idiot de la famille?" Littérature.
      No. 6, mai 1972, 111-120.

2377 Contat, Michel, et Rybalka, Michel. "Un entretien avec Jean-
      Paul Sartre: 'J'ai voulu montrer un homme et montrer une mé-
      thode dans L'Idiot de la famille'." Le Monde des Livres.
      No. 8190, 14 mai 1971, 17, 20-21. Hebdomadaire: No. 1178,
      20-26 mai 1971, 12-13.

2378 Daix, Pierre. "Le Flaubert de Sartre: I, Position du prob-
      lème." Lettres Françaises. No. 1386, 19-25 mai 1971, 3-4.

2379 Daix, Pierre. "Le Flaubert de Sartre: II, Une biographie cu-
      biste." Lettres Françaises. No. 1387, 26 mai-1 juin 1971,
      4-5.

2380 Daix, Pierre. "Le Flaubert de Sartre: III, Questions de mé-
      thode." Lettres Françaises. No. 1388, 2-8 juin 1971, 8-9.

2381 Debray-Genette, R. "La découvert de la forme." Le Monde des
      Livres. No. 8231, 2 juillet 1971, 2. Hebdomadaire: 16-17.

2382 Doubrovsky, Serge. "Une étrange toupie." Le Monde des
      Livres. No. 8231, 2 juillet 1971, 2. Hebdomadaire: 16-17.

2383 Fabre-Luce, Alfred. "Sartre par Flaubert." Revue des Deux
      Mondes. No. 10, octobre 1972, 44-61.

2384 Giron, Roger. "En 2136 pages (pour commencer) Sartre règle un
      compte avec Flaubert." France-Soir, 3 juin 1971.

2385 Jannoud, Claude. "Dans L'Idiot de la famille, Sartre est tour
      à tour philosophe, historien, critique, romancier, poète,
      classique et révolutionnaire." Le Figaro, 7 mai 1971, 1,
      33.

2386 Jannoud, Claude. "Flaubert vu par Sartre ou le bourgeois
      malgré lui." Figaro Littéraire. No. 1371, 26 août 1972,
      9-10.

2387 Juin, Hubert. "Le face-à-face Sartre-Flaubert." Combat, 3
      juin 1971.

2388 Lecarme, Jacques. "Sartre et son double." Nouvelle Revue
      Française. No. 232, avril 1972, 84-88.

2389 Léonard, J. "A propos de 'La conscience de classe chez Flau-
      bert', selon Sartre." Les Amis de Flaubert, décembre 1967,
      25-27.

2390 Marchand, Jacqueline. "L'Idiot de la famille." Courrier Ra-
      tionaliste, août 1974. A review.

2391 Marchand, Jacqueline. "Sartre, Flaubert et Dieu." Raison
      Présente. No. 33, mars 1975, 65-78.

2392 Matignon, Renaud. "Sartre a disparu." La Galerie. No. 106,
      juillet 1971, 66-67.

2393 Mergeai, Jean. "L'Idiot de la famille par Jean-Paul Sartre."
      Synthèses, XXVI, No. 304-305, octobre-novembre 1971, 71-74.

2394 Mouchard, Claude. "Un roman vrai?" Critique, XXVII, No. 295,
      décembre 1971, 1029-1049.

2395 Nabarra, Alain. "L'Idiot de la famille: Gustave Flaubert de
      1821 à 1857." Dialogue, XII, No. 2, juin 1973, 373-376.

2396 Nadeau, Maurice. "Flaubert 'écrivain du Second Empire'."
      Quinzaine Littéraire. No. 149, 1-15 octobre 1972, 19-20.

2397 Nadeau, Maurice. "L'Idiot de la famille: Monstreux, irritant
      et génial." Nouvelles Littéraires, XLVIV, No. 2284, 2 juil-
      let 1971, 16-17.

2398 Nadeau, Maurice. "Sartre et L'Idiot de la famille." Quin-
      zaine Littéraire. No. 119, 1-15 juin 1971, 3-4; Ibid., No.
      120, 15-30 juin 1971, 8-9; Ibid., No. 121, 1-15 juillet
      1971, 11-12.

2399 Ormesson, Jean d'. "Le premier de la classe." Nouvelles
      Littéraires, XLVIV, No. 2276, 21 mai 1971, 6.

2400 Peyret, Jean-François. "L'amateur d'échec." Nouvel Obser-
      vateur. No. 427, 15-21 janvier 1973, 56-58.

2401 Reichler, Claude. "Le Flaubert de Sartre: Au-delà d'un règle-
      ment de comptes, une esquisse d'une théorie de la connais-
      sance." Journal de Genève, 5 juin 1971.

2402 Revel, Jean-François. "Jean-François Revel a lu le Flaubert
      de Sartre." L'Express. No. 1036, 17-23 mai 1971, 69-71.
      Reimprimé "Le Flaubert de Sartre." Les Idées de notre
      temps: Chroniques de l'Express, 1966-1971. Paris: Robert
      Laffont, 1972, 167-171.

2403 Robert, Marthe. "Le tribunal ou l'analyse?" Le Monde des
      Livres. No. 8231, 2 juillet, 16.

2404 Roy, Claude. "L'oncle Gustave en flagrant délit." Nouvel
      Observateur, 31 mars, 1 avril 1969, 35-37.

2405 Rybalka, Michel. "Comment peut-on être Flaubert?" Nouvel Ob-
      servateur. No. 340, 17-23 mai 1971, 53-54.

2406 Simon, Pierre-Henri. "Flaubert disséqué par Sartre." Le
      Monde des Livres. No. 8231, 2 juillet 1971, 13.

STUDIES IN OTHER LANGUAGES

2407 Ambroise, Claude. "L'Idiot de la famille: una critica let-
      teraria anti strutturalista." Aut Aut. No. 136-137, July-
      October 1973, 85-115.

2408 Améry, Jean. "Die Wörter Gustave Flauberts: Uber Jean-Paul
      Sartres L'Idiot de la famille." Merkur, XXV, No. 12, Decem-
      ber 1971, 1197-1210.

2409   Faracovi, Ornella Pompeo. "Gustave, l'idiot de la famille:
       la metodologia sartriana alla misura dell' 'uomo' Flaubert."
       Ponte, XXVII, No. 8-9, August-September 1971, 970-978.

2410   Grössel, Hanns. "Jean-Paul Sartre: Gustaves Dummheit, Ein
       Kapitel aus der Flaubert-Monographie L'Idiot de la famille."
       Neue Rundschau, LXXXII, No. 4, 1971, 649-663. Introduction
       and translation.

2411   Guerena, Jacinto-Luis. "Ensayo." La Estafeta Literaria. No.
       475, 1 September 1971, 679-680.

2412   Mayer, Hans. "Sartre, Flaubert und die Dummheit." Anmerkun-
       gen zu Sartre. Pfüllingen: Gunther, Neske, 1972.

2413   Schlocker, George. "Forschungsreise zu Flaubert: Sartres
       neues Buch "Der Familientrottel"-Versuch einer Biographie."
       Die Welt, 11 June 1971, No. 133, 27.

PART IV

ITEMS ARRANGED BY PROPER NAMES

ADLER, Alfred.

2414   Barnes, Hazel E.   "Adler and Sartre: A Comment."   Journal of
        Individual Psychology, XXI, No. 2, November 1965, 163-168.

        Rom, Paul, and Ansbacher, Heinz L.   see 536.

2415   Stern, Alfred.   "Adler and Sartre: Comments."   Journal of In-
        dividual Psychology, XXI, No. 2, November 1965, 169-174.

2416   Stern, Alfred.   "Existential Psychoanalysis and Individual
        Psychology."   Journal of Individual Psychology, XIV, 1958,
        39-50.

2417   Stern, Alfred.   "El psicoanálisis existencialista."   Folia
        Humanistica, VIII, No. 94, October 1970, 781-793.

2418   Stern, Alfred.   "La psychologie individuelle d'Alfred Adler
        et la philosophie."   Revue Philosophique de la France et
        de L'Etranger, juillet-septembre 1960, 313-326.

        Stern, Alfred.   see 57.

ADORNO.

        Hannush, Mufid J.   see 1713.

ALAIN.

2419   Pascal, Georges.   L'Idée de philosophie chez Alain.   Paris:
        Bordas, 1970.

2420   Reboul, Olivier.   "Discussion: Alain et Sartre;" "L'inconsci-
        ent: Alain, Freud, et Sartre;" "La générosité: Alain, Des-
        cartes, et Sartre."   L'Homme et ses passions d'après Alain,
        2 vols.   Paris: Presses Universitaires de France, 1968, 127-
        132, 146-150, 262-268.

ALBEE.

        Falk, Eugene H.   see 899.

ALLEG (L'Affaire Alleg).

2421   Bondy, François.   "France, The New Puritans."   Censorship, I,
        Autumn 1964, 7-9.

2422   Karol, K.S. "The Prisoner of Paris." New Statesman, LV, No.
        1409, 15 March 1958, 328-329.

ALTHUSSER.

2423   Aron, Raymond. "Althusser ou la lecture pseudo-structural-
        iste de Marx." Marxismes imaginaires: D'une sainte famille
        à l'autre. Paris: Gallimard, 1970, 193-354.

ANOUILH, J.

        Beardsworth, P. see 414.

        Conradie, Pieter Jacobus. see 791.

2424   Erichsen, Sven. "Sartre og Anouilh." Athenaeum, I, No. 4,
        1946, 281-292.

2425   Marcel, Gabriel. "Sartre et Anouilh et le problème de Dieu."
        La Nouvelle Revue Canadienne, septembre-octobre 1951.

ARENDT, Hannah.

        McClusky, John E. see 344.

ARISTOTLE.

2426   Arboleda, T.J. "Tres miradas sobre Dios: Aristoteles, Buen-
        aventura, Sartre." Franciscanum, X, 1968, 43-53.

2427   Hahn, Paul. "A Note on Sartre and The Poetics." Educational
        Theater Journal, V, No. 1, March 1953, 12-13.

        Ray, F.L. see 376.

2428   Spanos, William V. "Modern Drama and the Aristotelian Tradi-
        tion: The Formal Imperatives of Absurd Time." Contemporary
        Literature, XII, No. 3, Summer 1971, 345-372.

ARLAND, Marcel.

2429   Arland, Marcel. Lettres de France. Paris: Albin Michel,
        1951.

ARON, Raymond.

2430   Brombert, Victor. "Raymond Aron and the French Intellectu-
        als." Yale French Studies. No. 16, 1955-1956, 13-23.

2431   Burnier, Michel-Antoine. "Raymond Aron: L'opium des conser-
       vateurs." Magazine Littéraire. No. 28, avril-mai 1969,
       36-39.

2432   Clavel, Maurice. "Le miroir de Raymond Aron." Nouvel Obser-
       vateur. No. 448, 9-17 juin 1973, 69.

2433   Lafaurie, Serge. "Les Bastilles de Raymond Aron." Le Nouvel
       Observateur, 19-25 1968. Cf. Les Ecrits de Sartre, 466.

2434   Nadeau, Maurice. "MM. Aron, Merleau-Ponty et les intellectu-
       els." Les Lettres Nouvelles, III, No. 28, juin 1955, 892-
       903.

2435   Patri, Aimé. "De l'opium des intellectuels à la cure de dé-
       sintoxication." Preuves, V, No. 53, juillet 1955, 81-85.

BACHELARD, Gaston.

2436   Grimsley, Ronald. "Two Philosophical Views of the Literary
       Imagination." Comparative Literature Studies. VIII, March
       1971, 42-57.

BALZAC, Honoré de.

2437   Buch, Stratton. "The Uses of Madness." Tennessee Studies in
       Literature, Vol. 3, 1958, 63-71. "La Chambre" and "Louis
       Lambert".

2438   Virtanen, Reino. "La Chambre et Louis Lambert: A Brief Com-
       parison." Symposium, VIII, No. 2, Winter 1954, 327-330.

BARRES, Maurice.

2439   Castex, Pierre G. "Le jeune Barrès et notre temps." L'In-
       formation Littéraire, X, 1958, 17-20.

2440   Fletcher, Dennis J. "Sartre and Barrès: Some Notes on La
       Nausée." Forum for Modern Language Studies, IV, No. 4,
       October 1968, 330-334.

BARTH, Karl.

2441   Carroll, O. "Sartre and Barth." Philosophy Today, IX, Summer
       1965, 101-111.

2442   Miskotte, Kornelis H. Barth Over Sartre. Dies-College, Lei-
       den: Universitaire Pers Leiden, 1951.

BEAUVOIR, Simone de.

2443   Anzieu, Didier. "Le moment de l'apocalypse." La Nef, XXIV,
       No. 31, juillet-octobre 1967, 127-132.

2444   Barry, J.L. "Sartre and Simone de Beauvoir." Carleton Mis-
       cellany. No. 21, February-March 1965, 62-66.

2445   Beauvoir, Simone de. La force de l'âge. Paris: Gallimard,
       1960. Trans. into English by Peter Green: The Prime of
       Life. Cleveland: World, 1962.

2446   Beauvoir, Simone de. La force des choses. Paris: Gallimard,
       1963. Trans. into English by Peter Green: Forces of Circum-
       stance. Cleveland: World, 1964.

2447   Beauvoir, Simone de. "Jean-Paul Sartre: Strictly Personal."
       Harper's Bazaar, January 1946, 113, 158, 160.

2448   Beauvoir, Simone de. Mémoires d'une jeune fille rangée.
       Paris: Gallimard, 1958. Trans. into English by James Kir-
       kup: Memoirs of a Dutiful Daughter. Cleveland: World, 1959.

2449   Beauvoir, Simone de. "Sartre and I." Books and Bookmen,
       VIII, March 1963, 10-11, 61.

2450   Beauvoir, Simone de. Tout compte fait. Paris: Gallimard,
       1972. Trans. into English by André Deutsch: All Said And
       Done. New York: Putnam, 1974.

2451   Bloch-Michel, Jean. "Les intermittences de la mémoire."
       Preuves. No. 155, 1964, 66-70.

2452   Bloch-Michel, Jean. "Sartre fanciullo e la Beauvoir adulta."
       Tempo Presente, VIII, No. 12, December 1963, 34-39.

2453   Cecchi, Anne. "Sartre's Ambiguous Friend." Yale French
       Studies. No. 32, Fall-Winter 1964, 133-137.

2454   Chapsal, Madeleine. "A Union Without Issue." Reporter,
       XXIII, No. 5, 29 September 1964, 40-46.

2455   Cismaru, Alfred. "Enduring Existentialists: Sartre and de
       Beauvoir in Their Golden Age." Antioch Review, XXXI, Win-
       ter 1971-1972, 557-564.

2456   Colombel, Jeannette. "Sartre et Simone de Beauvoir vus par
       Francis Jeanson." La Pensée, n.s., No. 129, octobre 1966,
       91-100.

2457 Durant, Will, and Durant, Ariel. "Jean-Paul Sartre and Si-
      mone de Beauvoir." Interpretations of Life: A Survey of
      Contemporary Literature. New York: Simon and Schuster,
      1970.

2458 Flanner, Janet (Genet). "Letter from Paris." New Yorker, 7
      January 1961, 66-68.

2459 Florence, Yves. "Simone de Beauvoir dans La force de l'âge."
      Le Monde, 12 novembre 1960, 11.

2460 Galey, Matthieu. "L'histoire d'un grand amour: Sartre par
      Simone de Beauvoir." Arts. No. 795, 9-15 November, 1960,
      3.

2461 Gobeil, Madeleine. "Sartre Talks of Beauvoir." Vogue, Amer-
      ican edition, No. 146, July 1965, 72-73. Reprinted "Entre-
      tien avec Jean-Paul Sartre." Serge Julienne-Caffie. Simone
      de Beauvoir. Paris: Gallimard, 1966, 38-43. Cf. Les Ecrits
      de Sartre, 417-418.

2462 Grande, Felix. "Los amores reñidos." Cuadernos Hispanoameri-
      canos, CCXXXII, 1967, 174-180.

2463 Houston, Mona Tobin. "The Sartre of Madame de Beauvoir."
      Yale French Studies. No. 30, 1962-1963, 23-30.

2464 Jonquille, Nepomucène. "Le crépuscule des dieux." Post-
      Scriptum. No. 1, décembre 1972, 13.

2465 Kanters, Robert. "De Sartre à Beauvoir." Figaro Littéraire.
      No. 927, 23-29 janvier, 1964, 4.

2466 Kaufman, Stanley. "Sartre and Friend." The New Republic,
      XLVIII, No. 19, 11 May 1968, 28, 41.

2467 Lilar, Suzanne. Le Malentendu du deuxième sexe. Paris:
      Presses Universitaires de France, 1969.

2468 Margolin, Jean-Claude. "Simone de Beauvoir, Jeanson, Sartre
      et le sartrisme." Etudes Françaises, III, No. 1, février
      1967, 61-73.

2469 Salvan, Jacques L. "Le scandale de la multiplicité des con-
      sciences chez Huxley, Sartre et Simone de Beauvoir." Sympo-
      sium, V, No. 2, November 1951, 198-215. Reprinted The Scan-
      dalous Ghost. Detroit: Wayne State Univ. Pr., 1967.

2470   Savanuzzi, Claudio. "Jean-Paul e Simone." Il Mondo, XII, No.
        39, 20 September 1960.

2471   Tristan, Raymond. "Deux auteurs en quête de personnage: Jean-
        Paul Sartre et Simone de Beauvoir." Revue Palladienne. No.
        12, 2e dizaine, juillet-août 1950, 105-107.

2472   Urmeneta, Fermín de. "Sobre estética sartreana-beauvoirana:
        Sartre o el existencialismo anticonformista; II: Simone de
        Beauvoir o el existencialismo antimasculinista." Revista
        de Ideas Estéticas, April-June 1965, 115-118.

2473   Watté, Pierre. "Enfances parallèls: Sartre, de Beauvoir,
        Julien Green." Revue Nouvelle, XLI, 1965, 102-112.

2474   Weightman, John. "The Unmarried Wife's Tale." The Observer.
        No. 9090, 19 September 1965, 28.

BECKETT, Samuel.

2475   Cohn, Ruby. "Philosophical Fragments in the Works of Samuel
        Beckett." Criticism, VI, Winter 1964, 33-43.

BENDA, Julien.

2476   Belvin, R.W. "Problems of Literary Artist's Detachment as
        Seen by Julien Benda, Jean-Paul Sartre and Thierry Maul-
        nier." Romantic Review, XLVII, December 1956, 270-284.

        Brigaud, Jacques. see 2667.

BERGMAN, Igmar.

2477   Lauder, R.E. "Bergman's Shame and Sartre's Stare." Catholic
        World, CCIX, September 1969, 247-250.

BERGSON, Henri.

2478   Delhomme, Jeanne. "Le problème de l'intériorité: Bergson et
        Sartre." Revue Internationale de Philosophie, XIII, No.
        48, 1959, 201-219.

2479   Hyppolite, Jean. "Du bergsonisme à l'existentialisme." Mer-
        cure de France. No. 1031, juillet 1949, 403-416.

2480   Maire, Gilbert. Une régression mentale d'Henri Bergson à
        Jean-Paul Sartre. Paris: Bernard Grasset, 1959.

2481   Maristany, J.   "La fantasía en Sartre, Freud y Bergson."
       Convivium.   No. 36, 1971, 45-82.

2482   Salvan, Jacques L.   "Les conceptions bergsonienne et sartri-
       enne de la liberté."   French Review, XXII, No. 2, December
       1948, 113-127.

2483   Selle, Mrg. H.   Un Deul à quatre: Saint Thomas, Kant, Bergson,
       Sartre.   La Chapelle du Chêne, Vion (Sarthe), 1954.

BERNANOS, Georges.

2484   Fitch, Brian T.   "Bernanos précurseur de Sartre: Aspects sar-
       triens de la dialectique du regard dans l'univers bernano-
       sien."   Etudes bernanosiennes 6.   Michel Estève, ed. Paris:
       Minard, Lettres Modernes, 1965.

2485   Raalte, L. van.   "Twee aspecten van het moderne franse denken:
       Bernanos en Sartre."   Levende Talen (Gröningen), 1959, 600-
       604.

BLANCHOT, Maurice.

2486   Douglas, Kenneth N.   "Blanchot and Sartre."   Yale French
       Studies, II, No. 1, Spring-Summer 1949, 85-95.

BLONDEL, Maurice.

2487   Romeyer, Blaise.   "Les 'autres' d'après Sartre, Camus, Blon-
       del."   Giornale di Metafisica, VIII, 1953, 185-206.

BONHOEFFER, Dietrich.

2488   Lochman, Jan M.   "Stationen auf dem Wege zue Freiheit: Frei-
       heit bei Sartre und bei Dietrich Bonhoeffer."   Die Zeichen
       der Zeit, XVI, 1962, 130-138.

BORCHERT, W.

2489   Weimer, K.S.   "No Entry, No Exit: A Study of Borchert With
       Some Notes on Sartre."   Modern Language Quarterly, XVII,
       June 1965, 153-165.

BOURGET, Paul.

2490   Laurent, Jacques.   Paul (Bourget) et Jean-Paul (Sartre).
       Paris: Grasset, 1951.   Reimprimé "Paul et Jean-Paul."   Au
       Contraire.   Paris: La Table Ronde, 1967, 57-83.

2491   Patri, Aimé. "Paul, Jean-Paul, François et Caroline." <u>Monde</u>
        <u>Nouveau-Paru</u>, VII, No. 48, 1951, 135-138.

2492   Talbot, Serge. "Jean-Paul Sartre a-t-il imité Paul Bourget?"
        <u>Arcadie</u>. No. 125, mai 1964, 251-257.

BRASILLACH, Robert.

2493   Bardèche, Maurice. "Jean-Paul Sartre et 'La Reine de César-
        ée." <u>La Bataille de</u> 'Bérénice'. Paris: Les Amis de Robert
        Brasillach, 1960, 95-101. Also <u>Les Cahiers des Amis de</u> Rob-
        ert <u>Brasillach</u>. No. 8, 6 février 1960.

BRASSEUR, Pierre.

        see 1135.

BRECHT, Bertold.

2494   Bach, Max, and Bach, Hughette L. "The Moral Problem of Po-
        litical Responsibility: Brecht, Frisch, Sartre." <u>Books</u>
        <u>Abroad</u>, XXXVII, No. 4, 1963, 378-384.

2495   Davis, R.G., and Berg, Peter. "Sartre Through Brecht." <u>TDR</u>:
        <u>The Drama Review</u>, XII, Fall 1967, 112-117.

        Loeb, E. see 904.

2496   Zehm, Günter Albrecht. "Uber den Nihilismus bei Brecht, Sar-
        tre und Camus." <u>Frankfurter Hefte</u>, XVII, 1962, 474-482.

        Zivanovich, Judith K. see 412.

BRETON, André.

2497   Breton, André. "Seconde arche." <u>Fontaine</u>, XI, No. 63, no-
        vembre 1947, 699-703. On surrealism and existentialism.

2498   Mauriac, Claude. "Sartre contre Breton." <u>Carrefour</u>, IV, No.
        156, 10 septembre 1947, 7.

BUBER, Martin.

2499   Friedman, Maurice. "Sex in Sartre and Buber." <u>Review of</u>
        <u>Existential Psychology and Psychiatry</u>, III, 1963, 113-124.

2500   Goldstein, Walter D. <u>Jean-Paul</u> Sartre <u>und</u> <u>Martin</u> <u>Buber</u>: <u>Eine</u>
       <u>vergleichende</u> <u>Betrachtung</u> <u>von</u> <u>Existentialismus</u> <u>und</u> <u>Dialogik</u>.
       Jerusalem: Massachusetts, 1965.

       Hellerich, G. see 313.

2501   Jest, Edward P. "Love and Two Kinds of Existentialism." <u>Eng-</u>
       <u>lish</u> <u>Record</u>, XVI, February 1966, 14-18.

       Shearson, William A. see 384.

BUDDHA.

2502   Siegmund, Georg. "Gotama Buddha und Jean-Paul Sartre: Das
       buddhistische Grunderlebnis." <u>Erbe</u> <u>und</u> <u>Auftang</u> <u>Benedekl</u>,
       XLIII, 1967, 294-310.

CAMUS, Albert.

2503   Anderson, D. "Images of Man in Sartre and Camus." <u>Modern</u>
       <u>Churchman</u>, VIII, October 1964, 33-45.

2504   Barilli, Renato. "Sartre et Camus jugés dans le <u>Journal</u>."
       <u>Gombrowicz</u>. Paris: Cahiers de l'Herne, 1971, 290-299.

2505   Bertmann, Martin A. "Existence Politics: Camus and Sartre."
       <u>Agora</u>, Fall 1969, 23-32.

2506   Blanchet, André. "La vie littéraire: La querelle Sartre-
       Camus." Etudes, Tome CCLXXV, No. 11, novembre 1953, 238-
       246. Reimprimé La <u>Littérature</u> <u>et</u> <u>le</u> <u>spirituel</u>. Paris:
       Aubier, 1959.

2507   Bodin, Paul. "Au delà de la querelle Sartre-Camus une grande
       bataille se poursuit-une polémique qui nous est finalement
       destinée." <u>Arts</u>. No. 378, 26 septembre-2 octobre 1953,
       1, 5.

2508   Boisdeffre, Pierre de. "La fin d'une amitié: Sartre contre
       Camus." La <u>Revue</u> <u>Libre</u>, décembre 1952, 51-57. Reimprimé
       Des <u>vivants</u> <u>et</u> <u>des</u> <u>morts</u>: <u>Témoignages</u> <u>1948-1953</u>. Paris:
       Editions Universitaires, 1953, 249-259.

2509   Brée, Germaine. <u>Camus</u> <u>and</u> <u>Sartre</u>: <u>Crises</u> <u>and</u> <u>Commitment</u>.
       New York: Delta, 1972.

2510   Brombert, Victor. "Camus and the Novel of the 'Absurd'."
       <u>Yale</u> <u>French</u> <u>Studies</u>. No. 1, Spring-Summer 1948, 119-123.

2511   Camus, Albert. "Lettre au directeur des Temps Modernes."
        Les Temps Modernes. No. 82, août 1952, 317-333. Reimpri-
        mé "Révolte et servitude." Actuelles II. Reimprimé Essais,
        754-774.

2512   Carat, Jacques. "La rupture Camus-Sartre." Preuves, II, No.
        20, octobre 1952, 53-56.

2513   Champigny, Robert. Humanism and Human Racism: A Critical
        Study of Essays by Sartre and Camus. (DPL: Séries prac-
        tique, 41). The Hague: Mouton, 1972, 82 pp.

2514   Chiaromonte, Nicolà. "Sartre Versus Camus: A Political Quar-
        rel." Partisan Review, XIX, November-December 1952, 680-
        686. Reprinted Camus: A Collection of Critical Essays.
        Germaine Brée, ed. Englewood Cliffs, New Jersey: Prentice-
        Hall, 1962.

2515   Coffy, Robert. Dieu des athées: Marx, Sartre, Camus. Lyon:
        Chronique Sociale de France, 1965.

2516   Cohn, Robert G. "Sartre-Camus Resartus." Yale French
        Studies. No. 30, Fall 1962, 73-78.

2517   Corsaro, Antonio. "Camus, Sartre, Jeanson." Astrattismo
        nella poesia francese del seicento e altri studi. Palmero:
        S.F. Flaccovio, 1968.

2518   Cruickshank, John. Albert Camus and the Literature of Revolt.
        London: Oxford Univ. Pr., 1959.

2519   Curtis, Jerry L. "Heroic Commitment, or the Dialectics of the
        Leap in Kierkegaard, Sartre and Camus." South Central Bul-
        letin, XXXI, No. 3, October 1971, 107.

2520   Curtis, Jerry L. "Heroic Commitment of the Dialectics of the
        Leap in Kierkegaard, Sartre and Camus." Rice University
        Studies, LIX, No. 3, 1973, 17-26.

2521   Domenach, Jean-Marie. "Camus-Sartre Debate: Rebellion versus
        Revolution." The Nation, 176, 7 March 1953, 202-203.

2522   Doubrovsky, Serge. "Sartre and Camus: A Study in Incarcera-
        tion." Yale French Studies. No. 25, Spring 1960, 85-92.

2523   Etcheverry, A. "La polémique Sartre-Camus: Les raisons d'une
        rupture." Revista Universitaria. No. 3, 1953, 1-2.

2524 Fiedler, Leslie A. "The Pope and the Prophet." Commentary,
       XXI, February 1956, 190-195.

2525 Gaillet, G. "Sartre contre Camus." France Illustrée, septem-
       bre 1952, 280.

2526 Galand, René. "Four French Attitudes on Life: Montherlant,
       Malraux, Sartre, Camus." New England Modern Language As-
       sociation Bulletin, XV, No. 1, February 1953, 9-15.

2527 Gershman, Herbert S. "The Structure of Revolt in Malraux,
       Camus and Sartre." Symposium, XXIV, No. 1, Spring 1970,
       27-35.

2528 Gillon, Adam. "The Absurd and 'les valeurs idéales' in Con-
       rad, Kafka and Camus." Polish Review, VI, Summer 1961, 3-
       10.

2529 Gonzales Mas, Ezequiel. Sartre y Camus: El nuevo espíritu de
       la literatura francesa. Universidad de Guayaquil, 1959.

2530 Guicharnaud, Jacques, and Beckelmans, June, eds. Modern
       French Theater from Giraudoux to Beckett. New Haven: Yale
       Univ. Pr., 1961, 131-152. "Man and His Acts: Sartre and
       Camus." reprinted Sartre: A Collection of Critical Essays.
       Edith Kern, ed. Englewood Cliffs, New Jersey: Prentice-
       Hall, 1962.

2531 Guignet, Jean. "Deux romans existentialistes: La Nausée et
       l'Etranger." French Review, XXIII, No. 2, December 1949,
       86-91.

2532 Hardee, A. Maynor: "Garcia and Sissyphus." Discourse, XII,
       No. 2, 1969, 226-230.

2533 Heppenstall, Rayner. "The Survivor (Camus, Sartre)." The
       Fourfold Tradition. London, 1961, 187-210.

2534 Hubscher, Arthur. "Camus-Marcel-Sartre." Welt und Wort. No.
       11, November 1949, 400-406.

2535 Jolivet, Régis. "El diálogo entre Jean-Paul Sartre y Alberto
       Camus." Sapientia, IX, 1954, 119-123.

2536 Klein, Maxine. "The Philosopher Dramatists." Drama Survey,
       VI, No. 3, Spring 1968, 278-287.

       Klein, Maxine. see 328.

2537 Legrand, Albert. "The Anguish on the Left." Culture (Quebec), XV, 1954, 164-174.

2538 LeWalter, Christian E. "Sartre contra Camus: Zur Krise im französischen Existentialismus." Merkur, VI, No. 12, December 1952, 1174-1176.

2539 Lobet, Marcel. "De l'ombre de Sartre à la lumière de Camus." Classiques de l'an 2000. Nivelles (Belgique): Editions de la Francite, 1970, 153-160.

2540 Marcel, Gabriel. "Sartre, Camus, Malraux-Philosophie und Dichtung des Existentialismus." Universitas, XXI, No. 10, 1966, 1019-1026.

Margadant, Ted W. see 419.

2541 Mayer, Hans. "Sartre und Camus." Anmerkungen zu Sartre. Pfüllingen: Günther, Neske, 1972, 53-58.

2542 Millholland, Donald. "Albert Camus and Existentialism." Religious Humanism, II, Fall 1968, 162-166.

2543 Murchland, T., trans. and author of an additional chapter on Sartre and Camus. "The Anatomy of a Quarrel." Choice of Action: The French Existentialists on the Political Front Line by Michel-Antoine Burnier.

Murchland, T. see 8.

2544 Netzer, Jacques. "Un dialogue sur le destin de la littérature: Sartre et Camus." Le Français dans le Monde. No. 8, avril 1962, 16-19.

2545 Peloux, Jean. "Comment, à huit clos, Sartre et Camus devenaient acteurs." Le Figaro Littéraire. No. 1213, 12-13 août, 1969, 18.

2546 Perroud, Robert. "La rottura tra Sartre e Camus." Da Mauriac a gli esistenzialisti. Milano: Società editrice Vita e Pensiero, 1955, 217-221.

2547 Perroud, Robert. "Ultime notizie esistenzialiste: La rottura Sartre e Camus." Vita e Pensiero, XXXV, November 1952, 641-642.

Pollman, Leo. see 47 and 167.

2548 Quillot, Roger.   Trans. from the French. The Sea and Prisons.
      University, Alabama: Univ. of Alabama Pr., 1970.

      Romeyer, Blaise.   see 2485.

2549 Schlotke-Schröder, Christa. "Patetische Grunzüge im litera-
      risch-philosophischen Werk von Sartre und Camus." Zeit-
      schrift für Französische Sprache und Literatur, LXXIII,
      No. 1-2, April 1963, 17-50.

2550 Simon, Pierre-Henri. "Sartre et Camus devant l'histoire."
      Terre Humaine. No. 23, November 1952, 9-20.

2551 Somers, Paul P. "Camus, si, Sartre, no or the Delightful M.
      Meursault." French Review, XLII, April 1969, 693-700.

2552 Thieriot, Jacques. "Ensayo de un paralelo entre Sartre y
      Camus." Letras del Ecuador, XIV, No. 118, January–June
      1960, 10-17.

2553 Thody, Philip. "A Note on Camus and the American Novel."
      Comparative Literature, IX, No. 3, Summer 1957, 243-249.

2554 Thomas, Charles. "Sartre as a Critic of Camus." New Black-
      friars, XLV, June 1964, 269-273.

2555 Tijeras, Eduardo. "Polémica Sartre-Camus." Cuadernos Hispan-
      oamericanos. No. 180, December 1964, 577-582.

2556 Todd, Oliver. "The French Reviews." Twentieth-Century,
      CLIII, January 1953, 36-43.

2557 Trocchi, Alexander. "Letter from Paris." Nimbus, II, No. 1,
      June-August 1953, 48-52.

2558 Troyat, Henri. "Réponse à M. Albert Camus." La Nef, III, No.
      14, janvier 1946, 144-148.

2559 Truc, Gonzague. "La querelle Sartre-Camus." Hommes et
      Mondes, VIII, No. 76, novembre 1952, 370-375.

2560 Vallejo, Remedios Castro. "Castro y el existencialismo." Pen-
      samiento, 29 April 1973, 227-236.

      Walters, Jennifer. see 1235.

      Wang, Joan P. see 402.

2561   Werner, Eric. De la violence au totalitarisme: Essai sur la
        pensée de Camus et de Sartre. Paris: Calmann-Lévy, 1972.

2562   Williams, Raymond. "Tragic Despair and Revolt." Critical
        Quarterly, V, Summer 1963, 103-115. Reprinted Modern Trag-
        edy, Stanford Univ. Pr., 1966, 174-189.

CASTRO, Fidel (and Cuba).

2563   Anonymous. "Ouragan sur le sucre: Réponse à Jean-Paul Sar-
        tre." France-Soir, 16 juillet 1960, 2.

2564   Bonosky, Philip. "Sartre's Cuba." Mainstream, XIV, No. 5,
        May 1961, 91-93.

2565   Cabus, José Domingo. Sartre, Castro y el azúcar. Mexico: Ed-
        itores Mexicanos Unidos, 1965.

2566   Mosley, James P. "Sartre on Cuba." Liberation, VI, Summer
        1961, 23-24.

2567   Otero, Lisandro. "Sartre y Beauvoir por la Provincia d'Or-
        iente." Revolución, 27 February 1961. Other interviews in
        Revolución, 26 February 1960, 11 March 1960, 15 March 1960.
        For Sartre's Cuban trips, Cf. Les Ecrits de Sartre, 343-351.

2568   Sartre, Jean-Paul. "L'assaut contre Castro." L'Express, 20
        avril 1961. On the Bay of Pigs invasion and American policy
        towards Cuba. Cf. Les Ecrits de Sartre, 364-365.

2569   Sauvage, Leo. "Le philosophe émerveillé . . . Quand Sartre
        découvre Fidel Castro." Le Figaro Littéraire, 24 septembre
        1960, 5.

2570   Szulc, Tad. "Visitors in Havana." New York Times Book Re-
        view, 23 July 1961, 10, 12.

2571   Ziegler, Jean. "Cuba, la révolution exemplaire." Dire (Gen-
        ève), No. 4, août 1960, 13. Cf. Les Ecrits de Sartre, 352.
        Interview with Sartre and de Beauvoir.

CELINE, Louis-Ferdinand.

2572   Boutet de Monvel, Denis. "Du Voyage au bout de la nuit à La
        Nausée." L'Action Nationale, LX, No. 2, octobre 1970, 168-
        172.

2573   Céline, Louis Ferdinand. <u>A l'agité du bocal</u>. Paris: P. La-
       nauve de Tartas, 1948.

2574   Thiher, A. "Céline and Sartre." <u>Philological Quarterly</u>,
       April 1971, 292-305.

CERVANTES.

   Mermier, G. see 1119.

CIORAN, E.M.

   Marks, Elaine. see 1715.

CLAUDEL, Paul.

2575   Haefner, Joseph. "Die Verlobung mit der Freiheit: Zum Problem
       der Freiheit bei Sartre und Claudel." <u>Priester und Arbeiter</u>
       (Köln), VI, 1956, 292-297.

2576   Oertel, Ferdinand. "Um die 'unverkurzte Wirlichkeit': Das
       Bild des Menschen und der Welt bei Sartre und Claudel."
       <u>Begegnung</u> (Koblenz), V, 1950, 193-195.

2577   Russell, John. "Sartre and Claudel." <u>World Review</u>, January
       1952, 34-38.

2578   Simon, Alfred. "Zwei Premieren: Sartre und Claudel." <u>Dok-
       umente 61: Französische Kultur</u> (Köln), 1961, 58-59.

2579   Weidner, Walther. "Sartre und Claudel." <u>Besinning</u> (Nürn-
       berg), II, 1947, 211-212.

CLAVEL, Maurice.

2580   Clavel, Maurice. "Clavel répond à Sartre." <u>Le Nouvel Obser-
       vateur</u>. No. 228, 24-30 mars, 1969, 46-47.

2581   Clavel, Maurice. "A propos de Sartre." <u>La Nef</u>, XXVI, Cahier
       No. 37, n.s., avril-août 1969, 214-218.

CONRAD, Joseph.

2582   Gillon, Adam. "Conrad and Sartre." <u>Dalhousie Review</u>, XL,
       Spring 1960, 61-71.

2583   Hay, Eloise Knapp. "Conrad Between Sartre and Socrates."
       <u>Modern Language Quarterly</u>, XXXIV, No. 1, March 1973, 85-97.

2584   Sadoff, Ira.   "Sartre and Conrad: Lord Jim as Existential
       Hero." Dalhousie Review, XLIX, No. 4, Winter 1969-1970,
       518-525.

2585   Tarnawski, Wil. "Conrad Versus Sartre." Wiadomosci, II, No.
       53-54, 13 Kwietnia 1947, 3.

       Wang, Joan P.   see 402.

CORNEILLE, Pierre.

2586   Doubrovsky, Serge. "Corneille et Sartre." L'Etre du héros
       chez Corneille et la dialectique du héros. Paris: Galli-
       mard, 1965.

       Gutwirth, M.   see 1055.

2587   Strozier, W.A.   "Motivation of Action in Corneille and Sar-
       tre." South Atlantic Bulletin, XV, No. 3, May 1954, 12.
       Abstract.

CROCE, Benedetto.

2588   Croce, Benedetto. "Impressioni sul Sartre." Nuove pagine
       sparse, Vol. 2. Napoli: Riccardo Ricciardi, 1948, 125-129.

DANTE.

2589   Vallone, Aldo. "L'uomo di Dante e l'uomo di Sartre." Idea,
       XIX, 1963, 613-622.

DE GAULLE, Charles.

2590   De Gaulle, Charles. "De Gaulle à Sartre: lettre du 19 avril
       1967." Le Nouvel Observateur. No. 128, 26 avril-3 mai
       1967, 4.

2591   Sartre, Jean-Paul. "Mis en cause pour son émission anti-
       gaulliste d'hier, Sartre m'a dit: 'Mon but est d'empêcher
       les auditeurs d'adhérer à l'un ou l'autre des blocs!"
       France-Soir, 22 octobre 1947. Interview.

2592   Sartre, Jean-Paul. "Sartre à De Gaulle." Le Nouvel Observa-
       teur, 26 avril-3 mai 1967. Cf. Les Ecrits de Sartre, 447.
       On the French government's interdiction of meeting of the
       'Russell Tribunal' on French territory.

2593   Flanner, Janet (Genet). "Letter from Paris." New Yorker,
       13 May 1960, 6.

DESCARTES, René.

2594 Boorsch, Jean. "Sartre's View of Cartesian Liberty." Yale
      French Studies, I, No. 1, Spring-Summer 1948, 90-96.

2595 Burkill, T.A. "Une critique de la tendance subjectiviste de
      Descartes à Sartre." Dialogue (Canada), VI, No. 3, décembre
      1967, 347-354.

2596 Caes, P. "De Descartes à Sartre." Synthèses, VII, No. 78,
      novembre 1952, 33-42.

2597 Fisher, Karl. René Descartes: Discours de la méthode. Abhan-
      lung über die Methode mit e. Vorwort von K. Jaspers und ein
      Beitrag über Descartes und die Freiheit von Sartre. Mainz
      Universum, 1948.

2598 Gullace, Giovanni. "Sartre et Descartes: le problème de la
      liberté." Revue de l'Université Laval, XXI, No. 2, octobre
      1966, 107-125.

2599 Heidsieck, François. "Honor and Nobility of Soul: Descartes
      to Sartre." International Philosophical Quarterly, I, De-
      cember 1961, 569-592.

2600 Lenoble, René. "Liberté cartésienne ou liberté sartrienne."
      Descartes (Cahiers de Royaumont, Philosophie, No. 11).
      Paris: Editions de Minuit, 1957, 302-324.

2601 Patri, Aimé. "Descartes, Sartre und Maritain." Merkur, I,
      No. 4, 1947, 615-624.

2602 Patri, Aimé. "Descartes vu par Sartre." Arche, III, No. 24,
      février 1947, 114-116.

2603 Patri, Aimé. "Descartes vu par Jean-Paul Sartre." Combat,
      24 janvier 1947, 2.

2604 Patri, Aimé. "La liberté selon Descartes vue par Sartre."
      Paru, février 1947, 99-100.

2605 Pêtrement, Simone. "La liberté selon Descartes et selon Sar-
      tre." Critique, I, No. 7, décembre 1946, 612-620.

2606 Poulet, Georges. "La 'nausée' de Sartre et le 'cogito' car-
      tésien." Studi Francesi, V, No. 15, septembre-décembre
      1961, 454-462.

2607   Reboul, Olivier. "La générosité: Alain, Descartes et Sartre."
       L'homme et ses passions d'après Alain, Tome 2. Paris:
       P.U.F., 1968.

2608   Sigaux, Gilbert. "Jean-Paul Sartre et la liberté cartési-
       enne." La Nef, IV, No. 30, mai 1947, 118-120.

2609   Wolff, Edgar. "Conscience et liberté chez Descartes et Sar-
       tre." Revue de Philosophie de la France et de l'Etranger,
       LXXX, 1955, 341-348.

DEWEY, John.

       Craver, Samuel M. see 280.

       Sanchez, Ray. see 380.

DOS PASSOS, John.

2610   Bruneau, Jean. "Existentialism and the American Novel." Yale
       French Studies, I, No. 1, Spring-Summer 1948, 66-72.

2611   Cumming, Robert D., ed. "Introduction." The Philosophy of
       Jean-Paul Sartre. New York: Random House, 1965.

2612   Desternes, Jean. see 2640. Cf. Les Ecrits de Sartre, 160.

2613   Lehan, Richard. A Dangerous Crossing: French Literary Exis-
       tentialism and the Modern American Novel. Carbondale:
       Southern Illinois Univ. Pr., 1973.

2614   Lehan, Richard. "The Trilogies of Sartre and Dos Passos."
       Iowa English Yearbook. No. 9, 1964, 60-64.

       Lehan, Richard. see 333.

2615   Stoltzfus, Ben. "John Dos Passos and the French." Compara-
       tive Literature, XV, No. 2, Spring 1963, 146-163.

       Thody, Philip. see 422.

2616   Thody, Philip. "French Novelists and the American Novel."
       Modern Language, XXXVII, 1955, 7-10.

DRIEU LA ROCHELLE, Pierre.

2617   Drieu la Rochelle, Pierre. Sur les écrivains. Paris: Galli-
       mard, 1964. Essais critiques réunis, préfacés et annotés
       par Frédéric Grover.

2618   Perrin, Marius. "Sartre and Drieu la Rochelle." Times Lite-
       rary Supplement, June 1971, 649.

DU BOS, Charles.

2619   Seznec, Jean. On Two Definitions of Literature. Oxford:
       Clarendon Pr., 1952.

DUHAMEL, Georges.

2620   Fitch, Brian T. "Portrait d'un aliéné, Salavin de Duhamel et
       quelques parallèles dans la littérature contemporaine."
       Bulletin des Jeunes Romantistes. No. 4, décembre 1961, 31-
       39.

2621   Onimus, Jean. "Folantin, Salavin, Roquentin: Trois étapes de
       la conscience malheureuse." Face au monde réel. Bruges:
       Desclée de Brouwer, 1962, 99-116. Originally published
       Etudes, CCXCVI, janvier 1958, 14-31.

DUMAS, Alexandre père.

       see 1216, 1221-1223, 1226, 1228.

DUVIVIER

2622   Broncel, Zdzislaw. "Sartre i Duvivier." Wiadomosci, IX, Nr.
       24/428, 13 czerwca 1954, 3.

EHRENBOURG, Ilya.

2623   Enrenbourg, Ilya. "Faulkner et Sartre vus par un écrivain
       soviétique." Les Lettres Françaises. No. 246, 1949, 1, 6.

ELIOT, T.S.

       Drese, Claud Helmut. see 934.

2624   Matthews, H.J. "The Hard Journey in the Plays of Eliot and
       Sartre." The Hard Journey: The Myth of Man's Rebirth. Lon-
       don: Chatto and Windus, 1968.

FAULKNER, William.

2635   Adams, Percy G.   "The Franco-American Faulkner."   Tennessee
       Studies in Literature, V, 1960, 1-14.

2636   Alter, Jean V.   "Faulkner, Sartre and the 'Nouveau roman'."
       Symposium, XX, Summer 1966, 101-112.

2637   Bruneau, Jean.   "Existentialism and the American Novel."   Yale
       French Studies, I, No. 1, 1948, 66-72.

2638   Church, Margaret.   Time and Reality: Studies in Contemporary
       Fiction.   Chapel Hill, North Carolina: The Univ. of North
       Carolina Pr., 1963, 253-275.

2639   Ciancio, Ralph A.   "Faulkner's Existentialist Affinities."
       Carnegie Studies in English.   No. 6, 1961, 69-91.

2640   Desternes, Jean.   "'Vous nous embêtez avec Faulkner le vieux'.
       disent les Américains."   Combat, 3 janvier 1947.   Cf. Les
       Ecrits de Sartre, 160.

       Harrington, Catherine S.   see 312.

       Richards, Lewis A.   see 378.

2641   Simon, John K.   "Faulkner and Sartre: Metamorphosis and the
       Obscene."   Comparative Literature, XV, No. 3, Summer 1963,
       216-225.

       Simon, John K.   see 389.

2642   Sowder, William J.   "Christ as Existentialist Hero."   The Uni-
       versity Review-Kansas City, XXX, No. 4, June 1964, 279-284.

2643   Sowder, William J.   "Colonel Thomas Sutpen as Existentialist
       Hero."   American Literature, XXXIII, No. 4, January 1962,
       484-499.

2644   Sowder, William J.   "Lucas Beauchamp as Existentialist Hero."
       College English, XXV, November 1963, 115-118.

2645   Sutherland, Donald.   "Time on Our Hands."   Yale French
       Studies.   No. 10, Fall-Winter 1952-1953, 5-13.

       Thody, Philip.   see 422 and 2616.

2646   Underwood, Henry J.   "Sartre on The Sound and the Fury: Some
       Errors."   Modern Fiction Studies, XII, Winter 1966, 477-479.

FAURE, Edgar.

2647 Faure, Edgar. "Réponse à Jean-Paul Sartre." Le Nouvel Obser-
      vateur. No. 229, 31 mars-6 avril 1969, 20-25.

2648 Lafaurie, Serge. "La jeunesse piégée." Le Nouvel Observa-
      teur, 17-23 mars 1969. Propos recueillis par S. Lafaurie
      sur l'opposition à 'la loi d'orientation' d'Edgar Faure. Cf.
      Les Ecrits de Sartre, 477.

FICHTE.

2649 Hübner, Kurt. "Fichte, Sartre und der Nihilismus." Zeit-
      schrift für Philosophische Forschung, X, No. 1, 1956, 29-43.

2650 Masullo, Aldo. La communità come fondamento: Fichte, Husserl,
      Sartre. (Filosofia e Pedagogia). Napoli: Libreria Scien-
      tifica Editrice, 1965.

FOUCAULT, Michel.

2651 Anonymous. "Rendre à Sartre ce qui est à Sartre (Michel Fou-
      cault)." Le Monde des Livres. No. 7214, 23 mars 1968, 2.

2652 El Kabbach, Jean-Pierre. "Foucault répond à Sartre." La
      Quinzaine Littéraire. No. 46, 1-15 mars 1968, 20-22.

2653 Foucault, Michel. "Réponse à une question." Esprit. No.
      371, mai 1968, 850-874.

2654 Foucault, Michel. "Réponse à Sartre." La Quinzaine Litté-
      raire. No. 47, 15-31 mars 1968, 21.

2655 Lebon, Sylvie. "Un positiviste désesperé: Michel Foucault."
      Les Temps Modernes. No. 248, janvier 1967, 1299-1319.

FREUD, Sigmund.

2656 Benayoun, Robert. Interview with John Huston on Sartre's se-
      nario for the film "Freud, The Secret Passion." Positif.
      No. 70, June 1965.

2657 Cole, Preston. "The Function of Choice in Human Existence."
      Journal of Religion, XLV, July 1965, 196-210. Concerning
      Freud and Sartre on determinism and free choice.

2658 Drefus, Dina. "De Freud à Sartre." Anhembi, ano I, I, No.
      2, January 1951, 190-198.

2659 Green, Martin. "British Marxists and American Freudians."
      Innovations: Essays on Art and Ideas. Edited with preface
      and introduction by Bernard Bergonzi. London: Macmillan,
      1968, 158-184.

2660 Herrera, José Luis. "Freud y Sartre: Supuestos antropológi-
      cos de sus teorías psicoanalíticas." Cuadernos Hispanoamer-
      icanos. No. 182, February 1965, 259-290.

      Lapointe, François H. see 5033.

      Maristany, J. see 2479.

      Nelson, J. see 1690.

2661 Pontalis, J.B. "Réponse à Sartre." Les Temps Modernes. No.
      273, avril 1969, 1820. Cf. "L'homme au magnétophone."
      Situations IX.

2662 Queiroz, Dinah. "Sartre, Freud." Leitura, ano 18, No. 39,
      September 1960, 26-28.

      Reboul, Oliver. see 2419.

2663 Tauxe, Henri-Charles. "Mise en question et fondement de la
      psychanalyse chez Sartre." Studia Philosophica, XXI, 1961,
      199-213.

FURLONG, E.J.

      Courtney, Richard. see 1758.

GARAUDY, Roger.

2664 Fagone, Virgilio. "Ideologia e prassi del communismo: Le
      ragioni del dissensi di Sartre e di Garaudy." Civilità
      Cattólica, CXXI, I, 1970, 448-462.

GATTI.

2665 Droit, Michel. "Gatti, Sartre et 'La Religieuse'." Le
      Figaro Littéraire, No. 1183, 6-12 janvier 1969, 36.

GIACOMETTI.

2666 Hubert, Renée Reese. "Lectures de Giacometti." Revue d'Es-
      thétique, XXIV, 1971, 75-90.

GIDE, André.

2667   Brigaud, Jacques. Gide entre Benda et Sartre. Paris: Minard, 1972.

2668   Chiaromonte, Nicolà. "Letter from Paris: Gide, Sartre and Café Communism." New Republic, CXXIV, 7 May 1951, 16-18.

2669   O'Nau, Martha. "'Musicalization' in Gide, Romains, Sartre." French Review, XXXI, No. 3, 1958, 211-216.

2670   Robichon, Jacques. "Sartre Successeur de Gide." Liberté de l'Esprit, III, No. 21, mai 1951, 157-158.

2671   Sackville-West, Edward. "Theseus and the Minotaur." Polemic. No. 8, 1947, 14-28.

GILSON, Etienne.

2672   Sérant, Paul. "De Jean-Paul Sartre à Etienne Gilson." Revue des Deux Mondes. No. 20, 15 octobre 1960, 727-735.

GIRAUDOUX, Jean.

2673   Magny, Claude-Edmonde. "M. Giraudoux et la philosophie d'Aristote." Précieux Giraudoux. Paris: Gallimard, 1945, 17-32.

2674   Pucciani, Oreste F. "The 'Infernal Dialogue' of Giraudoux and Sartre." Tulane Drama Review, III, May 1959, 57-76.

2675   Travers, P.L. "A Diatribe." New English Weekly, XXX, 17 October 1946, 8-9.

GOLDMANN, Lucien.

2676   Palmier, Jean-Michel. "Goldmann vivant." Praxis, 1971, 567-624.

GOMBROWICZ, Witold.

        Crawford, Maria A. see 281.

2677   Gombrowica, Witold. Journal Paris-Berlin. Trans. from the Polish by Allan Kosko. Paris: Christian Bourgeois, 1968.

GORZ, André.

2678   Brewster, Ben. "Presentation of Gorz in Sartre." New Left
       Review. No. 37, May-June 1966, 29-32.

2679   Thompson, Willie. "On André Gorz's 'Sartre and Marx'." New
       Left Review. No. 40, November-December 1966, 92-94.

GREEN, Julien.

       Watté, Pierre. see 2471.

GREENE, Graham.

2680   Evans, Oliver. "The Rise of Existentialism." South Atlantic
       Quarterly, XLVII, No. 2, April 1948, 152-156. Concerning
       Sartre's possible influence on Greene.

GUILLOUX, Louis.

       Greene, Francis J. see 439.

2681   Nadeau, Maurice. "A propos de Louis Guilloux et de Jean-Paul
       Sartre: Le romancier et ses personnages." Mercure de France,
       CCCVII, No. 1036, décembre 1949, 698-707.

GURVITSCH, Georges.

2682   Stack, George J. "The Background of Sartre's Social Dialec-
       tic." Journal of Social Philosophy, IV, Summer 1973, 4-8.

2683   Stack, George J. "Sartre's Hyperempirical Dialectic." Jour-
       nal of Thought, VIII, July 1973, 196-205.

HARDY, Thomas.

2684   May, Charles E. "Thomas Hardy and the Poetry of the Absurd."
       Texas Studies in Literature and Language, XII, No. 1, Spring
       1970, 63-73.

HARE, Norman.

       Fu, Charles. see 303.

HARTMANN, N.

2685   Vuillemin, Jules. "La dialectique négative dans la connais-
       sance et l'existence." Dialectica, IV, 1950, 21-42.

HEBBEL.

2686 Kreuzer, Helmut. "Die Jungfrau in Waffen: Hebbels Judith und
      ihre Geschwister von Schiller bis Sartre." Untersuchungen
      zu Literatur als Geschichte: Festchrift für Benino von
      Wiese. Günther Pivert et al, eds. Berlin: E. Schmidt,
      1973, 363-384.

HEGEL, F.W.

2687 Biemel, Walter. "Das Wesen der Dialektik bei Hegel und Sar-
      tre." Tijdschrift voor Filosofie, XX, 1958, 269-300.

2688 Duhrssen, Alfred. "Some French Hegelians." Review of Meta-
      physics, VII, No. 2, December 1953, 323-337.

2689 Gromczynki, Wieslaw. "Sartre et Hegel." Studia Filozoficzne
      (Warsaw), IV, 1970, 67-80.

2690 Hampshire, Stuart. "The Last Hegelian." New Statesman and
      Nation, XLVII, No. 1191, 2 January 1954, 19.

2691 Kemp, Peter. "Le non de Sartre à la logique de Hegel: L'in-
      terprétation et la critique de La Science de la logique dans
      L'Etre et le néant de Sartre." Revue de Théologie et Phil-
      osophie. No. 5, 1970, 289-300.

2692 Kline, George L. "The Existentialist Rediscovery of Hegel and
      Marx." Phenomenology and Existentialism. N. Lee and M.
      Mandelbaum, eds. Baltimore: Johns Hopkins Univ. Pr., 1967,
      113-138.

2693 Kopper, F. "Sartres Verständnis der Lehre Hegels von der
      Gemeinschaft." Kant-Studien, LII, No. 2, 1960-1961, 159-
      172.

2694 Poole, Roger C. "Indirect Communication, I: Hegel, Kierke-
      gaard, and Sartre." New Blackfriars. No. 554, July 1966,
      532-541.

HEIDEGGER, Martin.

2695 Aronson, Ronald. "Interpreting Husserl and Heidegger: The
      Roots of Sartre's Thought." Telos. No. 13, Fall 1972, 47-
      67.

2696 Beaufret, Jean. "Heidegger et Sartre." Confluences, I, 1945.

2697 Beaufret, Jean. "M. Heidegger et le problème de la vérité."
      Fontaine, XI, No. 63, novembre 1947, 758-785.

2698 Beschin, Giuseppe. "La morte in Heidegger e in Sartre." An-
      nali della Facoltà di Letteri, Filosofia, dell' Università
      di Macerata. No. 3-4, 1970-1971, 342-362.

2699 Braido, R.S. "L'umanesimo 'ontológico' di M. Heidegger contro
      l'umanesimo 'esistenzialistico' di Jean-Paul Sartre."
      Salesianum (Torino), XIV, 1952, 1-25.

2700 Champigny, Robert. "Sartre et Heidegger: Deux sensibilités."
      Modern Language Notes, LXX, 1955, 426-428.

2701 Cierlo, Hector Oscar. "Jean-Paul Sartre y Martin Heidegger:
      sobre el humanismo." Sur. No. 271, 1961, 73-77.

2702 Clarence. "Kant, Heidegger, Sartre et la querelle de l'human-
      isme." La Parisienne. No. 12, décembre 1953, 1604-1612.

2703 Cuisenier, Jean. "Heidegger et Sartre." La Nef, juillet
      1946, 133-137.

2704 Duval, R. "Présence et solitude: La question de l'être et le
      destin de l'homme." Revue des Sciences Philosophiques et
      Théologiques, LVII, July 1973, 377-396. Concerning Hei-
      deger and Sartre: L'Etre et le néant and Sein und Zeit.

2705 Delfgaauw, B.M.I. "Heidegger en Sartre." Tijdschrift voor
      Filosofie, X, 1948, 403-446.

2706 Delfgaauw, B.M.I. "Notes sur Heidegger et Sartre." Etudes
      Philosophiques, IV, No. 3-4, 1949, 371-374.

2707 Derisi, Octavio. "En torno a la moral de Heidegger y Sartre."
      Sapientia, XII, 1957, 139-141.

2708 Fumet, Stanislas. "Heidegger et les mystiques." La Table
      Ronde, numéro spécial de La civilization du néant. No.
      182, mars 1963, 82-89.

2709 Gabriel, Leo. "Existentialismus und Metaphysik, Martin Hei-
      degger zum 75. Gerburtstag gewidmet." Wissenschaft und
      Weltbild, 17. Jahrg., Helf 4, December 1964, 241-252.

2710 Garcia Baca, J.D. "Existencialismo alemán y existencialismo
      francés: Heidegger y Sartre." Cuadernos Americanos, XXXIV,
      No. 4, July-August 1947, 86-117.

2711   Grene, Marjorie. "Sartre and Heidegger: The Free Resolve."
       and "Sartre and Heidegger: The Self and Other Selves."
       Dreadful Freedom. Chicago: Chicago Univ. Pr., 1960, 41-94.

2712   Jolivet, Régis. Le problème de la mort chez Heidegger et Sar-
       tre. Abbaye de St. Wandrille: Fontenelle, 1950.

2713   Landgrebe, Ludwig. "Husserl, Heidegger, Sartre: Trois aspects
       de la phénoménologie." Revue de Metaphysique et de Morale,
       69e année, octobre-décembre 1964, 365-380.

       Lessing, Arthur. see 335.

2714   Muller-Schwefe, Hans R. "Aufstand gegen das Sein: Der Nihil-
       ismus bei Heidegger, Sartre, Jaspers und Marcel." Zeit-
       wende: Die Neue Furche (Hamburg), XXXII, 1961, 308-318.

2715   Pinera, Llera, Humberto. "Heidegger y Sartre o dos modos de
       la filosofía existencial." Revista Cubana, XXIII, January-
       December 1948, 22-54.

2716   Piorkowski, Henry. "The Path of Phenomenology: Husserl, Hei-
       degger, Sartre, Merleau-Ponty." Duns Scotus Philosophical
       Association, XXX, 1966, 177-221.

2717   Reding, Marcel. "Heidegger und Sartre." Der Mensch vor Gott:
       Festschrift für Theodor Steinbüchel. Düsseldorf, 1948, 333-
       348.

2718   Riu, Federico. "Sartre, Heidegger y el tema de la concien-
       cia." Cultura Universitaria (Caracas), No. 66-67, 1959,
       42-46.

2719   Uranga, Emilio. "Dos teorías de la muerte: Sartre y Hei-
       degger." Filosofía y Letras, XXXIII, January-March 1949,
       55-71.

2720   Van der Horven, J. "Waarheid in methode." Alg. Nederl. Tijd-
       schrift Wijsg. Psychologie, LVI, 1963-1964, 1-18. Inzake de
       Slotfase van het fenomenologisch denken bij Heidegger en
       Sartre.

2721   Van Hecke, Roger. "'Sartre? un bon écrivain, mais pas un phi-
       losophe', nous dit Martin Heidegger." Le Figaro Littéraire,
       4 novembre 1950, 4.

2722   Virasoro, Rafael. Existencialismo y moral: Heidegger y Sar-
       tre. Santa Fé (Argentina): Librería y Editorial Castellivi,
       1957.

2723   Waelhens, Alphonse de. "Heidegger et Sartre." <u>Deucalion</u>, I,
       Fascicule 1, 1946, 15-37.

2724   Wagner de Rayna, Alberto. "Sartre, Heidegger y el tema de la
       conciencia." <u>Cultura Universitaria</u> (Caracas), No. 66-67,
       January-June 1959, 47-54.

2725   Wind, Edgar. "Blood, Iron and Intuition: Jean-Paul Sartre,
       A French Heidegger." <u>Polemic</u>. No. 5, September-December
       1946, 54-57.

HELLER, J.

2726   Kennard, Jean. "Joseph Heller: At War with Absurdity." <u>Mo-
       saic</u>, IV, No. 3, Spring 1971, 75-87.

HEMINGWAY, Ernest.

2727   Killinger, John. <u>Hemingway and the Dead Gods: A Study in Ex-
       istentialism</u>. Lexington: Univ. of Kentucky Pr., 1960.

HERVE, P. (L'affaire).

2728   Garaudy, Roger. "A propos d'un article de Sartre sur Pierre
       Hervé." <u>La Nouvelle Critique</u>, VIII, No. 75, mai 1956, 38-
       44.

2729   Nadeau, Maurice. "Sartre et l'affaire Hervé." <u>Les Lettres
       Nouvelles</u>, 4e année, avril 1956, 591-597. Cf. <u>Le réformisme
       et les fétiches</u>.

HUME, David.

       Archer, Raymond. see 251.

HUSSERL, Edmund.

       Aronson, Ronald. see 2695.

2730   Beyer, Wilhelm Raimund. "Im Schatten Husserls." <u>Vier Kritik-
       en: Heidegger, Sartre, Adorno, Lukács</u>. Koln: Pahl Rugen-
       stein, 1970, 146-149.

2731   Brunet, Christian. "Husserl y Sartre frente al problema del
       conocimiento." <u>Dianoia</u>. Mexico: Fondo de Cultura Economi-
       ca, 1955, 311-349.

       Elveton, R.O. see 294.

2732   Hoche, U.U.   "Bemerkungen zum Problem der Selbst und Fremder-
       fahrung bei Husserl und Sartre."   Zeitschrift Philosophische
       Forschung, XXV, 1971, 172-186.

       Landgrebe, Ludwig.   see 2713.

2733   Lapointe, François H.   "Psicología fenomenológica de Husserl y
       Sartre."   Revista Latinoamericana de Psicología, II, No. 3,
       1970, 377-385.

       Masullo, Aldo.   see 2650.

       Murphy, Richard T.   see 354.

2734   Natanson, Maurice.   "The Empirical and Transcendental Ego."
       For Roman Ingarden: Nine Essays in Phenomenology.   The
       Hague: Nijhoff, 1959.   Reprinted Literature, Philosophy and
       the Social Sciences.   The Hague: Nijhoff, 1962, 44-54.

2735   Natanson, Maurice.   "Phenomenology and Existentialism: Husserl
       and Sartre on Intentionality."   The Modern Schoolman,
       XXXVII, November 1959, 1-10.   Reprinted Literature, Philoso-
       phy, and the Social Sciences.   The Hague: Nijhoff, 1962, 26-
       33.   Also reprinted Philosophy Today.   Jerry H. Gill, ed.
       No. 3.   New York: Macmillan, 1970, 61-71.

       Piorkowski, Henry.   see 2716.

2736   Pivecvic, Edo.   Husserl and Phenomenology.   London: Hutchinson
       Univ. Library, 1970.   Chapters 12 and 13.

       Scanlon, John D.   see 1750.

2737   Stamps, Ann.   "Shifting Focus from Sartre to Husserl."   Jour-
       nal of Thought, VIII, January 1973, 51-53.

       Stone, Robert V.   see 394.

2738   Sukale, Michael.   "The Ego and the Consciousness in Rival Per-
       spectives."   Iyyun, XXII, October 1971, 193-214.   A study of
       Husserl and the early Sartre in Hebrew.

2739   Theunissen, M.   "Die destruierende Wiederholung der transzen-
       dentalen Intersubjektivitätstheorie Husserls in der Sozialon-
       tologie Sartres."   Der Andere: Studien zur Sozialontologie
       der Gegenwart.   Berlin: de Gruyter, 1965, 187-240.

2740   Van de Pitte, M.M.   "On Bracketing the Epochè."   Dialogue, XI,
       No. 4, December 1972, 535-545.

2741   Van de Pitte, M.M.   "Sartre as Transcendental Realist."   Jour-
        nal of the British Society for Phenomenology, I, No. 2, May
        1970, 22-26.

HUXLEY, Aldous.

2742   Salvan, Jacques.   "De scandale de la multiplicité des consci-
        ences chez Huxley, Sartre, et Simone de Beauvoir."   Sympos-
        ium, V, No. 2, novembre 1951, 198-215.

IPHIGENIE.

2743   Leibrich, Louis.   "Iphigénie en Tauride à la lumière de la
        philosophie d'aujourd'hui."   Etudes Germaniques, 4e année,
        No. 2-3, avril-septembre 1949, 129-137.

IONESCO.

2744   Roud, Richard.   "Ionesco, the Opposite of Sameness."   Encore,
        III, No. 5, June-July 1957, 36-41.

JAMES, William.

        Blueston, Natalie S.H.   see 262.

2745   Edie, James M.   "William James and Phenomenology."   Review of
        Metaphysics, XXIII, March 1970, 481-526.

2746   Tibbetts, Paul.   "William James and the Doctrine of 'Pure Ex-
        perience'."   Univ. of Dayton Review, VIII, No. 1, Summer
        1971, 43-58.

JANKELEVITCH, V.

2747   Kanters, Robert.   "Le procès de la sincérité d'après Jankele-
        vitch et Sartre."   Les Lettres.   No. 1, 1945, 7-21.

JASPERS, K.

        Muller-Schwefe, Hans-Rudolf.   see 2714.

JEANSON, Francis.

2748   Colombel, Jeanette.   "Sartre et Simone de Beauvoir vus par
        Francis Jeanson."   La Pensée, n.s., No. 129, octobre 1966,
        91-100.

        Corsaro, Antonio.   see 2517.

Margolin, Jean-Claude. see 2468.

JOUVET.

2749 Forestier, Jacques. "Jouvet attend Sartre." _Opéra_. No. 291,
         7 février 1951, 1.

2750 Valogne, Catherine. "Querelle de ménage ou l'association Jou-
         vet-Sartre." _Arts_. No. 312, 1 juin 1951, 2.

JOYCE, James.

Mandler, Philip L. see 310a.

KAFKA, Franz.

2751 Bahr, E. "Kakfa and the Prague Spring." _Mosaic_, III, No. 4,
         Summer 1970, 15-29.

2752 Derins, Françoise. "Une conférence de Sartre: 'Kafka, écri-
         vain juif'." _La Nef_, IV, No. 33, juillet 1947, 165-166.

2753 Goth, Maja. "Existentialism and Franz Kafka: Sartre, Camus
         and Their Relationship to Kafka." _Proceedings of the Com-
         parative Literature Symposium_, Vol. 4: _Franz Kafka: His
         Place in World Literature_. W. Zyla, ed. 28-29 January
         1971, Lubbock: Texas Tech Univ., 1971.

Grangier, E. see 2763.

2755 Sokel, Walter H. "Kafka und Sartres Existenzphilosophie."
         Arcadia, V, No. 3, 1970, 362-377.

Witt, Mary. see 1299.

KANAPA, Jean.

2756 Werth, Jean. "Sartre and the Communists." _New Statesman and
         Nation_, XLVII, No. 1209, 8 May 1954, 590.

KANT, I.

Clarence, E. see 2702.

Selle, Mgr. H. see 2483.

2757 Rohatyn, Dennis A. "Sartre's Critique of Kant." _Indian Phi-
         losophical Quarterly_, Vol. 2, January 1975, 171-176.

KIERKEGAARD, Soren.

2758   Arnou, R. "L'existentialisme à la manière de Kierkegaard:
        Kierkegaard et Sartre." Gregorianum, XXVII, 1946.

2759   Cortese, Alessandre. "Kierkegaard-Sartre: Appunti di metodo-
        logie." Filosofia e Vita, VI, No. 2, 1965, 31-49.

2760   Cumming, Robert D. "Existence and Communication." Ethics,
        LXV, 1955, 79-101.

        Curtis, Jerry L. see 2519.

2761   Flam, Leopold. "Sartre tussen Kierkegaard en Marx." Tijd-
        schrift van de Vrije Universiteit van Brussel, IV, 1961-
        1962, 1-29.

2762   Flanner, Janet (Genet). "Letter from Paris." New Yorker,
        17 April 1965, 183-184. Concerning Sartre's reading of
        Kierkegaard.

2763   Grangier, E. "Abraham, oder Kierkegaard, wie Kafka und Sar-
        tre ihn sehen." Zeitschrift Philosophische Forschung, IV,
        1950, 412-420.

2764   Grooten, Johan. "Le soi chez Kierkegaard et Sartre." Revue
        Philosophique de Louvain, LI, février 1952, 64-69.

2765   Hohlenberg, Jahannes. "Jean-Paul Sartre og has forhold til
        Kierkegaard." Samtiden, LVI, No. 5, 1947, 310-322.

2766   Johnson, Howard A. "Kierkegaard and Sartre." Adam Interna-
        tional Review, XVI, No. 183, June 1948, 23-24.

2767   Johnson, Howard A. "On Sartre and Kierkegaard." American-
        Scandinavian Review, September 1947, 220-225.

2768   Kern, Edith. Existential Thought and Fictional Technique:
        Kierkegaard, Sartre, Beckett. New Haven: Yale Univ. Pr.,
        1970.

2769   Larson, Curtus W.R. "Kierkegaard and Sartre." The Personal-
        ist, XXXV, No. 2, Spring 1954, 128-135.

2770   Logstrup, K.E. "Sartres og Kierkegaards skildring of den
        daemoniske indeslutthed." Vindrhsen, XIII, No. 1, 28-42.

2771 Lowrie, W. "Existence as Understood by Kierkegaard and/or
      Sartre." Sewanee Review, LVIII, July 1950, 379-401.

2772 Ormesson, Jean d'. "Un colloque à l'UNESCO sur Kierkegaard
      vivant." Le Monde, 25 avril 1964, 4.

      Poole, Roger C. see 2694.

2773 Prenter, R. "Sartre's Conception of Freedom Considered in the
      Light of Kierkegaard's Thought." A Kierkegaard Critique.
      H.A. Johnson and N. Thulstrup, eds. New York: Harper, 1962,
      130-142.

2774 Roberts, D.E. "Faith and Freedom in Existentialism: A Study
      of Kierkegaard and Sartre." Theology Today, VIII, No. 4,
      January 1952, 469-482.

      Shearson, William A. see 384.

      Soper, William A. see 393.

KLEIST.

      Guthke, Karl. see 1010.

      Zimmermann, Hans J. see 1015.

KOJEVE, A.

2775 Sotelo, Ignacio. "El silencio de Alexandre Kojève." Revista
      de Occidente, XX, No. 60, March 1968, 363-371.

KRETSCHMER.

      Galler, Dieter. see 148.

LACAN, J.

2776 Lapouge, Gilles. "Sartre contre Lacan, bataille perdue,
      mais . . ." Le Figaro Littéraire. No. 1080, 29 décembre
      1966, 4.

2777 Revel, Jean-François. "Sartre en ballotage." L'Express. No.
      803, 7-13 novembre 1966, 47.

LAING, R.D.

2778 Gordon, Jan B. "The Meta-Journey of R. D. Laing." Salmagun-
      di. No. 16, Spring 1971, 38-63.

LAURENT, Jacques.

   Laurent, Jacques. see 2490.

2779 LeGrix, François. "La rencontre de Jacques Laurent et de
      Jean-Paul Sartre." Ecrits de Paris. No. 129, août 1955,
      96-104.

   Patri, Aimé. see 2491.

LAVELLE.

2780 Ecole, Jean. "Les conceptions sartrienne et lavellienne de la
      liberté." Atti XII Congresso Internazionale di Filosofia,
      Venezia, 12-18 September 1958, Vol. 12: Storia della filoso-
      fia moderna contemporanea. Firenze: Sansoni, 1961.

LAWRENCE, D.H.

2781 Kanters, Robert. "Deux humanismes paiens." La Gazette des
      Lettres, 30 mars 1946.

LENIN, V.

2782 Heerz, Herbert. "Philosophischer Materialismus und leninscher
      Materiebegriff." Deutsche Zeitschrift für Philosophie,
      XVII, December 1969, 1413-1437.

LEVI-STRAUSS, Claude.

   Abel, Lionel. see 2053.

2783 Aron, Raymond. "Le paradoxe du même et de l'autre." Echanges
      et communications: Mélanges offerts à Claude Lévi-Strauss.
      2 volumes. Jean Pouillon and Pierre Maranda, eds. The
      Hague: Mouton, 1970, 943-951.

2784 Gramont, Sanche de. "Says Lévi-Strauss: 'There Are No Super-
      ior Societies.'." New York Times Magazine, 28 January 1968,
      28-32 ff. Reprinted Claude Lévi-Strauss: The Anthropolo-
      gist as Hero. E.N. and T. Hayes, eds. Cambridge, Massa-
      chusetts: M.I.T. Press, 1970.

2785 Hartmann, Klaus. "Lévi-Strauss and Sartre." Journal of the
      British Society for Phenomenology, II, No. 3, October 1971,
      37-45.

2786 Jeanson, Francis. "On secoue trop tôt le cocotier . . ." Le
      Nouvel Observateur. No. 103, 2-8 novembre 1966, 33-34.

2787   Johansen, Svend. "En fortaelling om aegget og honen." Vin-
        drosen, XVI, No. 7, 1969, 26-33. Concerning continuity and
        discontinuity in Sartre and Lévi-Strauss.

2788   Lévi-Strauss, Claude. "Histoire et dialectique." La Pensée
        sauvage. Paris: Gallimard, 1962. Trans. into English: The
        Savage Mind. Chicago: Univ. of Chicago Pr., 1969.

        Mehlman, Jeffrey. see 348.

2789   Pouillon, Jean. "Sartre et Lévi-Strauss: Analyse dialectique
        d'une dialectique analytique." L'Arc. No. 26, 1965, 60-65.

2790   Pouillon, Jean. "Présentation: Un essai de définition." Les
        Temps Modernes. No. 246, novembre 1966, 769-790. Cf. Les
        Ecrits de Sartre, 434.

        Pouillon, Jean, and Maranda, Pierre. see 2783.

2791   Rosen, Lawrence. "Language, History and the Logic of Inquiry
        in Lévi-Strauss and Sartre." History and Theory, X, 1971,
        269-294. Reprinted The Unconscious in Culture: The Struc-
        turalism of Claude Lévi-Strauss in Perspective. Ino Rossi,
        ed. New York: E.P. Dutton, 1974.

2792   Rubio, J. "Estructura o dialectica? Nota sobre el debate
        entre Lévi-Strauss y Sartre." Estudio Agustiniano, IV,
        1969, 547-555.

2793   Scholes, Robert. "The Illiberal Imagination." New Literary
        History, IV, No. 3, Spring 1973, 521-540.

2794   Tibaldi, Giancarlo. "Storia e dialettica a proposito della
        polemica tra Lévi-Strauss e Sartre." Il Mulino, XIII, Fac-
        scilolo 143, September 1964, 969-973.

2795   Védrine, Hélène. Les Philosophes de l'histoire. Paris:
        Petite Bibliothèque Payot, 1974.

2796   Ziegler, Jean. "Sartre et Lévi-Strauss." Le Nouvel Observa-
        teur. No. 25, 6 mai 1965.

LUKACS, George.

2797   Bonnel, Pierre. "Lukács contre Sartre." Critique, IV, No.
        27, août 1948, 698-707. A propos de George Lukács. Exis-
        tentialisme ou marxisme?

2798   Erval, François. "L'existentialisme fait une apologie du ca-
        pitalisme." Combat, 13 janvier 1949. Cf. Les Ecrits de
        Sartre, 210.

2799   Erval, François. "Jean-Paul Sartre reproche à George Lukács
        de ne pas être marxiste." Combat, 20 janvier 1949. Cf.
        Les Ecrits de Sartre, 209-210.

2800   Erval, François. "Pour Lukács la terre ne tourne pas." Com-
        bat, 3 février 1949. Cf. Les Ecrits de Sartre, 210-211.

2801   Furter, Pierre. "La pensée de Georges Lukács en France."
        Revue de Théologie et de Philosophie, XI, No. 4, 1961, 353-
        361.

2802   Guérin, Daniel. "Sartre, Lukács et . . . la Gironde." Les
        Temps Modernes, XIII, 1957, 1132-1137. Concerning Question
        de méthode.

2803   Katin, Naim. "Entretien: Lukács-revenir au concret." La
        Quinzaine Littéraire. No. 17, 1-15 décembre, 1966, 4-5.

2804   Merleau-Ponty, Maurice. "Commentaire." Les Temps Modernes,
        IV, No. 50, décembre 1949, 1119-1121.

2805   Perlini, Tito. Utopia e prospettiva in Gÿorgÿ Lukacs. Bari:
        Dedalo Libri, 1968.

MACH, E.

2806   Sachs, Mendel. "Positivism, Realism and Existentialism in
        Mach's Influence on Contemporary Physics." Philosophy and
        Phenomenological Research, XXX, March 1970, 403-430.

MALLARME, P.

2807   Benamou, Michel. "Recent French Poetics and the Spirit of Mal-
        larmé." Contemporary Literature, XI, No. 2, Spring 1970,
        217-225.

2808   Bourgeois, Pierre. "Sartre et Mallarmé." Le Journal des Po-
        ètes, XXXVI, No. 2, avril 1966, 2.

2809   Jean, Raymond. "Sartre, Mallarmé et le langage." Le Monde.
        No. 6624, 30 avril 1966, 13; Ibid., 18 mai 1966, 10.

MALRAUX, André.

2810 Delaunay, Claude. "De Sartre à Malraux." Revue de la Medi-
      terranée, VIII, No. 2, mars-avril 1950, 215-223.

2811 Fitch, Brian T. "Le monde des objets chez Malraux et chez
      Sartre." Bulletin des Jeunes Romanistes. No. 1, juin 1960,
      22-25.

      Galand, René. see 2526.

2812 Galante, Pierre. Malraux. Paris: Plon, Paris-Match et
      Presses de la Cité, 1971. Avec le concours d'Yves Salgues;
      préface de Gaston Bonheur.

      Gershman, Herbert S. see 2527.

      Marcel, Gabriel. see 2540.

2813 Morawski, Stefan. L'absolu et la forme: L'esthétique d'André
      Malraux. Trans. into French from the Polish by Yolande
      Lamy-Grun. Paris: Klincksieck, 1972.

2814 Munster, G. J. "Irrational Commentaries." Nation (Sydney),
      No. 66, 8 April 1961, 21-22.

MANN, Henirich.

2815 Nerlich, Michael. "Der Herrenmensch bei Jean-Paul Sartre und
      Heinrich Mann." Akzente, XVI, No. 5, 1969, 460-479.

MARCEL, Gabriel.

2816 Armieri, Salvatore. "L'esistenzialismo fra Marcel e Sartre."
      Cenobio, VII, No. 7-8, 1958, 427-431.

2817 Chazel, Pierre. "Le tragique de la connaissance dans le thé-
      âtre de Sartre et de Gabriel Marcel." Revue d'Histoire et
      de Philosophie Réligieuses, XXX, 1950, 81-92.

2818 Corte, Marcel de. "Réflexions sur Gabriel Marcel et Jean-Paul
      Sartre." Revue de Philosophie. No. 2, 1946. Réimprim'
      L'Existentialisme. Paris: Tequi, 1947, 34-38.

2819 Glenn, John D. Jr. "Gabriel Marcel and Sartre: The Philosophy
      of Communion and the Philosophy of Alienation." The Philos-

ophy of Gabriel Marcel. (The Library of Living Philosophers, 15, Paul A. Schilpp, ed.). La Salle, Illinois: Open Court, 1974.

2820   Gonzalez Paredes, Ramon. "La mirada según Sartre y Marcel." Ateneo. No. 79, 1955, 14-24.

Hubscher, Arthur. see 2534.

2821   Mendoza, Esther C. "'Being-For-Others' in Sartre and Gabriel Marcel." St. Louis Quarterly (Philippines), IV, 1966, 5-36.

Muller-Schwefe, Hans-Rudolph. see 2714.

2822   Schaldenbrand, Mary Aloysius. "Freedom and the 'I': An Existential Inquiry." International Philosophical Quarterly, III, December 1963, 571-599.

2823   Schaldenbrand, Mary Aloysius. Phenomenologies of Freedom: An Essay on the Philosophies of Sartre and Gabriel Marcel. Washington, D.C.: Catholic Univ. of America Pr., 1960.

MARCUSE, Herbert.

2824   Holz, Hans Heinz. Utopie und Anarchismus: Zur Kritik der kritischen Theorie Herbert Marcuses. Köln: Pahl-Rugenstein, 1968, 53-58.

2825   Struyker Boudier, C.E.M. "Alienation and Liberation: Evil and Redemption in the Thought of Sartre and Marcuse." Man and World, VI, No. 2, May 1973, 115-142.

2826   Vircillo, Domenico. "L'uomo a una dimensione di Marcuse e l'immaginario di Sartre." Teorisi, XXVII, January-June 1972, 51-76.

MARITAIN, Jacques.

2827   Patri, Aimé. "Descartes, Sartre und Maritain." Merkur, I, No. 4, 1947, 615-624.

MARTIN (L'Affaire Henri Martin).

2828   Astre, G.A. "'Il faut rétablir la justice'." Action. 24 janvier 1952. Interview. Cf. Les Ecrits de Sartre, 246.

2829   Maulnier, Thierry. "Henri Martin et Jean-Paul Sartre." La Table Ronde. No. 72, décembre 1953, 29-39.

2830 Maulnier, Thierry. "L'ironie de Jean-Paul Sartre." La Table
      Ronde. No. 73, janvier 1954, 37-48.

2831 Montigny, Serge. "'Le devoir d'un intellectuel est de dénon-
      cer l'injustice partout.'" Combat, 31 octobre-1 novembre
      1953. Interview. Cf. Les Ecrits de Sartre, 266.

2832 Villefosse, Louise de. "Jean-Paul Sartre: L'affaire Henri
      Martin." La Pensée. No. 52, décembre 1953, 89-92.

MARX, Karl.

      Carricaburu, A. see 275.

      Flam, Leopold. see 2761.

2833 Gorz, André. "Sartre and Marx." New Left Review. No. 37,
      May-June 1966, 33-52.

2834 Hildebrandt, Walter. "Existenz und Gesellschaft: Die Marx-
      kritik Jean-Paul Sartre als Teil eines zeitgemässen Humanis-
      mus." Deutsche Studien, C, 1972, 338-353.

2835 Marlet, M. "Marx oder Sartre: Der humanistische Neomarxis-
      mus." Zeitschrift Katholische Theologie, XCV, 1973, 123-
      131.

2836 Mazzola, Michel. "De l'intellectuel chez Marx au marxisme
      des intellectuels." Arguments. No. 20, 1960, 22-26.

2837 Parsons, Howard L. "Marx's Humanism versus Sartre's Existen-
      tialism." Humanism and Marx's Thought. Springfield, Illi-
      nois, Charles C. Thomas, 1971, 190-207.

2838 Schaff, Adam. Marx oder Sartre? Versuch eine Philosophie d.
      Menschen. Berlin: Deutscher, 1965.

2839 Schaff, Adam. "Sartre und Marx oder Moral und Politik."
      Forum (Wien), XI, No. 123, March 1964, 135-139.

MAURIAC, François.

2840 Anonymous. "Sartre et le silence de François Mauriac." Le
      Monde des Livres. No. 7506, 1 mars 1969, 3.

2841 Blot, Jean. "François Mauriac et la forêt magique." Nouvelle
      Revue Française, XVII, No. 199, July 1969, 80-84.

2842   Heppenstall, Rayner. "Mauriac and Sartre." The Double
        Image. London: Secker and Warburg, 1947, 57-60.

2843   Holdheim, William W. "Mauriac and Sartre's Mauriac Criti-
        cism." Symposium, XVI, No. 4, Winter 1962, 245-258.

2844   Jurt, Joseph. "François Mauriac und Jean-Paul Sartre."
        Schweizer Monatshefte, December 1970, 775-786.

2845   Parinaud, André. "Sartre, Mauriac et l'honneur." Arts et
        Loisirs. No. 20, 9-16 février, 1966, 3.

        Patri, Aimé. see 2491.

2846   La Rédaction. "A propos du François Mauriac de Sartre." La
        Nouvelle Revue Française. No. 306, mars 1939.

2847   Rousseaux, André. "Sartre et Mauriac." La Revue Universelle,
        15 février 1939.

2848   Saraiva, M.M. "Sartre, Mauriac e o problema de liberdade."
        Revista da Facultade de Letras (Lisboa), No. 13, 1971, 401-
        424.

MEAD, George H.

2849   Ames, Van Meter. "Mead and Sartre on Man." Journal of Phi-
        losophy, LV, 15 March 1956, 205-219.

MERLEAU-PONTY, Maurice.

2850   Anonymous. "'Sartre est un ultra-bolchéviste' . . . déclare
        Merleau-Ponty." Le Figaro Littéraire, 7 mai 1955, 1.

2851   Arntz, Joseph. "L'athéisme au nom de l'homme? L'athéisme de
        Jean-Paul Sartre et de M. Merleau-Ponty." Concilium. No.
        16, 1966, 59-64.

2852   Bannon, John F. "Merleau-Ponty and Sartre." The Philosophy
        of Merleau-Ponty. New York: Harcourt, Brace and World, 1967,
        229-243.

2853   Beauvoir, Simone de. "Merleau-Ponty et le pseudo-sartrisme."
        Les Temps Modernes, Vol. 10, 1955, 2072-2122. Reprinted
        Privilèges. Paris: Gallimard, 1955, 203-272.

2854   Bonomi, Andrea. "La polemica contra Sartre." Aut Aut. No.
        66, 1961, 562-567.

2855   Capizzi, Antonio. "Su una divergenza fra Sartre e Merleau-
       Ponty." La Cultura, VI, 1968, 147-150.

       Dunne, R.   see 290.

2856   Daniels, Graham. "Sartre and Merleau-Ponty: An Existential-
       ist Quarrel." French Studies, XXIV, 1970, 379-392.

2857   Dillon, M. C. "Sartre on the Phenomenal Body and Merleau-
       Ponty's Critique." Journal of the British Society for
       Phenomenology, V, May 1974, 144-157.

2858   Discordia Concors: "Rencontres Est-Ouest à Venise." Compren-
       dre (Venise), No. 16, septembre 1956, 201-301; "Entre Mer-
       leau-Ponty, Sartre, Silone et les écrivains soviètiques,
       premier dialogue Est-Ouest à Venise." L'Express, 19 octob-
       re 1956. Excerpts from Discordia Concors. Cf. Les Ecrits
       de Sartre, 299-304.

2859   Flynn, Bernard. "The Question of Ontology: Sartre and Mer-
       leau-Ponty." The Horizons of the Flesh: Critical Perspec-
       tives on the Thought of Merleau-Ponty. Garth Gillan, ed.
       Carbondale: Southern Illinois Univ. Pr., 1972.

       Gahamanyi, Célestin.   see 305.

2860   Grene, Marjorie. "The Aesthetic Dialogue of Sartre and Mer-
       leau-Ponty." Journal of the British Society for Phenome-
       nology, I, May 1970, 59-72.

2861   Holz, Hans Heinz. "Nachwort zur deutschen Ubersetzung von
       'Merleau-Ponty vivant'." Wiesbaden, 1962.

2862   Hyppolite, Jean. "Merleau-Ponty vivant." Les Temps Modernes.
       No. 184-185, octobre-novembre 1961, 228-244.

2863   Kwant, Remy C. The Phenomenological Philosophy of Merleau-
       Ponty. Pittsburgh: Duquesne Univ. Pr., 1963.

2864   Lessing, Arthur. "Sartre and Merleau-Ponty." Barat Review,
       V, 1970, 55-59.

2865   Lessing, Arthur. "Walking in the World: Sartre and Merleau-
       Ponty." Human Inquiries, XI, 1971, 43-55.

2866   Maier, Willi. Das Problem des Leiblichkeit bei Sartre und
       Merleau-Ponty. Tübingen: Niemeyer, 1964.

2867 Moreland, John M. "For-Itself and In-Itself in Sartre and
      Merleau-Ponty." Philosophy Today, XVII, Winter 1973, 311-
      318.

      Murphy, Richard T. see 354.

      Nadeau, Maurice. see 2434.

2868 Parain, Brice. "Querelle de khagneux." Monde Nouveau-Paru,
      XI, No. 92, septembre 1955, 45-51.

2869 Patocka, Jan. "Die Kritik des psychologischen Objektivismus
      und das Problem der phänomenologischen Psychologie bei Sar-
      tre und Merleau-Ponty." Akten der 14th International Kon-
      gress für Philosophie. Vienna, 1969, 175-184.

2870 Patri, Aimé. "Sartre et Merleau-Ponty." Preuves. No. 135,
      mai 1962, 84-86.

2871 Pingaud, Bernard. "Merleau-Ponty, Sartre et la littérature."
      L'Arc. No. 46, 1971, 80-91.

      Piorkowski, Henry. see 2716.

2872 Podleck, A. Der Leib als Weise des in-der-Welt-Seins. Bonn:
      Bouvier, 1956.

2873 Rabil, Albert Jr. "Merleau-Ponty and Sartrian Existential-
      ism." Merleau-Ponty, Existentialist of the Social World.
      New York: Columbia Univ. Pr., 1967, 116-140.

2874 Rauch, Leo. "Sartre, Merleau-Ponty and the 'hole' in being."
      Philosophical Studies (Ireland), XVIII, 1969, 119-132.

      Senofonte, Ciro. see 200.

2875 Sheridan, James F. "On Ontology and Politics: A Polemic."
      Dialogue (Canada), VII, December 1968, 449-460.

2876 Smith, Colin. "Sartre and Merleau-Ponty: The Case for a Mod-
      ified Essentialism." Journal of the British Society for
      Phenomenology, I, No. 2, May 1970, 73-79.

2877 Sorel, Jean-Jacques. "Merleau-Ponty contre Sartre." France-
      Observateur, VI, No. 263, 26 mai 1955, 16-18.

2878 Toscano, Giuseppe. "L'in-der-Welt-Sein di Maurice Merleau-
      Ponty." Teorisi, XIX, No. 3-4, July-December 1964, 162-
      177.

2879   Truc, Gonzague. "Jean-Paul Sartre, Merleau-Ponty et l'athé-
       isme radical." Ecrits de Paris. No. 131, octobre 1955, 27-
       31.

2880   Weightman, John. "The French Debate." New Statesman and Na-
       tion, LII, No. 1329, 1 September 1956, 245-246.

MICHEL, Georges.

2881   Zand, Nicole. "L'Agression de Georges Michel." Bref (Pério-
       dique du T.N.P.), No. 103, février-mars 1967, 46-48. Inter-
       view. Cf. Les Ecrits de Sartre, 440.

MITTERAND, François.

2882   Barillon, Raymond. "M. Jean-Paul Sartre se rallie à M. Mitte-
       rand." Le Monde. No. 6498, 4 décembre 1965, 1-2.

MOLIERE.

2883   Larnaudie, Suzanne. "Molière et Jean-Paul Sartre: Visages
       du Dom Juanisme." Annales Publiées Trimestriellement par
       l'Université de Toulouse-Le Mirail, n.s., VII, Fas-
       cicule 2, 1971, Littératures XVIII, 67-85.

MONTHERLANT, Henri de.

       Galand, René. see 2526.

MURDOCH, Iris.

       Allen, Diogenes. see 423.

2884   Pondrom, Cyrena Norman. "Iris Murdoch, an Existentialist?"
       Comparative Literature Studies, V, No. 4, December 1964,
       403-419.

NAGEL.

2885   Anonymous. "Sartre gagne son procès contre les Editions Na-
       gel." Le Monde. No. 7711, 29 octobre 1969, 18.

NIETZSCHE, F.

2886   Friedmann, Maurice. "The Atheist Existentialist: Nietzsche
       and Sartre." To Deny Our Nothingness: Contemporary Images
       of Man. New York: Random House, 1966.

2887   Frigeri, Pier-Ricardo. "Nietzsche e Sartre." Cenobio, VII,
       1958, 432-441.

2888   Hofer, Hans. Existenz und Nihilismus bei Nietzsche und drei
       verwandten Denkern. Bern: Francke, 1953.

2889   Kaufmann, Walter. "Euripides, Nietzsche, Sartre." Tragedy
       and Philosophy. New York: Doubleday, 1969, 283-315.

2890   Kaufmann, Walter. "Nietzsche Between Homer and Sartre: Five
       Treatments of the Orestes Story." Revue Internationale de
       Philosophie, XVIII, No. 67, 1964, 50-73.

2891   Louis, Chanoine Michel. Humanisme et réligion, I: L'experi-
       ence athée, Nietzsche, Sartre, Malraux. Paris: Aumônerie
       Catholique du Lycée Jeanson de Sailly, 1965.

NIZAN.

2892   Aubarède, Gabriel d'. "Rencontre avec Jean-Paul Sartre." Les
       Nouvelles Littéraires, 1 février 1951. Cf. Les Ecrits de
       Sartre, 241-242.

2893   Fe, Franco. "Nizan oggi." Il Ponte, Facscicolo 11-12, 1971.

2894   Hurtin, Jean. "Le vrai Nizan." Magazine Littéraire. No. 15,
       février 1968, 25-27.

2895   Juquin, Pierre. "Critiques sans bases." La Nouvelle Cri-
       tique. No. 118, août-septembre 1960, 109-114.

2896   Leiner, Jacqueline. Le Destin littéraire de Paul Nizan.
       Paris: Klincksieck, 1970.

2897   Lemar, Yves. "Sartre donne un maître à la jeunesse: Le trou-
       ble-fête Paul Nizan." Arts. No. 776, 25-31 mai 1960, 3.

2898   Martelli, Giampaolo. "Nizan e Sartre." Dialogui, IX, 1961,
       335-342.

2899   Merleau-Ponty, Maurice. "Préface." Signes. Paris: Galli-
       mard, 1960. Trans. into English: Signs. Evanston, Illinois:
       Northwestern Univ. Pr., 1964.

2900   Pautasso, S. "L'incontro Sartre-Nazan." L'Europa Letteria,
       II, No. 9-10, June-August 1961, 163-165.

2901   Redfern, W.D. Paul Nizan: Committed Literature in a Conspira-
       torial World. Princeton: Princeton Univ. Pr., 1972.

2902   Senart, Philippe.   "Sartre et Nizan."   Combat.   No. 6228, 2
       July 1964, 7.

O'NEILL, Eugene.

       Stamm, Rudolf   see 822.

ORTEGA Y GASSET, José.

2903   Rodriguez Alcala, Hugo.   "Existencia y destino del hombre se-
       gún José Ortega y Gasset y Jean-Paul Sartre."   Revista Uni-
       versidad de Buenos Aires, V, No. 1, January-March 1960,
       63-80.   Also Cuadernos Americanos, Mexico, XIX, No. 110,
       1960, 89-110.

2904   Rodriguez Alcala, Hugo.   "Ortega y Gasset and Jean-Paul Sar-
       tre on Existence and Human Destiny."   Research Studies of
       the State College of Washington, XXIV, No. 3, September
       1956, 193-211.

OSBORNE, John.

       Flint, Martha, and Gerrard, Charlotte.   see 1115.

PARIS.

2904   Maublanc, René.   "Paris sous l'occupation."   La Pensée.   No.
       7, avril-juin 1946, 112-116.

2905   Robert, Jacques.   Dictionnaire des Parisiens.   Paris: Solar
       Editeur, 1970.

PARMENIDES.

2906   Pettit, Philip.   "Parmenides and Sartre."   Philosophical
       Studies (Ireland), XVII, 1968, 161-184.

PAZ.

2907   Paz, Octavio.   "Octavio Paz contre Sartre et Fidel Castro."
       Figaro Littéraire.   No. 1417, 14 juillet 1973.

PEGUY, Charles.

       Adereth, Maxwell.   see 1.

2908   Viard, Jacques.   "Péguy, le socialiste: du côté de chez Sar-
       tre, Péguy aux outrages.   Feuillets de l'Amitié Charles
       Péguy.   No. 97, décembre 1962, 3-78.

PICASSO, Pablo.

2909 Brassai (Pseudonym for Gyullia Halasz). Conversations avec
      Picasso. Paris: Gallimard, 1964.

2910 Karol, K.S. "Sartre, Picasso and the Party." New Statesman
      and Nation, LII, No. 1352, 9 February 1957, 163-164.

2911 Manegat, Julio. "De Picasso a Sartre con pausa para otras
      cosas." La Estafeta Literaria. No. 392, 23 March 1968, 13.

2912 Mortimer, Raymond. "A Note on Picasso and Sartre." Adam
      International Review, XIV, No. 154-155, January-February
      1946, 4-5.

PICO.

2913 King-Farlow, John and Coby, Arthur. "Creation and Human Free-
      dom: Pico's Answer to Sartre." Darshana International,
      II, No. 2, 1962, 22-28.

PINERA.

2914 McLees, Ainslie A. "Elements of Sartrian Philosophy in Elec-
      tra Garrigó." Latin American Theater Review, VII, No. 1,
      1973, 5-11.

PIRANDELLO, Luigi.

2915 Bishop, Thomas. Pirandello and the French Theater. New York:
      New York Univ. Pr., 1960, 122-127.

2916 Cambon, Glauco, ed. Pirandello: A Collection of Critical
      Essays. Englewood Cliffs, New Jersey: Prentice-Hall, 1967.

2917 Chiappa, Vincenzo. Pirandello e Sartre. Firenze: Kursaal,
      1967.

      Gouhier, Henri. see 1384.

      Kripinksi, Wlodnemierz. see 331.

2918 Lanza, Giuseppe. "Pirandello e Sartre." Osservatore Politico
      Lettarario, VII, No. 8, August 1961, 59-62.

PLATO.

2919 Hühnerfeld, Paul. "Platon und Sartre." Die Zeit, IV, No. 9,
      1949, 5.

POLITZER, Georges.

    Lapointe, François H. see 5033.

    Rom, Paul, and Ansbacher, Heinz. see 536.

POLIN.

    Lauth, Reinhardt. see 5038.

PONGE.

2920 Douthat, B. Margaret. "Le parti pris des choses?" French
      Studies, XIII, 1959, 39-51.

PROUST, Marcel.

    Bost, Pierre. see 464.

2921 Coe, J.M. "Proust's World Seen Through Sartre, or Transcen-
      dence Transposed." Forum for Modern Language Studies, III,
      No. 2, April 1967, 172-175.

2922 Cohn, Robert G. "Sartre Versus Proust." Partisan Review,
      XXVIII, September-November 1961, 633-645.

2923 Grubbs, Henry A. "Sartre's Recapturing of Lost Time." Modern
      Language Notes, LXXIII, November 1958, 515-522.

2924 Isère, Jean. "Sartre Versus Proust." Kenyon Review, IX, No.
      2, Spring 1947, 287-289.

2925 Kuhn, Rheinard. "Proust and Sartre: The Heritage of Romanti-
      cism." Symposium, XVIII, Winter 1964, 293-304.

    Seifert, Stéfanie. see 495.

2926 Shattuck, Roger. "Making Time: A Study of Stravinsky, Proust,
      and Sartre." Kenyon Review, XXV, Spring 1963, 248-263.

2927 Stockwell, H.C.R. "Proust and Sartre." Cambridge Journal,
      VII, No. 8, May 1954, 476-487.

2928 Zimmerman, Eugenia N. "The Metamorphosis of Adam: Names and
      Things in Sartre and Proust." Twentieth Century French Fic-
      tion: Essays for Germaine Brée. George Stambolean, ed. New
      Brunswick, New Jersey: Rutgers Univ. Pr., 1975.

RADIGUET.

2929   Laurent, Jacques.   "Pour Radiguet contre Jean-Paul Sartre."
       Arts.   No. 358, 8-14 May 1952, 1, 6.

RILKE, Rainer M.

       Aycock, Charles B.   see 254.

2930   St. Aubyn, F.C.   "Rilke, Sartre and Sarraute: The Role of the
       Third."   Revue de Littérature Comparée, XLI, 1967, 275-284.

RIMBAUD, Arthur.

2931   Paillour, P.H.   Arthur Rimbaud, père de l'existentialisme.
       Paris: Perrin, 1947.

ROBBE-GRILLET, Alain.

2932   Connerton, Paul.   "Alain Robbe-Grillet: A Question of Self-
       Deception."   Forum for Modern Language Studies, October
       1968, 347-359.

2933   Kermode, Frank.   "A Hero in Bad Faith: Sartre and the Anti-
       Novel."   New Statesman and Nation.   No. 1802, 24 September
       1965, 439-440.

2934   Morrissette, Bruce.   "Oedipus and Existentialism: Les gommes
       de Robbe-Grillet."   Wisconsin Studies in Contemporary Lite-
       rature, Vol. 1, Fall 1960, 47-73.

2935   Pingaud, Bernard.   "De Sartre à Robbe-Grillet."   Education
       Nationale.   No. 20, 31 mai 1962, 16-18.

2936   Porter, Dennis.   "Sartre, Robbe-Grillet and the Psychotic
       Hero."   Modern Fiction Studies, XVI, Spring 1970, 13-25.

ROLLAND, Romain.

       Blumel, Adolf.   see 2326.

ROMAINS, Jules.

       O'Nau, Martha.   see 2669.

       Wilson, Clotilde.   see 460.

ROUSSEAU, Jean-Jacques.

> Delue, Steven M.   see 284.

> Lapassade, Georges.   see 2154.

RUSSELL, Bertrand (Tribunal).

2937   Anders, Gunther, and Bondy, François.   "Das 'Russell Tribunal' im Für und Wider."   Merkur, XXI, Heft 11, No. 236, November 1967, 1098-1102.

2938   Lafaurie, Serge.   "Douze hommes sans colère."   Le Nouvel Observateur, 24-30 mai 1967.   Cf. Les Ecrits de Sartre, 448-
449.

2939   Lafaurie, Serge.   "Le génocide."   Le Nouvel Observateur, 6-12
décembre 1967.   Cf. Les Ecrits de Sartre, 454.

2940   Sartre, Jean-Paul.   "Le crime."   Le Nouvel Observateur, 30 no-
vembre-6 décembre 1966.   Trans. "Imperialist Morality."   New
Left Review.   No. 41, January-February 1967, 3-10.   Cf. Les
Ecrits de Sartre, 445-446.

2941   Sartre, Jean-Paul.   "Sartre à de Gaulle."   Le Nouvel Observateur, 26 avril-3 mai 1967.   Cf. Les Ecrits de Sartre, 447.

RYLE, Gilbert.

> Courtney, Richard.   see 1758.

> Lycos, Kimon.   see 1768.

> Miedzianogora, Miriam.   see 349.

2942   Walker, Leslie J.   "Gilbert Ryle and Jean-Paul Sartre."   The
Month, CLXXXIX, 1950, 432-443.

SACHS.

2943   Mascolo, Dionys.   "Mauvaise foi et bonne foi en littérature:
les exemples de Sachs et de Sartre."   Le Communisme: Révolution et communication ou la dialectique des valeurs et des
besoins.   Paris: Gallimard, 1953.

SADE.

2944   Taylor, Robert E.   "The SEXpressive in Sade and Sartre."   Yale
French Studies.   No. 11, Spring-Summer 1953, 18-24.

SALACROU, A.

Fauve, Jacques.   see 794, 1114.

SALAVIN.

Fitch, Brian T.   see 2620.

Onimus, Jean.   see 2621.

SARRAUTE, Natalie.

St. Aubyn, F.C.   see 2930.

SCHAFF, Adam.

Burkle, Howard R.   see 2070.

2945   Piersanti, Umberto.   "Umanesimo e marxismo: Riflessioni su
       La Critique de la raison dialectique e su Adam Schaff."
       Studi Urbinati, n.s., B. XLVI, 1972, 222-258.

SCHELER, Max.

2946   Mateo, M.S.   "Los juicios del valor moral."   Investigación y
       Docencia (Tucuman), No. 6-7, 1967, 73-90.

SCHILLER, F.

2947   Forster, Kurt W.   "The Image of Freedom: An Inquiry Into the
       Aesthetics of Schiller and Sartre."   British Journal of Aes-
       thetics, V, June 1965, 46-54.

2948   Hamburger, Kate.   "Schiller und Sartre: Ein Versuch zum Ideal-
       ismus-Problem Schillers."   Jahrbuch der Deutschen Schiller-
       Gesellschaft, III, 1959, 118-141.

2949   Hell, Victor.   "Poésie et philosophie: Considérations sur un
       parrellèle entre Schiller et Sartre."   Revue de Littérature
       Comparée, XLIII, No. 1, January-March 1969, 83-97.

       Kowatzki, Irmgard.   see 330.

SCIACCA, M.F.

2950   Ruig, Felix.   "Humanismo y anti-humanismo: Sciacca y Sartre."
       Augustinus, V, 1960, 537-545.

SKINNER, B.F.

2951   Kvale, Steinar, and Grenness, Carl E.   "Skinner and Sartre:
       Toward a Radical Phenomenology of Behavior?"   Review of Ex-
       istential Psychology and Psychiatry, VII, Spring 1967, 128-
       150.

STALIN.

2952   Pivert, Marceau.   "Jean-Paul Sartre la classe ouvrière et le
       stalinisme."   Revue Socialiste.   No. 63, janvier 1953, 76-
       84.

UNAMUNO, Miguel de.

2953   Abrams, Fred.   "Sartre, Unamuno and the 'Hole Theory'."   Ro-
       mance Notes, V, No. 1, Autumn 1963, 6-12.

2954   Frank, Rachel.   "Unamuno: Existentialism and the Spanish Nov-
       el."   Accent, IX, No. 2, Winter 1949, 80-88.

2955   Serrano-Plaja, Arturo.   "Nausea y Niebla."   Revista de Occi-
       dente.   No. 78, September 1969, 295-328.

VALERY, Paul.

2956   Hyppolite, Jean.   "Note sur Paul Valéry et la crise de la con-
       science."   La Vie Intellectuelle, XIV, No. 3, mars 1946,
       121-126.

2957   LeSage, Laurent.   "Paul Valéry and Jean-Paul Sartre: A Con-
       frontation."   Modern Language Quarterly, XXXII, No. 2, June
       1971, 189-205.

VIAN, Boris.

2958   Duchateau, Jacques.   Boris Vian.   (Collection 'Les vies per-
       pendiculaires').   Paris: La Table Ronde, 1969.

2959   Vian, Boris.   "Sartre et la . . ."   La Rue.   No. 6, 12 juillet
       1946.

VOLTAIRE.

2960   Allen, Marcus.   "Character Development in the Oreste of Vol-
       taire and Les Mouches of Jean-Paul Sartre."   College Lan-
       guage Association Journal, XVIII, No. 1, September 1974, 1-
       21.

WARREN, Robert Penn.

Ellis, Helen E.   see 295.

WHITEHEAD, Alfred N.

2961   Grange, Joseph.   "Whitehead's Tragic Vision: Process, Prog-
       ress and Existentialism."   Bucknell Review, XX, No. 2, Fall
       1972, 127-144.

WHITMAN, Walt.

2962   Harrison, Stanley R.   "Sacrilege of Preference in Whitman and
       Sartre."   Walt Whitman Review, XV, 1969, 51-54.

WOLS.

2963   Inch, Peter.   "The Destruction of Wols."   Art and Artists, VI,
       No. 9, December 1971, 34-37.

WRIGHT, Richard.

2964   Widmer, Kingsley.   "The Existential Darkness: Richard Wright's
       'The Outsider'."   Wisconsin Studies in Contemporary Litera-
       ture, I, Fall 1960, 13-21.

ZOLA, Emile.

2965   Hartley, Anthony.   "Sartre and Emile Zola."   Encounter, XXIII,
       No. 3, September 1964, 94-95.

PART V

ITEMS ARRANGED BY SUBJECTS

ABSOLUTE

2966   Colin, Pierre. "La phénoménologie, l'existence et l'absolu."
       Recherches et Debats, X, 1950, 91-107.

2967   Cournot, Patrice. "Les grands contemporains à la recherche
       d'un absolu: No. 1, Sartre et les jeunes." Le Semeur. No.
       7-8, février 1960, 2-5. Cf. Les Ecrits de Sartre, 352-353.

2968   Fabro, Cornelio. "L'assoluto di Jean-Paul Sartre." Idea, II,
       No. 20, 14 May 1950, 4.

2969   Fabro, Cornelio. "L'escluzione dell'assoluto in Sartre."
       L'Assoluto nell'esistenzialismo. Catania: Guido Miano,
       1954.

2970   Stefanini, Mario. "Esistenzà e assoluto." Acts of the Inter-
       national Congress of Philosophy, Rome, November 1946.

2971   Virieux-Reymond, Antoinette. "Quelques aspects du déclin des
       absolus classiques dans la pensée contemporaine de langue
       française." Revue de Théologie et de Philosophie, 3e série,
       Tome IV, No. 3, 1954, 197-215.

ABSURD and ABSURDITY

       Haug, Wolfgang F. see 155.

2972   Iriarte, Joaquin. "Sartre o la filosofía del absurdo." Razón
       y Fé, XLIX, No. 140, July-December 1949, 149-161.

2973   Peyre, Henri. "The Notion of the Absurd in Contemporary
       French Literature." Prose. No. 4, Spring 1972, 109-131.

ACT

2974   Bouchardy, François. "Note sur l'acte gratuit de Gide à Sar-
       tre." Nova et Vetéra, XXVI, No. 2, April-June 1951, 101-
       109.

2975   Jameson, Fredric R. "The Problem of Acts." Modern Drama:
       Essays in Criticism. T. Bogard and W.I. Oliver, eds. New
       York: Oxford Univ. Pr., 1965, 276-289.

ACTION

2976   Atwell, John E. "Sartre's Conception of Action and His Utili-
       zation of 'Wesensschau'." Man and World, V, May 1972,
       143-157.

2977   Bernstein, Richard J. "Consciousness, Existence and Action:
        Kierkegaard and Sartre." Praxis and Action: Contemporary
        Philosophies of Human Activity. Philadelphia: Univ. of
        Pennsylvania Pr., 1971, 84-164.

2978   Gandillac, Maurice. "Apories de l'action et la liberté dans
        la philosophie de Sartre." Cahiers de la Nouvelle Epoque.
        No. 1, 1945, 81-103.

        McCall, Dorothy K. see 343.

        McIntire, Russell Martin Jr. see 346.

AESTHETIC (see ART)

2980   Altieri, Charles. "Jean-Paul Sartre: The Engaged Imagina-
        tion." The Quest for Imagination: Essays in Twentieth Cen-
        tury Aesthetic Criticism. O.B. Hardison, Jr., ed. Cleve-
        land: Case Western Reserve Univ. Pr., 1971, 167-190.

        Bonnet, Henri. see 74.

2981   Glucksmann, Christine. "Jean-Paul Sartre et le gauchisme es-
        thétique." La Nouvelle Critique: Sartre est-il marxiste?
        No. 173-174, mars 1966, 167-198.

2982   Hogan, Homer. "Structures of Wonder in Aesthetic Experience."
        Dialogue (Canada), XI, No. 2, June 1972, 224-240.

2983   Isère, Jean. "Ambiguité de l'esthétique de Sartre." French
        Review, XXI, No. 5, March 1948, 357-360.

        Kaelin, Eugene F. see 29.

2984   Kaelin, Eugene F. Art and Existence: A Phenomenological Aes-
        thetics. Lewisburg, Pennsylvania: Bucknell Univ. Pr., 1970.

2985   Kopeczi, Béla. "A propos des vues esthétiques de Sartre."
        Acta Litteraria Academiae Scientiarum Hungaricae. No. 9,
        1967, 243-260.

2986   Maione, Pasquale. "L'estetica di Sartre." Baretti. No. 45-
        46, 1967, 69-81.

        Morawski, S. see 2813.

2987   Morpurgo-Tagliabue, Guido. "Estetica ed etica in Sartre."
        Aut Aut. No. 51, May 1959, 195-203; Ibid., No. 52, July
        1959, 254-266.

2988   Morpurgo-Tagliabue, Guido. L'Esthétique contemporaine: Une
       enquête. Milano: Marzorati, 1960. Trans. into English by
       Sterlin Haig of one chapter: "L'existentialisme et l'esthé-
       tique." Sartre: A Collection of Critical Essays. Edith
       Kern, ed. Englewood Cliffs, New Jersey: Prentice-Hall,
       1962, 129-135.

2989   Oxenhandler, Neal. "Towards the New Aesthetic." Contemporary
       Literature, XI, No. 2, Spring 1970, 169-191.

2990   Rau, Catherine. "The Aesthetic Views of Sartre." Journal of
       Aesthetics and Art Criticism, IX, December 1950, 139-147.

2991   Royle, Peter. "Théâtre et roman dans l'esthétique de Sartre."
       Revue de l'Université Laurentienne, IV, No. 1, novembre
       1971, 68-75.

2992   Subercaseaux, S. Bernardo. "Recuento critico de las ideas e
       estéticas de Sartre." Boletín del Instituto de Filologia de
       la Universidad de Chile, 22, 1971, 149-175.

       Urmeneta, Fermín de. see 2472.

AFRICA

2993   Erickson, John. "Sartre's African Writings: Literature and
       Revolution." L'Esprit Créateur, X, No. 3, Fall 1970, 182-
       196.

2994   Jeanson, Francis. "Sartre et le monde noir." Présence Afri-
       caine. No. 7, 1949, 189-214.

2995   Larson, Charles R. The Emergence of African Fiction. Bloom-
       ington: Indiana Univ. Pr., 1972.

2996   Salgues, Yves. "Sartre de retour d'Afrique." Paris-Match. 20
       mai 1950. Cf. Les Ecrits de Sartre, 226.

ALGERIAN WAR

2997   Blumenthal, Simon, and Spitzer, Gerard. "Bilan et perspec-
       tives de la lutte antifasciste." La Voie Communiste, n.s.,
       No. 29, juin-juillet 1962. Interview. Cf. Les Ecrits de
       Sartre, 379.

2998   Deville, Arrieux, Labre. "Entretien avec Sartre." La Voie
       Communiste, n.s., No. 20, février 1961. Cf. Les Ecrits de
       Sartre, 363.

2999   Jeanson, Francis. "Interview de Sartre." Vérités pour . . .
        (mensuel clandestin). No. 9, 2 juin 1959, 14-17. Cf. Les
        Ecrits de Sartre, 334-335.

3000   Karol, K.S. "Jeunesse et guerre d'Algérie." Vérité-Liberté.
        No. 3, juillet-août 1960. Cf. Les Ecrits de Sartre, 356.

3001   Martinet, Gilles. "Comment faire face au terrorisme."
        France-Observateur. 18 mai 1961. Cf. Les Ecrits de Sar-
        tre, 366.

3002   Smith, Tony. "Idealism and People's War: Sartre on Algeria."
        Political Theory, I, November 1973, 426-449. Concerning
        Sartre's historical method applied to the Algerian War.

ALIENATION

3003   Balliu, Julien. "L'aliénation et les avatars de l'ontologie."
        Revue de l'Université de Bruxelles, XX, No. 5, août-septem-
        bre 1968, 403-419.

3004   Bychowski, Gustav. "The Archaic Object and Alienation." In-
        ternational Journal of Psychoanalysis, XLVIII, Part 3, 1967,
        384-393.

        Chung, Ha Eun. see 276.

3005   Finkelstein, Sidney. Existentialism and Alienation in Ameri-
        can Literature. New York: Internation, 1965, 113-135.

        Glenn, John D. Jr. see 2819.

        Joubert, Ingrid. see 321.

3006   Knecht, Ingbert. Sartres Theorie der Entfremdung. Bonn:
        Selbstverl, 1972, 375 pp.

3007   Levi, Albert W. "Existentialism and the Alienation of Man."
        Phenomenology and Existentialism. Edward N. Lee and Maur-
        ice Mandelbaum, eds. Baltimore: The Johns Hopkins Pr, 1967,
        243-265.

3008   Marantz, Enid. "The Theme of Alienation in the Literary Works
        of Sartre." Mosaic, II, No. 1, 1968, 29-44.

3009   Schact, Richard L. "Alienation in Sartre's Major Works."
        Alienation. London: George Allen and Unwin, 1971, 218-231.
        Introductory essay by Walter Kaufmann.

Schact, Richard L.   see 380a.

Sist, Arthur J.   see 390.

ALONENESS

3010 Owens, Thomas. "Absolute Aloneness as Man's Existential
      Structure: A Study of Sartrean Ontology." New Scholasti-
      cism, XL, 1966, 341-360.

AMERICA

3011 Anonymous. "Sartre Cancels U.S. Visit in Protest." Christian
      Century, 82, 31 March 1965, 388.

3012 Anonymous. "Why I Will Not go to the United States."
      Meanjin, XXIV, No. 3, 1965, 340-344.

3013 Baker, Joseph E. "How the French See America." Yale Review,
      XLVII, December 1957, 239-253.

3014 Bentley, Eric. "A Note of American Culture." American
      Scholar, XVIII, No. 2, Spring 1949, 173-194. Concerning the
      influence of American writers on the French.

3015 Grossvogel, David I. "Letter on Sartre's Cancellation of His
      Cornell Conferences." Le Nouvel Observateur, 8 avril 1965.
      Cf. Les Ecrits de Sartre, 413. With Sartre's reply.

3016 Levin, Harry. "France-Amérique: The Transatlantic Refrac-
      tion." Comparative Literature Studies, I, No. 2, 1964, 87-
      92.

3017 Roza, Robert. "Modern French Writers Look at America." Amer-
      ican Society Legion of Honor Magazine, XXXVII, No. 1, 1966,
      25-41.

3018 Savoini, Guilliana. "Studi sull'esistenzialismo in America."
      Rivista di Filosofia, LXI, October-December 1970, 405-418.

L'AMI DU PEUPLE

3919 Hallier, Jean-Edern and Savignat, Thomas. "Jean-Paul Sartre:
      'L'ami du peuple'." L'Idiot International. No. 10, sep-
      tembre 1970, 33-35.

ANGOISSE (Anxiety)

3020 Capizzi, Antonio. "Variazioni sul tema dell'angoscia."
      Giornale Critico della Filosofia Italiana, XXI, July-September 1967, 441-457.

3021 Eck, Marcel. "L'angoisse chez Jean-Paul Sartre," "Phénoménologie de l'angoisse," "La fuite devant l'angoisse,"
      "L'angoisse et la sexualité." L'Homme et l'angoisse.
      Paris: Arthème Fayard, 1964, 63-69, 13-28, 81-86, 99-121.

3022 Guyot, Charly. "Sartre et l'expérience de l'angoisse." Labyrinthe (Genève), No. 4, 1945, 6, 9.

3023 Miro Quesada, Francisco. "Nausea, angustia y amor en la filosofía de Sartre." Archivas de la Sociedad Peruana de Filosofía, III, 1950, 43-70.

3024 Salinas, Laurent Marcel. "Jean-Paul Sartre et l'expérience de l'angoisse." Labyrinthe (Genève), No. 4, 1945, 6, 9.

3025 Wurtenberg, Gustav. "Sartre, Heiseler und die Angst." Zeitwende (München), XXII, 1949-1950, 374-376.

ANHISTORICAL thought of Sartre

3026 Ferrier, Jean-Louis. "La pensée anhistorique de Sartre."
      Studia Philosophica, XII, 1952, 4-17. Also Bâle: Verlag für Recht und Gesellschaft, 1952.

ANTHROPOLOGY (Philosophical)

      Brufau-Prats, Jaime. see 1982.

      Flynn, Bernard C. see 299.

3027 Herra, R.A. Sartre y los prolegómenos a la antropología. (Pulicación de la Universidad de Costa Rica, Serie Filosofía,
      28). Costa Rica: Ciudad Univ. Rodrigo Facio, 1968.

      Herrera, José Luis. see 2658.

      Jones, William R. see 320.

3028 Nuño, Juan A. "La prueba ontológica como determinante de la concepción antropológica sartriana." Memoirs of the Thirteenth International Congress of Philosophy, Vol. III, 282-293. Also Episteme (Caracas), 1961-1962, 323-335.

3029   Penalves Simo, Patricio. "Sobre la antropología negativa de
Sartre." Atlandida, VI, No. 40, July-August 1969, 374-386.

3030   Roosli, Joseph. Die Existenzphilosophie: Anthropologie von
Jean-Paul Sartre. (Annalen der Philosophischen Gesellschaf-
tin Inner-Schweiz und Ostschweiz), V, No. 1-2, 1949.

3031   Sheridan, James F. Once More From the Middle: A Philosophical
Anthropology. Athens, Ohio: Ohio Univ. Pr., 1973.

3032   Strasser, Stephan. "Wesen und Grenzen des Schöpherischen im
Menschen: Betrachtungen im Zusammenhang mit der philosophi-
sche Anthropologie Sartres." Jahrbuch für Psychologie und
Psychotherapie (Wurzburg), I, 1952-1953, 46-58.

3033   Wein, Hermann. "Sartre und philosophische Anthropologie."
Zeitschrift Philosophische Forschung, XXII, October-December 1968, 569-574.

ANTI-HEROS

3034   Girard, René. "L'anti-héros et les salauds." Mercure de
France, mars 1965, 422-449.

ANTI-NOVEL

Kermode, Frank.   see 2933.

ANTI-SEMITISM

see 1708-1738.

APARTHEID

3035   Geoffroy, Jean. "Sartre et L'apartheid." Le Nouvel Observateur. No. 105, 16-22 novembre 1966, 12-13.

APRES BUDAPEST SARTRE PARLE

3036   Anonymous. "Komunismus: Der arme Mitlaufer Jean-Paul Sartre."
Spiegel, X, No. 49, 1956, 30-39.

3037   Anonymous. "Sartres Absage ist endgültig." Kultur, Stuttgart, V, No. 78, 1956-1957, 3.

3038   Garaudy, Roger. "Réponse à Sartre." France Nouvelle, No.
570, 15 novembre 1956, 6-8.

3039   Lochak, Pierre. "Le fantôme de Staline hante Sartre."
       Preuves. No. 73, mars 1957, 55-57.

3040   Parain, Brice. "Sartre a parlé." Monde Nouveau, XI, No. 106,
       décembre 1956, 1-8.

3041   Sales, Edouard. "Sartre und der Komunismus." Ost-Probleme,
       IX, 1957, 413-418.

3042   Sartre, Jean-Paul. "Après Budapest, Sartre parle." L'Ex-
       press, supplément au numéro 281, 9 novembre 1956. Cf. Les
       Ecrits de Sartre, 304-306.

3043   Verret, Michel. "Jean-Paul Sartre ou le compte des responsa-
       bilités." La Nouvelle Critique, VIII, No. 80, décembre
       1956, 60-81. Trans. into German "Jean-Paul Sartre oder die
       Frage nach den Schuldigen." Geist und Zeit (Düsseldorf),
       No. 1, 1957, 142-159.

ART (and Artist)

3044   Ames, Van Meter. "Existentialism and the Arts." Journal of
       Aesthetics and Art Criticism, IX, March 1951, 252-256.

       Aronson, Alan R. see 252.

3045   Bauer, George H. Sartre and the Artist. Chicago: Univ. of
       Chicago Pr., 1969.

       Bauer, George H. see 255.

       Binnie, Donald. see 415.

3046   Borrello, Oreste. L'Estetica dell'esistenzialismo. Firenze:
       G. D'Anna, 1956.

3047   Borrello, Oreste. "Il soggettivismo nel pensiero estetico di
       Jean-Paul Sartre." Rassegna di Scienze Filosofici, XII,
       1959, 317-339.

3048   Borrello, Oreste. "Ontologia e fenomenologia estetica di
       Jean-Paul Sartre." Aut Aut. No. 51, 1959, 204-210.

3049   Borrello, Oreste. "La psicanalisi esistenziale e il problema
       dell'arte in Jean-Paul Sartre." Aspetti dell'estetica
       odierna. Napoli: Primo Editorial del Mezzogiorno, 1962.

3050 Bousoño, Carlos. "Arte y moral." Revista de Occidente, XXVI,
      No. 77, August 1969, 159-175.

3051 Brinker, Menachem. "The Doctrine of L'engagement and the Evo-
      lution of Sartre's Aesthetics: 1938-1964." Hasifrut, I,
      1968, 640-664. In Hebrew; summary in English.

3052 Egebak, Niels. Indskirfter: Essays om Faenomenologi og aes-
      tetik. Fredensborg: Arena, 1967.

3053 Fallico, Arturo B. Art and Existentialism. Englewood Cliffs,
      New Jersey: Prentice-Hall, 1962.

3054 Grandjean, L. "De l'art et de la beauté d'un point de vue ex-
      istentiel." Revue Générale Belge, juin 1947, 161-167.

3055 Grene, Marjorie. "The Aesthetic Dialogue of Sartre and Mer-
      leau-Ponty." Journal of the British Society for Phenome-
      nology, I, May 1970, 59-72.

3056 Leibowitz, René. "Réponse à Jean-Paul Sartre." L'Artiste et
      sa conscience: Esquisse d'une dialectique de la conscience
      artistique. Paris: L'Arche, 1950, 131-159.

3057 Major, Jean-Louis. "Pensée concrète, art abstrait." Dia-
      logue, I, No. 2, 1962, 188-201.

3058 Mandel, Oscar. "Artists Without Masters." Virginia Quarterly
      Review, XXXIX, Summer 1963, 401-419.

3059 Mendes, Joao. "Itinerario da arte moderna." Revista Portu-
      guesa de Filosofia, XX, 1964, 222-234.

3060 Somenzi, Vittorio. "Arte e conoscenza in Jean-Paul Sartre."
      Sigma. No. 3, May-June 1947, 173-190.

3061 Veloso, A. "Filosofia e arte." Brotéria, LXVII, No. 6, 1958,
      541-546.

ATHEISM

3062 Alceste (pseudonym). "Jean-Paul Sartre ou le romantique
      athée." Terre Humaine. No. 25, janvier 1953, 136-140.

3063 Arntz, Joseph. "L'athéisme au nom de l'homme? L'athéisme de
      Jean-Paul Sartre et de M. Merleau-Ponty." Concilium. No.
      16, 1966, 59-64.

3064   Ateismo: tentación o estimuli?   Madrid: Fax, 1965, 322 pp.
       Various authors.

3065   Balzer, Carmen.   "El problema del ateismo en Sartre."   Sapi-
       entia, XXI, 1966, 17-26.

3066   Barjon, Louis.   Le silence de Dieu dans la littérature contem-
       poraine.   Paris: Centurion, 1955.

3067   Beis, R.   "Atheistic Existentialism Ethos: A Critique."
       The Modern Schoolman, XLII, January 1965, 153-177.

3068   Blanchard, P.   "L'existentialisme athée et le monde."   Chron-
       ique Sociale de France, janvier-mars 1946.

3069   Breton, Stanislas.   "Le principe d'intentionalité de la con-
       science implique-t-il l'athéisme?"   Sapientia Aquinatis, I,
       1947, 409-417.

3070   Buber, Martin.   "Religion und modernes Denken."   Merkur, VI,
       No. 48, February 1952, 101-120.

3071   Buske, Thomas.   "Gottes Gottlosigkeit: Religionsphilosophische
       Elemente eines existentiellen Atheismus."   Neue Zeitschrift
       Systematische Theologie, XII, 1970, 383-390.

3072   Cappizzi, Antonio.   "Figure dell'ateismo francese del dopo-
       guerra."   Giornale della Filosofia Italiana, XLV, October-
       December 1966, 541-586.

       Caradang, A.L.   see 274.

3073   Collins, James.   "Sartre's Postulatory Atheism."   The Existen-
       tialists: A Critical Study.   Chicago: Henry Regnery, 1960,
       38-79.

3074   Copleston, Frederick C.   "Existentialism and Religion."   Dub-
       lin Review.   No. 440, Spring 1947, 45-63.

3075   Copleston, Frederick C.   "Man Without God."   The Month,
       CLXXIV, No. 961, July-August 1947, 18-27.

3076   Descoqs, Pedro.   "L'athéisme de Sartre."   Revue de Philoso-
       phie.   No. 2, 1946.   Also L'Existentialisme.   Paris: Téqui,
       1947, 39-90.

3077   Duméry, Henry.   "L'athéisme sartrien."   Esprit, XVIII, 1950,
       240-252.

3078   Duméry, Henry. "La clef de l'existentialisme sartrien." Regards sur la philosophie contemporaine. Paris: Castermann, 1956, 181-184.

3079   Duméry, Henry. Foi et interrogation. (Collection Notre Monde, 9). Paris: Téqui, 1953.

3080   Durand, R.P. Sartre ou la liberté sans Dieu. Marseille: Conférences C.I.T.A., 1953.

3081   Earle, William. "Man as the Impossibility of God." Christianity and Existentialism. Evanston, Illinois: Northwestern Univ. Pr., 1963.

3082   Essey, Albert. Atheismus. Köln: Hegner, 1971.

3083   Figurelli, Roberto. Jean-Paul Sartre: Do ateismo ao antiteismo. Porto Alegre: Grafica da Universidad do Rio Grande do Sul, 1962.

3084   Gerber, Rudolph F. "Causality and Atheism." Proceedings Catholic Philosophical Association, XLIV, 1970, 232-240.

3085   Gerber, Rudolph F. "Causality and Atheism: The Difficulty With the Creative God in Existential Phenomenology." The Personalist, LI, Fall 1970, 522-534.

3086   Giannaras, Christos. "An Orthodox Comment on 'The Death of God'." Sobornost, Series 5, No. 4, Winter 1966, 249-257.

3087   Glicksberg, Charles I. Modern Literature and the Death of God. The Hague: Nijhoff, 1966.

       Hassenhüttl, Gotthold. see 771.

3088   Hossfeld, P. "Die 'Bekehrung' von Simone de Beauvoir und Jean-Paul Sartre zum Atheismus." Theologie und Glaube, LX, 1970, 144-157.

3089   Iriarte, Joaquin. "La gran filosofía nunca ha sido atea." Razón y Fé. No. 145, June 1952, 565-574.

3090   Lacroix, Jean. "Sens et valeur de l'atheisme actuel." Esprit, XXII, 1954, 167-191.

3091   Lapointe, François H. "Sartre's Atheism or the Possibility to be Man." Diafora, VI, No. 3, 1974, 15-20.

3092   Lepp, Ignace. "L'athéisme de Sartre." Psychanalyse de L'ath-
        éisme moderne. Paris, 1961, 192-202.

3093   Llambias de Azevedo, Juan. "Sobre el argumento de Sartre con-
        tra la existencai de Dios." Stromata, XIII, 1967, 91-101.

3094   Lotz, J.B. "L'ateismo in Jean-Paul Sartre." L'ateismo con-
        temporaneo, Vol 2. Torino: SEI, 1968.

        Louis, Chanoine Michel. see 2891.

3095   Lotz, J.B. "Gotteserfahrung im modernen Denken." Stimmen
        der Zeit, 171, August 1963, 321-334.

3096   Luipjen, William A. and Koren, Henry J. "The Atheism of Sar-
        tre." A First Introduction to Existential Phenomenology.
        Pittsburgh: Duquesne Univ. Pr.; Louvain: Editions E. Nau-
        welaerts, 1969.

3097   Luipjen, William A. Phenomenology and Atheism. Pittsburgh:
        Duquesne Univ. Pr., 1968.

3098   Mark, James. "Sartre and the Atheism Which Purifies." Prism.
        No. 65, September 1962, 5-22.

3099   Marson, M.J. "The Atheism of Jean-Paul Sartre." Modern
        Churchman, XLIV, March 1954, 49-54.

3100   Masterson, Patrick. Atheism and Alienation: A Study of the
        Philosophical Sources of Contemporary Atheism. Notre Dame,
        Indiana: Univ. of Notre Dame Pr., 1971.

3101   Monthaye, Gaston. L'athéisme, le communisme, l'existential-
        isme. Paris: Librairie Mercure, 1949.

3102   Montull, Tomas. "Anti-teismo en Sartre." Ciencia Tomistica,
        LXXXIX, 1962, 69-138.

3103   Muller-Schwefe, Hans-Rudolph. Atheismus. Stuttgart, 1962.

3104   Patté, Daniel. L'athéisme d'un chrétien ou un chrétien à
        l'écoute de Sartre. Paris: Nouvelles Editions Latines,
        1965.

3105   Pinto, Juan-Luis. El ateismo del último Sartre: la linea evo-
        lutiva de su actitud atea. Madrid: Editorial Razón y Fé,
        1968.

3106   Pinto, Juan-Luis. "Trayectoria vital del ateismo sartriano."
       Revista de Filosofía, XXV, 1966, 367-369.

3107   Pruche, Benoît. "Pourquoi l'existentialisme est-il athée?"
       Revue de l'Université d'Ottawa, XXI, No. 3, septembre 1951,
       287-301.

3108   Siguenza, José J. "Genesis de la libertad en el ateismo de
       Sartre." Verdadera Vida, XXVI, 1968, 5-59.

3109   Smith, Vincent E. "Sartre's Refuge in Atheism." Idea-Men of
       Today. Milwaukee: Bruce, 1952, 288-310.

3110   Strobl, W. "Sartre und die letzte Konsequenz des Atheismus."
       Besinnung (Nürnberg), II, 1947, 231-235.

3111   Truc, Gonzague. "Sartre, Merleau-Ponty et l'athéisme radi-
       cal." Ecrits de Paris. No. 131, octobre 1955, 27-31.

3112   Vahanian, Gabriel. "Existentialism and the Death of God."
       The Death of Our Post-Christian Era. New York: G. Barzil-
       ler, 1961, 203-227.

3113   Vietta, Egon. Theologie ohne Gott. Zürich: Artemis, 1948.

3114   Weidle, Wladmir. The Dilemma of the Arts. Trans. by Martin
       Jarrett-Kerr. London: S.C.M. Pr., 1948, 92-95. Concerning
       the godless struggle in the works of Sartre.

3115   Wicker, Brian. "Atheism and the Avant-Garde." New Black-
       friars, LI, No. 606, novembre 1970, 527-535.

AUTHENTICITY

3116   Albérès, René-Marill. "Autenticidad y libertad en Jean-Paul
       Sartre." Sur. No. 162, April 1948, 86-101.

       Garris, N. Norman. see 307.

3117   Grene, Marjorie. "Authenticity: An Existential Virtue."
       Ethics, LXII, July 1952, 266-274.

3118   Lauder, R. "Choose Freedom! Sartre and Search for Authenti-
       city." New Catholic World, 216, November 1973, 269-272.

3119   Olafson, Frederick A. "Authenticity and Obligation." Sar-
       tre: A Collection of Critical Essays. Mary Warnock, ed.
       Garden City, New York: Doubleday, Anchor Books, 1971, 121-
       175.

3120 Olson, Robert G. "Authenticity, Metaphysics and Moral Respon-
      sibility." Philosophy, XXXIV, 1959, 99-110.

3121 Smoot, William. "The Concept of Authenticity in Sartre." Man
      and World, VII, No. 2, May 1974, 135-148.

3122 Trilling, Lionel. "The Heroic, the Beautiful, the Authentic."
      Sincerity and Authenticity. London: Oxford Univ. Pr., 1972,
      81-105.

3123 Wild, John. "Authentic Existence." Ethics, LXXV, No. 4, July
      1965, 227-235.

BAD FAITH (see Sincerity)

      Blundo, Virginia C. see 263.

3124 Elkin, Henry. "Comment on Sartre From the Standpoint of Exis-
      tential Psychotherapy." Review of Existential Psychology
      and Psychiatry, I, Fall 1961, 189-194.

3125 Code, Lorraine and King-Farlow, John. "Bonne foi, mauvaise
      foi, sincérité et espoir." Dialogue, XII, No. 3, septembre
      1973, 502-514.

3126 Dugué, Gabrielle. "Critique de la mauvaise foi du privilégié
      dans l'oeuvre de Sartre." Doctoral Dissertation in progress,
      City Univ. of New York.

3127 Fingarette, Herbert. Self-Deception. New York: Humanities
      Pr., 1969, 92-100.

3128 Garcia Baca, J.D. "La mala fé y la mentira según Sartre."
      Revista Nacional de Cultura. No. 63, 1950, 97-104.

3129 Gilbert, Margaret. "Vices and Self-Knowledge." Journal of
      Philosophy, LXVIII, 5 August 1971, 443-452.

3130 Herrera, José-Luis. "La 'mal fé' en Jean-Paul Sartre." Mer-
      curio Peruano, XXXVI, No. 410, June 1961, 496-509.

3131 Monasterio, X.O. "La mauvaise foi et l'analyse sartrienne de
      la conscience." Archives de Philosophie, XXXV, No. 4, 1972.

3132 Santoni, Ronald E. "Sartre on 'Sincerity': Bad Faith or Equi-
      vication?" The Personalist, LIII, 1972, 150-160.

BEING (see Ontology)

    Champigny, Robert. see 1828.

3133 Derisi, Octavio. "El ser en el existencialismo materialista
    de Sartre." Témas de Filosofía contemporanea. Emilio S.
    Lopéz and Alberto Caturelli, eds. Buenos Aires: Sudamerica,
    1971, 33-44.

    Ecole, Jean. see 1921.

3134 Henry, Michel. L'Essence de la manifestation, 2 vols. Paris:
    Presses Universitaires de France, 1963. Trans. into English
    by Etzkorn: The Essence of Manifestation. The Hague:
    Nijhoff, 1973, 740 pp.

3135 Lynch, L.E. "Past and Being in Jean-Paul Sartre." American
    Catholic Philosophical Association Proceedings, XXII, 1947,
    212-220.

3136 Napoli, Giovanni di. La concezione dell'essere nella filoso-
    fia contemporanea. Roma: Studium, 1953.

BEING-IN-THE-WORLD

3137 Ferrier, Jean-Louis. L'homme dans le monde. Neuchâtel: Edi-
    tion de la Baconnière, 1957.

    Lessing, Arthur. see 2864.

    Toscano, Giuseppe. see 2878.

'BEING-WITH'

    Hellerich, G. see 313.

BEHAVIOR

3138 Jeanson, Francis. "Les caractères existentialistes de la con-
    duite humaine selon Sartre." Morale chrétienne et requêtes
    contemporaines, 173-194. Reimprimé Lignes de départ. Paris:
    Editions du Seuil, 1962, 153-177.

    Kvale, Steinar and Grenness, Carl E. see 2951.

BLACK AMERICAN LITERATURE

    Reid, Joel O. see 377.

BUDDHIST CONCEPT OF MAN

Wisadavet, Wit. see 407.

Le 'CAS' Sartre

3148 Brisson, Pierre. "Le cas Sartre." Propos de théâtre. Paris:
Gallimard, 1957, 21-53.

3149 Ehrenbourg, Ilya. "Le cas Sartre." Le Figaro Littéraire, XX,
No. 1002, 1-7 juillet 1965, 1, 7.

3150 Treves, Renato. "El 'caso' Sartre en Italia." Realidad, II,
No. 6, November-December 1947, 414-417.

CAUSALITY

Dina, Stephen. see 287.

La CAUSE du Peuple

3151 Améry, Jean. "Der Weg zum Aufwiegler: Jean-Paul Sartres Prozess gegen die Wirklichkeit." Die Zeit. No. 35, 27 August
1971, 14.

3152 Anonymous. "L'enfer sartrien." L'Express. No. 1004, 5-11
octobre 1970, 14-15.

3153 Anonymous. "A Paris: Jean-Paul Sartre et dix-sept personnes
qui distribuaient La Cause du Peuple sont interpellés sur
les grands Boulevards." Le Monde. No. 7917, 28-29 juin
1970, 10.

3154 Anonymous. "Print and Be Seized." Time, XCVI, 10 November
1970, 76 ff.

3155 Contat, Michel and Rybalka, Michel. "Sartre 1969-1970: Bibliographie commentée." Adam International Review. No. 343-
345, 1970. Avec un appendice: "Textes relatifs à la reprise
par Sartre de la direction de La Cause du Peuple.

CHARACTER

3156 Boros, Marie-Denise. "L'antinaturalisme des personnages de
Sartre." French Review, XL, October 1966, 77-83.

Burdick, Dolores M. see 788.

Galler, Dieter. see 1280.

3157   Goldberg, M.A.   "Chronology, Character and Human Condition."
       Criticism, V, No. 1, Winter 1963, 1-12.

3158   Harvey, W.J.   "Character and the Context of Things," "Charac-
       ter, Essence and Existence," "Conclusion: An End to Theory."
       Character and the Novel.   London: Chatto and Windus, 1963,
       31-51, 150-190.

3159   Will, Frederick.   "Sartre and the Question of Character in Li-
       terature."   PMLA, LXXVI, September 1961, 455-460.   Reprinted
       Literature Inside Out: Ten Speculative Essays.   Cleveland:
       Western Reserve Univ. Pr., 1966, 94-109.

CHINA

3160   Heutges, Pierre.   "Tout dans ce pays est émouvant."   L'Human-
       ité, 1 novembre 1955.   Interview.

3161   Karol, K.S.   "Sartre Views the New China."   New Statesman,
       LIV, 3 December 1955, 737-739.

3162   Tillard, Paul.   "Une soirée à Pékin avec Sartre et Simone de
       Beauvoir."   L'Humanité-Dimanche, 23 octobre 1955.

CHILDHOOD

       Hoy, Nancy.   see 316.

CHOICE

       Cole, Preston.   see 2657.

3163   Fruchter, Norm.   "Sartre and the Drama of Choice."   Encore,
       IX, No. 4, July-August 1962, 35-42.

3164   Reck, Rima Drell.   "Sartre: Ambiguity of Moral Choice."   Lite-
       rature and Responsibility: The French Novelists in the Twen-
       tieth Century.   Baton Rouge, Louisiana: Louisiana State
       Univ. Pr., 1970, 3-41.

3165   Ridge, George R.   "Meaningful Choice in Sartre's Drama."
       French Review, XXX, No. 6, May 1957, 535-541.

3166   Shapiro, Gary.   "Choice and Universality in Sartre's Ethics."
       Man and World, VII, No. 1, February 1974, 20-35.

3167   Smith, Colin.   "Toward a Definition of Authenticity: Choice."
       Contemporary French Philosophy: A Study in Norms and Val-
       ues.   London: Methuen, 1964, 216-233.

(Original) CHOICE

Lindermayer, E.R.   see 336.

CHRISTIANITY

3168   Champigny, Robert. "Sartre and Christianity." Renascence,
        VII, No. 2, Winter 1954, 59-62, 69.

3169   Chiari, Joseph. "Marxism, Existentialism, and Christianity."
        The Aesthetics of Modernism. London: Vision, 1970, 25-48.

3170   Daniélou, Jean. "Dialogue: Communisme, existentialisme, chri-
        stianisme." Etudes. No. 8, 1947.

3171   Daniélou, Madeleine. "Sartre et les Chrétiens." Cahiers de
        Neuilly. No. 12, 1946, 1-8.

3172   Earle, William, et al. Christianity and Existentialism.
        Evanston, Illinois: Northwestern Univ. Pr., 1963.

3173   Itterbeck, Eugène van. "Sartre en het Kristendom." Dietsche
        Warande en Belfort, CVII, 1962, 70-71.

3174   Kroner, R.J. "Existentialism and Christianity." Encounter,
        XVII, Summer 1956, 219-244.

3175   Mikeleitis, Edity. "Sartre und des Christentum." Christen-
        gemeinschaft, XXXIII. Stuttgart, 1961, 91-92.

3176   Moeller, Charles. L'Homme moderne devant le salut. Paris:
        Editions Ouvrières, 1965. Trans. into English by Charles
        Underhill Quinn: Man and Salvation in Literature. Notre
        Dame, Indiana: Univ. of Notre Dame, 1970.

3177   Moeller, Charles. Littérature du vingtième siècle et Chris-
        tianisme II: La foi en Jésus-Christ. Paris: Edition Cas-
        terman, 1953.

3178   Moeller, Charles. Littérature du vingtième siècle et Chris-
        tianisme III: Espoir des hommes. Paris-Tournai: Casterman,
        1957.

3179   Mindan, Manero, Manuel. "Existencialismo y Christianismo:
        Les doctrinas existentialistas a la luz de Humani Generis."
        Revista de Filosofía, X, No. 39, 1951, 746-755.

3180 Rideau, Emile. "Un humanisme social athée: Jean-Paul Sartre
      et le christianisme." Nouvelle Revue de Théologie, LXXXV,
      décembre 1963, 1039-1062.

3181 Rideau, Emile. Paganisme et christianisme. Paris-Tournai:
      Casterman, 1953.

CHURCH

3182 Anonymous. "The Church and French Writers." Transition. No.
      3, 1948, 129-150; Ibid., No. 4, 1948, 113-134.

CINEMA (see LES JEUX SONT FAITS)

3183 Loriot, Patrick. "Sartre à l'écran." Le Nouvel Observateur.
      No. 395, 5-11 juin 1972, 42-43.

3184 Rybalka, Michel. "Sartre et le cinéma." L'Esprit Créateur,
      VIII, No. 4, Fall 1968, 284-292.

CIVILIZATION

3185 Rao, M.V. Venkata. "Sartre on the Crisis of Civilization."
      Thought (Delhi), V, No. 2, 10 January 1953, 10-12.

CLASS

3186 Diavoletto, Concetta. "Sartre tra classe e partito." Rivista
      di Studi Salernitiani, 4, 1971, 329-338.

3187 Vailland, Roger. "Un phénomène de classe qui sert la réac-
      tion." Pour et contre l'existentialisme, grand débat. Co-
      lette Audrey, ed. Paris: Atlas, 1948.

CLASS CONSCIOUSNESS

3188 Massolo, Arturo. "Frammento etico-politico." La Storia della
      filosofia come problema. Firenze: Vallechi, 1967, 234-243.
      Massolo respinge la concezione spontaneistica della coscien-
      za di classe, rifacendosi a Lenin e a Sartre.

COEXISTENCE

      Hermann, Friedrich W. von. see 2194.

COLOR

      Fletcher, Dennis J. see 434.

3189   Matore, Georges. "A propos du vocabulaire des couleurs."
       Annales de l'Université de Paris, XXVIII, No. 2, avril-juin
       1958, 137-150.

COMIC

3190   Prince, Gerald J. "Le comique dans l'oeuvre romanesque de
       Sartre." PMLA, LXXXVII, mars 1972, 295-303.

COMEBACK

3191   Horodinca, Georgeta. "Sartre's Comeback in Strength." Adam
       International Review, XXXV, No. 343-345, 1970, 99-100.

COMMITMENT (see Engagement)

       Adereth, Maxwell. see 1.

3192   Clowes, George. "Sartre and Commitment." Prism. No. 83,
       March 1964, 72-73.

3193   Cranston, Maurice W. "Sartre's Commitment." Encounter,
       XXIII, August 1964, 43-45.

       Curtis, Jerry L. see 2519, 2520.

3194   Davidson, Robert F., ed. "The Commitment of the Existential-
       ist." The Search for Meaning in Life: Readings in Philos-
       ophy. New York: Holt, 1962, 333-394.

3195   Halle, Louis J. "The Question of Commitment." Virginia Quar-
       terly Review, XLIX, No. 2, Spring 1973, 161-181.

3196   Mander, John. The Writer and Commitment. Philadelphia: Du-
       four, 1962, 8-15.

3197   O'Brien, Conor Cruise. "Thoughts on Commitment." The Listen-
       er, LXXXVI, No. 2229, 16 December 1971, 834-836.

COMMUNICATION

       Cumming, Robert D. see 2760.

       Poole, Roger C. see 2694.

COMMUNION

       Markus, Thomas B. see 341.

Patterson, Olanda.   see 364.

COMMUNISM

3198   Anonymous.   "Communistas contra Sartre."   Hispano Americano,
       CIII, No. 1368, 22 July 1968, 39.

3199   Aron, Raymond.   "Jean-Paul Sartre, le prolétariat et les Com-
       munistes."   Revue de Paris, LXI, juin 1954, 88-89.

3200   Aron, Raymond.   L'opium des intellectuels.   Paris: Gallimard,
       1955.   Trans. into English by Terence Kilmartin: The Opium
       of the Intellectuals.   London: Secker and Warburg, 1957.

3201   Benckiser, Nikolas.   "'Klebrige Ratte': Wie steht Jean-Paul
       Sartre zum Kommunismus?"   Wort und Wahrheit, VIII, Frieberg,
       1953, 74-76.

3202   Boisdeffre, Pierre de.   "Sartre et le communisme."   Des Vi-
       vants et des morts: Témoignages 1948-1953.   Paris: Éditions
       Universitaires, 1954, 219-248.

3203   Boisdeffre, Pierre de.   "Sartre face au communisme."   L'Age
       Nouveau.   No. 79, février 1953, 34-50.

3204   Burnier, Michel Antoine.   Les existentialistes et la poli-
       tique.   Paris: Gallimard, 1966.   Trans. into English.

3205   Caldwell, Malcolm.   "Expertise and Dexterity."   Tribune,
       XXXIV, No. 17, 24 April 1970, 14.   Concernant le spectre de
       Staline, les Communistes, et la paix.

3206   Carat, Jacques.   "Sartre and the Communists."   Thought (Del-
       hi), VI, No. 35, 28 August 1954, 10-12.

3207   Caute, David.   Communism and the French Intellectuals 1914-
       1960.   London: André Deutsch, 1964.

3208   Caute, David.   The Fellow-Travellers: A Postscript to the En-
       lightenment.   London: Weidenfelt and Nicholson, 1973.

       Chiaromonte, Nicolà.   see 2668.

3209   Chiaromonte, Nicolà.   Il tempo della malafeda, il communismo
       degli intelletuali.   Roma: Italia por la Libertà della Cul-
       tura, 1959.

3210   Domarchi, Jean.   "Questions du communisme."   Confluences,
       VIII, No. 18-20, 1947, 111-119.

Fagone, Virgilio. see 2664.

3211   Fe, Franco. Sartre e il communismo. (Nostro tempo, 15). Fi-
        renze: La Nuova Italia, 1970.

3212   Flanner, Janet (Genet). "Letter from Paris." New Yorker, 13
        December 1952, 161 ff.

3213   Heist, Walter. "Die Wandlungen des Jean-Paul Sartre: Er und
        die Kommunisten." Frankfurter Hefte, XII, No. 4, April
        1957, 257-264.

3214   Kanapa, Jean. Comme si la lutte entière . . . Paris: Nagel,
        1946.

3215   Kanapa, Jean. "Un 'nouveau revisionisme' à l'usage des intel-
        lectuels." L'Humanité, 22 février 1954.

3216   Kanapa, Jean. "Sartre, les communistes et la paix." La Nou-
        velle Critique, IV, No. 39, septembre-octobre 1952, 23-42.

        Karol, K.S. see 2910.

3217   Mounier, E. "Récents critiques du communisme." Esprit, XIV,
        No. 10, 1946, 482-484.

3218   P.P. "Jean-Paul Sartre demande aux Communistes: 'Etes-vous
        fous'?" Preuves, IV, No. 38, avril 1954, 95-96.

3219   Sales, Edouard. "Sartre und der Kommunismus." Ost-Probleme,
        IX, 1957, 413-418.

3220   Simier, Pierre. "Quand Sartre se tait . . . l'écho commu-
        niste répète . . ." Le Populaire, 28 mai 1954. Cf. Les
        Ecrits de Sartre, 276.

3221   V.P., P. "Selon Jean-Paul Sartre, les Communistes ont peur de
        la révolution." Le Monde. No. 7526, 26 mars 1969, 18.

3222   Wall, Bernard. "The French Reviews." Twentieth Century,
        CLIII, April 1953, 276-282.

3223   Walther, Elizabeth. "Sartre und die Kommunisten." Augen-
        blick, I, No. 4, 1958, 13-18.

3224   Werth, Alexander. "Sartre and the Communists." New Statesman
        and Nation, XLVII, No. 1209, 8 May 1954, 590.

COMPLEX

3225 Naesgaard, Sigurd. "Le complexe de Sartre." Psyché. No. 20, juin 1948, 655-665.

CONSCIOUSNESS

3226 Anderson, Thomas C. "Neglected Sartrean Arguments for the Freedom of Consciousness." Philosophy Today, XVII, Spring 1973, 28-38.

3227 Banerjee, A.K. "Consciousness in Sartre." Journal of the Indian Academy of Philosophy, X, No. 2, December 1971.

Bhadra, Mrinal K. see 260.

Blueston, Natalie. see 262.

3228 Bowes, Pratina. Consciousness and Freedom: Three Views. London: Methuen; New York: Barnes and Noble, 1971.

3229 Chavez Santillan, Francisco J. "La conciencia en J." Logos, I, September-December 1973, 359-378.

3230 Christensen, William. "Sartre's Interpretation of Consciousness as Spontaneous." Philosophical Studies (Ireland), XXI, 1972, 172-185.

Coleman, Michael. see 277.

3231 Corvez, Maurice. "L'être de la conscience dans la philosophie de Sartre." Revue Thomiste, LI, 1950, 563-574.

Dina, Stephen. see 287.

3232 Engelberg, Edward. The Unknown Distance: From Consciousness to Conscience, Goethe to Camus. Cambridge, Massachusetts: Harvard Univ. Pr., 1972.

3233 Funishi, H. "La structure de la conscience dans la philosophie de Sartre." Bunka, XXII, No. 2, 1958, 156-174. In Japanese; summary in French.

Goldthorpe, Rhiannon. see 437.

Kersten, Fred. see 1847.

McIntire, Russell M. see 346.

Mole, Jack. see 5016.

Murphy, Richard T. see 354.

3234   Piancella, Cesare. "La reificazione della coscienza nei primi
       scritti di Sartre." Rivista di Filosofia, LVII, 1966, 36-
       52.

Riu, Federico. see 2718.

Salvan, Jacques L. see 2742.

Scanlon, John D. see 1750.

3235   Sukale, Michael. "The Ego and the Consciousness in Rival Per-
       spectives: A Study of Husserl and the Early Sartre." IYYUN,
       XXII, October 1971, 193-214. In Hebrew.

3236   Tibbetts, Paul. "Some Recent Philosophical Contributions to
       the Problem of Consciousness." Philosophy Today, XIV,
       Spring 1970, 3-22.

Wagner de Reyna, Alberto. see 2724.

3237   Wolff, Edgar. "Conscience et liberté chez Descartes et Sar-
       tre." Revue de Philosophie de la France et de l'Etranger,
       LXXX, 1955, 341-348.

3238   Zurro Rodriguez, Maria R. "El campo de conciencia: Preperson-
       alidad y prerreflexión en Jean-Paul Sartre." Anales del Se-
       minaro de Metafisica, 1971, 57-83.

COURT (Sartre on trial in 1971)

Améry, Jean. see 3151.

3239   Anonymous. "Manifestations devant le Ministère de la Jus-
       tice." Le Figaro, 18 janvier 1972, 8. Edition départemen-
       tale.

3240   Anonymous. "Sartre convoqué au Palais pour diffamation en-
       vers la police." Le Figaro, 24 septembre 1971, 15.

3241   Anonymous. "Sartre en prison?" Le Nouvel Observateur. No.
       286, 4-10 mai 1970, 20.

3242   Anonymous. "Sartre inculpé de diffamation." Le Figaro, 18
       janvier 1972, 9.

3243   Anonymous. "Sartre inculpé d'injures envers La Caisse d'as-
       surance vieillesse artisanale." Le Figaro, 15 mars 1972,
       16.

3244   Anonymous. "Sartre kämpft um seinen politischen Prozess."
       Die Welt. No. 143, 24 June 1971, 6.

3245   Frossard, André. "Procès (tient à son procès populaire de la
       police, qui aura lieu le 27 juin)." Le Figaro, 26 juin
       1971, 1.

CRAB (Metaphor of)

3246   Boros, Marie-Denise. "La métaphore du crabe dans l'oeuvre
       littéraire de Sartre." PMLA, LXXXI, October 1966, 446-450.

CREATIVITY

3247   Bedford, Mitchel. Existentialism and Creativity. New York:
       Philosophical Library, 1972.

CRISIS (of Sartre's generation)

3248   Moravia, S. "La crisi della generazione sartriana." Rivista
       di Filosofia, LVIII, October-December 1967, 426-470.

CRITIC (Sartre as critic)

3249   Brée, Germaine and Zimmerman, E. "Contemporary French Criti-
       cism." Comparative Literature Studies, I, No. 3, 1964, 175-
       196.

3250   Colwell, C. Carter. "Literary Criticism and Process Thought:
       Blackmur, Sartre, Brooks, and Whitehead." Process Studies,
       II, Fall 1972, 183-192.

3251   Donato, Eugenio. "The Two Languages of Criticism." The Lan-
       guage of Criticism and the Science of Man. Richard Macksey
       and Eugenio Donato, eds. Baltimore: Johns Hophins Univ.
       Pr., 1969, 89-97, 110-124.

3252   Hahn, Paul. "L'oeuvre critique de Sartre." Modern Language
       Notes, LXXX, No. 3, May 1965, 347-363. Trans. into English:
       "Sartre's Literary Criticism." Sartre: A Collection of
       Critical Essays. Mary Warnock, ed. Garden City, New York:
       Doubleday, Anchor Books, 1971, 221-243.

3253   Hardré, Jacques. "Jean-Paul Sartre: Literary Critic."
       Studies in Philology, LV, January 1958, 98-106.

Halpern, Joseph. see 310.

3254 Jameson, Fredric. "Three Methods in Sartre's Literary Criticism." Modern French Criticism from Proust and Valéry to Structuralism. John K. Simon, ed. Chicago: Chicago Univ. Pr., 1972, 193-228.

3255 Laufer, Roger. "Sartre as Literary Critic." Meanjin Quarterly, XVIII, 1950, 427-434.

3256 O'Brien, Conor Cruise. "Sartre as Critic." Writers and Politics. New York: Pantheon, 1965, 72-75.

3257 Payne, Michael. "La critique engagée: Littérature and Politics." CEA Critic, XXXV, No. 2, January 1973, 4-8.

3258 Rossi, Lino. "Sartre e il problema della critica." Arte, critica, Felix Sofia (Studi di Estetica). Bologna: R. Patron, 1965, 231-267.

Suhl, Benjamin. see 59, 141.

3259 Thody, Philip. "Sartre as a Literary Critic." London Magazine, VII, No. 11, November 1960, 61-64.

3260 Ungar, Steven R. "Sartre as Critic." Diacritics, I, No. 1, Fall 1971, 32-37.

3261 Vivaldi, Cesare. "Sartre critico." Europa Letteraria, I, No. 2, 1960, 197-198.

3262 Wardman, Harold. "Sartre as Critic." Sartre: A Collection of Critical Essays. Mary Warnock, ed. Garden City, New York: Doubleday, Anchor Books, 1971, 186-220.

Yon, André-François. see 409.

CRITICISM

3263 Doubrovsky, Serge, Pourquoi la nouvelle critique? Critique et objectivité. Paris: Mercure de France, 1966.

3264 Fowlie, Wallace. The French Critic 1594-1967. Carbondale: Southern Illinois Univ. Pr., 1968.

3265 Hannsen, Alfonso. "Sartre y la crítica inglesa." Boletín Cultural y bibliográfico (Bogotá), No. 10, 1967, 343-347.

3266 Jones, Robert E. "L'école existentialiste: Sartre." Panor-
      ama de la nouvelle critique, de Gaston Bachelard à Jean-Paul
      Weber. Paris: SEDES, 1968, 101-133.

3267 Lawall, Sarah N. Critics of Consciousness: The Existential
      Structures of Literature. Cambridge, Massachusetts: Harvard
      Univ. Pr., 1968.

3267a Lawall, Sarah N. "Recent Existential Criticism." Unpublished
      Doctoral Dissertation, Yale Univ., 1961.

3268 LeSage, Laurent. The French New Criticism: An Introduction
      and a Sampler. University Park: Pennsylvania Univ. Pr.,
      1967.

3269 Pingaud, Bernard. "Critique traditionelle et nouvelle cri-
      tique." La Nef, XXIV, No. 29, janvier-mars 1967, 41-56.

3270 Rossi, Lino. "Specchio e contesto della nuova critica fran-
      cese." Paragone, XIV, No. 162, n.s., June 1963, 38-75.

3271 Strarobinski, Jean. "Considerations on the Present State of
      Literary Criticism." Diogenes. No. 74, Summer 1974, 57-84.

3272 Weber, Jean-Paul. "Sartre et la nouvelle critique." Bulletin
      de la Société des Professeurs Français en Amérique, 1971.

3273 Wellek, René. "The Main Trends of Twentieth Century Criti-
      cism." Yale Review, LI, Autumn 1951, 102-118.

CULPABILITY

      Doherty, Cyril M. see 288.

DANDY

3274 Carassus, Emilien. Le Mythe du dandy. Paris: Armand Colin,
      1971.

DEATH

      Beschin, Giuseppe. see 2698.

3275 Choron, Jacques. Death and Western Thought. New York: Col-
      lier, 1967. Trans. into French: La mort et la pensée occi-
      dentale. Paris: Payot, 1970.

3276 DeFranco, Raffaella. "La idea della morte e il suicidio." Giornale Critico della Filosofia Italiana, LI, October-December 1970, 566-579.

3277 DeFranco, Raffaella. "Morte e alienazione." Giornale Critico della Filosofia Italiana, LIII, April-June 1972, 263-272.

3278 Hoffman, Fredrick J. "Existentialist Living and Dying." The Mortal No: Death and the Modern Imagination. Princeton: Princeton Univ. Pr., 1964, 424-452.

3279 Jolivet, Régis. Le Problème de la mort chez Heidegger et Sartre. Abbaye de Saint Wandrille: Editions de Fontenelle, 1950.

3280 Kaufmann, Walter. "Existentialism and Death." Chicago Review, XIII, No. 2, Summer 1959, 75-93.

3281 Kaufmann, Walter. "Existentialism and Death." The Meaning of Death. Hermann Feifel, ed. New York: McGraw-Hill, 1959.

3282 Natanson, Maurice. "Death and Situation." American Imago, XVI, 1959. Reprinted Literature, Philosophy, and the Social Sciences. The Hague: Nijhoff, 1962, 212-220.

3283 O'Mahoney, E.B. "Martin Heidegger's Existential of Death." Philosophical Studies (Ireland), XVIII, 1969, 58-75.

3284 O'Mara, Joseph. "Death and the Existentialists." Studies (Ireland), XXXIX, No. 156, December 1950, 427-437.

3285 Pirlot, Jules. "La mort et la liberté." Revue Philosophique de Louvain, LVI, 3e série, No. 52, novembre 1958, 573-585.

Uranga, Emilio. see 3719.

DESPAIR

3286 Lain Entralgo, Pedro. "Sartre y la desesperanza." Cuadernos Hispanoamericanos, XXX, No. 85, January 1957, 7-23.

DIALECTIC and DIALECTICAL (see Critique de la raison dialectique)

3287 Abel, Lionel. "Sartre e la ragione dialettica." Tempo Presente, IX, No. 11, November 1964, 12-26.

3288 Amoros, Celia. "El concepto de razón dialectica en Sartre." Teorema, I, No. 2, June 1971, 103-116.

3289 Aron, Raymond. "Aventures et mésaventures de la dialectique."
      Preuves, janvier 1956. Reimprimé Marxismes imaginaires.
      Paris: Gallimard, 1970. Trans. into English: Marxism and
      the Existentialists. New York: Harper and Row, 1969.

      Biemel, Walter. see 2687.

3290 Buehl, Walter. "Dialeckische Soziologie und soziologische
      Dialektik." Köelner Zeitschrift fur Soziologie, XXI, 1969,
      717-751.

      Canilli, Adele. see 181.

3291 Daghiri, Giairo. "Materialismo objettivato ed esistenzialismo
      dialettico." Aut Aut. No. 82, 1965, 18-39.

3292 Dufrenne, Mikel. "Notes sur Les aventures de la dialectique."
      Combat, 29 septembre 1955.

3293 Gurvitch, Georges. "La dialectique chez Jean-Paul Sartre."
      Dialectique et sociologie. Paris: Gallimard, 1962.

3294 Kopper, Joachim. "Die Dialektik in französischen Denken der
      Gegenwart." Zeitschrift für Philosophische Forschung, XI,
      1957, 142-164.

3295 Kourim, Zdenek. "¿Adonde va la dialectica?" Sapientia,
      XXVII, January-March 1972, 15-36.

3296 Lefebvre, Henri. "Les dilemmes de la dialectique." Média-
      tions. No. 2, 1961, 79-105.

3297 Kryger, Edna. "L'activité négative." Journal History of Phi-
      losophy. July 1973, 337-362. See Hegel, History.

3298 Maccio, Marco. "La dialettica sartriana e la critica della di-
      alettica oggettivistica." Aut Aut, July 1964, 58-92.

3299 Merleau-Ponty, Maurice. Les Aventures de la dialectique.
      Paris: Gallimard, 1955.

3300 Nauta, Lolle W. "Dialektik bei Sartre." Studium Generale,
      XXI, July 1968, 591-607.

      Pagano, Giacoma M. see 196.

      Panou, S. see 166.

      Seel, Gerhard. see 170.

3301   Sève, Lucien. "Sartre et la dialectique en 1960." La Nou-
       velle Critique. No. 123, février 1961, 78-100.

       Sotelo, Ignacio.   see 222.

3302   Stack, George J.   "Sartre: Dialéctica y realidad social."
       Folia Humanistica, XI, 1973, 621-646.

       Stack, George J.   see 2682, 2683.

       Tibaldi, Giancarlo.   see 2794.

DON JUANISM

       Larnaudie, Suzanne.   see 2883.

DREAD

3303   Grimsley, Ronald.   "'Dread' as a Philosophical Concept."   Phi-
       losophical Quarterly, VI, No. 24, July 1956, 245-255.

DREAM

3304   Fowler, Albert.   "Sartre's World of Dream."   Southwest Review,
       XLI, No. 3, Summer 1956, 264-269.

       Hering, Jean.   see 1764.

3305   Lefebvre, Maurice-Jean.   "The Surreal Dream and Dreamed Real-
       ity."   Diogenes.   No. 44, Winter 1963, 81-103.

DRUG

3306   Bonnet, Nicole.   "Une génération spontanée d'alexandrins."
       dans 'Cinq écrivains racontent leur expérience de la
       drogue."   Arts, 14-21 juin 1961.   Cf. Les Ecrits de
       Sartre, 367-368.

DUALISM

3307   Bonilla, Luis.   "El dualismo del bien y del mal."   La Esta-
       feta Leteraria.   No. 353, 24 September 1966, 12-13.

3308   Wieczynski, Joseph.   "A Note on Jean-Paul Sartre: Monist or
       dualist?"   Philosophy Today, XII, 1968, 184-189.

ECONOMICS

3309   Lagueux, Maurice.   "Sartre et la praxis économique."   Dialogue, XI, No. 1, mars 1972, 35-47.   Concernant Critique de
la raison dialectique.

EDUCATION

3310   Benhaminda, Khemais.   "Sartre's Existentialism and Education:
The Missing Foundations of Human Relationships."   Educational Theory, XXIII, Summer 1973, 230-238.

3311   Broudy, S.H.   "Sartre's Existentialism and Education."   Educational Theory, XXI, Spring 1971, 155-177.

3312   Cerf, Walter.   "Existentialist Mannerism and Education."
Journal of Philosophy, LII, No. 6, 17 March 1955, 141-152.

Craver, Samuel M.   see 280.

Garris, N. Norman.   see 307.

Hellerich, G.   see 313.

3313   Lesnoff-Caravaglia, Gari.   Education as Existential Possibility.   New York: Philosophical Library, 1972.

O'Neill, William F.   see 361.

Overholt, George E.   see 362.

3314   Vandenberg, Donald.   "Who is 'Pseudo'?"   Educational Theory,
XXIV, Spring 1974, 183-193.

3315   Weldhen, Margaret.   "The Existentialists and Problems of Moral
and Religious Education."   Journal of Moral Education, I,
June 1972, 187-194.

EGOISM

3316   Royle, Peter.   "Egoism and the Pre-reflexive volo."   Humanities Association Bulletin (Canada), XXI, No. 2, 1970, 57-
59.

ELECTRA

3317   Brunel, Pierre.   Le mythe d'Electre.   Paris: Armand Colin,
1971.

ENACTMENT

3318   Edie, James M. "The Problem of Enactment." Journal of Aes-
       thetics and Art Criticism, XXIX, Spring 1971, 308-318.

ENCOUNTER

       Shearson, William A. see 384.

ENGAGEMENT (see Commitment)

3319   Adorno, Theodor W. "Zur Dialektik des 'Engagements'." Die
       Neue Rundschau, LXXIII, No. 1, 1962, 93-110.

       Baude, Pierre-André. see 1041.

       Brinker, Menachem. see 3051.

3320   Choisy, Marsye. "Liberté ou engagement?" Psyché, IV, No. 29,
       mars 1949, 194-221.

       Clowes, George. see 3193.

3321   Desanti, Dominique. "Sartre et l'engagement." Adam Interna-
       tional Review, XXXV, No. 343-345, 1970, 33-35.

3322   Jamet, Dominique. "Sartre écrivain rengagé." Le Figaro Litté-
       raire. No. 1250, 4-10 mai 1970, 8-9.

3323   Keene, Dennis. "Engagement." Essays in Criticism, XIV, No.
       3, July 1963, 285-300.

3324   Paris, Jean. "L'engagement d'aujourd'hui." Liberté, III, No.
       17, novembre 1961, 683-690.

3325   Schmidt, Albert-Marie. "Dégageons-nous de l'engagement."
       Chroniques de Réforme 1945-1966. Lausanne: Editions Ren-
       contres, 1970, 50-53.

3326   Steinova, Dagmar. "Aujourd'hui plus que jamais-l'engagement."
       La Vie Tchécoslovaque, mars 1969, 14-15. Interview. Cf.
       Les Ecrits de Sartre, 478.

       Sulzer, Elisabeth. see 142.

EN-SOI (In-itself)

3327   Corvez, Maurice. "L'être-en-soi dans la philosophie de Sar-
       tre." Revue Thomiste, L, No. 3, 1950, 360-372.

Moreland, John M.   see 2867.

3328   Prince, Gérald J.   "La main et la menace de l'en-soi dans
       l'oeuvre romanesque de Sartre."   Romance Notes, X, Autumn
       1968, 7-10.

3329   Yolton, John W.   "The Metaphysics of En-soi and Pour-soi."
       Journal of Philosophy, XLVIII, 1951, 548-556.

ENSNAREMENT

3320   Brombert, Victor.   "Sartre and the Drama of Ensnarement."
       Ideas in the Drama.   J. Gassner, ed.   New York: Columbia
       Univ. Pr., 1964, 155-174.

EPISTEMOLOGY

Brunet, Christian.   see 2731.

Dina, Stephen.   see 287.

3331   Thyssen, Johannes.   "Vom Gegebenen zum Realen: Mit Blick auf
       die Erkenntnis-Metaphysik von Sartre."   Kant-Studien, XLVI,
       No. 1, 1954-1955, 68-87; Ibid, No. 2, 1954-1955, 157-171.
       Reprinted Realismus und moderne Philosophie.   Bonn: Bou-
       vier, 1959, 92-138.

Vuillemin, Jules.   see 2685.

EPOCHE

Van de Pitte, M.M.   see 2740.

EROTISME

3332   Bodart, Marie-Thérèse.   "De l'érotisme à l'érotique, ou Sartre
       est-il cathare?"   Synthèses, XXII, No. 253, juin 1967, 110-
       114.

3333   Varin, René.   Anthologie de l'érotisme: De Pierre Louys à
       Jean-Paul Sartre.   Paris: Éditions Nord-Sud, 1948.   Essai.

3334   Varin, René.   L'Erotisme dans la littérature, Tome I: Morceaux
       choisis de la littérature française moderne de Pierre Louys
       à Jean-Paul Sartre.   Lyon: Editions Champsfleuris, 1951.

ESSAY

3335   Champigny, Robert. Pour une esthétique de l'essai: Analyses
       critiques. Paris: Minard, 1967.

ESSENTIALISM

       Smith, Colin. see 2876.

ETHICS

3336   Anderson, Thomas C. "Is a Sartrean Ethics Possible?" Philos-
       ophy Today, XIV, Summer 1970, 116-140.

       Arras, John D. see 253.

3337   Barnes, Hazel E. "Sartre's Choice." An Existentialist Eth-
       ics. New York: Knopf, 1967.

       Binnie, Donald J. see 415.

3338   Bollnow, Otto F. "Existentialismus und Ethik." Die Sammlung,
       VI, 1949, 103-113. Reprinted Französischer Existentialis-
       mus. Stuttgart: Kohlhammer, 1965, 53-78.

3339   Borrajo, Mahin. "Moral Perspectives in the Existentialism
       of Jean-Paul Sartre." Philippiniana Sacra (Manila), III,
       1968, 531-570.

3340   Boucher, Rémi. "Quelques aspects moraux de la pensée de Sar-
       tre." Revue Philosophique de Louvain, LXXI, août 1973,
       539-574.

       Bousoño, Carlos. see 3050.

3341   Brisbois, Edmond. "Le sartrisme et le problème moral." Revue
       Philosophique de Louvain, Tome XLVIII, 3e série, 1952, 30-
       48; Ibid., 124-145.

3342   Bruch, Jean-Louis. "Perspectives morales de la philosophie
       existentielle." La Revue du Caire, 17e année, No. 172, sep-
       tembre 1954, 99-103.

3343   Brufau-Prats, Jaime. Moral, vida social y derecho en Jean-
       Paul Sartre. Salamanca, Universidad, 1967.

3344   Bukala, C.R. "Sartrean Ethics: An Introduction." The New
       Scholasticism, XLI, Fall 1967, 450-464.

3345   Coates, J.B. "Existentialist Ethics." Fornightly, CLXXXI,
        mai 1954, 338-344.

3346   Colombel, Jeannette. "Y a-t-il une morale marxiste?" La Nou-
        velle Critique. No. 160, novembre 1964, 22-54.

3347   De Brie, G.A. "Ontologie en ethiek bij Sartre." Tijdschrift
        voor Filosofie, XXIV, 1962, 180-188.

3348   De Gonzalez, Judith Botti. "Etapas en la evolución del pen-
        samiento de Sartre desde el punto de vista ético." Sapien-
        ta, XXII, 1967, 41-59.

        Derisi, Octavio. see 2707.

3349   DiGona, Goriano. "Sartre, il moralista senza morale." Hu-
        manitas, V, No. 3, March 1950, 244-246.

3350   Flam, Leopold. De krisis van de burgerlijke moraal: Van Kier-
        kegaard tot Sartre. Antwerpen: Uitgeverij Ontwikkeling,
        1956.

3351   Foulk, Gary J. "Plantinga's Criticism of Sartre's Ethics."
        Ethics, LXXXII, July 1972, 330-333.

3352   Frutos, Eugenio. El humanismo y la moral de Sartre. Sara-
        gossa, 1949.

        Fu, Charles. see 303.

3353   Gambra, Rafael. "Possibilidades éticas en el existencialis-
        mo." Revista de Filosofía, XI, No. 42, 1952, 401-442.

3354   Garaudy, Roger. "Bourgeois Morality and Communist Morality."
        Marxism Today, III, No. 8, August 1959, 243-246.

3355   Garaudy, Roger. "Problèmes moraux dans la philosophie fran-
        çaise contemporaine." Voprosy Filosofi, XIV, No. 10, 1960,
        64-77.

3356   Greene, Norman N. Jean-Paul Sartre: The Existentialist Eth-
        ic. Ann Arbor: Univ. of Michigan Pr., 1960; London: Cres-
        set Pr., 1961.

3357   Hellerich, G. "What is Often Overlooked in Existentialist-
        Ethics." Journal of Thought, V, January 1970, 46-54.

3358 Jaroszewski, T.W. "La philosophie de l'existence et l'éthique de la situation chez Sartre." Etyka. Marek Fritzhand, ed., VII, Warsaw: Panstwowe Wydawnictwo Naukowe, 1970.

3359 Jeanson, Francis. Le problème moral et la pensée de Sartre, 2e éd. Paris: Editions du Seuil, 1947. Avec un nouveau chapitre: "Un quidam nommé Sartre," 1965.

Jones, William R. see 320.

3360 Kolnai, Aurel, "Existence and Ethics, II." The Aristotelian Society, Supplementary XXXVII, 1963, Harrison and Sons, 1963, 27-50.

3361 Las Vergnas, Raymond. "La morale de l'écrivain." Hommes et Mondes. No. 6, January 1947, 123-131.

3362 Luisi, Giuseppe M. "Etica, ontologia, anthropologia." Giornale Critico della Filosofia Italiana, XXIII, October-December 1969, 561-582.

3363 Macgregor, Joaquin. "Hay una moral existencialista?" Filosofía y Letras, April-June 1948, 267-278.

3364 MacIntyre, Alasdair C. "Modern Moral Philosophy." A Short History of Ethics. London: Routledge and Kegan Paul, 1966, 249-269.

3365 MacNiven, D.C. "Analytic and Existential Ethics." Dialogue, IX, No. 1, June 1970, 1-19.

3366 Macrae, D.G. "Private and Public Morality in Sartre's Existentialism." Ideology and Society. New York: Free Pr., 1961, 198-207.

3367 Madinier, Gabriel. La Conscience morale, 5e éd. Paris: Presses Universitaires de France, 1966.

3368 Maritain, Jacques. "L'existentialisme sartrien." La Philosophie morale: Examen historique et critique des grands systèmes. Paris: Gallimard, 1960, 460-489.

3369 Manno, Ambrogio. "La morale di Jean-Paul Sartre." Studi Francescani, 1961, 252-268.

3370 Manser, A.R. "Existence and Ethics." The Aristotelian Society. Supplementary XXXVII, 1963. London: Harrison and Sons, 1963.

3371   Olafson, Frederick A. Principles and Persons: An Ethical In-
       terpretation of Existentialism. Baltimore: Johns Hopkins
       Pr., 1967.

3372   Pilkington, A.E. "Sartre's Existentialist Ethics." French
       Studies, XXIII, No. 1, January 1969, 38-48.

3373   Plantinga, Alvin. "An Existentialist's Ethics." Review of
       Metaphysics, XII, December 1958, 235-258.

3374   Portman, Stephen G. "Existential Ethics and Being as Value."
       Dialogue, XIV, October 1971, 11-15.

3375   Rau, Catherine. "The Ethical Theory of Sartre." Journal of
       Philosophy, XLVI, August 1949, 536-545.

3376   Rees, D.A. "Philosophical Surveys, IV: A Survey of Literature
       on Ethics and the History of Ethics, 1945-1950; Part 2: Eth-
       ics." Philosophical Quarterly, II, No. 6, January 1952,
       71-81.

3377   Rtischsaew, W.I. "Einige Aspekten der buergerlichen Kritik an
       der existenzialischen Ethik." Sowiet Gesselschaftswissen-
       schaftliche Beitraege, IX, 1969, 953-961.

3378   Schrag, Calvin O. "The Structure of Moral Experience: A Phe-
       nomenological and Existential Analysis." Ethics, LXXIII,
       July 1963, 255-265.

3379   Schwartzmann, K.A. "Apologiia individualizma von Ekziztent-
       siaslissk etike." Voprosy Filosofi, XIII, No. 10, 1950, 20-
       30.

3380   Shapiro, Gary. "Choice and Universality in Sartre's Ethics."
       Man and World, VII, No. 1, February 1974, 20-35.

3381   Teo, Wesley K.H. "Self-Responsibility in Existentialism and
       Buddism." International Journal of Religion, IV, Summer
       1973, 80-91.

3382   Verstraeten, Pierre. "Grâce et destin: Esquisse d'une morale
       dialectique à travers le théâtre de Sartre." Morale Enseig-
       nante, XVI, No. 62-63, 1967, 38-119.

3383   Verstraeten, Pierre. Violence et éthique: Esquisse d'une
       critique de la morale dialectique à partir du théâtre poli-
       tique de Sartre. (Les Essais, 165). Paris: Gallimard,
       1972.

3384   Verstraeten, Pierre.   "Violence et morale: Esquisse d'une
       morale dialectique à travers le théâtre de Sartre." Morale
       Enseignante, IX, No. 35, 1960, 1-43; Ibid., X, No. 37-38,
       1961, 1-35.

       Virasoro, Rafael. see 2722.

3385   Warnock, Mary. Ethics Since 1900. London: Oxford Univ. Pr.,
       1960, 162-199.

3386   Warnock Mary. "Jean-Paul Sartre." Existentialist Ethics.
       London: Macmillan; New York: St. Martin's, 1967, 18-52.

3387   Warnock, Mary. "The Moral Philosophy of Sartre." The Listen-
       er, LXI, No. 1554, 8 January 1959, 64-65; Ibid., No. 1555,
       15 January 1959, 105-106, 146.

EUROPE

3388   Domenach, Jean-Marie. "Sartre et l'Europe." Esprit, XXXI,
       No. 3, 1962, 454-463; Ibid., No. 4, 1962, 634-645.

3389   Rougemont, Denis de. "Sartre contre l'Europe." Arts. No.
       852, 17-22 janvier 1962, 1,4.

EVIL

       Bonilla, Luis. see 3307.

3390   Champigny, Robert. "Sartre on Good and Evil: Translations and
       Comments on Saint Genet, commedien et martyr." Journal of
       Philosophy, LIV, 23 May 1957, 314-335.

       Dreyfus, Dina. see 2134.

3391   Faleni, Cornelio. "Sartre e la giustificazione del male."
       Idea, IV, No. 47, 24 November 1952, 2.

3392   Gaillard, Pol. Le Mal de Blaise Pascal à Boris Vian. Paris:
       Bordas, 1971.

3393   Hannedouche, S. "Le problème du mal chez quelques écrivains
       contemporains." Cahiers d'Etudes Cathares. No. 30, Summer
       1957, 67-74.

3394   Jackson, Christopher. "The Dark Passages: A Study in the
       Knowledge of Evil in Twentieth Century Literature." The
       Adelphi, XXIII, No. 1, October-December 1946, 29-35.

Nordstrom, Louis D.   see 358.

Struyker Boudier, C.E.M.   see 2825.

EVOLUTION

Carp, E.A.D.E.   see 230.

EXISTENCE and ESSENCE

3395   Atwell, John E.   "Existence Precedes Essence."   Man and World,
       II, November 1969, 580-591.

3396   Bertrand, R.   "Notes sur l'essence et l'existence."   Revue de
       Métaphysique et de Morale, LI, 1946, 193-199.

3397   Corvez, Maurice.   "Existence et essence."   Revue Thomiste, LI,
       No. 2, 1951, 305-330.

3398   Ecole, Jean.   "Essence et existence chez Sartre."   Les Etudes
       Philosophiques, VI, No. 2-3, 1951, 161-174.

3399   Fabre, Lucien.   "Essentialisme et existentialisme."   Revue de
       Paris, LIV, No. 4, April 1947, 91-112.

3400   Forest, Aime.   "L'essence et l'existence."   Témoignages.
       Paris: Cahiers de la Pierre-qui-vit, 1947, 212-225.

3401   Lavelle, Louis.   "Dissociation de l'essence et de l'existence."
       Revue de Métaphysique et de Morale, LII, 1947, 201-227.

Smith, Colin.   see 2876.

EXISTENTIAL

see Psychology, Psychiatry, Psychotherapy, Psychopathology

EXISTENTIALISM

STUDIES IN ENGLISH

3402   Alexander, Ian W.   "Sartre and Existentialist Philosophy."
       Cambridge Journal, 19 September 1947, 721-738.

3403   Angrand, Cécile.   "Existentialism: An Anti-Democratic Philos-
       ophy."   Modern Quarterly, III, Summer 1947, 357-365.

3404   Ayer, A.J.   "Reflexions on Existentialism."   Modern Languages,
       XLVIII, March 1967, 1-12.

3405   Ayer, A.J. "Some Aspects of Existentialism." The Rationalist Annual for the Year 1948. London: Watts, 1948.

3406   Bailey, Roland. What is Existentialism? The Creed of Commitment and Action. London: S.P.C.K., 1950.

3407   Barrett, William. What is Existentialism? New York: Partisan Review, 1947.

3408   Benda, Clemens E. "Existentialism in Philosophy and Science." Journal of Existential Psychiatry, I, 1960, 284-314.

        Bettler, Alan R. see 259.

3409   Bhattacharya, B.K. "Existentialism: A Modern Craze." Calcutta Review.

3410   Braun, Sidney D. "Existentialism in the Classroom." Modern Language Journal, XXXIX, No. 7, November 1955, 348-350.

3411   Bigelow, Gordon E. "A Primer of Existentialism." College English, XXII, December 1961, 171-178.

3412   Brome, Vincent. "Existentialism: A New Philosophy-Or Is It Only a Word?" Picture Post (London), XXXVI, No. 5, 2 August 1947, 4,31. Cf. Les Ecrits de Sartre, 168-169.

3413   Brown, M. Jr. "The Atheistic Existentialism of Sartre." Philosophic Review, LVII, No. 2, March 1948, 158-166.

3414   Bruch, Jean-Louis. "Sartre's Existentialism." Thought (Delhi), IX, No. 22, 1 June 1957, 16-17.

3415   Buchler, Justus. "Concerning Existentialism." The Nation, CLXV, October 1947, 449-450.

3416   Burgelin, Pierre. "Existentialism and the Tradition of French Thought." Yale French Studies. No. 16, Winter 1955-1956, 103-105.

3417   Collins, James. "Annual Review of Philosophy." Cross Currents, XIII, No. 2, 1963, 187-215.

3418   Collins, James. "The Appeal of Existentialism." The Commonweal, LXI, 6 October 1954, 7-9.

3419   Collins, James. "Existential Thinking: A Bibliography." Thought, XXVI, March 1951, 154-158.

3420   Copleston, Frederick C. "Concerning Existentialism." The
        Month, January 1949, 46-54.

3421   Copleston, Frederick C. "From Kierkegaard to Sartre." The
        Month, February 1951, 123-135.

3422   Copleston, Frederick C. "Existentialism." Philosophy, XXIII,
        No. 84, January 1947, 19-37.

3423   Copleston, Frederick C. "Existentialism and Religion." Dub-
        lin Review, No. 440, Spring 1947, 45-63.

3424   Copleston, Frederick C. "The Philsophy of the Absurd." The
        Month, CLXIII, No. 957, March 1947, 157-164.

3425   Copleston, Frederick C. "What is Existentialism?" Month,
        CLXXXIII, January 1947, 13-21.

3426   Cruickshank, John. "Existentialism After Twelve Years-An
        Evaluation." Dublin Review, CCXXXI, Summer 1957, 52-65.

3427   De Ruggiero, C. Existentialism. Rayner Heppenstall, ed.
        Trans. into English by M. Cocks. London, 1946.

3428   De Soto, Anthony E. "The Challenge of Existentialism-A Cri-
        tical Analysis." Journal of Thought, V, April 1970, 72-79.

3429   Dieckmann, Herbert. "French Existentialism Before Sartre."
        Yale French Studies, I, No. 1, 1948, 33-41.

3430   Douglas, Kenneth N. "A Critical Bibliography of Existential-
        ism." Yale French Studies, 1950. New York: Krauss Reprint,
        1966. Concerning the Paris School of Existentialism.

3431   Dru, A. "What Existentialism Is: The Error of Sartre and Mou-
        nier." The Tablet, LXXVIII, 2 November 1946, 225-226.

3432   Dufrenne, Mikel. "Existentialism and Existentialisms." Phi-
        losophy and Phenomenological Research, XXVI, No. 1, Septem-
        ber 1965, 51-62.

3433   Dutt, K.G. Existentialism and Indian Thought. New York: Phi-
        losophical Library, 1960.

3434   Estall, H.M. "Existentialism as a Philosophy." University of
        Toronto Quarterly, XXIX, April 1948, 297-309.

3435   Evans, Oliver. "The Rise of Existentialism." South Atlantic
        Quarterly, XLVII, No. 2, April 1962, 152-156.

3436   Ferre, Frederick. "Existentialism and Persuasion." Philo-
       sophical Quarterly, XII, No. 47, April 1962, 153-161.

3437   Friedmann, Maurice. The Worlds of Existentialism: A Critical
       Reader. New York: Random House, 1964.

3438   Gabriel, Leo. "Was ist Existenzphilosophie?" Wissenschaft
       und Weltbild, 3. Jahrg., Heft 10, December 1950, 441-449.

3439   Georgiades, Niki. "What is Existentialism?" World Review,
       October 1945, 14-19.

3440   Gibson, A. Boyce. "Existentialism: An Interim Report." Mean-
       jin Quarterly, VII, No. 1, Autumn 1948, 41-52.

3441   Gilson, Etienne. "Philosophical Movements in France." The
       Listener, XXXVII, 6 February 1947, 251-252.

3442   Glicksberg, Charles I. "Existentialism and the Tragic Vi-
       sion." The Tragic Vision in Twentieth Century Literature.
       Carbondale: Southern Illinois Univ. Pr., 1963.

3443   Glicksberg, Charles I. "Literary Existentialism." Arizona
       Quarterly, IX, No. 1, Spring 1953, 24-39.

3444   Gregory, J.C. "Sartre's Existentialism." Contemporary Re-
       view, CLXXVI, September 1949, 163-168.

3445   Guicharnaud, Jacques. "Those Years: Existentialism 1943-
       1945." Yale French Studies. No. 16, Winter 1955-1956. Re-
       printed Sartre: A Collection of Critical Essays. Edith
       Kern, ed. Englewood Cliffs, New Jersey: Prentice-Hall,
       1962.

3446   Hardré, Jacques. "The Existentialism of Sartre." Carolina
       Quarterly, I, No. 2, March 1949, 49-55.

3447   Hassan, Ihab. "Interlude: From Existentialism to Alitera-
       ture." The Dismemberment of Orpheus: Toward a Postmodern
       Literature. New York: Oxford Univ. Pr., 1971.

3448   Heinemann, F.H. Existentialism and the Modern Predicament.
       New York: Harper, 1958.

3449   Heinemann, F.H. "What is Alive and What is Dead in Existen-
       tialism." Revue Internationale de Philosophie, III, No.
       9, 15 July 1949.

       Hoffmann, K.   see 315.

3450 Hyppolite, Jean. "A Chronology of French Existentialism."
      Yale French Studies. No. 16, Winter 1955-1956, 100-102.

3451 Kaplan, Abraham. "Existentialism." The New World of Philos-
      ophy. New York: Vintage, 1963, 97-128.

3452 Kappler, Frank. "Sartre and Existentialism." Life, LVII, No.
      19, 6 November 1964, 86-96.

3453 Kaufmann, Walter. Existentialism from Dostoevsky to Sartre.
      New York: Meridian, 1956, 11-51.

3454 Kecskemeti, Paul. "Existentialism: A New Trend in Philoso-
      phy." Modern Review, I, No. 1, March 1947, 34-51. Reprint-
      ed New Directions, X, 1949, 290-318.

3455 Kingston, F. Temple. "An Introduction to Existentialist
      Thought." Dalhousie Review, XL, No. 2, Summer 1960, 181-
      188.

3456 Kingston, F. Temple. French Existentialism: A Christian Cri-
      tique. Toronto: Univ. of Toronto Pr., 1961, 207-216.

3457 Kuhn, Helmut. Encounter With Nothingness: An Essay on Exis-
      tentialism. Chicago: Henry Regnery, 1949.

3458 Kuhn, Helmut. "Existentialism." A History of Philosophical
      Systems. Vergilius Ferm, ed. New York: Philosophical Li-
      brary; Ames, Iowa: Littlefield Adams, 1958.

3459 Kuhn, Helmut. "Existentialism: Christian Versus Antichris-
      tian." Theology Today, VI, October 1949, 311-323.

3460 Langan, Thomas. "Existentialism and Phenomenology in France."
      Recent Philosophy, Hegel to the Present. E. Gilson et al.,
      eds. New York: Random House, 1964, 374-408.

3461 Löwith, Karl. "Jean-Paul Sartre: Existentialism." Sociology
      and Social Research, XVI, 1949, 122-124.

3462 Loyens, W. "Existentialism: A Bibliography on Sartre."
      Modern Schoolman, XXXI, 1953, 29-33.

3463 Macgregor, G. "Sartre and Existentialism." Modern Church-
      man, March 1948, 33-44.

3464 MacIntyre, Alasdair C. "Existentialism." Sartre: A Collec-
      tion of Critical Essays. Mary Warnock, ed. Garden City,
      New York: Doubleday, 1971, 1-58.

3465 Mansfield, Lester. "Existentialism: A Philosophy of Hope and
      Despair." Rice Institute Pamphlet, XLI, No. 3, October
      1954, 1-25.

3466 Marcel, Gabriel. The Philosophy of Existentialism. Trans.
      from the French by Manya Harari. New York: Citadel Pr.,
      1961.

3467 Maritain, Jacques. "From Existential Existentialism to Aca-
      demic Existentialism." Sewanee Review, LXVI, No. 2, 1948,
      210-229.

3468 McEachran, F. "The Existential Philosophy." Hibbert Journal,
      XLVI, April 1948, 232-238.

3469 Merleau-Ponty, Maurice. "The Battle Over Existentialism."
      Sense and Non-Sense. Trans. from the French by H.L. Dre-
      fus. Evanston, Illinois: Northwestern Univ. Pr., 1964.

3470 Michalson, Carl. "Existentialism is a Mysticism." Theology
      Today, XII, No. 3, October 1955, 353-368.

3471 Mihalich, Joseph. Existentialism and Thomism. New York: Phi-
      losophical Library, 1960.

3472 Molina, Fernando. Existentialism as a Philosophy. Englewood
      Cliffs, New Jersey: Prentice-Hall, 1962.

3473 Newman, Fred. "The Origins of Sartre's Existentialism."
      Ethics, LXXVI, No. 3, April 1966, 178-191.

3474 Olafson, Frederick A. "Jean-Paul Sartre." The Encyclopedia
      of Philosophy, Vol. 7. Paul Edwards, ed. New York: Mac-
      millan, 1967, 287-293.

3475 Olson, Robert C. An Introduction to Existentialism. New
      York: Dover; London: Constable, 1962.

3476 O'Mara, Joseph. "The Meaning and Value of Existentialism."
      Studies (Dublin), XL, No. 147, March 1951, 11-22.

3477 Passmore, J.A. "Existentialism and Phenomenology." A Hun-
      dred Years of Philosophy, 2nd revised ed. New York: Basis,
      1966.

3478 Patka, Frederick, ed. Existential Thinkers and Thought. New
      York: Philosophical Library, 1962.

3479 Peyre, Henri. "Existentialism-A Literature of Despair?" Yale
      French Studies. No. 1, Spring-Summer 1948, 21-32.

3480 Prosch, Harry. "Analytical Philosophy and Existentialism."
      The Genesis of Twentieth Century Philosophy. New York:
      Doubleday, 1964.

3481 Pucciani, Oreste F. "Existentialism." Modern Language Forum,
      XXXV, No. 1-2, March-June 1950, 1-13.

3482 Rheinhardt, Kurt F. Existentialist Revolt: The Main Themes
      and Phrases of Existentialism, 2nd revised ed. New York:
      Ungar, 1960.

3483 Rhoades, Donald H. "Essential Varieties of Existentialism."
      The Personalist, XXXV, No. 1, January 1954, 32-40.

3484 Rintelen, Fritz J. von. Beyond Existentialism. Trans. from
      the German by Hilda Graef. London: Allen and Unwin, 1961.

3485 Roberts, D.E. "Jean-Paul Sartre." Existentialism and Relig-
      ous Belief. New York: Oxford Univ. Pr., 1956, 193-226.

3486 Roubiczek, Paul F. "Some Aspects of French and German Exis-
      tentialism." Existentialism For and Against. Cambridge:
      Cambridge Univ. Pr., 1964, 117-134.

3487 Schact, Richard. "On 'Existentialism', Existenz-Philosophy
      and Philosophical Anthropology." American Philosophical
      Quarterly, XI, No. 4, October 1974.

3488 Schmidt, Paul F. "The Real Basis of Existentialism." Hibbert
      Journal, LXIII, No. 248, Autumn 1964, 12-15.

3489 Sellars, Roy W. "Existentialism, Realistic Empiricism and
      Materialism." Philosophy and Phenomenological Research,
      XXV, No. 3, March 1965, 315-332.

3490 Shrivastava, S.J.L. "Existentialism." The Aryan Path, XXXI,
      No. 7, July 1960, 306-312.

3491 Sinari, Ramakant. Reason in Existentialism. New York: Human-
      ities Pr., 1968.

3492 Smith, Vincent E. "The Existentialism of Sartre." Catholic
      Mind, XLV, April 1947, 202-207.

3493   Solomon, Robert C.   "Sartre and French Existentialism."   From
       Rationalism to Existentialism: The Existentialists and Their
       Nineteenth Century Background.   New York: Harper and Row,
       1972.

3494   Somit, A.   "Sartre's Existentialism as a Political Theory."
       Social Science, XXV, January 1950, 40-47.

3495   Srinivasan, G.   "Some Aspects of Existentialism."   The Aryan
       Path, XXVII, No. 10, October 1956, 457-463.

3496   Stern, Alfred.   "Sartre and French Existentialism."   The Per-
       sonalist, XXIX, No. 1, January 1949, 17-31.

3497   Stern, Alfred.   "What is Existentialism?"   Pacific Spectator,
       IV, No. 4, Autumn 1950, 388-403.

3498   Stockwell, H.C.R.   "Sartre's Existentialist Philosophy."
       Cambridge Journal, VI, No. 12, September 1953, 753-760.

3499   Straelen, Van H.   Man the Lonely: Preface to Existentialism.
       London, 1952.

3500   Thomson, J.S.   "The Existential Philosophy."   Philosophy To-
       day, II, 1958, 93-106.

3501   Titus, Harold H.   "Existentialism and Related Movements."
       Living Issues in Philosophy.   New York: American, 1964.

3502   Titus, Harold H.   "What is Existentialism?"   The Range of Phi-
       losophy.   New York: American, 1964.

3503   Troisfontaines, Roger.   "What is Existentialism?"   Thought,
       XXXII, No. 127, Winter 1957-1958, 516-532.

3504   Tulloch, D.M.   "Sartrean Existentialism."   Philosophical Quar-
       terly, II, No. 6, January 1952, 31-53.

3505   Unger, Eric.   "Existentialism."   Nineteenth Century and After,
       CXLII, No. 850, December 1947, 278-288; Ibid., No. 851, Jan-
       uary 1948, 28-38.

3506   Ussher, Arland.   "The Existentialism of Sartre."   Dublin Re-
       view, XXI, No. 2, April-June 1946, 32-35.

3507   Ussher, Arland.   Postscript on Existentialism and Other
       Essays.   Dublin: Sandymount Pr.; London: Williams and Nor-
       gate, 1946.

3508   Ussher, Arland. "Sartre's Existentialism." Dublin Magazine,
       October-December 1954, 5-13; Ibid., January-March 1955, 18-
       20.

3509   Vial, Fernand. "Existentialism in France." American Society
       Legion of Honor Magazine, XIX, No. 1, Spring 1948, 33-52.

3510   Wahl, Jean. "Existentialism: A Preface." New Republic,
       CXIII, 1 October 1945, 442-444.

3511   Wahl, Jean. A Short History of Existentialism. New York:
       Philosophical Library, 1949.

3512   Warnock, Mary. "Jean-Paul Sartre, I and II." Existentialism.
       London: Oxford Univ. Pr., 1970, 92-130.

3513   Weil, Eric. "French Philosophy Today." The Listener, XLVII,
       1 May 1952, 710-711.

3514   Weil, Eric. "The Strength and Weakness of Existentialism."
       The Listener, XLVII, 8 May 1952, 473-477.

3515   White, Morton G. "Existentialism: Jean-Paul Sartre." The Age
       of Analysis: Twentieth Century Philosophy. Boston: Houghton
       Mifflin, 1955.

3516   Wild, John. The Challenge of Existentialism. Bloomington:
       Indiana Univ. Pr., 1955.

3517   Wild, John. "Existentialism: A New View of Man." University
       of Toronto Quarterly, XXVII, October 1957, 79-95.

3518   Wild, John. "Existentialism as a Philosophy." Journal of
       Philosophy, LVII, January 1960, 45-62.

3519   Wilson, Colin. Introduction Into the New Existentialism.
       London: Hutchinson, 1966.

3520   Wilson, Colin. The Outsider. London: Gollancz; Boston:
       Houghton Mifflin, 1956.

3521   Yanitelli, Victor R. "A Bibliographical Introduction to Exis-
       tentialism." Modern Schoolman, XXVI, May 1949, 345-363.

3522   Yanitelli, Victor R. "Types of Existentialism." Thought,
       XXIV, September 1949, 495-508.

STUDIES IN FRENCH

3523   Alexander, Ian W. "La philosophie existentialiste en France:
Ses sources et ses problèmes fondamentaux." French Studies,
I, No. 2, Spring 1947, 95-114.

3524   Audry, Colette, et al. Pour ou contre l'existentialisme:
Grand débat. Paris: Atlas, 1948.

3525   Aury, Dominique. "Qu'est-ce que l'existentialisme? Bilan
d'une offensive." Les Lettres Françaises. No. 83, 24 novembre 1945; Ibid, No. 84, 1 décembre 1945.

3526   Bataille, Georges. "De l'existentialisme au primat de l'éco-
nomie." Critique, III, 1948, 127-143.

3527   Beaufret, Jean. "A propos de l'existentialisme." Confluences, I, No. 2, mars 1945, 193-199; Ibid, No. 3, avril 1945,
307-314; Ibid, No. 4, mai 1945, 415-422; Ibid, No. 5, juin-
juillet 1945, 531-538; Ibid, No. 6, août 1945, 637-642;
Ibid, No. 7, septembre 1945, 764-771.

3528   Berdiaeff, Nicolai. "Sartre et le déclin de l'existentialisme." Au Seuil de la nouvelle époque. Neuchâtel: Delachaux
et Niestlé, 1947, 129-140.

3529   Benda, Julien. "L'existentialisme? C'est la forme moderne
d'une position philosophique éternelle." Pour ou contre
l'existentialisme: Grand débat. Paris: Atlas, 1948, 107-
126.

3530   Benda, Julien. Tradition de l'existentialisme ou les philosophes de la vie. Paris: Téqui, 1947.

3531   Bénèze, G, et Cuénot, Claude. Qu'est-ce que l'existentialisme? Paris: 1947.

3532   Blondel, Maurice. "L'existentialiste est-il un philosophe vé-
ritable?" Atti del Congresso Internationale di Filosofia à
Rome, 15-20 novembre 1946. Vol. 2: L'Esistenzialismo.
Castelli, ed. Milano, 1948, 95-100.

3533   Bordry, Paul. "Existentialisme: Drôle de mot." Poetry, LXIX,
No. 3, December 1946, 152-158.

3534   Bourbousson, Edouard. "La littérature existentialiste et son
influence." French Review, XXIII, No. 6, May 1950, 36-48.

3535   Brisbois, Edmond. "Qu'est-ce que l'existentialisme?" Revue
       Philosophique de Louvain, Tome XLVIII, 3e série, No. 18,
       mai 1950, 185-218.

3536   Chastaing, Marc. "Existentialisme et imposture." La Vie In-
       tellectuelle, XX, novembre 1952, 57-68.

3537   Croteau, Jacques. "Introduction à l'existentialisme." Revue
       de l'Université d'Ottawa. XXII, 1952, 90-110.

3538   Cuviller, André. "Les courants irrationalistes dans la phi-
       losophie contemporaine." Cahiers Rationalistes. No. 95,
       mars-avril 1947.

3539   Cuvillier, André. "A propos de l'existentialisme." Les Nou-
       velles Littéraires, 31 mai 1946, 11.

3540   Daniel, R. "Courrier français." Cahiers du Témoignage Chré-
       tien, 12 octobre 1945, 7.

3541   Daniélou, Jean. Dialogue avec les existentialistes. Paris:
       Le Portulan, 1948.

3542   Duché, Jean. "A la recherche de l'existentialisme: Sartre
       s'explique." Le Littéraire, 13 avril 1946. Reimprimé "As-
       sumer pleinement sa condition d'homme." Liberté européenne.
       Paris: Flammarion, 1949, 133-140. Cf. Les Ecrits de Sar-
       tre, 146-147.

3543   Dufrenne, Mikel. "Existentialisme et sociologie." Cahiers
       Internationaux de Sociologie, I, 1946, 161-171.

3544   Eubé, Charles. "Le pour et le contre de l'existentialisme."
       Poésie 46. No. 31, mars 1946, 79-84.

3545   "L'existentialisme devant l'opinion philosophique." Revue
       Internationale de Philosophie, III, No. 9, juin 1949.

3546   Féraud, Henri. "Une philosophie de naufrage: L'existentialis-
       me." Cahiers du Sud, XXVI, No. 281, 1947, 96-103.

3547   Gak, G. "Un courant à la mode de la philosophie bourgeoise."
       Cahiers du Communisme, XXIV, No. 5, mai 1947, 380-397.

3548   Garaudy, Roger. "L'existentialisme athée: Jean-Paul Sartre,"
       et une lettre écrite par Sartre: "Marxisme et philosophie de
       l'existentialisme." Perspectives de l'homme: Existentialis-

me, pensée catholique, marxisme. 2e éd. revisée et cor-
igée. Paris: Presses Universitaires de France, 1960, 59-
113.

3549 Gérard, Jacques. "Origines et climat de l'existentialisme."
Revue des Langues Vivantes, XIV, No. 1, 1948, 6-13; Ibid,
No. 2, 72-81; Ibid, No. 4, 203-216; Ibid, No. 5, 260-280.

3550 Gérel, André. "De l'existentialisme à Saint-Germain-des-
Prés." Introduction à La Nausée. (Les grands romans de
notre temps). Paris: Culture, Art, Loisirs; Bibliothèque
de Culture Littéraire.

3551 Gignoux, Victor. La Philosophie existentielle. 2e éd.
Paris: Lefebvre, 1955.

3552 Jeanson, Francis. "L'oeuvre philosophique de Sartre." Bib-
lio, I, No. 5, mai-juin 1950.

3553 Jeanson, Francis. "Situation de l'existentialisme." La Gazette des Lettres, VII, No. 14, 15 novembre 1951, 31-36.

3554 Joussain, André. "La farce de l'existentialisme sartrien."
Ecrits de Paris. No. 213, mars 1963, 72-76.

3555 Lacroix, Jean. Marxisme, existentialisme, personalisme. 6e
éd. Paris: Presses Universitaires de France, 1966.

3556 Lacroix, Jean. "La philosophie de l'existence." Le Monde, 7
février 1946.

3557 LeBlond, Jean-Marie. "Qu'est-ce que l'existentialisme?"
Etudes, Tome CCXLVIII, février 1946, 336-350.

3558 Leclerc, Guy. "L'existentialisme est une mystification."
Lettres Françaises. No. 143, 1947, 4.

3559 Lefebvre, Henri. L'existentialisme. Paris: Sagittaire, 1956.

3560 Lefebvre, Luc J. "L'existentialisme est-il une philosophie?
Paris: Editions Alsatia, 1946.

3561 Lemarchand, Jacques. "L'existentialisme vu de la terrasse."
Rencontres. No. 1, 1946.

3562 LeMeur, L. "Un nouveau système philosophique: L'existentialisme de Sartre." Recherches et Travaux, I, No. 2, décembre
1946, 26-47; Ibid, No. 2, mai-août 1947, 68-76.

3563 Loranquin, Albert. "L'existentialisme en faillite." Bulletin des Lettres. No. 256, 15 mars 1964, 97-101.

3564 Merleau-Ponty, Maurice. "La philosophie de l'existence." Dialogue (Canada), V, No. 3, décembre 1966, 307-322.

3565 Merleau-Ponty, Maurice. "La querelle de l'existentialisme." Les Temps Modernes, I, No. 2, novembre 1945, 344-356. Reimprimé Sens et non-sens. Paris: Nagel, 1948, 123-144.

3566 Micha, Alexandre. "Origines littéraires de l'existentialisme." Cahiers du Sud, XXVI, No. 283, 1947, 469-474.

3567 Mortimer, Raymond. "Sartre et l'existentialisme." Revue de la Méditerranée, III, No. 12, 1946, 212-218.

3568 Mougin, Henri. "Courte histoire de l'existentialisme." La Pensée, No. 8, juillet-août 1946, 23-30; Ibid., No. 9, octobre-décembre 1946, 3-14; Ibid., No. 10, 32-43.

3569 Mougin, Henri. La sainte famille existentialiste. Paris: Editions Sociales, 1947.

3570 Mounier, Emmanuel. "L'existentialisme." Esprit, XIV, No. 121, avril 1946, 521-539; Ibid., No. 122, mai 1946, 744-767; Ibid., No. 123, juin 1946, 935-954; Ibid., No. 124, juillet 1946, 74-102; Ibid., No. 126, octobre 1946, 413-436. Reimprimé Introduction aux existentialismes. Paris: 1948.

3571 Mounier, Emmanuel. "De l'existentialisme à nos conditions d'existence." Esprit, XVI, No. 141, janvier 1948, 143-150.

3572 Mounier, Emmanuel. "Journal à plusieurs voix." Esprit, XVI, No. 143, mars 1948.

3573 Mounier, Emmanuel. "Perspectives existentialistes et perspectives chrétiennes." C. Audry, et al. Pour et contre l'existentialisme, grand débat. Paris: Atlas, 1948, 127-164.

3574 Mounin, Georges. "Position de l'existentialisme." Cahiers d'Action, mai 1946.

3575 Mouy, Paul. "L'existentialisme." Revue Synthèses, XXI, 1947, 123-125.

3576 Mueller, Fernand-Lucien. "La nouvelle philosophie de l'existence." Présence (Genève), V, No. 1, avril 1946, 20-42.

3577   Ouy, Achille.   "Déclin de l'existentialisme."   Mercure de
       France.   No. 1002, 1947, 359-363.

3578   Paillour, P.H.   Arthur Rimbaud, père de l'existentialisme.
       Paris: Perrin, 1947.

3579   Parain-Vial, Jeanne.   "L'existentialisme, philosophie du néant
       absolu."   La Table Ronde.   No. 182, mars 1963, 31-39.

3580   Pesch, E.   L'Existentialisme.   Paris: Editions Dynamo, 1948.

3581   Picard, G.   "L'existentialisme de Sartre."   Mélanges de Sci-
       ence Religieuses, III, 1946, 315-328.

3582   Plinval, George de.   "Les idées-pièges de l'existentialisme."
       Ecrits de Paris, septembre 1956, 57-73.

3583   Roenet, Louis.   "Existentialistes, marxistes et personalites."
       La Vie Intellectuelle, XIV, No. 6, juillet 1946, 143-151.

3584   Soustelle, Jacques.   "L'inexistentialisme de Sartre."   Carre-
       four, V, No. 218, 16 novembre 1948, 1, 3.

3585   Sylvestre, Guy.   "Qu'est-ce que l'existentialisme?"   La Nou-
       velle Relève, IV, No. 10, avril 1946, 891-902.

3586   Troisfontaines, Roger.   Existentialisme et pensée chrétienne.
       Paris: Vrin, 1946, 34-39.

3587   Waelhens, Alphonse de.   "Les constances de l'existentialisme."
       Revue Internationale de Philosophie, III, No. 9, 1949, 249-
       269.

3588   Waelhens, Alphonse de.   "Sartre."   Les Philosophes célèbres.
       Maurice Merleau-Ponty, ed.   Paris: Lucien Mazenod, 1956,
       344-350.

3589   Waelhens, Alphonse de.   "Sartre."   Les philosophes français
       d'aujourd'hui par eux-mêmes.   Textes recueillis et présentés
       par G. Deledalle et D. Huismans.   Paris: C.D.U., 1963.
       Autobiographie de la philosophie française contemporaine.

3590   Wahl, Jean.   Esquisse pour une histoire de l'existentialisme
       de Kierkegaard à Kafka, Heidegger à Sartre.   Paris: Editions
       de l'Arche, 1949.

3591   Wahl, Jean.   Petite histoire de l'existentialisme.   Paris:
       Edition du Club Maintenant, 1947.

3592   Wahl, Jean. Les philosophies de l'existence. Paris: Colin, 1954.

3593   Wahl, Jean. "La vogue de l'existence." Poésie, pensée, perception. Paris: Calmann Lévy, 1948, 170-178.

3594   Wahl, Jean. "La vogue de l'existentialisme." Labyrinthe (Genève), No. 17, 1946.

3595   Zeegers, Victor. "L'existentialisme de Kierkegaard à Sartre." Revue Générale Belge, XCV, No. 8, 1959, 1-18.

STUDIES IN OTHER LANGUAGES

3596   Belleza, A. "Bilancio del esistenzialismo in 1946 in Italia." L'Italia che Scrive. November 1946.

3597   Bense, Max. "Existentialismus und Marxismus." Neue Literarische Welt, III, No. 9, 1952, 2.

3598   Bollnow, Otto F. "Existentialismus." Die Sammlung, II, 1947, 654-666. Reprinted Französischer Existentialismus. Stuttgart: Kohlhammer, 1965, 11-22.

3599   Bollnow, Otto F. "Deutsche Existenzphilosophie und französischer Existentialismus." Zeitschrift für Philosophische Forschung, II, 1948, 231-242. Reprinted Französischer Existentialismus. Stuttgart, Kohlhammer, 1965, 23-38.

3600   Bruch, Jean-Louis. "Wo steht heute der Sartresche Existentialismus." Antares (Hamburg), V, No. 5, 1957, 48-49.

3601   Bubner, Rudiger. "Kritische Fragen zum Ende des französischen Existentialismus." Philosophische Rundschau, XIV, October 1967, 241-257.

3602   Caminero, Nemesio G. "Panorama existencialista." Pensamiento, XVI, 1948, 66-74.

3603   Castelli, Enrico, ed. L'Esistenzialismo. Roma, 1946.

3604   Champly, Henry. "Brochazos sobre el existencialismo sartriano." Revista Universidad de Buenos Aires. No. 8, 1948, 449-472.

3605   Chiodi, Pietro. L'Esistenzialismo. Torino: Loescher, 1957.
        Trans. into Spanish: El pensamiento existencialista. Ma-
        drid: Alianza, 1962.

        D'Alberti, Sarah. see 188.

3606   Delfgaauw, B.M.I. Existentiele verwondering. Amsterdam,
        1947.

3607   Delfgaauw, B.M.I. "Het existentialisme van Sartre." Studiën,
        1944, 63-68.

3608   Delfgaauw, B.M.I. Praeadviezen over het existentialisme. The
        Hague, 1947.

3609   Delfgaauw, B.M.I. What is Existentialisme? Door Bernard Del-
        fgaauw, 7 herz. druk; Baarn: Het Wereldvenster, 1969.

3610   Dresden, S. Existentialisme en literatuur beschouwing. Am-
        sterdam: Meidenhoff, 1946.

3611   Dunham, Barrows. "Eszistentializm." Voprosy Filosofi, XIV,
        No. 9, 1960, 63-80.

3612   Ell, Johannes. Der Existenzialismus in seinem Wesen und Wer-
        den. (Mensch und Welt, 6). Bonn: Bouvier, 1955.

3613   Fabro, Cornelio. Problemi dell'esistenzialismo. Roma, 1945.

3614   Fingal, Stefan. "Unfug des Existentialismus." Aufbau, IV,
        No. 11, 1948, 1014-1016.

3615   Fogeler, G. "Kritike ekzistentzialisskoi ontseptsii sushchet-
        vononaniia." Vestnik Moskovskogo Universiteta, XVII, No. 5,
        September-October 1962, 53-63.

3616   Fredericia, W. "Bestätigen Sartres Dramen und Romane sein
        existenzialistisches Denken?" Die Zeit, V, No. 17, 1950, 4.

3617   Gemmer, Anders. Sartre Ecksistentialism en kritisk Vurder-
        ing. Copenhagen: Munksgaard, 1947.

3618   Guerra, Ricardo. "Sartre, el existencialismo." Hombres y
        ideas de nuestro tiempo. Mexico: U.N.A.M., 1969.

3619   Holz, Hans Heinz. "Sartre." Der französische Existentialis-
        mus: Theorie und Aktualität. München: Speyer, 1958.

3620   Horst, G.   "Der Existentialismus bei Sartre." Neues Europa,
       II, No. 4, 1947, 32-36.

3621   Iturrioz, J.   "A los veinticinco años de existencialismo."
       Razón y Fé, L, Tome CXLII, July-December 1950, 230-250.

3622   Knittenmeyer, Heinrich. Die Philosophie der Existenz von der
       Renaissance bis zur Gegenwart. Wien: Humbolt, 1952, 366-
       400.

3623   Kohky, Dario Valcarcel. "Aún y todavia y siempre sobre el ex-
       istencialismo." Escorial, XX, No. 61, September 1949, 195-
       209.

3624   Kuiper, V.M.   "Aspectos del existencialismo." Revista de Fi-
       losolosofía, III, 1944.

3625   Lamana, Manuel.   "Jean-Paul Sartre: El existencialismo y la
       literatura." La Torre, VII, No. 27, July-September 1959,
       22-47.

3626   Larroyo, Francisco. El existencialismo, sus fuentes y direc-
       ciones. Mexico: Editorial Stylo, 1951.

3627   Lascaris-Commena, P.   "En torno al existencialismo." Nubis
       (Valencia), IX, 1948.

3628   Lenz, Joseph. Der moderne deutsche und französische Existen-
       tialismus. Trier: Paulinus, 1951. Trans. into Spanish:
       El moderno existencialismo alemán y francés. Madrid: Gre-
       dos, 1955.

3629   Lenz, Joseph.   "Sartres atheistischer Existentialismus." Tri-
       erer Theologische Zeitschrift, LIX, 1950, 73-80, 150-160,
       216-226.

3630   Leutis, Alexander.   "Die Philosophie auf allen vieren." Neue
       Welt (Berlin), II, No. 12, 1947, 57-72.

3631   Lindblom, Paul.   "Vem är existentialist?" Studiekamraten,
       XLVIII, 1966, 161-163.

3632   Lusset, F. Ch. Eube.   "Die Philosophie des Nichts: Für und
       wider den Existentialismus." Sonntag, III, No. 1, 1948, 2.

       Manno, Ambrogio. see 194.

3633   Muller, Max. Existenzphilosophie im geistigen Leben der Ge-
       genwart. Heidelberg, 1958.

3634 Muller-Schwefe, Hans R. Existenzphilosophie: Das Verständnis
      von Existenz in Philosophie und christlichen Glauben, Eine
      Begegnung. Zürich, 1961.

3635 Neto, Silveira. "Sartre und Existentialismus." Kriterion,
      XV, 1962, 703-705.

3636 Nore, Peter. "Mennesker uten sammenheng og Eksistensialis-
      men." Vinduet, IV, No. 3, 1950, 170-172.

3637 Paci, Enzo. Ancore sull'esistenzialismo. 2nd ed. revised and
      augmented. Firenze: C.C. Sansoni, 1950.

3639 Pedersen, Olaf. Van Kierkegaard tot Sartre. 3rd ed. Amster-
      dam: Het Wereldvenster, 1956.

3640 Perez-Señac, Ramón. "El existencialismo, filosofía de nuestro
      época." Revista Nacional (Montevideo), XVI, No. 175, July
      1953, 63-86.

3641 Pessis, B. "In der Kloake der Existentialisten." Deutsch-
      sprachige Sowjetliteratur (Moscow), No. 2, 1949, 170-174.

3642 Rajecki, Jan. "Sartre i egzystencjonalizw." Wiadomosci, II,
      No. 53-54, 13 Kwietnia 1947, 3.

3643 Redeker, Hans. Existentialisme: Een doortocht door philoso-
      phisch frontgebied. Amsterdam: De Bezige bij, 1956.

3644 Reding, Marcel. Die Existenzphilosophie. Düsseldorf: L.
      Schwann, 1949.

3645 Rintelen, Fritz J. von Philosophie der Endlichkeit. West-
      kulturverlag, Anton Hain, 1951.

      Roosli, Joseph. see 3030.

3646 Rozin, N.V. "Auf der Suche nach der humanistischen Philoso-
      phie; Zur Kritik von Sartres Existentialismus." Wissen-
      schaft Zeitschrift Friedrich-Schiller Universitat, Jena
      Geschicht uber Sprache R, XX, No. 6, 1971, 115-127.

3647 Sanchez, J.F. "Si y no a Sartre." Revista Dominicana de Fi-
      losofía, I, No. 4, 1958, 11-52.

3648 Sorensen, Ernst. "Sartre og ekistensialismen." Spektrum,
      III, No. 1, 1948, 38-52.

3649   Svitsov, V.I.   "Kritika Eksistentsialisskish."   Voprosy Filo-
       sofi, XVII, No. 1, 1963, 167-172.

3650   Tejada, Ricardo Guerra.   "Sartre, filosofo de la libertad."
       Filosofía y Letras, April 1948, 295-312.

3651   Thonnard, F.J.   "El existencialismo francés contemporáneo."
       Sapientia, No. 5, 1947, 238-247.

3652   Triolo, Carmela.   "Appunti sull'esistenzialismo."   Teorisi.
       No. 1-2, January-June 1958, 150-178.

3653   Van der Leuw, G.   Het Existentialisme.   Wending, 1947.

3654   Vandienst, Julien.   "Balans van het existentialisme."   Nieuw
       Vlaams Tijdschrift, XVII, No. 1, 1964, 79-108; No. 2, 208-
       235; No. 3, 305-330; No. 7, 675-698; No. 8-9, 813-837; No.
       10, 945-964; No. 11, 1081-1100.

3655   Vanni Rovighi, Sofia.   "Esistenzialismo o esistenzialisti?
       Panorama della filosofia dell'angoscia."   Vita e Pensiero,
       XXX, 1947, 203-208.

3656   Vedaldi, A.   Esistenzialismo.   Verona: M. Lecce, 1947.

3657   Vietta, Egon.   "Existentielles Philosophieren in Frankreich."
       Universitas, I, No. 7, October 1946, 909-910.

3658   Weier, Winfried.   "Die nihilistischen Wurzeln der Existenzphi-
       losophie."   Sophia (Italy), XLI, January-December 1973, 93-
       106.

3659   Weischedel, Wilhelm.   "Wessen und Grenzen der Existenzphiloso-
       phie."   Frankfurter Hefte, III, No. 8, August 1948, 726-
       735; No. 9, September 1948, 804-813.

FACTICITY

       Cottier, Georges.   see 469.

       Goldthorpe, Rhiannon.   see 437.

       Overholt, George E.   see 362.

FANTASY

       Maristany, J.   see 2481.

FAITH

Roberts, D.E.   see 2774.

FLESH

3660   Artinian, Robert W.   "The Flesh Degenerate: Imagery in Sartre." New Contemporary Literature. No. 3, 1971, 7-9.

FOR-ITSELF (see En-soi)

Bordreaux, Michael M.   see 265.

Moreland, John M.   see 2867.

O'Brien, Robert J.   see 359.

FETICHISM

3661   Ames, Van Meter.   "Fetichism in the Existentialism of Sartre." Journal of Philosophy, XLVII, 6 July 1950, 407-411. Concerning L'Etre et le néant.

3662   Ames, Van Meter.   "Reply to Mr. Natanson." Journal of Philosophy, XLVIII, 4 January 1951, 99-102.

3663   Natanson, Maurice.   "Sartre's Fetichism: A Reply to Van Meter Ames." Journal of Philosophy, XLVIII, February 1951, 95-99.

FREEDOM

3664   Albérès, René-Marill.   "Autenticidad y libertad en Jean-Paul Sartre." Sur. No. 162, April 1948, 86-101.

3665   Allen, E.L.   "Man and His Freedom." Existentialism from Within. London: Routledge and Kegan Paul; New York: Macmillan, 1953.

Anderson, Thomas C.   see 3226.

3666   Anonymous.   "L'esprit et la liberté." Le Nouvel Observateur. No. 204, 18-24 novembre 1968, 46.

3667   Astruc, Alexandre.   "Sartre, le théâtre et la liberté." Verger. No. 2, juin 1947, 13-16.

3668   Ayer, A.J.   "The Definition of Liberty: Sartre's Doctrine of
        Commitment." The Listener, XLIV, No. 1135, 30 November
        1950, 633-634.

        Baürle, Wilhelm. see 859.

3669   Bauzyte, G.   "Asmenybes laisves problema Sartre dramaturgijo-
        je." Literatura, X, 1967, 99-113.

3670   Bohme, Wolfgang. "Freiheit und Liebe: Bemerkungen zu Sartres
        Existential-Philosophie." Der Christliche Student. Tübin-
        gen, No. 15, 1949, 14, 21-22.

3671   Boisdeffre, Pierre de. "Sartre ou l'impossible liberté."
        Métamorphose de la littérature, Vol. 2. Paris: Alsatia,
        1950, 185-258.

        Boorsch, Jean. see 2594.

        Bowes, Pratina. see 3228.

        Bremen, Rudolph S. see 267.

        Brunner, August. see 1983.

        Bukala, C.R. see 787.

3672   Bull, R. "Freedom." Marxism Today, IV, No. 7, July 1960,
        220-222.

3673   Buonajuto, Maria. "Libertà e storia." Giornale Critica della
        Filosofia Italiana, XXIII, July-September 1969, 400-445.

        Burke, David R. see 272.

        Burkle, Howard R. see 2068, 2070.

3674   Cebik. L.B. "Freedom: An Existential Illusion." Georgia Re-
        view, XXV, No. 4, Winter 1971, 395-423.

3675   Champigny, Robert. "Position philosophique de la liberté."
        Revue de Métaphysique et de Morale, LXIII, janvier-mars
        1959, 225-235.

        Choisy, Maryse. see 3220.

3676   Collins, James. "Freedom as Atheistic Heroism." Giornale di
        Metafisica, 1949, 573-580.

3677   Cook, Gladys C. "Jean-Paul Sartre's Doctrine of Human Freedom
        and Responsibility." Bucknell Review, I, No. 2, June 1949,
        12-21.

        Cording, Richard A. see 279.

3678   Cristaldi, Mariano. "La libertà in pericolo e la psicanalisi
        transcendentale." Libertà e metafisica. Bologna: Casa Edi-
        trice Prof. Riccardo Patron, 1964, 61-88.

3679   Dalbiez, Roland. "Le moment de la liberté." Revue Thomiste,
        XLVIII, 1948, 180-190.

3680   Davenport, Manuel M. "A Critique of Sartre's Concept of Free-
        dom." Philosophy Today, XVII, Spring 1973, 22-27.

        Ecole, Jean. see 2780.

        Edmondson, P.E. see 293.

        Emonet, Pierre-Marie O.P. see 296.

3681   Emonet, Pierre-Marie O.P. "La notion de la liberté chez Jean-
        Paul Sartre." Nova et Vetera, XXVII, No. 3, juillet-septem-
        bre 1952, 168-184.

        Fautone, Vicente. see 207.

3682   Félix, Henri. "Une philosophie nouvelle de la liberté." Va-
        leurs. No. 6, juillet 1946, 78-88.

        Fisher, Karl. see 2597.

        Fisher, Rosemary F. 298.

        Forster, Kurt W. see 2947.

3683   Foueré, R.A. "Sur la conception sartrienne de la liberté."
        Revue Palladienne. No. 3, juin-juillet-août 1948, 81-86.

3684   Fox, Richard M. "The Concept of Freedom in Sartre's Philos-
        ophy of Man." Philosophy in Context, III, 1973, 56-70.

3685   Gahamanyi, Célestin. "La conception de la liberté chez Sartre
        et Merleau-Ponty." Thèse de Lettres, Université de Fri-
        bourg, 1967.

3686   Galkowski, J. "Le développement de la notion de liberté: Duns
        Scot, Kant, Sartre." Deus et homo ad mentem. I: Duns Scoti.

Acta Tertii Congressus Scotistici Internationalis, Vinde-
bonae, 29 septembre-2 octobre 1970. Romae: Societas Internationalis Scotistica, 1972.

3687 Gandara, Carmen R.L. de. "La otra libertad." Realidad, III,
No. 8, March-April 1948, 251-253.

Gandillac, Maurice de. see 2978.

3688 Greenlee, Douglas. "Sartre: Presuppositions of Freedom."
Philosophy Today, XII, Fall 1968, 176-183.

3689 Guerra Tejada, R. "Jean-Paul Sartre, filósofo de la libertad." Filosofía y Letras, XV, No. 30, 1948, 295-312.

3690 Guillet, Henri. "Sartre: une liberté sans chemins." Livres
et Lectures (Issy-Bruxelles), I, No. 104, 1956, 501-508.

Gullace, Giovanni. see 2598.

Haefner, Joseph. see 2575.

3691 Hana, Ghanem-George. Freiheit und Person: Eine Auseinandersetzung mit d. Darstellung Jean-Paul Sartres. München:
Beck, 1965.

Hanly, C.M.T. see 311.

3692 Hanly, C.M.T. "Phenomenology, Consciousness and Freedom."
Dialogue, V, No. 3, December 1966, 323-345.

3693 Havard, René. Les problèmes de la liberté. (Coll. Le monde
et la foi). Tournai: Desclée et Cie, 1957.

3694 Helstrom, K.L. "Sartre's Notion of Freedom." Southwestern
Journal of Philosophy, III, No. 3, Winter 1972, 111-120.

3695 Henrich, Dieter. "Sartres Versuch über die Freiheit." Das
Neue Forum, Darmstadt, X, 1960-1961, 113-119.

3696 Hyppolite, Jean. "La liberté chez Sartre." Mercure de
France, CCCXII, 1951, 396-413. Reimprimé Figures de la pen-
sée philosophique: Ecrits (1931-1968), Vol. 2. Paris:
Presses Universitaires de France, 1971, 759-779.

3697 Jeanson, Francis. "Das Thema der Freiheit in Sartres dramatischen Werk." Antares, II, No. 7, 1954, 67-75.

3698   Jolivet, Régis. "Liberdade e valor em Sartre." Revista Portuguesa de Filosofia, VI, 1950, 292-299.

3699   Jolivet, Régis. "Le problème de la liberté selon Jean-Paul Sartre." Humanitas (Tucuman), II, No. 4, 1954, 205-208.

Joubert, Ingrid. see 321, 585.

3700   Kahn, Ludwig W. "Freedom: An Existentialist and an Idealist View." Publications of Modern Language Association, LXIV, No. 1, March 1949, 5-14. Concerning Les Mouches.

3701   Kerlin, Michael. "Freedom and Identity." Philosophy Today, XVI, Summer 1972, 148-159.

3702   Killinger, John. "Existentialism and Human Freedom." English Journal, L, May 1961, 303-313.

King-Farlow, John and Coby, Arthur. see 2913.

3703   Kingston, F. Temple. "Freedom and Being Free." Anglican Theological Review, XXXVIII, No. 2, 1956, 153-160.

3704   Lauder, R. "Choose Freedom! Sartre and Search for Authenticity." New Catholic World, CCXVI, November 1973, 269-272.

3705   Leahy, Louis. "Réflexions sur la liberté." Dialogue, II, No. 1, June 1963, 42-57.

3706   Le Blond, Jean-Marie. "Histoire et liberté selon Sartre." Etudes, juillet-août, 1960, 62-76.

Lenoble, R. see 2600.

3707   Leon Tello, F.J. "Ibañez: Libertad y compromiso en Sartre." Revista de Ideas Estéticas, XIX, No. 75, 1961, 250-254.

Lessing, Arthur. see 335.

3708   Lewis, G. "La liberté d'indifférence ou l'acte gratuit." Travaux et Documents, IV, décembre 1945, 1-8.

Lochman, Jan M. see 2488.

Macleod, Norman. see 2100.

3709   Marcel, Gabriel. "Existence and Human Freedom." The Philos-
       ophy of Existence. London: Harvill Pr., 1948; New York:
       Philosophical Library, 1949.

3710   Marcel, Gabriel. "L'existentialisme et la liberté humaine
       chez Sartre." E. Georges, et al. Les grands appels de
       l'homme contemporain. Paris: Editions du Temps Présent,
       1946, 111-176.

3711   Marcel, Gabriel. "M. Sartre's Conception of Liberty."
       Thought, XXII, No. 84, March 1947, 15-18.

3712   Marin Ibañez, Ricardo. Libertad y compromiso en Sartre. Va-
       lencia, 1959. Disputación provincial de Valencia.

       McClusky, John Evans. see 344.

3713   McGill, J.V. "Sartre's Doctrine of Freedom." Revue Interna-
       tionale de Philosophie, III, 15 July 1949, 329-342.

3714   Mihalich, Joseph. "Some Aspects of Freedom in Sartre's Exis-
       tentialism." Four Quartets, VIII, January 1959, 10-25.

3715   Moliner, Fernando Mautero. "La interpretación dialectica de
       la libertad." Teorema, I, March 1971, 75-90.

3716   Mottier, G. Déterminisme et liberté. Neuchâtel: Editions de
       la Baconnière, 1948, Chapitre 8.

       Moyano, Pedro B. see 353.

3717   Natanson, Maurice. "Sartre's Philosophy of Freedom." Social
       Research, XIX, 1952, 364-380. Reprinted Literature, Philos-
       ophy and the Social Sciences. The Hague: Nijhoff, 1962.

3718   Naville, Pierre. Les conditions de la liberté. Paris: Sagit-
       taire, 1947.

       Neveux, Georges. see 1663.

3719   Nott, Kathleen. "Freedom From and For." Philosophy and Human
       Nature. London: Houder and Staughton, 1970, 100-126.

3720   Oisermann, T.I. "Determinismus und Freiheit." Deutsche Zeit-
       schrift für Philosophie. No. 12, 1971, 1460-1470.

       O'Neill, William F. see 361.

3721   Onimus, Jean.   "L'existentialisme et le piège de la liberté."
       Cahiers Universitaires Catholiques. No. 3-4, décembre 1965-
       janvier 1966, 106-128.

3722   Otto, Marie. Reue und Freiheit: Versuch über ihre Beziehung
       im Ausgang von Sartres Drama. (Symposium Philosophische
       Schriften, 6). Freiburg: Alber, 1961.

3723   Paseyro, R. "Una libertad sin compromiso: Acerca de Sartre."
       Indice. No. 191, 1964, 16-18.

3724   Patri, Aimé. "Remarques sur une nouvelle doctrine de la li-
       berté." Deucalion. No. 1, 1946, 75-92.

       Patri, Aimé. see 2604.

       Pètrement, Simone. see 2605.

3725   Picato Sotela, S. "Jean-Paul Sartre: una filosofía de la li-
       bertad." Revista de Filosofía de la Universidad de Costa
       Rica, July 1964-June 1965, 301-322.

3726   Pleydell-Pearce, A.G. "Freedom, Emotion and Choice in the
       Philosophy of Sartre." Journal of the British Society for
       Phenomenology, I, May 1970, 35-46.

3727   Potoacki, Charles. "Freedom à la Sartre." Annual Report,
       Duns Scotus Philosophical Association, XXIX, 1965, 128-159.

3728   Pouillon, Jean. "Une philosophie de la liberté." Colette
       Audrey, et al. Pour et contre l'existentialisme, grand
       débat. Paris: Editions Atlas, 1948.

       Prenter, R. see 2773.

       Ratanakum Pinit. see 374.

       Roberts, D.E. see 2774.

3729   Rose, H.H. "Freedom Without a Framework." Judaism, VII, Fall
       1958, 320-328.

       Salvan, Jacques L. see 2482.

       Saraiva, M.M. see 2848.

       Schaldenbrand, Mary Aloysius. see 2822, 2823.

Schmauch, Jochen. see 877.

3730   Schrag, Calvin O. Existence and Freedom: Towards an Ontology
       of Human Finitude. Evanston, Illinois: Northwestern Univ.
       Pr., 1961.

Shouery, Imad T. see 387.

Sigaux, Gilbert. see 2608.

Siguenza, José J. see 3108.

3731   Stack, George J. "Sartre: De la libertad abstracta a la con-
       creta, I-II." Folia Humanistica, XI, 1973, 19-35, 147-159.

3732   Stefanini, Mario. La libertà esistenziale in Jean-Paul Sar-
       tre. Milano: Vita e Pensiero, 1949.

3733   Steffen, Günther. "Die schreckliche Freiheit." Berliner
       Hefte für Geistiges Leben, III, No. 2, 1948, 130-138.

Stur, Edward J. see 395.

3734   Sultan, Ather. "Sartre's Theory of Freedom and Choice." Pa-
       kistan Philosophical Journal, IX, April 1966, 13-18.

3735   Thyssen, Johannes. "Sartre und das Problem der Willensfrei-
       heit." Erkenntnis und Verantwortung: Festschrift für Theo-
       dor Litt. Düsseldorf, 1960. Hg. von Joseph Derbolar und
       Freidhelm Nicolin.

Upchurch, N. see 401.

Vogel, Heinrich. see 883.

3736   Wahl, Jean. "Freedom and Existence in Some Recent Philoso-
       phies." Philosophy and Phenomenological Research, VIII,
       No. 4, June 1948, 538-556.

3737   Wahl, Jean. "La liberté chez Sartre." Deucalion, I, 1946.

3738   Warnock Mary. "Freedom in the Early Philosophy of Jean-Paul
       Sartre." Essays in Freedom and Action. Tod Honderick, ed.
       London: Routledge, 1973.

3739   Werner, Eric. "Sartre et la liberté." Contrepoint. No. 5,
       Winter 1971, 37-50.

3740   Wild, John.   Existence and the World of Freedom.   Englewood
       Cliffs, New Jersey: Prentice-Hall, 1963.

       Wolff, Edgar.   see 2609.

       Wyschogrod, Michael.   see 5035.

3741   Yadava, B.S.   "The Dialectic Existence and the Existential
       Freedom."   Darshana International, X, April 1970, 50-57.

3742   Zdarzill, Herbert.   "Der unbedingte Mensch: Sartres Philoso-
       phie der Freiheit."   Wissenschaft und Weltbild.   June 1964,
       133-141.

GEMEINSCHAFT

       Kopper, F.   see 2693.

GENEROSITY

       Heidsieck, François.   see 2599.

       Reboul, O.   see 2420.

GENOCIDE

3744   Lafaurie, Serge.   "Le génocide."   Le Nouvel Observateur, 6-12
       décembre 1967.   Cf. Les Ecrits de Sartre, 454.

GERMANY

3745   Anonymous.   "Sartre in Frankfurt."   Allgemeine Wochenzeitung
       der Juden in Deutschland, V, No. 14, 1950, 7.

3746   Anonymous.   "Sartre und das ewige Deutschland."   Das Ganze
       Deutschland (Heidelberg), III, No. 2, 1951, 2.

3747   Jourdan, Henri.   "Sartre à Berlin."   Adam International Re-
       view, XXXV, No. 343-345, 1970, 22-28.

3748   Langasser, E.   "Der Schutzverband deutscher Autoren empfing
       Sartre."   Aussaat.   No. 10-11, 1948, 6-7.   Lorch Wurt.

3749   Nott, Kathleen.   "German Influence on Modern French Thought."
       The Listener, LIII, No. 1350, 13 January 1955, 73-75.

GOD

       Arboleda, T.J.   see 2426.

3750   Bellafiore, Luigi. "Il problema de Dio in Sartre e nel to-
       mismo." Sapientia Aquinatis, I, 1948, 89-104.

3751   Bouchard, Claude. "Sartre et Dieu." Incidences (Ottawa),
       No. 7, janvier 1965, 18-26.

3752   Buber, Martin. Eclipse of God: Studies in the Relation Be-
       tween Religion and Philosophy. New York: Harper, 1957.

3753   Burkle, Howard R. The Non-existence of God. New York: Herder
       and Herder, 1969.

3754   Champigny, Robert. "God in Sartrean Light." Yale French
       Studies. No. 12, Fall-Winter 1953, 81-88.

3755   Christensen, William and King-Farlow, John. "Two Sides to a
       Theist's Coin." Philosophical Studies (Ireland), XIX, 1970,
       172-180.

3756   Cochrane, Arthur C. The Existentialists and God. Philadel-
       phia: Westminster Pr., 1956.

3757   Coffy, Robert. Dieu des athées: Marx, Sartre, Camus. Lyon:
       Chronique Social de France, 1965.

3758   Colin, Pierre. "Phénoménologie et connaissance de Dieu." Re-
       cherches de Philosophie. Paris: Desclée de Brouwer, 1958,
       299-405.

3759   Copleston, Frederick C. "Man Without God." The Month,
       CLXXIV, No. 961, July-August 1947, 17-27.

3760   da Costa, M. Franklin. "O problema de Deus em Jean-Paul Sar-
       tre." Revista Portuguesa de Filosofia, XXVI, 1970, 285-312.

3761   Del Colle, G. "Il rapporto fra l'uomo e Dio in Sartre."
       Laurentianum (Roma), XII, No. 4, 1971, 369-386.

3762   Denat, Antoine. "Le moi, le monde et Dieu." Vu des anti-
       podes: Synthèses critiques. Paris: Didier, 1969, 11-17.

       Earle, William, et al. see 3172.

3763   Ecole, Jean. "Das Gottesproblem in der Philosophie Sartres."
       Wissenschaft und Weltbild, X, December 1957, 265-267.

3764   Ecole, Jean. "La problème de Dieu dans la philosophie de Sar-
       tre." Giornale di Metafisica, XIII, 1958, 606-618.

3765 Fabro, Cornelio. "Aporie teologiche dell'esistenzialismo."
      Doctor Communis, X, 1957, 119-145.

3766 Fabro, Cornelio. "Patent Atheism in French Existentialism."
      God in Exile: Modern Atheism. Trans. and edited by A. Gib-
      son. Westminster, Maryland: New Man Pr., 1968, 938-957
      (Part 7, Chapter 5).

3767 Falconi, Carlo. "L'istinto del divino nell'opera di Sartre."
      Humanitas, III, 1948, 824-831. Reprinted Letras del Ecuad-
      or. No. 69, July 1951.

      Giannaras, Christos. see 3086.

      Glicksberg, Charles I. see 3087.

3768 Gromczynski, Wieslaw. Czlowiek Swiatrzeczy: Bog w filosofii
      Sartre's a. Warsaw: Panstwowe Wyndawnictwo Naukowe, 1969.

3769 Hammer, Felix. "Menschenbild und Gottesbild." Wissenschaft
      und Weltbild, XXV, No. 2, April-June 1972, 123-138.

3770 Kanters, Robert. "Dieu devant Sartre." Le Figaro Littéraire.
      No. 1071, 27 October 1966, 5.

3771 Kemp, Pierre. "Le concept de Dieu chez sartre." Revue d'Hi-
      stoire Philosophie Réligieuse, XLVII, 1967, 327-337.

3772 Llambias de Azevedo, Juan. "Sobre el argumento de Sartre con-
      tra la existencia de Dios." Stromata, XIII, 91-101.

3773 Lotz, J.B. "Gotteserfahrung im modernem Denken." Stimmen der
      Zeit, CLXXI, August 1963, 321-334.

3774 Marcel, Gabriel. "Sartre et Anouilh et le problème de Dieu."
      La Nouvelle Revue Canadienne. septembre-octobre 1951.

3775 Meritt, Richard N. "God, Sartre and the New Theologian."
      Journal of General Education, XVII, 1965, 125-134.

3776 Miceli, Vincent. "Sartre's Rage Against God." Wahrheit,
      Wert, und Sein: Festgabe für Dietrich von Hildebrand.
      Regensburg: Hobbel, 1970. Hrsg. van Balduin Schwarz.

3777 Mourgue, Gérard. Dieu dans la littérature d'aujourd'hui.
      Paris: Editions France-Empire, 1961.

3778   Mow, Joseph J.   "Jean-Paul Sartre: Christian Theist?"   Chris-
       tian Century, LXXXIII, 23 November 1966, 1437-1439.

3779   Mow, Joseph J.   "Sartre Again."   Christian Century, LXXXIV,
       1 February 1967, 146-148.

3780   Paissac, Henri.   Le Dieu de Sartre.   Paris: Arthaud, 1950.

3781   Paniker, Salvador.   "A propósito de Sartre, la fé y los di-
       oses."   Revista de Occidente, VIII, No. 3, January 1965,
       108-112.

3782   Pfeil, H.   "The Modern Denial of God: Its Origin and Tragedy."
       Philosophy Today, III, 1959, 19-27.

3783   Salmona, Bruno.   "Dio nel teatro di Sartre."   Epheremides
       Carmeliticae.   No. 1, 1965, 173-186.

3784   Sanabria, José Ruben.   "El tema de Dios en Jean-Paul Sartre."
       Sapientia, XII, 1957, 201-205.

3785   Scheltens, D.F.   "Contingency and the Proofs for the Existence
       of God."   International Philosophical Quarterly, XII, Decem-
       ber 1972, 572-586.

3786   Turienzo, S.A.   "Absence of God and Man's Insecurity."   Phi-
       losophy Today, III, 1959, 135-139.

3787   Vietta, Egon.   Theologie ohne Gott.   Zürich: Hauswedell, 1948.

3788   Visentin, Giovanni.   "La presenza di Dio nel teatro contempo-
       raneo."   Idea, V, No. 36, 6 September 1953, 5.

3789   Walter, Robert.   "Existentialism and God."   Ashridge Quarter-
       ly, II, October 1948, 81-88.

3790   Yale French Studies.   No. 12, 1953.   "God and the Writer."

GRAPHOLOGIE

3791   Delamain, Maurice.   "Graphologie et critique."   Almanac des
       Lettres.   Paris: Editions de Flore, 1946, 148-150.

GREEKS

3792   Szogyi, Alex.   "Sartre and the Greeks: A Vicious Magic Cir-
       cle."   The Persistent Voice: Essays on Hellenism in French
       Literature Since the Eighteenth Century in honor of Profes-

sor <u>Henri M. Peyre</u>. Walter G. Langlois, ed. New York: New
York Univ. Pr.; Geneva: Droz, 1971, 159-172.

HAITI

3793 Altman, Georges. "J'ai vu à Haiti un peuple noir fier de sa
      tradition de liberté." <u>Franc-Tireur</u>, 21 octobre, 1949;
      "Haiti se jette avec passion sur tout ce qui évoque la cul-
      ture française . . . et parmi les riches Antilles, cette ré-
      publique noire est la seule à crever de faim." <u>Franc-
      Tireur</u>, 22-23 octobre 1949; "Haiti vu par Jean-Paul Sartre."
      <u>Franc-Tireur</u>, 24 octobre 1949. Cf. <u>Les Ecrits de Sartre</u>,
      218-219.

HALLUCINATION

3794 Faure, Henri. <u>Hallucination et réalité perceptive</u>. Paris:
      Presses Universitaires de France, 1965.

HAND

      Prince, Gerald J. see 3328.

HAPPINESS

3795 Burdick, Dolores Mann. "The Concept of Happiness in the Mo-
      dern French Theater." <u>Papers of the Michigan Academy of
      Science, Arts and Letters</u>, L, 1965, 609-620.

HEBREW

3796 Brinker, Menachem. "Sartre in Hebrew: A Misleading Transla-
      tion." <u>Hasifrut</u>, I, 1968, 728-730. In Hebrew; summary in
      English.

HERO

3797 Thomas, J. James. "The Sartrean Hero." <u>The Revolutionary
      Hero</u>. Michigan: Univ. Center, 1971, 16-47. A phenomen-
      ological investigation of the literature of Sartre and four
      American novelists.

HEROISM

3798 Arcocha, Juan. "Sartre o el heroismo del hombre en situa-
      ción." <u>Espiral</u>, LXXVII, June 1960, 14-27.

HISTORY

      Buonajuto, Maria. see 3673.

3799 Hernandez de Alba, G. "En torno a Sartre y el problema de la
      historia." Humanitas (Univ. de Nuevo Leon), IV, No. 4,
      1963, 29-44.

3800 Hincker, François. "Jean-Paul Sartre et l'histoire." Sartre
      est-il marxiste?, 157-166. La Nouvelle Critique. No. 173-
      174, mars 1966, 157-166.

3801 Jameson, Fredric. "Sartre and History." Marxism and Form:
      Twentieth-Century Dialectical Theories of Literature.
      Princeton: Princeton Univ. Pr., 1971, 206-305.

3802 Krieger, Leonard. "History and Existentialism in Sartre."
      The Critical Spirit: Essays in Honor of Herbert Marcuse.
      Kurt H. Wolff and Barrington Moore, eds. Boston: Beacon
      Pr., 1967.

3803 Kryger, Edna. "L'activité négative." Journal of the History
      of Philosophy. July 1973, 337-362.

3804 Le Blond, Jean-Marie. "Histoire et liberté selon Sartre."
      Etudes, juillet-août 1960, 62-76.

3805 Lichtheim, George. "Sartre, Marxism and History." History
      and Theory, III, No. 2, 1963-1964, 222-246.

3806 Munford, C.J. "Sartrean Existentialism and the Philosophy of
      History." Journal of World History, XI, No. 3, 1968, 392-
      404.

3807 Nicol, Eduardo. Historicismo y existencialismo, la temporali-
      dad del ser y la razón. Mexico: Colegio de México, 1950.

      Petruzzellis, Nicola. see 2215.

      Rosen, Lawrence. see 2791.

3808 Simon, Pierre-Henri. L'Esprit et l'histoire: Essai sur la
      conscience historique dans la littérature du vingtième si-
      ècle. Paris: A. Colin, 1954.

      Simon, Pierre-Henri. see 2550.

      Tibaldi, Giancarlo. see 2794.

3809 Védrine, Hélène. Les Philosophies de l'histoire. Paris:
      Petite Bibliothèque Payot, 1974.

3810 Wein, Hermann. "Sartre und das Verhältnis von Geschichte und
      Wahrhreit: Glossen zu Sartres Kritik der dialektischen Ver-
      nunft. Verstehen und Vertrauen: Otto F. Bollnow zum 65.
      Geburtstag. Johannes Schwartlander, et al, ed. Stuttgart:
      Kohlhammer, 1968, 245-255.

3811 Zehm, Günter Albrecht. Historische Vernunft und direkte Ak-
      tion: Zur Politik und Philosophie Sartres. Stuttgart:
      Klett, 1964.

'HOLE IN BEING'

      Abrams, Fred. see 2953.

      Rauch, Leo. see 2874.

HONOR and NOBILITY

      Heidsieck, François. see 2599.

HUMANISM

3812 Ayraud, Pierre. "Les livres et le problème de l'humanisme."
      Témoignages, XIII, 1949, 431-434.

3813 Bortolaso, Giovanni. "Umanismo ateo." La Civiltà Cattolica.
      No. 55, January 1960, 535-544.

3814 Bouillon, Georges. "Discours sur l'humanisme." Dryade. No.
      19, Autumn 1959, 5-19.

3815 Bustabad Alonso, Indalecio. El humanismo sartriano. Tesis de
      Lic., Univ. de Costa Rica, 1965.

3816 Etcheverry, A. Le conflit actuel des humanismes. New ed.
      Rome: Presses de l'Université Gregorienne, 1964.

3817 Eube, Charles. "Humanités d'aujourd'hui." Poésie 46. No.
      30, février 1946, 79-84.

3818 Fernaud, Jacques. "Humanism in Contemporary French Fiction."
      American Society Legion of Honor Magazine, XXII, No. 4, Win-
      ter 1951, 341-353.

3819 Fragata, J. "O humanismo existencialista de Sartre." Revista
      Portuguesa de Filosofia, XIX, January-March 1963, 48-59.

3820 Gallegos, Racafull, J.M. "El hombre de Sartre y el hombre
      eterno." Latinoamerica, I, 1949, 337-340.

3821   Gallegos, Racafull, J.M.   "El pretendido humanismo de Sartre."
       Latinoamerica, I, 1949, 157-165.

3822   Garin, Eugenio.   "Quel 'humanisme?   Variations historiques."
       Revue Internationale de Philosophie, XXII, 1968, 263-275.

3823   Hardré, Jacques.   "Sartre's Existentialism and Humanism."
       Studies in Philology, XLIX, No. 3, July 1952, 534-547.

3824   Heidegger, Martin.   Lettre sur l'humanisme.

3825   Jerunca, Virgil.   "Existentialist Humanism."   Agora, I, 1945,
       72-78.

3826   Kanters, Robert.   "Deux humanismes paiens."   La Gazette des
       Lettres.   30 mars 1946.

3827   Maulnier, Thierry.   "Notes sur un nouvel humanisme."   La Table
       Ronde.   No. 14, 1949, 241-249.

3828   Polimeni, Dante O.   "Sartre: del Humanismo como ética formal
       al humanismo de la libertad."   Actas de las Segundas Jorna-
       das Universitarias de Humanidades.   Mendoza: Instituto de
       Filosofía, 1964, 147-150.

3829   Salem, E.D.   "Is Sartre Becoming a Humanist?"   The Humanist,
       LXXIX, No. 10, October 1964, 319-321.

3830   Stinivasan, G.   "The Humanism of Sartre."   Philosophical Quar-
       terly (Asian), XXVIII, 1955, 185-190.

       Zivanovic, Judith K.   see 412.

HUMANITY

3831   Ghose, Ramedra Nath.   "Humanity as an End."   Pakistan Philo-
       sophical Journal.   April 1966, 30-45.

HUMOUR

       Easterling, Ilda M.   see 291.

IDEOLOGUE

3822   De Olaso, Ezequiel.   "Sartre ideólogo."   Cuadernos.   No. 73,
       1963, 57-61.

3833   Mesnard, Pierre. "L'idéologue Jean-Paul Sartre." Les grands courants de la philosophie contemporaine. Vol. II: Portraits. Paris: Fischbacher, 1964.

3834   Molnar, Thomas. Sartre: Ideologue of our time. New York: Funk and Wagnalls, 1968. Trans. into French: Sartre: Philosophie de la contestation. Paris: le Prieure, 1970.

IDEOLOGY

3835   Marcuse, Ludwig. "Der Kunstler und die Ideologie." Der Monat. October 1961, 14-19.

3836   Petruzzellis, Nicola. "Jean-Paul Sartre tra filosofia e ideologia." Rassegna Scienze Filosofici, XV, 1962, 1-27.

3837   Wein, Hermann. "The Concept of Ideology in Sartre: 'Situatedness' as an Epistemological and Anthropological Concept." Dialogue, VII, 1968-1969, 1-15.

IDENTITY

       Kerlin, Michael. see 3701.

IMAGE   (see L'Imagination et l'Imaginaire)

3838   Baladie, Naguib. "La structure de l'image d'après Jean-Paul Sartre." Valeurs (Alexandrie), No. 1, April 1945, 45-65.

3839   Durand, Gilbert. Les structures anthropologiques de l'imaginaire. Paris: PUF, 1963.

3840   Lefebvre, Maurice-Jean. L'image fascinante et le surréel. Paris: Plon, 1965.

3840a Salinas, Laurent M. "La structure de l'image d'après Sartre." Valeurs, avril 1945, 65-72.

IMAGERY

       Artinian, Robert. see 3660.

3841   John, S. "Sacrilege and Metamorphosis: Two Aspects of Sartre's Imagery." Modern Language Quarterly, XX, March 1959, 57-66.

       John, S. see 319.

3842   Ullman, Stephen. "Image in the Modern Novel." Style in the
       French Novel. Oxford: Basil Blackwell, 1964. Concerning
       Les Chemins de la liberté.

IMAGINAIRE

3843   Duvignaud, Jean. Spectacle et société: La fonction de l'imag-
       inaire dans les sociétés. Paris: Denoël-Gonthier, 1960.

IMAGINATION

       see L'Imagination et l'Imaginaire, Part III.

IMMANENTISM

3844   Sciacca, Michele F. "Sartre o l'immanentismo ridotta all'as-
       surdo." Idea, V, No. 14, 5 April 1953, 1,5.

3845   Sciacca, Michele F. "Sartre o el inmanentismo reducido al
       absurdo." Ciudad de Dios (El Escorial), CLXV, 1953, 157-
       161.

IMMORTALITY

3846   Challaye, Félicien. "Immortalité et existentialisme." Syn-
       thèses, XI, No. 128, janvier 1957, 286-296.

3847   Thomas, J.H. "Immortality and Humanism." Modern Churchman.
       December 1959, 33-40.

INCEST

3848   Hochland, Janina. "Incest: A Theme in Sartre's Literary
       Work." Journal of the British Society for Phenomenology,
       I, No. 2, May 1970, 93-99.

INDEX   (librorum prohibitorum)

3849   Copleston, Frederick C. "Sartre on the Index: The Church
       Judges His Philosophy of Decadence." The Tablet, CXCII, No.
       5659, 6 November 1948, 292-293.

3850   Dickel, J.S. "M. Sartre on the Index." The Tablet, CXCII,
       13 November 1948, 314.

3851   E.G. "The Works of Sartre Condemned." Clergy Review, XXXI,
       1949, 59-60.

3852   Mahoney, E.J.   "Works of Sartre Condemned: Decretum."   <u>Clergy</u>
       <u>Review</u>, XXXI, January 1949.

INDIVIDUAL

3853   Odajnjk, Walter.   "The Individual and Marxism."   <u>Darshana In-</u>
       <u>ternational</u>, III, No. 3, August 1963, 46-56.

3854   Warnock, Mary.   "L'individu dans la philosophie de Sartre."
       <u>Philosophie</u> et <u>littérature</u>.   Deuxième Colloque de la Société
       Britannique de Philosophie de Langue Française.   Hull: Fret-
       wells, 1963, 31-38.

INTELLECTUAL

3855   Alvarez del Vayo, J.   "Politics and the Intellectual."   <u>The</u>
       <u>Nation</u>, CLXIII, 28 September 1948, 346-349.

3856   Bo, Carlo.   "I poteri dell'intellectuale: Carlo Bo a colloquio
       con Jean-Paul Sartre dall rubrica televisiva 'Incontri'."
       <u>L'Approdo</u> <u>Letterario</u>, XII, No. 34, April-June 1966, 97-110.

       Brombert, Victor.   see 546.

       Chiaromonte, Nicola.   see 2668.

3857   Cranston, Maurice W.   "Intellectuals of the World: 3, Paradox
       of the French Intellectual."   <u>New</u> <u>Society</u>, V, 7 January
       1965, 12-14.

3858   Garot, Jean-Claude.   "L'intellectuel face a la révolution."
       <u>Le</u> <u>Point</u>.   No. 13, janvier 1968, 18-23.   Trans. into English
       by B. Rice: "Intellectuals and Revolution."   <u>Ramparts</u> <u>Maga-</u>
       <u>zine</u>, IX, December 1970, 52-55.   Cf. <u>Les</u> <u>Ecrits</u> <u>de</u> <u>Sartre</u>,
       458-459.

3859   Gerassi, J.   "Iron in His Soul."   <u>Guardian</u>.   4 September 1971,
       9; <u>Guardian</u> <u>Weekly</u>, CV, No. 12, 18 September 1971, 18-19.

3860   Gerassi, J., ed.   "Sartre Accuses the Intellectuals of Bad
       Faith."   <u>New</u> <u>York</u> <u>Times</u> <u>Magazine</u>.   17 October 1971, 38-39 ff.
       Interview.

3861   Gorkin, Julian.   "La crise des intellectuels et le masochisme
       communiste de Sartre."   <u>Revue</u> <u>Socialiste</u>.   No. 66, avril
       1953, 424-435.

3862   Gorkin, Julian. "A proposito de Jean-Paul Sartre: La crisis
       de los intelectuales y el masoquismo communista." Cuadernos
       (Del Congreso por la libertad de la Cultura), No. 11, March-
       May 1953, 74-81.

3863   Jurt, Joseph. "Jean-Paul Sartre, die Intellektuellen und die
       Arbeiter." Profil, XLIX, No. 12, 1970, 354-359.

3864   Laurent, Jacques. "Lettre de Souslov, membre du Praesidium
       du Comité central à Jean-Paul Sartre, intellectuel." Au
       contraire. Paris: La Table Ronde, 1967, 197-199.

3866   Lüthy, Herbert. "Sartre et le drama de l'intellectuel bour-
       geois." Preuves. No. 215-216, février-mars 1969, 118 ff.

3867   Mazzola, Michel. "De l'intellectuel chez Marx au marxisme des
       intellectuels." Arguments. No. 20, 1960, 22-26.

3868   Naville, Pierre. "L'intellectuel communiste." Lettres Nou-
       velles, 4e année, juin-octobre 1956, 442-457; Ibid., No. 39,
       juin 1956, 871-866; Ibid., No. 40, juillet-août 1956, 60-79;
       Ibid., No. 42, octobre 1956, 442-457. Publié en volume:
       L'intellectuel communiste. Paris: Rivière, 1956.

3869   Ormesson, Jean d'. "Portrait de l'intellectuel en militant de
       base." Nouvelles Littéraires, L, No. 2316, 14-20 février
       1972, 8.

3870   Ratté, John. "Literature and Freedom: The Crisis of the Bour-
       geois Intellectual in France." The University of Denver
       Quarterly, V, No. 2, Summer 1970, 19-55.

3871   Reblitz, Irma. "Vorbemerkung." Der Intellektuelle und die
       Revolution. Aus dem Französischen von Irma Reblitz; Vor-
       bemerkung von Irma Reblitz. Neuwied und Berlin: Luchter-
       hand, 1971, 5-8.

INTENTIONALITY

       Breton, Stanislas. see 3069.

       Butts, R.E. see 1827.

       Dina, Stephan A. see 1834.

       Goldthorpe, Rhinannon. see 438.

3872   Mohanty, J.N. The Concept of Intentionality. St. Louis: War-
       ren H. Green, 1972.

3873   Mohanty, J.N. "Husserl and Intentionality." Analecta Husser-
       liana, Vol. I. Anna-Teresa Tymieniecka, ed. Dordrecht: D.
       Reidel, 1971.

3874   Natanson, Maurice. "Husserl and Sartre on Intentionality."
       Literature, Philosophy, and the Social Sciences. The Hague:
       Nijhoff, 1962.

       Rauch, Leo. see 375.

INTERIORITY

       Delhomme, Jeanne. see 2478.

INTERSUBJECTIVITY

       Bukula, Casimir R. see 270.

3875   Tollenaere, M. de. "Intersubjectivity in Jean-Paul Sartre."
       International Philosophical Quarterly, V, May 1965, 203-220.

INTERVIEWS, PORTRAITS, and GENERAL PRESENTATION

STUDIES IN ENGLISH

3876   Ahadjanian. "Existential Confusion." Religion and Society,
       1957.

3877   Allen, E.L. "Existentialism." The Adelphi, XXIV, April-June
       1948, 157-160.

3878   Anonymous. "Alone in a Loveless World." Times Literary Sup-
       plement. No. 2380, 13 September 1967, 460.

3879   Anonymous. "Existentialist." New Yorker, XXII, 16 March
       1946, 24-25. Concerning Sartre's speech in New York City in
       1946.

3880   Anonymous. "The Far Side of Despair." New Statesman and Na-
       tion, LI, No. 1320, 30 June 1956, 764-765.

3881   Anonymous. "A Few Sartrean Reflections." Times Literary Sup-
       plement. No. 2380, 13 September 1967, 460.

3882   Anonymous. "Miscellena." The Guardian. 2 February 1971, 11.

3883   Anonymous. "Successively Sartre." Times Literary Supplement.
       No. 3560, 21 May 1970, 565.

3884   Arnold, W.E. "Sartre as Performer and Literary Illusionist."
       The Commonweal, LXXXII, 6 August 1965, 566 ff.

3885   Arnou, R. "Existentialism in France Today." Modern School-
       man, XXIV, May 1947, 193-207.

3886   Barry, Joseph. Left Bank, Right Bank: Paris and Parisians.
       New York: Norton, 1951.

3887   Barry, Joseph. The People of Paris. Garden City, New York:
       Doubleday, 1966.

3888   Bartholomew, R.L. "The Star of the Lost." Thought (Delhi),
       V, No. 22, 30 May 1953.

3889   Benichou, P. "What's Sartre Thinking Lately?" Esquire,
       LXXVIII, December 1972, 204-208 ff.

3890   Benthall, Jonathan. "Beyond Despair: Reflections on Sartre."
       Granta, LXIV, No. 1209, 13 May 1961.

3891   Brown, J.M. "Chief Prophet of the Existentialists." New York
       Times Magazine. 2 February 1947, 20-21, 50, 52.

3892   Bruckberger, R.L. "A View of Sartre." New York Times Book
       Review. 15 November 1964, 2.

3893   Campbell, Michael. "Hell in Heaven or the Swiss Sofa." The
       Listener, LXXI, 14 May 1964, 793-795.

3894   Cebik, L.B. "Two Premature Epitaphs for Sartre." Denver
       Quarterly, VIII, No. 1, Spring 1973, 99-104.

3895   Chapsal, Madeleine. "Jean-Paul Sartre." Yale French Studies.
       No. 30, 1962.

3896   Connolly, Cyril. Ideas and Places. London: Weidenfeld and
       Nicholson, 1953.

3897   Crozier, Michel. "The Cultural Revolution: Notes on the
       Changes in the Intellectual Climate of France." A New Eu-
       rope? Stephen R. Graubard, ed. Boston: Houghton Mifflin,
       1964, 597-630.

3898   Cruickshank, John. "Looking at Sartre." Time and Tide, XLII,
       No. 29, 20 July 1961, 1201.

3899   Davenport, Guy. "A Rebel Reappraised." New York Times Book
       Review. 31 June 1968, 10.

3900   Douglas, Kenneth N. "Sartre Expounds His Views." Yale Re-
       view, XXXVII, No. 2, December 1947, 268-269.

3901   Drell, R. " . . . said Jean-Paul Sartre." Yale French Stud-
       ies. No. 16, 1956, 3-7.

3902   Duncan, Elmer H. "Something About Sartre." Forum (Houston),
       VI, No. 1, Fall-Winter 1968, 22-24.

3903   Dupee, F.W. "An International Episode." Partisan Review,
       XIII, Spring 1946, 259-265.

3904   Ecole, Jean. "New Look in Philosophy." Philosophy Today, IV,
       1960, 44-54.

3905   Ehrenbourg, Ilya. Post-War Years: 1945-1954. Men, Years,
       Life, Vol. VI. Trans. by T. Shebunina. London: MacGibbon
       and Keel, 1966.

3906   Ehrmann, Jacques. "Of Rats and Men: Notes on the Preface."
       Yale French Studies. No. 30, Winter 1962-1963, 78-85.

3907   Frazer, G.S. "Meet Jean-Paul Sartre." World Review. No. 1,
       March 1949, 61-64.

3908   Gabriel, M. "Poor Man's Snobbery." Thought (Delhi), XVI,
       No. 18, 2 May 1964, 13-14.

3909   Gobeil, Madeleine. "Playboy Interview: Jean-Paul Sartre."
       XII, No. 5, May 1965, 69-75. Reprinted Playboy Interview.
       Chicago: Playboy Pr., 1967, 162-179. Cf. Les Ecrits de Sar-
       tre, 415-416.

3910   Grindea, Miron. "Voltaire 1970." Adam International Review,
       XXXV, No. 343-345, 1970, 2-3.

3911   Gross, George. "Sartre Interviews." Human Context, IV, Aut-
       umn 1972, 608-618.

3912   Hardwick, Elisabeth. "We Are All Murderers." New York Review
       of Books. 3 March 1966, 4, 9.

3913   Hartley, Anthony. "A Long Bitter, Sweet Madness: An Inter-
       view with Sartre." Encounter, XXII, June 1964, 61-63.

3914   Hartley, Anthony. "The Spirit of Abstraction." The Bedside
       Guardian, Vol. X. A Selection from The Guardian. London:
       Collins, 1961.

3915   Hughes, Stuart H. "Jean-Paul Sartre." Ramparts Magazine.
       March 1966.

3916   Johnstone, Lesley. "The Uncertain Oracle." Prairie Schooner,
       XXXIX, No. 4, Winter 1965-1966, 340-356.

3917   Justus, Pal. "Sartre as Seen by a Hungarian Translator."
       New Hungarian Quarterly, VI, No. 18, Summer 1965, 168-173.

3918   Kazin, Alfred. "The Useful Critic." Atlantic, CCXVI, No. 6,
       December 1965, 73-80.

3919   Kitchen, Paddy. "Sartre's Total Relevance." Tribune. No.
       45, 6 November 1970, 11.

3920   Kitchen, Lawrence. "The Cage and the Scream." The Listener.
       No. 1765, 24 January 1963, 157-159.

3921   Kitchen, Lawrence. "The Lion-Tamers." The Listener. No.
       1842, 16 July 1964, 87-89.

3922   Knowles, Peter. "Two Commentaries." Prism International,
       VIII, No. 2, Autumn 1968, 97-103.

3923   Laing, Dilys. "From God to Sartre." The Nation. 27 June
       1959, 579-580.

3924   Lehmann, John. The Ample Proposition: Autobiography III.
       London: Ayre and Spottiswoode, 1966.

3925   Lehmann, John. "In Daylight-I." New Writing and Daylight,
       VI, 1946, 7-15.

3926   Lehmann, John. "The Search for the Myth." The Open Night.
       London: Green, 1952; Also The Penguin New Writing. No. 30,
       1947, 142-158.

3927   Lehmann, John. The Whispering Gallery: Autobiography I. Lon-
       don: Longmans Green, 1955.

3928   Lotthe, Etienne. "Modern French Philosophy." Circle Maga-
       zine. No. 1, January 1964, 6-9.

3929 Lüthy, Herbert. "The Void of Sartre." Anchor Review, II,
      1957, 241-257.

3930 Mallinson, V. "Note on Sartre." New Statesman and Nation,
      XXX, No. 773, 15 December 1954, 403-404.

3931 Mays, Wolfe. "Introduction." Journal of the British Society
      for Phenomenology, I, No. 2, May 1970. Special issue on
      Sartre.

3932 McCarthy, Mary. The Writing on the Wall and Other Essays.
      New York, 1972.

3933 McMahon, Joseph J. "A Reader's Hesitation." Yale French
      Studies. No. 30, Fall-Winter 1962-1963, 96-107.

3934 Merleau-Ponty, Maurice. "A Scandalous Author." Sense and
      Non-Sense. Evanston, Illinois: Northwestern Univ. Pr.,
      1964.

3935 Meyerhoff, Hans. "The Return to the Concrete." Chicago Re-
      view, XIII, No. 2, Summer 1959, 27-39.

3936 Moore, Sebastian. "Reflections on the Thought of Sartre."
      Downside Review, LXXII, No. 228, April 1954, 146-152.

3937 Morgan, E. "Immigration of a Fad: Existentialist Books Come
      to the USA." America, LXXVII, 7 June 1947, 259-270.

3938 Mukerjea, S.V. "Sartrism: Will It Live?" Disjecta membra.
      Bangalore, India, 1959, 184-190.

3939 Nott, Kathleen. A Soul in the Quad. . . London: Routledge and
      Kegan Paul, 1969.

3940 Ohye, Kenzaburo. "Portrait of Sartre." Orient West, VII, No.
      9, September 1962, 331-341.

3941 Ottensmeyer, O.S.B. "The Epoch of the Classic Hero." Ameri-
      can Benedictine Review, XVI, September 1965, 455-464.

3942 Parisot, Paul. "Keeping Up With M. Sartre." Thought (Delhi),
      VI, No. 18, 1 May 1954, 5-6.

3943 Paz, Octavio. "The Exception to the Rule." Alternating Cur-
      cents. Trans. from the Spanish by Helen R. Lane. New York:
      Viking, 1973, 169-174.

3944 Rowland, John. "Sartre Speaks Out." Thinker's Weekly, I, 27
      June 1947, 1-2.

3945 Saint-René Taillandier, M. "French Youth Today." National
      Review, CXXVI, No. 759, May 1946, 411-414.

3946 Siepmann, E.O. "The Ass's Face, 2." Nineteenth Century and
      After, CXLV, March 1949, 150-156.

3947 Sinari, Ramakant. "Sartre's Prophecy: 'Life Is Hell'."
      Thought (Delhi), XVII, No. 49, 4 December 1965, 14-15.

3948 Smith, Colin. "The Philosophical Drama of Sartre." Prompt.
      No. 4, 1964, 25-29.

3949 Solotaroff, T. "Sartre: The View From the Void." The Red Hot
      Vacuum and Other Pieces on the Writing of the Sixties. New
      York: Atheneum, 1970, 192-197.

3950 Szogyi, Alex. "Found Wanting." New York Times Book Review.
      2 April 1961, 4, 22.

3951 Tanaka, Ryo. "An Interview With Sartre." Orient West, VII,
      No. 5, May 1962, 63-69. Cf. Les Ecrits de Sartre, 376.

3952 Thomas, Peter H. "Jean-Paul Sartre: A Portrait." Dalhousie
      Review, XLV, No. 1, Spring 1965, 78-89.

3953 Untermeyer, Louis. "Jean-Paul Sartre." Makers of the Modern
      World. New York: Simon and Schuster, 1955, 741-746.

3954 Ustinov, Peter. "Super-Intellectuals - and Sartre." Literary
      Digest, II, Winter 1947, 8-11.

3955 Warnock, Mary. "Gurus of Our Time-4: Sartre." New Society,
      X, No. 263, 12 October 1967, 508-510.

3956 Weightman, John. "What Happened to Commitment?" The Listen-
      er. No. 1782, 23 May 1963, 867-868.

3957 West, Paul. "The Fear of Possibility: American Myth and
      French Mimesis." Chicago Review, XIV, Summer 1960, 1-33.

3958 Wilson, Colin. "To Be or Not To Be: Sartre's Dilemma." The
      Humanist, LXXXVI, No. 12, 1970, 363-368.

3959 Wilson, Colin. "Existential Criticism." Chicago Review, Sum-
      mer 1959, 152-181.

3960 Winner, Percy. "Outside America." New Republic, CXX, No. 25,
      1959, 9-10.

STUDIES IN FRENCH

3961 Anonymous. "Deux heures avec Sartre." L'Express. No. 431,
      17 septembre 1959, 35-37.

3962 Anonymous. "Jean-Paul Sartre." La Gazette des Lettres, VI,
      No. 9, 1951, 65-69.

3963 Anonymous. "Penseurs d'hier et d'aujourd'hui." La Libre Bel-
      gique, LXXXVII, No. 191, 10 juillet 1970, 7.

3964 Anonymous. "Portraits par un inconnu: V, Jean-Paul Sartre, ou
      l'humanisme révolutionnaire." Revue des Deux Mondes. No.
      11, novembre 1973, 257-263.

3965 Anonymous. "Sartre donne les clefs de 'L'enfer c'est les au-
      tres'." Le Figaro Littéraire, XX, No. 977, 7-13 janvier
      1965, 2.

3966 Aubarade, Gabriel d'. "Rencontre avec Sartre." Les Nouvelles
      Littéraires. 1 février 1951. Cf. Les Ecrits de Sartre,
      241-242.

3967 Audry, Colette. "Interview avec Sartre." Les Lettres Fran-
      çaises. 24 novembre 1945.

3968 Audry, Colette. "La vie d'un philosophe." L'Express. 11
      mars 1964, 34.

3969 Barrault, Jean-Louis. "Jean-Paul Sartre." Souvenirs pour
      demain. Paris: Editions du Seuil, 1972, 151-154.

3970 Barrère, Jean-Bertrand. "Sartre, métaphysicien hanté." Cri-
      tique de chambre. Paris: La Palatine, 1964, 175-201.

3971 Bechtel, Guy. "M. Sartre, vous êtes devenu celui dont vous
      vous moquiez hier." Carrefour, XV, No. 715, 29 mai 1958,
      13.

3972 Beigbeder, Marc, ed. "Introduction." Jean-Paul Sartre.
      Paris: Bordas, 1968.

3973 Bellour, Raymond. "Homme pour homme." L'Arc. No. 30, décem-
      bre 1966, 10-14.

3974   Belmont, Georges. "Bout à bout." La Revue de Poche. No. 7,
       janvier 1966, 175-185.

3975   Berger, Pierre. "Sartre dans Paris et dans le monde." Spec-
       tateur. 1 octobre 1946. Cf. Les Ecrits de Sartre, 151.

3976   Berger, Pierre. "Sartre et sa légende." La Gazette des Let-
       tres. No. 38, 14 juin 1947.

3977   Berger, Yves and Simon, Claude. "Deux écrivains répondent à
       Sartre. Berger: 'Nous ne sommes pas des traitres'; Simon:
       'Pour qui donc écrit Sartre?'." L'Express. 28 mai 1964,
       30-33.

3978   Bernson, B. "Connaissance d'un homme: Jean-Paul Sartre. Con-
       naissance de l'homme. No. 4, 1954, 34-38.

3979   Boisdeffre, Pierre de. "Qui est Jean-Paul Sartre?" A la
       Page. No. 8, février 1965, 188-195.

3980   Bonnefoy, Claude. "Sartre à vingt ans: Un bel avenir univer-
       sitaire." Arts. No. 804, 11-17 janvier 1961, 13-14.

3981   Bonnefoy, Claude. "Les souvenirs de Jean-Paul Sartre: 'Ma vo-
       cation d'écrivain est née au sixième étage'." Arts. No.
       932, 16-22 octobre 1963, 5.

3982   Borde, Raymond. L'Extricable. Paris: Eric Losfeld, 1970.

3983   Bory, Jean-François. "Une histoire d'amour dont les héros
       sont Debussy, Barrès, Rostand, Sartre." Paris Match. No.
       1141, 20 mars 1971, 67.

3984   Bosquet, Alain. "Lettre ouverte à Jean-Paul Sartre." Injus-
       tice. Paris: La Table Ronde, 1969, 147-152.

3985   Bouillon, Georges. "Provinciales: Telles quelles (XII)."
       Dryade. No. 42, Summer 1965, 47-53.

3986   Bouillon, Georges. "Provinciales: Telles quelles." Dryade.
       No. 45, Spring 1966, 57-61.

3987   Campbell, Robert. "Jean-Paul Sartre." Espace (Clermont-Fer-
       and), 1 mars 1945, 98-101.

3988   Caradec, François. Trésors du pastiche . . . Paris: Pierre
       Hornay, 1971.

3989   Chapsal, Madeleine. "Jean-Paul Sartre." Les Ecrivains en
       présence. Paris: Juillard, 1960, 203-230. Reimprimé Situ-
       ations IX. Paris: Gallimard, 1972, 3-39. Cf. Les Ecrits
       de Sartre, 342-343.

3990   Charbonneau, Bernard. "Sartre ou le malheur d'être libre."
       Arts et Loisirs. No. 26, 23-29 mars 1966, 9-11.

3991   Chazel, Jean. "Situation de Sartre." Pretextes. mai-juin
       1950, 2-5.

3992   Chevalier, Gabriel. "Jean-Paul Sartre." L'Envers de Cloche-
       merle: Propos d'un homme libre. Paris: Flammarion, 1966,
       221-224.

3993   Chevalier, Gabriel. "Lettre à Sartre." Monde Nouveau-Paru,
       XII, No. 102, juillet 1956, 56-58.

3994   "Civilisation du néant." La Table Ronde. No. 182, mars 1963.
       Special Issue devoted to Sartre.

3995   Controverses. Recherches et Débats. No. 32, septembre 1960.
       Concernant Les Séquestrés d'Altona.

3996   Cuénot, Claude. "Jean-Paul Sartre." Rencontres. No. 121,
       1947.

3997   Curtis, Jean-Louis. "Un huis clos très public." Le Nouvel
       Observateur. No. 47, 6-12 octobre 1965, 31.

3998   Deleuze, Gilles et Axelos, Kostas. "Deux philosophes s'ex-
       pliquent. Deleuze: 'Il a été mon maître'; Axelos: 'Il a
       fait descendre la métaphysique dans les cafés'." Arts.
       28 octobre-3 novembre 1964, 8-9.

3999   Delhomme, Jeanne. "L'absurdité de l'existence." Espace 4,
       1946.

4000   Delpeyrou, Jacques. "La passion de l'explicable." Esprit,
       XXXII, No. 327, avril 1964, 660-664.

4001   Déon, Michel. "Quand le guide a du génie: La littérature tou-
       ristique." Les Nouvelles Littéraires, XLV, No. 2087, 31
       août 1970, 1, 8.

4002   Diop, Al. "A propos d'une phrase de Sartre." La Vie Intel-
       lectuelle, XIV, août 1946, 164-170.

4003   Duhamel, Marcel. Raconte pas ta vie. Paris: Mercure de
       France, 1972.

4004   Dullin Charles. Ce sont les dieux qu'il nous faut. Edition
       établie et annotée par Charles Charras. Paris: Gallimard,
       1969.

4005   Dumur, Guy. "Le spectacle Sartre." L'Arche. No. 22, décem-
       bre 1946, 117-122.

4006   Ehrenbourg, Ilya. "Le cas Sartre." Le Figaro Littéraire, XX,
       No. 1002, 1-7 juillet 1965, 1, 7.

4007   Estève, Michel. "Notes sur le Festival de Venise." Etudes,
       Tome CCCXXVII, novembre 1967, 528-534.

4008   Fabre-Luce, Alfred. Journal 1951. Paris: Amot-Dumond, 1951.

4009   Farnoux-Raynaud, Lucien. "Un faux génie, Jean-Paul Sartre."
       dans "Faux génies, faiseurs et vrais méconnus." Crapouil-
       lot. No. 53, juin 1961, 49-52.

4010   Fedida, Pierre. "Le huis clos." La Nef. No. 46-47, février-
       mai 1972, 235-238.

4011   Ferrier, Jean-Louis. L'Homme dans le monde. Neuchâtel: La
       Baconnière, 1957.

4012   Fouchet, Max-Pol. "Mal d'aurore." La Gazette des Lettres,
       III, 28 juin 1947, 1.

4013   Fouchet, Max-Pol. "Chronique d'un incident." Les Appels.
       Paris: Mercure de France, 1967, 149-155.

4014   Frank, Bernard. "Souvenirs." Les Cahiers des Saisons. No.
       11, juin-juillet 1957, 377-380.

4015   Galey, Matthieu. "Un maudit de mauvaise foi." Arts, 28 oct-
       tobre-3 novembre 1964, 5-6.

4016   Gorz, André. Le Traître. Paris: Editions du Seuil, 1959.

4017   Gozlan, Serge. "De la morale de l'ambiguité à la vieillesse."
       Le Magazine Littéraire. No. 39, avril 1970, 13-15.

4018   Guendline, D. and Razgonov, S. "Deux heures avec Sartre." La
       Culture et la Vie (Mensuel publié en français à Moscou), No.
       9, septembre 1962, 35-36. Cf. Les Ecrits de Sartre, 382-
       383.

4019   Guilbert, Jean-Claude. "Les nouveaux maîtres à penser de la
        jeunesse." Combat. No. 7318, 24 janvier 1968, 8-9.

4020   Hachin, André. "Une visite à Sartre." Bulletin du Cercle
        Thomiste de St. Nicolas de Caen. No. 1, 1954, 27-29.

4021   Hallier, Jean E. "Un intellectuel bourgeois mais infiniment
        utile à la revolution." Le Figaro Littéraire. No. 1280,
        30 novembre-6 décembre 1970, 13.

4022   Hector, Josette. "La présence de Sartre." Synthèses, XXVII,
        No. 309-310, mars-avril 1972, 91-93.

4023   Jean, Raymond. "Quand sonne le glas: La technique de la lu-
        cidité divine." Le Monde. No. 1065, 20-26 mars 1969, 13.

4024   Jeanson, Francis. "Sur Sartre." La Quinzaine Littéraire.
        15 avril 1966, 19-20.

4025   Laurent, Jacques. "Les mauvaises rencontres." La Parisienne.
        No. 14, février 1954, 181-192.

4026   Laurent, Jacques. "Pour Radiguet contre Sartre." Arts. No.
        358, 8-14 mai 1952, 1, 6.

4027   Lavaud, Guy. "L'Hérésiarque et le Pontife." La Revue Palla-
        dienne. No. 21, 1952, 30-33.

4028   Lazard, Didier. "Sartre." Réalités. No. 11, novembre 1946.

4029   Lebesque, Morvan. "Sartre et le compotier." La loi et le
        système: Chroniques du 'Canard'. Paris: Editions du Seuil,
        1965.

4030   LeClezio, J.M.G. "Un homme exemplaire." L'Arc. No. 30, dé-
        cembre 1966, 5-9.

4031   Lorquet, Pierre. "Qui est Jean-Paul Sartre ou l'interview
        sans interview." Mondes Nouveaux. No. 2, 21 décembre 1944,
        3.

4032   Maquet, Albert. "Sartre et les deux points." Vie et Langage.
        No. 210, septembre 1969, 497-500.

4033   Marcel, Gabriel. "Réfutation de Sartre." Ici-France. 18
        septembre 1947.

4034   Marcheix, Claude. "Revue des revues." Tendances. No. 5,
        mars 1960, 133-164.

4035   Massis, Henri. _Au Long d'une vie_. Paris: Plon, 1967.

4036   Merle, Robert. "Sur une lettre de Sartre." _Les Lettres Fran-
       çaises_. No. 844, 6-12 octobre 1960, 1, 7.

4037   Merleau-Ponty, Maurice. "Jean-Paul Sartre ou un auteur scan-
       daleux." _Le Figaro Littéraire_. 6 décembre 1947, 1, 3. Ré-
       imprimé _Sens et non sens_. Paris: Nagel, 1948, 83-96.

4038   Morelle, Paul. "'La poésie pour la jeunesse russe c'est le
       contrepoids de la technique." _Libération_. 11 juillet 1962.
       Interview. Cf. _Les Ecrits de Sartre_, 380.

4039   Palmier, Jean-Michel. "Le dialogue avec Sartre ou l'histoire
       d'une amitié." _Le Monde des Livres_. No. 7857, 18 avril
       1970, 4-5.

4040   Paulhan, Jean. "Jean-Paul Sartre: _Situations_." _Le Figaro
       Littéraire_, V, No. 2, février 1949, 119-121.

4041   Peillard, Léonce. "Entretien avec Sartre." _Biblio et Livres
       de France_, XVII, janvier 1966, 14-18. Cf. _Les Ecrits de
       Sartre_, 426.

4042   Peillard, Léonce. "Sartre parle." _Le Figaro Littéraire_, XXI,
       No. 1029, 6 janvier 1966, 1, 4.

4043   Péju, Marcel. "Lettre au Directeur des _Temps Modernes_." _Les
       Temps Modernes_. No. 194, juillet 1962, 181-189. Also Sar-
       tre's answer in "Correspondence."

4044   Péju, Marcel. "Lettre de Marcel Péju." _Le Monde_. 17 juin
       1962, 2.

4045   Perros, Georges. "Notes sur Sartre." _Nouvelle Revue Fran-
       çaise_, XII, No. 144, décembre 1964, 1027-1037.

4046   Pfeiffer, Jean. "A propos d'_Un Beau ténébreux_." _Arche_, III,
       No. 16, juin 1946, 166-173.

4047   Philip, André. "Tribune libre: Réponse à Sartre." _Le Nouvel
       Observateur_. No. 34, 7 juillet 1965, 32. Commentaire sur
       'Achever la gauche ou la guérir' de Sartre.

4048   Pingaud, Bernard. "Culture de poche et culture de masse."
       Les Temps Modernes. No. 228, mai 1965, 1994-2001. Cf. _Les
       Ecrits de Sartre_, 414.

4049   Pingaud, Bernard. "Interview: Sartre répond." La Quinzaine
           Littéraire. No. 14, 15-31 octobre 1966, 4-5.

4050   Pingaud, Bernard. "Réponse à Sartre." Les Temps Modernes.
           No. 274, avril 1969, 1821-1823. Cf. Situations IX, 329-
           338; 361-364.

4051   Pingaud, Bernard, ed. "Sartre aujourd'hui." L'Arc. No. 30,
           décembre 1966, 87-96.

4052   Pingaud, Bernard. "Sartre répond." L'Arc. No. 30, décembre
           1966, 87-96.

4053   Poirot-Delpech, Bertrand. "Sartre trop justifié: Salut l'ar-
           tiste!" Le Monde des Livres. No. 8992, 13 décembre 1973,
           17.

4054   Pontalis, J.B. "L'entreprise de l'écrivain." Pour et contre
           l'existentialisme, grand débat. Colette Audrey, ed. Paris:
           Atlas, 1948.

4055   Poulet, Georges. "Sartre." La Conscience critique. Paris:
           José Corti, 1971, 261-265.

4056   Pucciani, Oreste F. "Sartre et notre culture." Adam Inter-
           national Review, XXXV, No. 343-345, 1970, 4-8.

4057   Robert, Guy. "Sartre ou la nostalgie d'un équilibre." Revue
           Dominicaine (Montréal), LXIV, octobre 1948, 153-162.

4058   Rostenne, Paul. "Les idées: Sartre ou la mauvaise conscience
           athée." La Revue Nouvelle, VII, No. 4, 15 avril 1948, 390-
           394.

4059   Roux, Dominique de. Maison jaune. Paris: Christian Bour-
           geois, 1969.

4060   Sérant, Paul. "De Sartre à Gilson." Revue des Deux Mondes.
           15 octobre 1960, 727-735.

4061   Sollers, Philippe. "Un fantasme de Sartre." Tel Quel. No.
           28, Winter 1967, 84-86.

4062   Tavernier, René. "Dialogue sans issue." Centre, I, No. 5, 1
           août 1946, 40-44.

4063   Truc, Gonzague. "Sartre ou l'homme et lui-même." Ecrits de
           Paris. No. 189, janvier 1961, 58-69.

4064   Vervin, Claire. "Lectures de prisonniers." Lettres Fran-
        çaises. 2 décembre 1944, 3.

STUDIES IN OTHER LANGUAGES

4065   Andersch, Alfred. Europäische Avantgarde. Frankfurt am Main:
        Verlag der Frankfurter Hefte, 1949.

4066   Anonymous. "Die Welt urteilt uber Sartre." Christ und Welt,
        II, No. 1, 1949, 12.

4067   Anonymous. "Interview mit Sartre." Geist und Zeit (Düssel-
        dorf), No. 1, 1957, 130-142.

4068   Arean, Carlos Antonio. "Sartre." Arbor, LX, No. 229, January
        1965, 49-62.

4069   Bachmann, Jakob. "Das heutige Denken von Sartre: Situation
        und Freiheit." Universitas, XXVII, 1972, 693-698.

4070   Bajnovic, Luka. "Sartre, escritor comprometido." Nuestro
        Tiempo, XXII, 1965, 668-675.

4071   Bondy, François. "Jean-Paul Sartre, zwischen Freiheit und
        Gewalt." Der Rest ist Schreiben: Schriftsteller als Akti-
        visten, Aufklärer und Rebellen. Wien: Europaverlag, 1972,
        62-85.

4072   Caruso, Paolo. "Una intervista a Sartre." Le Mani sporche.
        Torino: Einaudi, 1964, 137-149. Trad, di V. Sermonti; con
        una intervista a Sartre e una testimonianza di Simone de
        Beauvoir. Cf. Les Ecrits de Sartre, 182-184.

4073   Costantini, Costanzo. "Sartre spega la crisi della gioventu
        di oggi." Il Messagero di Roma. 25 August 1959, 4. Cf.
        Les Ecrits de Sartre, 335.

4074   Dehn, Fritz. "Werner Kohlschmidt: Die entzweite Welt." Orbis
        Litterarum, X, No. 1-2, 1956, 110-118.

4075   Della Terza, Dante. "Sartre." Belfagor, VII, No. 4, 31 July
        1952, 420-438.

4076   Falconi, Carlo. "Decadenza di Sartre." Idea, I, No. 33, 25
        December 1949.

4077   Faraconi, Ornella P. "Jean-Paul Sartre: un compagno di
        strada?" Ponte, XXVII, No. 4, April 1971, 451-471; Ibid,
        No. 5-6, May-June 1971, 684-698.

4078   Französische Kultur 1962. Köln: Verlag des Dokumente, 1962.

4079   Guereña, Jacinto Luis. "Sartre entre escritores." La Torré.
        No. 49, January-April 1965, 45-57.

4080   Haenssler, Ernst. "Sartre." Freigeistige Aktion, III, No.
        2, February 1959, 9-10.

4081   Konder, Leandro. "Sartre, suas contradicoes formais e seus
        meritos." Estuos Sociais (Rio de Janeiro), IX, No. 3,
        August 1960, 89-94.

4082   Lietzmann, S. "Anmerkung zu Sartre." Berliner Hefte für
        Geistiges Leben, II, 1947, 716-717.

4083   Loetscher, Hugo. "Sartre 1960." Kulturelle Monatsschrift
        (Zürich), XX, No. 9, 1960, 61-65.

4084   Lüthy, Herbert. Nach dem Untergang des Abendlandes. Köln,
        1964.

4085   Marcelli, Augusto. "La luna: Una vittoria o una trappola?"
        Paese Sera. 30 August 1969. Interview. Cf. Les Ecrits de
        Sartre, 479-480.

4086   Massi, U. "A propósito de Sartre." Studium, XLIX, No. 4,
        1953, 246-248.

4087   Mondrome, D. "Il messagio disperato di Sartre." Civiltà
        Cattólica, XCIX, No. 1, 7 February 1948, 252-266.

4088   Mondrome, D. "Pessimismo e ottimismo di certa narrativa."
        Civilità Cattólica, CIII, No. 2454, 20 September 1952, 598-
        608.

4089   Montesi, Gotthard. "Sartre und die Sartristen, oder Hubris
        und Erniedrigung des Menschen." Wort und Wahrheit, VII, No.
        9, September 1952, 656-674.

4090   Pelligrini, Alessandro. "Sartre oggi." Il Ponte, XV, 1959,
        474-485.

4091   Perez-Señac, Ramón. "Sartre, el novelista e el filósofo."
        Revista Nacional (Montevideo), XVII, No. 182, February 1954,
        199-221.

4092   Perroud, Robert. "L'incontro del critico e del filosofo con
        l'artista in Sartre." Vita e Pensiero, XXXIV, No. 4, 1951,
        208-218.

4093   Piater, J. "Entrevista con Sartre." Indice. No. 185, 1964,
       3.

4094   Polybois, E. "Sartre als Schriftsteller." Befreiung (Aarau-
       Schweiz), I, 1953, 156-160; Ibid, 169-176.

4095   Ruig, Rainaldo. "Sartre otra vez." Revista. No. 408, 1960.

4096   Sanavio, Piero. "Dopo la detronizzazione di Sartre hanno vo-
       luto la loro parte anche l'art decco, i femetti e il magis-
       mo: Questa nostra realtà non basta." La Fiera Letteraria,
       XLIII, No. 1, 4 January 1968, 7-8.

4097   Sanavio, Piero. "Due gruppi di giovani scrittori si conten-
       dono in Francia l'eredità si Sartre: L'incruenta guerra dei
       diadochi." La Fiera Letteraria, XLIII, No. 52, 29 Decem-
       ber 1967, 5-6.

4098   Saporta, Marcelo. "Entrevista Jean-Paul Sartre." Insula.
       No. 32, 15 August 1948. Cf. Les Ecrits de Sartre, 192-193.

4099   Saporta, Marcelo. "Una entrevista con Jean-Paul Sartre."
       Cuadernos Americanos, XIII, Vol. LXXIII, No. 1, January-Feb-
       bruary 1954, 57-64. Cf. Les Ecrits de Sartre, 272.

4100   Schrifsteller. "Sartre: Hölle im Ich." Der Spiegel. No. 7,
       17 January 1964, 74-76.

4101   Souviron, J.M. "Acerca de algunos infiernos." Humanidades,
       XVIII, 1966, 149-163.

4102   Spender, Stephen. "Un poeta en la Sorbonna." Convivium,
       XXXI, 1970, 27-45.

4103   Steffen Günther. "Die verdrangten Prügel: Sartre und Oedipus-
       komplex." Die Zeit, VI, No. 8, 1951, 4.

4104   Steinhoff, Peter A. "Jean-Paul Sartre und die Menschenverach-
       tung." Aufbau, IV, No. 2, February 1949, 97-105.

4105   Strohm, E. "Der totalengagierte Professor: Zum 50. Geburtstag
       Jean-Paul Sartres." Das Ganze Deutschland, VII, No. 26,
       1955, 5.

4106   Tschernjak, B. "Der Sartrismus, ein Zeichen der Verfalls der
       bürgerlichen Kultur." Neue Welt (Berlin), III, No. 9, 1948,
       96-103.

4107   Wahl, François. "Von Sartre zu Teilhard de Chardin." Doku-
       mente 61: Französische Kultur 1961. Köln: Dokumente, 1962,
       7-21.

4108   Walz, Hans H. "Sartre." Die Neue Furche (Tübingen), VI,
       1952, 403-407.

4109   Wurtenberg, Gustav. "Sartre und die menschliche Existenz."
       Begegnung (Koblenz), III, 1948, 447-454.

INTUITION

4110   Borrello, Oreste. "L'intuizione nella psicologia fenomeno-
       logica di Sartre." Rassegna di Scienze Filosofici, XV,
       1962, 169-199, 319-339.

ISRAEL

4111   Anonymous. "Sartre, Israël et les Arabes." Le Nouvel Obser-
       vateur. No. 33, 1 July 1965, 11.

4112   Biollay, Emile. "Jean-Paul Sartre, escamoteur d'Israël?" La
       Revue Juive de Genève, X, No. 6-7, juin-juillet 1947, 212-
       213. Cf. Les Ecrits de Sartre, 167.

ITINERARY

4113   Anderson, Perry, et al. "Itinerary of a Thought: An Interview
       with Sartre." New Left Review. No. 58, November-December
       1969, 43-66. Reprinted The New York Review of Books, XIV,
       No. 6, 26 March 1970, 22-31.

4114   Anonymous. "L'itinéraire mouvementé de Sartre." Le Figaro.
       18 mars 1972, 15.

4115   Anonymous. "Thirty Years On." Times Literary Supplement.
       No. 3241, 21 September 1967, 839.

4116   Beigbeder, Marc. "Ce qui a pu le faire." Les Philosophes
       français d'aujourd'hui par eux-mêmes. Paris: C.D.U., 1963,
       302-313. Textes recueillis et présentés par G. Deledalle
       et Denis Huisman. Autobiographie de la philosophie
       française contemporaine.

4117   Egabak, Niels. "L'itinéraire de Jean-Paul Sartre: de la psy-
       chanalyse existentielle à la méthode progressive-regres-
       sive." Revue Romane, II, 1967, 28-37.

Fergnani, Franco. see 1198, 2188.

Fields, Madelaine. see 1325.

4118   Goldmann, Lucien. "Problèmes philosophiques et politiques
       dans le théâtre de Sartre: Itinéraire d'un penseur."
       L'Homme et la Société. No. 17, juillet-septembre 1970, 1-
       42.

Huertas-Jourda, D. see 2256.

4119   Javet, Pierre. "De L'Etre et le néant à la Critique de la ra-
       ison dialectique." Revue de Théologie et Philosophie, XI,
       No. 1, 1961, 51-60. Trans. into English: Philosophy Today,
       IX, Fall 1965, 176-183.

'J'ACCUSE'

4120   Anonymous. "Sartre défend 'J'accuse'." Le Figaro. 3 mars
       1972, 12.

4121   Frossard, André. "Tous en justice." Le Figaro. 16 janvier
       1971, 1. 'J'accuse' dans le mensuel de gauche où il colla-
       bore.

JOURNAL

Bingham, William L. see 261.

JUDAISM

4122   Fachenheim, Emil L. Encounters Between Judaism and Modern
       Philosophy. New York: Basic, 1973, 201-214.

JUSTICE

4123   Allen, E.L. "Justice and Self-Justification in Sartre." The-
       ology Today, XVIII, July 1961, 150-158.

JUSTIFICATION

4124   Olafson, Frederick A. "Existentialism, Marxism and Historical
       Justification." Ethics, LXV, January 1955, 126-134.

LANGUAGE

4125   Baudoin, Dominique. "Sartre et le langage." Pacific Coast
       Philology, VII, 1972, 11-19.

4126   Berckmans, J.P. and Garot, J.C. "Une structure du langage."
        Le Point. No. 8, février 1967. Interview with Sartre. Cf.
        Les Ecrits de Sartre, 439.

4127   Berkvam, Michael. "Les pouvoirs du mot." Revue des Sciences
        Humaines. Fasicule 148, octobre-décembre 1972, 545-566.

4128   Brochier, Jean-Jacques. "Les Huns et les autres." L'Arc,
        Sartre aujourd'hui. No. 30, décembre 1966, 65-70.

4129   Champigny, Robert. "Langage et littérature selon Sartre."
        Revue d'Esthétique, XIX, avril-juin 1966, 131-148.

4130   Dieguez, Manuel de. "Jean-Paul Sartre." L'Ecrivain et son
        langage. Paris: Gallimard, 1960, 234-293.

4131   Cortez y Vasquez, Luis L. Cinco estúdios sobre el hablar po-
        pular en la litteratura francesa: Molière, Balzac, Maupas-
        sant, Giono, Sartre. Salamanca: Univ. de Salamanca, Acta
        Salmanticensa, Filosofia y Letras, Tomo XVII, No. 4, 1964.

4132   Ehrmann, Jacques. "De l'articulation: Langage de l'histoire
        et terreur du langage." Critique, XXI, No. 253, juin 1968,
        603-618. Trans. into English: "On Articulation: The Lan-
        guage of History and the Terror of Language." Literature
        and Revolution. J. Ehrmann, ed. Also Yale French Studies.
        No. 39, 1967 and Beacon paperback, Boston, 1970.

4133   Faye, Jean-Pierre. "Huns et satrapes." Tel Quel. No. 28,
        Winter 1967, 87-96.

4134   Faye, Jean-Pierre. Le Récit hunique. Paris: Editions du
        Seuil, 1967.

4135   Faye, Jean-Pierre. "Sartre entend-il Sartre?" Tel Quel.
        No. 27, Autumn 1966, 72-al.

4136   Faye, Jean-Pierre. "Sartre et les Huns." Lettres Françaises.
        No. 1122, 10 mars 1966.

4137   Gallup, John R. "Le verbe français contre Sartre." Dialogue
        (Canada), VIII, mars 1970, 663-677.

4138   Gandon, Yves. Cent ans de jargon, ou de l'écriture artiste au
        style canaille.

4139   Genette, Gérard. "La rhétorique et l'espace du langage." Tel
        Quel. No. 19, Autumn 1964, 44-54.

4140   Goff, Robert. "On Sartre's Language." Man and World, III,
       No. 3-4, September-November 1970, 370-374.

4141   Halloran, Stephen M. "Language and the Absurd." Philosophy
       and Rhetoric, VI, Spring 1973, 97-108.

4142   Jean, Raymond. "La parole poétique." L'Arc: Sartre aujourd'
       hui. No. 30, 1966, 60-64.

       Jean, Raymond. see 2809.

4143   Larthomas, Pierre. Le Langage dramatique: Sa nature, ses pro-
       cédès. Paris: Armand Colin, 1972.

4144   Lefebvre, Maurice-Jean. "La présentification (suite) et le
       discours comme image." Structure du discours et du récit.
       Neuchâtel: Editions de la Baconnière, 1971, 92-103.

4145   Plessen, Jacques. "Sartre et le langage." Het Franse Boek.
       janvier 1968, 49-65.

4146   Roche, Maurice. Phenomenology, Language and the Social Sci-
       ences. London: Routledge and Kegan Paul, 1973, 19-25, 134-
       139, 167-169, 195-204 ff.

4147   Rudolf, Anthony, ed. Languages. (Cambridge Opinion/Circuit
       Publication). London: Circuit Magazine, 1969.

4148   Saisselin, Rémy G. "De la terminologie sartrienne et de ses
       possibilités." Bayou. No. 76, 1959, 238-240.

LAUGHTER

4149   Douchin, Jacques. "Source et signification du rire dans le
       théâtre de Sartre." Revue des Sciences Humaines. No. 130,
       avril-juin 1968, 307-314.

       Jameson, Fredric. see 441.

LAW

       McBride, William L. see 39, 342.

       Poulantzas, N. see 2163.

4150   Romano, Bruno. "Sui fondamenti della fenomenologia giuridico-
       sociale di Sartre." Rivista Internazionale di Filosofia del
       Diritto, XLVII, 1970, 76-126.

4151   Scholler, Heinrich. "Interpretazione del diritto nell corren-
ti contemporanee della filosofia." Revista Internazionale
di Filosofia del Diritto, L, July-September 1973, 498-518.

4152   Van Overbeke, P.M. "Philosophie du droit." Revue Thomiste,
LXIX, juillet 1969, 435-462.

4153   Villey, Michel, ed. Philosophes d'aujourd'hui en présence
du droit. Archives de Philosophie du Droit, X. Paris:
Sirey, 1965.

LEAP

Curtis, Jerry L. see 2519.

LEFT

4154   Bloch-Michel, Jean. "Letter from Paris: On the French Left."
Encounter, XXI, October 1963, 53-55.

4155   Bourniquel, Camille. "Frankreich Literatur des Linken."
Literatur zwischen Links und Rechts: Deutschland-Frankreich
U.S.A. München, 1962, 103-124.

4156   Emmanuel, Pierre. "The 'Leftist' Group in France." The Listener. No. 1261, 30 April 1953, 706-707.

Legrand, Albert. see 2537.

4157   Montaldi, Danila. "Cronache della 'gauche'." Questioni. No.
3, May 1956, 4-11.

4158   Plumyene, Jean and La Sierre, Raymond. Le complexe de gauche.
Paris: Flammarion, 1967.

4159   Priouret, Roger. "La gauche sartrienne." L'Express. No.
910, 21-22 décembre 1968, 65.

4160   Ritsch, Frederick. The French Left and the European Idea,
1947-1949. New York: Pageant Pr., 1966.

4161   Steffen, Günther. "Die französische Linke: Mythos und Reali-
tät." Merkur, X, No. 99, 1956, 471-481.

4162   Winner, Percy. "The 'New Left' in France: Why the Intellectuals Are Cooling Toward Communism." New Republic, CXXXIII,
No. 3, 18 July 1955, 14-15.

'LIBERATION'

4163   Anonymous.   "Exclusif: Avec Jean-Paul Sartre dans la barque de
       'Liberation'."   Paris Match.   No. 1262, 14 juillet 1973, 59-
       60.

LITERATURE

STUDIES IN ENGLISH

4164   Barnes, Hazel E.   "Litterature and the Politics of the Fu-
       ture."   Denver Quarterly, V, No. 1, Spring 1970, 41-64.

4165   Bède, Jean-Albert.   "Sartre."   Columbia Dictionary of Modern
       European Literature.   New York: Columbia Univ. Pr., 1947.

4166   Blackham, Harold J.   "Sartre on Literature and Life."   Lite-
       rary Guide, LXX, No. 5, May 1955, 11-12.

4167   Block, Haskell and Salinger, Herman, eds.   The Creative Vis-
       ion.   New York: Grove Pr.; London: Evergreen, 1960.

4168   Brombert, Victor.   "Sartre: Techniques and 'Impossible Situ-
       ation'."   Modern Language Quarterly, XXX, September 1969,
       439-445.

4169   Calvino, Italo.   "Crosscurrents III: Philosophy and Litera-
       ture."   Times Literary Supplement.   No. 3422, 28 September
       1967, 871-872.

4170   Clouart, Henri and Leggewie, Robert, ed.   French Writers of
       Today.   New York: Oxford Univ. Pr., 1965.

4171   Cumming, Robert D.   "The Literature of Extreme Situations."
       Aesthetics Today.   M. Philipson, ed.   Cleveland: Meridian,
       1961, 377-412.

       Doherty, C.   see 288.

4172   Fletcher, John.   New Directions in Literature: Critical Appro-
       aches to a Contemporary Phenomenon.   London: Calder and
       Boyars, 1968.

4173   Fowlie, Wallace.   "Existentialism."   Climate of Violence: The
       French Literary Tradition from Baudelaire to the Present.
       New York: Macmillan, 1967.

4174   Garaudy, Roger.   "New Currents in French Writing."   Soviet
       Literature, VII, 1955, 129-143.

4175   Glicksberg, Charles I. The Ironic Vision in Modern Litera-
        ture. The Hague: Nijhoff, 1969.

4176   Glicksberg, Charles I. Literature and Religion: A Study in
        Conflict. Dallas: Southern Methodist Univ. Pr., 1960.

4177   Glicksberg, Charles I. Literature and Society. The Hague:
        Nijhoff, 1972.

4178   Green, Peter, ed. Essays by Divers Hands, being the trans-
        actions of the Royal Society of Literature of the United
        Kingdom, XXXI. London: Oxford Univ. Pr., 1962.

4179   Grieve, James. "Twentieth Century French Literature in Trans-
        lation." Australasian Universities Language and Literature
        Association. J.R. Ellis, ed. Clayton, Victoria (Austral-
        ia): Monash Univ., 1970, 161-191.

4180   Grossman, Morris. "How Sartre Must be Read: An Examination of
        a Philosophical Method." Bucknell Review, XVI, No. 1,
        March 1968, 18-29.

4181   Hassan, Ihab. "Beyond a Theory of Literature: Intimation of
        Apocalypse?" Comparative Literature Studies, I, No. 4,
        1964, 261-271.

4182   Heppenstall, Rayner. The Intellectual Part. London: Barrie
        and Rockliff, 1963.

4183   Hollis, James R., ed. Modern Life Styles. Glenview, Illi-
        nois: Scott, Foresman, 1971.

4184   Holsinger, Rosemary, et al, eds. The Creative Encounter.
        Glenview, Illinois: Scott, Foresman, 1971.

4185   Kern, Edith. "Abandon Hope, All Ye . . ." Yale French Stud-
        ies. No. 30, 1962-1963, 56-62.

4186   Kern, Edith. "Introduction." Sartre: A Collection of Criti-
        cal Essays. Englewood Cliffs, New Jersey: Prentice-Hall,
        1962.

4187   Knight, Everett W. Literature Considered as Philosophy: The
        French Example. London: Routledge and Kegan Paul; New York:
        Macmillan, 1958; Collier, 1962.

4188   Lakich, John. "Metaphysical, Ethical and Political Issues in
        Expressionism and the Literature of Commitment." Kentucky
        Romance Quarterly, XV, No. 1, 1968, 37-56.

4189 LeSage, Laurent. "French Literature Since World War II, Criticism and Research, 2: The Novel." Symposium, XI, Spring 1957, 16-24.

4190 Levin, Harry. "Literature as an Institution." Accent, VI, No. 3, Spring 1946, 159-168.

4191 "Literature and Alienation." Mosaic, II, No. 1, Fall 1968.

4192 Magliola, Robert. "The Phenomenological Approach to Literature: Its Theory and Methodology." Language and Style, V, No. 2, Spring 1972, 79-99.

4193 Maulnier, Thierry. "Towards a New Classicism." Horizon, XII, No. 71, May 1945, 301-309.

4194 Mayer, Hans. "Observations on the Situation of Sartre." Steppenwolf and Everyman. Trans. from the German by D. Zipes. New York: Thomas Y. Crowel, 1971.

4195 Mendel, Sydney. "From Solitude to Salvation: A Study in Regeneration." Yale French Studies. No. 30, Fall-Winter 1962-1963, 45-55.

4196 Natanson, Maurice. "Existentialism and the Theory of Literature." The Critical Matrix. Paul R. Sullivan, ed. Washington, D.C.: Georgetown Univ., 1961. Also "Sartre and Literature." Forum, Fall 1959. Reprinted Literature, Philosophy and the Social Sciences. The Hague: Nijhoff, 1962, 101-115.

4197 Nikolaiev, V. "Fighting France." Soviet Literature. No. 11, 1948, 177-184.

4198 Observer Profiles. London: Allan Wingate, 1948. Introduction by Ivor Brown.

4199 Oxenhandler, Neal. "Literature as Perception in the Work of Merleau-Ponty." Modern French Criticism from Proust and Valéry to Structuralism. John K. Simon, ed. Chicago: Univ. of Chicago Pr., 1972, 229-254.

Peyre, Henri. see 2973.

4200 Ransom, John Crowe, ed. The Kenyon Critics: Studies in Modern Literature from the Kenyon Review. Cleveland: World, 1951.

4201 Read, Herbert. The Tenth Muse: Essays in Criticism. London: Routledge and Kegan Paul, 1957.

4202   Scott, Nathan A. Jr.   "Prolegomenon to a Christian Poetic."
       Modern Literature and the Religious Frontier. New York:
       Harper, 1968, 46-64.

4203   Simon, Claude.   "Whom Does Sartre Write For?" Trans. by A.M.
       Sheridan Smith.   London Magazine, IV, No. 5, August 1964,
       56-61.

4204   Stern, Alfred.   "Some Philosophical Considerations of Litera-
       ture." The Personalist, XLIX, No. 2, Spring 1968, 163-181.

4205   Strickland, Geoffrey.   "Jean-Paul Sartre." Delta. No. 28,
       Winter 1962, 3-13.

4206   Strickland, Geoffrey.   "The Respectability of Jean-Paul Sar-
       tre." Cambridge Quarterly, I, Spring 1966, 198-201.

4207   Votan, A.   "Literature of Extreme Situations: Existentialism
       and the Romantic Protest." Horizon, XX, Summer 1949, 145-
       150.

STUDIES IN FRENCH

4208   Balmas, E.   Aspects et problèmes de la littérature contempor-
       aine. Milan, 1959.

4209   Beau de Loméie, E.   "Les doctrines littéraires et politiques
       de Sartre." Chroniques de la quatrième. Paris: Denoël,
       1956, 151-169.

4210   Beauvoir, Simone de.   "Littérature et métaphysique." Les
       Temps Modernes, I, No. 7, avril 1946, 1153-1163.

4211   Blanchot, Maurice.   "La passion de l'indifférence." Nouvelle
       Revue Française, VI, No. 67, juillet 1958, 93-101.

4212   Bloch-Michel, Jean.   "Une littérature d'ennui." Preuves. No.
       131, 1962.

4213   Boisdeffre, Pierre de.   "Aura-t-il une postérité littéraire?"
       Arts, 28 octobre-3 novembre 1964, 7.

4214   Brenner, Jacques.   Journal de la vie littéraire: 1962-1964.
       Paris: Julliard, 1965.

4215   Buin, Yves.   Que peut la littérature? Paris: E.G.E., 1965.

4216   Bessède, Robert. "Les rapports de la littérature et de l'his-
       toire de la pensée." Annales de la Faculté des Lettres de
       l'Université d'Aix-Marseille, XLIV, 1968, 67-79.

4217   Daix, Pierre. "Situation de Sartre." Lettres Françaises.
       No. 1030, 21-27 mai 1964, 1-2.

4218   Delaunay, Claude. "De Sartre à Malraux." Revue de la Médi-
       terranée, VIII, No. 2, mars-avril 1950, 215-223.

4219   Dupriez, B. L'Etude des styles ou la commutation en littéra-
       ture. Paris: Didier, 1969.

4220   Elsen, Claude. "La bibliothèque noire." La Table Ronde. No.
       26, février 1950, 134-138.

4221   Freustié, Jean. Chroniques d'humeur. Paris: Mercure de
       France, 1969.

4222   Ganne, Gilbert. Interviews impubliables. Paris: A. Bonne,
       1952.

4223   Georgin, R. La Prose d'aujourd'hui. Paris, 1956.

4224   Glucksmann, Christine. "L'origine de la littérature." Sartre
       aujourd'hui, numéro spécial de L'Arc. No. 30, décembre
       1966, 53-59.

4225   Grenier, Jean. "L'époque des sybilles." Nouvelle Revue Fran-
       çaise, I, No. 2, février 1953, 203-213.

4226   Hendericks, Paul. "Propos sur Sartre." Revue des Langues Vi-
       vantes, XXXIV, No. 6, 1968, 637-642.

4227   Jamet, Claude. Images mêlées de la littérature et du théâtre.
       Paris: Edition de l'Elan, 1947.

4228   Jean, Raymond. "Le jeune homme et la mer." La Littérature et
       le réel: De Diderot du 'nouveau roman'. Paris: Albin Mi-
       chel, 1965, 125-132.

4229   Jeanson, Francis. De Gide à Sartre. Buenos Aires: Paidos,
       1970.

4230   Kanters, Robert. "Panorama 1960." Cahiers du Sud, XLVIII,
       No. 358, décembre 1960-janvier 1961, 455-461.

4231   Lablénie, Edmond. <u>Recherches</u> <u>sur</u> <u>la</u> <u>technique</u> <u>des</u> <u>arts</u> <u>litté</u>-<u>raires</u>. Paris: Société d'Edition d'Enseignement Superieur, 1962.

4232   Lavers, Annette. <u>L'Usurpateur</u> <u>et</u> <u>le</u> <u>prétendant</u>, <u>essai</u>: <u>Le</u> <u>psychologue</u> <u>dans</u> <u>la</u> <u>littérature</u> <u>contemporaine</u>. Paris: Minard, 1964.

4233   LeClech, Guy S. "Que peut la littérature? Sartre et de Beauvoir ont posé la question à la Mutualité: Quatorze écrivains répondent à leur tour." <u>Le</u> <u>Figaro</u> <u>Littéraire</u>, XIX, No. 974, 17 décembre 1964, 1.

4234   Maurois, André. <u>Nouvelles</u> <u>directions</u> <u>de</u> <u>la</u> <u>littérature</u> <u>fran</u>-<u>çaise</u>. Oxford: Clarendon Pr., 1967.

4235   Maulnier, Thierry. "La littérature est-elle justifiable?" <u>L'Arche</u>, III, No. 12, décembre 1945, janvier 1946, 29-30.

4236   Moeller, Charles. "De la littérature existentialiste à l'exploration du monde." <u>La</u> <u>Revue</u> <u>Nouvelle</u>, X, 15 décembre 1954, 588-601.

4237   Montigny, R. <u>Sartre</u> <u>et</u> <u>l'existentialisme</u> <u>ou</u> <u>le</u> <u>problème</u> <u>de</u> <u>la</u> <u>littérature</u> <u>philosophique</u>. Lindau Im Bodensee: Frish und Perneder, 1948.

4238   Mouillaud, Maurice. "Sartre ou le trafiquant des lettres." <u>La</u> <u>Nouvelle</u> <u>Critique</u>, II, No. 15, avril 1950, 32-43.

4239   Patri, Aimé. "Responsabilité de l'écrivain selon Daniel Parker et Jean-Paul Sartre." <u>Paru</u>. No. 36, novembre 1947, 9-11.

4240   Paulhan, Jean. "Sartre n'est pas en bons termes avec les mots." <u>La</u> <u>Table</u> <u>Ronde</u>. No. 35, novembre 1950, 9-20. Réimprimé <u>Petite</u> <u>préface</u> <u>à</u> <u>toute</u> <u>critique</u>. Paris: Editions de Minuit, 1951, 79-88.

4241   Paulhan, Jean. "Sartre voit la littérature à l'envers." <u>Petite</u> <u>phrase</u> <u>à</u> <u>toute</u> <u>critique</u>. Paris: Editions de Minuit, 1951, 97-106.

4242   Perruchot, H. "La littérature engagée." <u>Larousse</u> <u>Mensuel</u>, XIV, 1956-1957, 232-234.

4243   Prémont, Laurent. <u>Le</u> <u>mythe</u> <u>de</u> <u>Prométhée</u> <u>dans</u> <u>la</u> <u>littérature</u> <u>française</u> <u>contemporain</u>. Québec: Les Presses de l'Université de Laval, 1964.

4244 Rainoird, Manuel. "De Sartre aux barbes nobles." Monde Nou-
      veau-Paru, X, No. 94, novembre 1955, 160-163.

4245 Rétif, André. "Sartre et le dictionnaire." Vie et Langue.
      No. 232, juillet 1971, 373-384.

4246 Robichon, Jacques. "La défaite de M. Sartre." Liberté de
      l'Esprit, IV, No. 27, janvier 1952, 31.

4247 Rousselot, Jean. "Sartre et l'avenir de la littérature."
      France-Asie, IV, No. 39, juin 1949, 1088-1092.

4248 Saget, Justin. "Sartre à n'en finir." Terre des Hommes. No.
      10, 1 décembre 1945, 7.

4249 Saillet, Maurice. Billets doux de Justin Saget. Paris: Mer-
      cure de France, 1952.

4250 Sénart, Philippe. Chemins critiques d'Abellio à Sartre.
      Paris: Plon, 1966.

4251 Sylvestre, Guy. "Existentialisme et littérature." Revue de
      l'Université Laval, I, No. 6, février 1947, 423-433.

4252 Vettard, Camille. "Note cursive sur M. Sartre." Du Côté de
      chez . . . Albi, 1946, 87-96.

4253 Vier, Jacques. "'Monstres sacrés' de la littérature contempo-
      raine." Pensée Catholique, XII, No. 54, 1958, 76-92.

4254 Wiriath, Marcel. Notes du soir. Paris: Plon, 1968.

4255 Zéraffa, Michel. "Aspects structuraux de l'absurde dans la
      littérature contemporaine." Journal de Psychologie Normale
      et Pathologique. octobre-décembre 1964, 437-456.

STUDIES IN OTHER LANGUAGES

4256 Balmas, E. "Il filosofo Sartre." Situazioni e profili, I.
      Milan, 1960, 45-79.

4257 Bo, Carlo. "La letteratura di domani." L'Approdo Letterario,
      IX, No. 23-24, July-December 1963, 3-22.

4258 Czaykowski, Bohdan. "Literatura i polityka, I." Kultura
      (Paris), No. 259, 1967, 98-106.

4259 Dyserinck, H. "Das Werk Sartres als Wendepunkt in der franzö-
      sischen Gegenwartsliteratur." Die Neueren Sprachen. No. 6,
      1953, 246-258.

4260 Enzensberger, Hans Magnus. "Sartre im truben 'Spiegel'."
      Texte und Zeichen (Berlin-Frohau), III, No. 12, 1957, 199-
      204.

4261 Escudero, Gonzalo. "Aventura demoniaca de Sartre." Letras
      del Ecuador. No. 69, July 1951, 1-17.

4262 Grenzmann, Wilhelm. "Sartre." Weltdichtung der Gegenwart:
      Probleme und Gestalten. Frankfurt am Main: Athenäum, 1961.

4263 Hirth, Friedrich. "Vier französische Dichter unsere Tage."
      Romanische Beitrage, I, 1950, 3-25.

4264 Ihlenfeld, Kurt. Poeten und Propheten. Witten, 1951.

4265 Kaltofen, Gunther. "Partei ergreifen für den Menschen und den
      Forstchritt: Der Schaffensweg von Sartre." Heute und Mor-
      gen. Schwerin, 1954, 426-430.

4266 Lange, Wolf-Dieter, ed. Französische Literatur der Gegenwart.
      Stüttgart: Alfred Kröner, 1971.

4267 Magny, Claude-Edmonde. "Ein Portrait Sartres." Besinnung
      (Nürnberg), II, 1947, 212-214.

4268 Mayer, Hans. "Anmerkungen zu Sartre." Ansichten zur Litera-
      tur der Zeit. Hamburt: Reinbeck, 1962, 139-154.

4269 Mendes, Joao. "Se a palavra e uma 'coisa'." Brotéria, LVVI,
      1960, 254-257.

4270 Minder, Robert. Wozu Literatur? Reden und Essays. Frankfurt
      am Main: Suhrkamp, 1971.

4271 Rattaud, Janine. "Sartre." Praxis des Neusprachlichen Unter-
      richts. 11 January 1964, 163-164.

4272 Roger, Juan. Figuras de la literatura francesa contemporanea.
      Madrid: Rialp, 1962.

4273 Ruhle, Jürgen. Literatur und Revolution: Die Schrifsteller
      und der Kommunismus. Köln: Kiepenheuer und Witsch, 1960.

4274   Stutzer, Herbert. "Existentialistische und humanistische Literatur." Die Literatur der Gegenwart. Recklinghausen, 1948, 1-5.

4275   Thumann, Albert. "1945-1947: Die markanteste Werke der französischen Literatur." Besinnung, II, No. 5-6, 1947, 215-219.

4276   Torre, Guillermo de. Problemática de la literatura. Buenos Aires: Losada, 1951.

4277   Walz, Hans Hermann. "Jean-Paul Sartre." Die Neue Furche (Tübingen), VI, 1952, 403-407.

4278   Weinert, Hermann-Karl. "Von Sartre bis Ionesco-die französische Literatur unserer Zeit, ihre Standorte und Richtungen." Universitas, XVIII, No. 8, August 1963, 825-833.

4279   Weinrich, Harald. Literatur für Leser: Essays und Aufsätze zur Literaturwissenschaft. Stüttgart: W. Kohlhammer, 1971.

LITERARY

4280   Blair, Gordon. "Sartre in British and American Literary Criticism." Adam International Review, XXXV, No. 343-345, 1970, 100-104.

4281   Denat, Antoine. "Critique littéraire et langage philosophique." Vu des antipodes: Synthèses critiques. Paris: Didier, 1969.

4282   Dufrenne, Mikel. "Critique littéraire et phénoménologie." Revue Internationale de Philosophie, XVIII, No. 68-69, 1964, 193-208.

4283   Fowlie, Wallace. "The French Literary Mind." Accent, VIII, No. 2, Winter 1948, 67-81.

4284   LeSage, Laurent. "The New French Literary Critics." American Society of Honor Magazine, XXXVII, 1966, 75-86.

4285   Lobet, Marcel. "Littérature: Perdition ou salut?" Revue Générale Belge, mai 1967, 73-84.

4686   Lobet, Marcel. "Que faut-il penser de l'existentialisme littéraire?" Revue Générale Belge. No. 5, mars 1946, 551-559.

4287   Lobet, Marcel. La Science du bien et du mal: Essai sur la connaissance littéraire. Paris: La Nef de Paris, 1954.

4288   Lundquist, Arthur. "Kring den litterara situationen." Pris-
        ma. No. 6, 1948, 6-13.

4289   Pollman, Leo. Literaturwissenschaft und Methode, 2 vols.
        Frankfurt am Main: Athenäum, 1971.

4290   Richard, J.P. "The Literary Year in France." International
        Literary Annual, I, 1958, 197-203.

LOGIC

4291   Blondel, Maurice. "The Inconsistency of Jean-Paul Sartre's
        Logic." The Thomist, X, No. 4, October 1947, 393-397.

        Farrell, B.A.   see 4870.

        Rosen, Lawrence.   see 2791.

LOOK   (the gaze)

4292   Arias Muñoz, J. Adolfo. "Valor ontológico de Le regard en
        Jean-Paul Sartre." Studium, X, 1970, 471-489.

        Fitch, Brian T.   see 2484.

4293   Gonzalez Paredes, Ramon. "La mirada según Sartre y Marcel."
        Ateneo. No. 79, 1955, 14-24.

        Lauder, R.E.   see 2477.

4294   Shouery, Imad T. "The Phenomena of the 'Look', 'Shame', and
        the 'Other' in Sartre." Darshana International, XI, April
        1971, 43-57.

        Simon, John K.   see 2641.

LOVE

4295   Arntz, A.J. Het Aanvaarden der Lichamelijkheid. Brussels,
        1951.

4296   Arntz, Joseph T.C. De liefde in de ontologie van Jean-Paul
        Sartre: L'amour dans l'ontologie de Jean-Paul Sartre. Nij-
        megen: Drukkerij Gebr. Janssen, 1960.

4297   Aubrun, J.L. "Sartre et l'amour." Quo Vadis. Montigny-les-
        Metz, 1949.

        Bohme, Wolfgang.   see 3670.

Chauffier, Louis Martin et al. see 1138.

Cronkite, Roland F. see 282.

Jest, Edward F. see 2501.

4298   Lilar, Suzanne. A propos de Sartre et de l'amour. Paris:
       Grasset, 1967.

4299   Lilar, Suzanne. "Sartre contre l'amour." Les Nouvelles Lit-
       téraires. 16 février 1967.

       Miro Quesada, Francisco. see 3023.

4300   Moreno, Julio. "El amor en la filosofía de Sartre." Número,
       III, No. 15-17, juillet-décembre 1951, 367-373.

4301   Noulet, E. "Suzanne Lilar: A propos de Sartre et de l'amour."
       Revue de l'Université de Bruxelles, XX, No. 1-2, octobre-
       janvier 1968, 147-152.

MADNESS

       Buch, Stratton, see 525.

4302   Mackay, David. "Sartre and the Problem of Madness." Journal
       of the British Society for Phenomenology, I, May 1970, 80-
       82.

       Simon, John K. see 527.

MAN

4303   Anderson, D. "Image of Man in Sartre and Camus." Modern
       Churchman, VIII, October 1964, 33-45.

4304   Anderson, D. "Man at Absolute Zero," and "Phonies and Sa-
       lauds." The Tragic Present: A Christian Study of Some Mod-
       ern Literature. London: John Knox, 1970, 49-64.

4305   Anonymous. "Der Mensch ist, wozu er sich macht." Das Neue
       forum, Darmstadt, X, 1960-1961, 123-126.

4306   Carp, E.A.D.E. Zelfonthulling in het mensbeeld van Jean-Paul
       Sartre. Antwerpen: Standaard Wetenschappelijke Uitgeverij;
       Rotterdam: Universitaire Pers Rotterdam, 1970.

Crawford, Maria A.   see 281.

4307   De George, R.   "The Soviet Concept of Man and Western Philosophical Tradition."   Philosophy Today, VIII, Winter 1964,
258-271.

4308   Desan, Wilfrid.   "The Anti-Cartesian Man or Man in the Collective."   American Catholic Philosophical Association Proc.,
XXXVIII, 1964, 119-128.

4309   Fritzch, Robert.   "Der Mensch in Jean-Paul Sartres erzähler-
ischen Werk."   Welt und Wort, XI, No. 3, March 1956, 72-
76.

4310   Gallegos, Racafull, J.M.   "El hombre de Sartre y el hombre
eterno."   Latinoamerica, I, 1949, 337-340.

4311   Glicksberg, Charles I.   "The Sartrean Man."   The Self in Modern Literature.   University Park, Pennsylvania: Pennsylvania
State Univ. Pr., 1963, 136-148.

4312   Grene, Marjorie.   "L'homme est une passion inutile: Sartre and
Heidegger."   Kenyon Review, IX, No. 2, Spring 1947, 167-185.

4313   Hayen, E. Henri.   Sartre contre l'homme.   Annemasse: Editions
L'Effort Humain, 1947.

4314   Hopkins, Jasper.   "Theological Language and the Nature of Man
in Sartre's Philosophy."   Harvard Theological Review, LXI,
No. 1, January 1968, 27-38.

4315   Jones, Robert E.   "The Existentialist and the Absurd Man."
Alienated Hero in Modern French Drama.   Athens, Georgia:
Univ. of Georgia Pr., 1962, 95-111.

4316   Mahmud, Z.N.   "Contemporary Man in Modern Literature: For Them
and For Us."   Al Magallah (Egypt), December 1961, 23-31.

4317   Mayerhoff, Milton.   "Sartre on Man's Incompleteness: A Critique and Counter-Proposal."   International Philosophical
Quarterly, III, December 1963, 600-609.

4318   Marcel, Gabriel.   "L'homme selon Sartre."   Les grands appels
de l'homme contemporain.   R. Georges, et al., eds.   Paris:
Editions du Temps Présent, 1946.

4319   Pieper, Josef.   "'Creaturidad' y 'naturaleza humana': Notas
sobre su planteamiento filosofico en Jean-Paul Sartre."
Folia Humanistica, X, 1972, 417-427.

4320   Rousseau, Richard W.   "Secular and Christian Images of Man."
        Thought, XLVII, No. 185, Summer 1972, 165-200.

4321   Scott, Nathan A. Jr.   "Jean-Paul Sartre: Advocate of Responsi-
        bility in Solitude." The Unquiet Vision: Mirrors of Man in
        Existentialism. New York: World, 1969, 120-149.

4322   Stevensen, Leslie. Seven Theories of Human Nature. New York:
        Oxford Univ. Pr., 1974.

        Thomas, J.J. see 399.

        Vallone, Aldo. see 2589.

        Wisadavet, Wit. see 407.

MAOISM

4323   Burnier, Michel-Antoine. "On Maoism: An Interview with Sar-
        tre." Telos, Summer 1973, 92-101.

MARXISM

4324   Antunes, M. "Sartre e o marxismo." Brotéria, LXXV, 1962,
        540-550.

4325   Aron, Raymond. "Althusser ou la lecture pseudo-structuraliste
        de Marx." Marxismes imaginaires, 193-354.

4326   Aron, Raymond. "Aventures et mésaventures de la dialectique."
        Preuves, janvier 1956. Réimprimé Marxismes imaginaires, 63-
        116. Trans. into English: Marxism and the Existentialists,
        45-80.

4327   Aron, Raymond. "Bagarre à l'ombre du sénat romain entre L'ex-
        istentialisme et le marxisme." Journal Le Littérature. No.
        38, 1947.

4328   Aron, Raymond. "Le fanatisme, la prudence et la foi."
        Preuves, février 1956. Réimprimé Marxismes imaginaires,
        117-159 et Marxism and the Existentialists, 81-108.

4329   Aron, Raymond. "The Impact of Marxism in the Twentieth Cen-
        tury." Marxism in the Modern World. Milorad K. Drachko-
        vitch, ed. Stanford, California: Stanford Univ. Pr., 1965,
        1-46. Reprinted Marxism and the Existentialists, 111-163.

4330   Aron, Raymond. "Introduction." Marxismes imaginaires.

4330a Aron, Raymond. L'Opium des intellectuels. Paris: Gallimard, 1955. Trans. into English: The Opium of the Intellectuels. London: Secker and Warburg, 1957.

4331 Aron, Raymond. "Of Passions and Polemics." Encounter, XXXIV, No. 5, May 1970, 49-55.

4332 Aron, Raymond. "Remarques sur les rapports entre l'existentialisme et le marxisme." Conférence donnée au Collège Philosophique, 1946. Réimprimé L'Homme, le monde et l'histoire. Paris: Arthaud, 1948. Réimprimé aussi Marxismes imaginaires. Paris: Gallimard, 1970, 27-61. Trans. into English: Marxism and the Existentialists. New York: Harper, 1969, 19-41.

4333 Aron, Raymond. "Sartre and the Marxist-Leninists." Marxism and the Existentialists, 19-41.

4334 Aron, Raymond. "Sartre et le marxisme." Le Figaro Littéraire, 29 octobre-4 novembre 1964, 1, 6. Trans. into English: "Sartre's Marxism." Encounter, XXIV, June 1965, 34-39. Reprinted Marxism and the Existentialists, 164-176 and Marxismes imaginaires, 163-191.

4335 Beaufret, Jean. "Vers une critique marxiste de l'existentialisme." La Revue Socialiste. No. 2, 1949.

4336 Bell, David R. "Marx, Sartre and Marxism." The Listener, LXIX, 23 May 1963, 867-868.

4337 Bell, David R. "Marx, Sartre and Marxism." Manchester Literary and Philosophical Society Publications, CIV, 1961-1962, 47-64.

4338 Bense, Max. "Existentialismus und Marxismus." Neue Literarische Welt, Heidelberg, III, No. 9, 1952, 2 ff.

4339 Bitschko, I.". "Friedrich Engels und die Begruendung des marxistischen Humanismus." Deutsche Zeitschrift für Philosophie, XVIII, 1970, 1184-1192.

4340 Burkle, Howard R. Review of Desan, The Marxism of Sartre. International Philosophical Quarterly, VI, 1966, 132.

       Burnier, Michel-Antoine. see 8, 78.

4341 Busch, Thomas W. "Sartre: From Phenomenology to Marxism." Research in Phenomenology, II, 1972, 111-120.

4342 Chiodi, Pietro. <u>Sartre</u> <u>e</u> <u>il</u> <u>marxismo</u>. Milano: Feltrinelli,
      1965.

4343 Chiodi, Pietro. "Sartre e il marxismo." <u>Rivista</u> <u>di</u> <u>Filoso</u>-
      <u>fia</u>, LVI, No. 1, 1965, 47-55.

4344 Collazo, Celso. "Sartre y el marxismo." <u>Revista</u>. No. 16, 31
      July 1952, 8.

      Colombel, Jeannette. see 2129, 2130, 3346.

      Compagnolo, Umberto. see 2178.

4345 Copleston, Frederick. "Existentialism and Marxism." <u>Specta</u>-
      <u>tor</u>, CCXXVI, No. 7438, 16 January 1971, 83-84.

4346 Cotroneo, Girolamo. "Il marxismo fra storia e struttura."
      <u>Rivista</u> <u>di</u> <u>Studi</u> <u>Crociani</u>, X, April-June 1973, 184-191.

4347 Cranston, Maurice W. "Le marxisme et l'existentialisme: Quel-
      ques réflexions sur la philosophie politique de Sartre."
      <u>Studi</u> <u>Internazionali</u> <u>di</u> <u>Filosofia</u>, V, Autumn 1973, 183-198.

      Cranston, Maurice W. see 2073.

4348 Delasnerie, Charles. "Des actuelles tentatives de synthèse
      entre l'existentialisme et le marxisme." <u>Revue</u> <u>Internatio</u>-
      <u>nale</u>. No. 13, 1947, 184-186.

4349 Diaz, Carlos. "Marxismos, hoy." <u>Pensamiento</u>, XXIX, April
      1973, 195-207.

4350 Domarchi, Jean. "Lettre ouverte à Sartre: Le marxisme reste
      inachevé, l'existentialisme ne lui apporte rien." <u>Arts</u>.
      No. 792, 19-25 octobre 1960, 1-2.

4351 Dufrenne, Mikel. "Note sur <u>Les</u> <u>Aventures</u> <u>de</u> <u>la</u> <u>dialectique</u>."
      <u>Combat</u>, 29 septembre 1955. Réimprimé <u>Jalons</u>. The Hague:
      Nijhoff, 1966, 169-173.

      Dunne, R. see 290.

4352 Duvignaud, Jean. "Der marxistisch-existentialistische Dis-
      put." <u>Französische</u> <u>Kultur</u> <u>1962</u>. Köln: Verlag der Doku-
      mente, 1962, 39-46.

4353 Espiau de la Maestre, André. "Sartre." <u>Der</u> <u>Sinn</u> <u>und</u> <u>das</u>
      <u>Absurde</u>. Salzburg: Muller, 1961, 87-133.

4354   Espiau de la Maestre, André. "Sartres Auseinandersetzung mit
       dem Marxismus." Stimmen der Zeit, June 1965, 161-170.

4355   Fell, Joseph J. "Sartre as Existentialist and Marxist."
       Bucknell Review, XIII, No. 3, December 1965, 63-74.

4356   Fergnani, Franco. "Marxismo ed esistenzialismo nell'ultimo
       Sartre." Il Pensiero Critico. January-March 1959, 46-78.

4357   Fetscher, Irving. Der Marxismus im Spiegel der französischen
       Philosophie. Schriften der Studiengemeinschaft der Evan-
       gelischen Akadmeien. Tübingen, 1961.

4358   Fieschi, Pascal. "Sartre a enfin célébré les noces du marxis-
       me et de l'existentialisme." Arts. No. 772, 27 avril-3 mai
       1960, 16.

4359   Finklestein, Sidney. "Marxism and Existentialism." Science
       and Society, XXXI, Winter 1967, 58-66.

4360   Finklestein, Sidney. "Sartre, Existentialism and Marxism."
       Political Affairs, XLIV, No. 10, October 1965, 52-64.

       Flam, Leopold. see 2761.

4361   Fossdal, Alf. "Eksistensialisme og marxisme." Samtiden,
       LXVIII, No. 4, 1959, 226-240.

4362   Gallo, Blas Raul. Jean-Paul Sartre y el marxismo. Buenos
       Aires: Quetzal, 1966.

4363   Garaudy, Roger. "Un faux prophète: Jean-Paul Sartre." Les
       Lettres Françaises, 29 décembre 1945, 8 ff.

4364   Garaudy, Roger. "Un faux prophète: Jean-Paul Sartre." Une
       littérature de fossoyeurs. Paris: Editions Sociales, 1948.
       Trans. into English by Joseph Bernstein: Literature of the
       Graveyard. New York: International, 1949.

4365   Garaudy, Roger. Marxisme du vingtième siècle. Paris: Edi-
       tion La Palatine, 1966. Trans. into English by René Hague:
       Marxism in the Twentieth Century. New York: Scribners; Lon-
       don: William Collins and Sons, 1970.

4366   Garaudy, Roger, et al. Marxisme et existentialisme: contro-
       verses sur la dialectique. Paris: Plon, 1962.

4367   Gervais, Charles. "Le marxisme de Sartre: Mystification ou
       réalité?" Dialogue, X, December 1971, 727-742.

4368   Gervais, Charles. "Le marxisme de Sartre: Signification et projet." _Dialogue_, VIII, septembre 1969, 272-292.

4369   Gervais, Charles. "Y a-t-il un deuxième Sartre? A propos de la _Critique de la raison dialectique_." _Revue Philosophique de Louvain_, LXVII, février 1969, 74-103.

4370   Gisselbrecht, André. "Présentation." _Sartre est-il marxiste?_ Numero spécial de _La Nouvelle Critique_. No. 173-174, mars 1966.

4371   Glicksberg, Charles I. "Existentialism Versus Marxism." _Nineteenth Century and After_, CXLVII, May 1950, 335-341. Reprinted _The Tragic Vision in Twentieth Century Literature_. Carbondale: Southern Illinois Univ. Pr., 1963, 335-341.

4372   Goldmann, Lucien. _Marxisme et sciences humaines_. Paris: Gallimard, 1960.

4373   Girardin, Jean-Claude. "Sartre's Contribution to Marxism." Dick Howard and Karl E. Klar. _The Unknown Dimension: European Marxism Since Lenin_. New York: Basic, 1972, 307-321.

4374   Girardin, Jean-Claude. "Sartre et le marxisme." _Magazine Littérature_. No. 55-56, septembre 1971, 20-23.

4375   Gorz, André. "Sartre et le marxisme." _Le socialisme difficile_. Paris: Editions du Seuil, 1967, 215-244.

Gorz, André. see 2833.

4376   Grassi, Ernesto. "Marxismus und existentielle Philosophie." _Neue Schweizer Rundschau_, XIV, No. 10, February 1947, 618-624.

Hartmann, Klauss. see 2087.

4377   Hartmann, Norbert. "Marxismus und Existentialismus." _Wissenschaft und Weisheit_, XVIII, 1955, 219-224.

4378   Hook, Sydney. "Marxism in the Western World: From 'Scientific Socialism' to Mythology." _Marxist Ideology in the Contemporary World: Its Appeals and Paradoxes_. M.M. Drachkovitch, ed. New York: Praeger, 1966.

4379   Kruithof, J. "Sartre en het marxisme." _Dialoog_, I, 1960-1961, 41-60.

Kwant, Remy C.   see 2200-2202.

4380   Lacroix, Jean. Marxisme, existentialisme, personalisme. 6e
       éd. Paris: PUF, 1966.

4381   Lapointe, François H. and Lapointe, Claire C. "Jean-Paul
       Sartre's Marxism: A Bibliographical Essay." Journal of the
       British Society for Phenomenology, V, No. 2, May 1974, 184-
       192.

4382   Lefebvre, Henri. "Existentialisme et marxisme: Réponse à une
       mise au point." Action. No. 40, 8 juin 1945.

4383   Lefebvre, Henri. "Le marxisme et la pensée française." Les
       Temps Modernes, juillet-août 1957.

4384   Lefort, Claude. "Le marxisme de Sartre." Les Temps Modernes,
       VIII, No. 89, avril 1953, 1541-1570. Réponse de Sartre:
       "Réponse à Claude Lefort." Ibid., 1571-1629.

4385   Lefort, Claude. "De la réponse à la question." Les Temps
       Modernes, X, 1954-1955, 157-184.

4386   Lewis, John. "Marxism and Its Critics." Marxist Quarterly,
       II, No. 4, October 1955, 203-216.

4387   Lewis, John. "Sartre and Marxism." Marxism Today, V, No. 4,
       April 1961, 120-122.

4388   Lichtheim, George. Marxism in Modern France. New York: Co-
       lumbia Univ. Pr., 1970.

4389   Lichtheim, George. "Rebel." The New York Review of Books,
       28 janvier 1965, 8-9. Concerning Desan's The Marxism of
       Sartre.

4390   Lichtheim, George. "Sartre, Marxism and History," and "Phi-
       losopher in Revolt." The Concept of Ideology and Other
       Essays. New York: Random House, 1967, 282-315.

Lichtheim, George. see 2097.

4391   Lukács, Georges. Existentialisme ou marxisme? Paris: Nagel,
       1948, 141-160.

4392   Lukács, Georges. "Sartre pèche contre la probité intellectu-
       elle." Combat, 3 février 1949.

Macleod, Norman. see 2100.

Maurois, André. see 2158.

4393   Molnar, Thomas. "The Manichean Marxist." _Modern Age_, IX,
      No. 3, Summer 1965, 319-322.

4394   Naville, Pierre. "Marxisme et existentialisme." _Revue Inter-
      nationale de Philosophie_, III, juillet 1949.

4395   Naville, Pierre. _Psychologie, marxisme, matérialisme_. Paris,
      1945.

4396   _Nouvelle Critique (La)_. _Sartre est-il marxiste?_ No. 173-174,
      1966, 96-198.

4397   Novack, George. _Existentialism Versus Marxism_. New York:
      Dell, 1966, 69-109, 175-206.

4398   Odajnyk, Walter. "Marxism and Existentialism." _Darshana
      International_, VI, 1966, 31-38.

Odajnyk, Walter. see 2105, 2106, 3853.

Odini, Eleni M. see 360.

Oisermann, T.I. see 2209.

Olafson, Frederick A. see 4124.

4399   Onimus, Jean. "Technique et désespoir." _Etudes_, mai 1948,
      194-202.

4400   Pagano, Giacoma Maria. "Sartre e l'insuperabile filosofia del
      nostro tempo." _Rivista di Studi Crociani_, VI, October-De-
      cember 1969, 435-446.

Parsons, Howard L. see 2837.

4401   Patri, Aimé. "Le marxisme existentialiste de Sartre."
      Preuves. No. 114, 1960, 63-69.

4402   Patri, Aimé. "Sartre y el marxismo." _Arco_, XXII, June 1962,
      364-372.

Patri, Aimé. see 2870.

4403   Pierce, Roy. "Biography of a Generation," and "Jean-Paul
      Sartre: Existentialist Marxist." _Contemporary French Po-
      litical Thought_. New York: Columbia Univ. Pr., 1966, 24-
      48, 148-184.

4404   Read, Herbert. Existentialism, Marxism, and Anarchism. London: Freedom Pr., 1949.

4405   Rovatti, Pier Aldo. "Sartre e il marxismo strutturale." Aut Aut. No. 136-137, July-August 1973, 41-64.

4406   Ruig, Rainaldo. "El existencialismo filo-marxista de Jean-Paul Sartre." Convivium. No. 11-12, 1961, 181-186.

4407   Sabetti, A. "L'esistenzialismo marxista di Jean-Paul Sartre." Società, XV, 1959, 1199-1224.

4408   Schaff, Adam. Marxism and the Human Individual. Trans O Wojtaswewicz, McGraw Hill, 1970.

        Schaff, Adam. see 2165.

4409   Sotelo, Ignacio. "Sartre y el marxismo." Boletín Informativo del Seminario de Derecho Político (Universidad de Salamanca), October 1964, 203-217.

4410   Tordai, Zador. "Sartre and Marxism." The New Hungarian Quarterly, X, No. 34, Summer 1969, 128-131.

4411   Torrevejano, Mercedes. "Sartre, del existencialismo al marxismo." Eidos, July-December 1964, 9-24.

4412   Tran-duc-Thao. "Existentialisme et marxisme." Revue Internationale de Philosophie, II, juillet 1948.

4413   Valentini, Francesco. "Esistenzialismo e marxismo." Giornale Critico della Filosofia Italiana, Series 3, VI, No. 1, 1952, 78-96.

4414   Valentini, Francesco. "Sartre e il marxismo." Aut Aut. No. 51, May 1959, 189-194.

4415   Wroblewski, Vincent von. "Sartres Existenzialistische Hegeldeutung und Revision des Marxismus." Deutsche Zeitschrift Philosophie, XVIII, 1970, 869-878.

MATTER

4416   Bambrough, André. "Principia metaphysica." Philosophy, XXXIX, No. 148, April 1964, 97-109.

        Heerz, Herbert. see 2782.

MATERIALISM

4417 Daghiri, Giairo. "Materialismo objettivato ed esistenzialismo dialettico." Aut Aut. No. 82, 1965, 18-39.

4418 Derisi, Octavio. "El materialismo subyacente en la concepción antropológica y ontológica de Sartre." Revista Filosofía (La Plata), No. 5, 1952, 48-52.

Derisi, Octavio. see 3133.

4419 Fergnani, Franco. "Soggettività e materialismo in Sartre." Aut Aut. No. 136-137, July-August 1973, 65-84.

4420 Jolivet, Régis. "Jean-Paul Sartre et le matérialisme." Giornale di Metafisica, IV, 1949, 510-518.

MAY 1968

4221 Anonymous. "Again the Days of May." Time, XCV, 8 June 1970, 37.

4422 Epistémon. Ces idées qui ont ébranlé la France. Paris: Fayard, 1968.

4423 Epistémon. Interview on Sartre's Influence on the May 1968 'Revolution' in France. Le Monde, 30 novembre 1968. Cf. Les Ecrits de Sartre, 462.

4424 George, François. "Sartre après mai." Le Nouvel Observateur. No. 384, 20-26 mars 1972, 50-51.

4425 Gilles, Françoise. Interview with Sartre on the Student Revolt. The text of this interview has been recorded, in part, "Les Journées de mai 1968 par les journalistes de R.T. L., Philips, B77757L Cf. Les Ecrits de Sartre, 461.

4426 Lafaurie, Serge. "L'imagination au pouvoir." Le Nouvel Observateur, supplément spécial, 20 mai 1968. Entretien de Sartre avec Daniel Cohn-Bendit; texte transcrit par S. Lafaurie. Cf. Les Ecrits de Sartre, 464-465. Réimprimé J.A. Sauvageot, et al. "Entretiens Sartre-Cohn Bendit." La révolte étudiante: Les animateurs parlent. Paris: Editions du Seuil, 1968.

4427 Lafaurie, Serge. "L'idée neuve de mai 1968, propos recueillis par S. Lafaurie." Le Nouvel Observateur, 26 juin-2 juillet 1968. Cf. Les Ecrits de Sartre, 466-467.

4428 Lafaurie, Serge. "Les Bastilles de Raymond Aron." Le Nouvel
      Observateur, 19-25 juin 1968. Cf. Les Ecrits de Sartre,
      466.

MEANING

4429 Greene, Theodor. "Anxiety and the Search for Meaning." Texas
      Quarterly, I, No. 3, Summer-Autumn 1958, 172-191.

4430 Smith, Colin. "The Pursuit of Meaning . . ." Contemporary
      French Philosophy: A Study in Norms and Values. London:
      Methuen, 1964, 27-47.

MESSAGE

4431 Brun, Jean. "Un prophète sublime à la recherche d'un mes-
      sage: Jean-Paul Sartre." Cahiers du Sud, XLVIII, No. 364,
      décembre 1961-janvier 1962, 287-295.

METAPHYSICS

4432 Bornheim, Gerd A. Sartre: Metafisica e existenticalismo.
      Sao Paulo, 1971, 315 pp.

4433 Fink, Paul F. "Sartre: An Existentialist Approach to Meta-
      physics." The Challenge of Philosophy. San Francisco:
      Chandler, 415-426.

      Pires, Celestino. see 4530.

4434 Porcarelli, Vanio. "La metafisica di Sartre." Rivista Filo-
      sofia Neoscolastica, XL, 1948, 249-258.

      Prince, Gerald J. see 370.

4435 Prince, Gerald J. Métaphysique et technique dans l'oeuvre ro-
      manesque de Sartre. Genève: Droz, 1968.

      Thyssen, Johannes. see 3331.

4436 Trotignon, Pierre. "Le dernier métaphysicien." L'Arc: Sartre
      aujourd'hui. No. 30, 1966, 27-34.

4437 Vircillo, D. "Metafisica dialettica e critica dell'integral-
      ità." Aquinas, XVI, 1973, 58-84.

      Vuillemin, Jules. see 2685.

4438   Whittemore, Robert C.   "Metaphysical Foundations of Sartre's
       Ontology."   Tulane Studies in Philosophy, VIII, 1959, 111-
       121.

METHOD

       Duméry, Henry.   see 1920.

MIND

       Miedzianogora, Miriam.   see 349.

4439   Morris, Phyllis.   "Sartre and the Existence of Other Minds."
       Journal of the British Society for Phenomenology, I, No. 2,
       May 1970, 17-22.

MONIST

       Wieczynski, Joseph.   see 3308.

MORTALITY

4440   Wilder, Amos N.   "Mortality and Contemporary Literature."
       Harvard Theological Review, LVIII, No. 1, January 1965, 1-
       20.

MOTIVATION

4441   Fell, Joseph.   "Sartre's Theory of Motivation: Some Clarifi-
       cations."   Journal of the British Society for Phenomenology,
       I, No. 2, May 1970, 27-34.

4442   Olson, Robert G.   "The Three Theories of Motivation in the
       Philosophy of Sartre."   Ethics, LXVI, April 1956, 176-186.

       Strozier, W.A.   see 2587.

MUSIC

       Bost, Pierre.   see 464.

       O'Nau, Martha.   see 2669.

4443   Robinson, Paul E.   "Sartre on Music."   Journal of Aesthetics
       and Art Criticism, XXXI, Summer 1973, 451-457.

4444   Souris, André.   "Sartre chez les musiciens."   Critique.   No.
       49, 1959, 579-590.

(1a) MUTUALITE

4445   Anonymous. "Sartre n'est pas venu à la Mutualité hier, ma-
       lade." Le Figaro, 1 juillet 1971, 10.

4446   Cotta, Michèle. "Le Concile et Sartre à la Mutualité." L'Ex-
       press. No. 705, 21-27 décembre 1964, 72-73.

4447   Romero, J.L. and Paseyro, R. "Discusión sobre la conferencia
       de Sartre en La Mutualité." Indice. No. 195, 1965, 23-24.

MYTH

       Andrews, Jeffery. see 250.

       Dickenson, Donald H. see 286, 793.

4448   Diez del Corral, Luis. La función del mito clássico en la
       literatura contemporánea. Madrid: Gredos, 1957.

4449   Hakim, Eleanor. "Jean-Paul Sartre: The Dialectics of Myth."
       Salmagundi, I, No. 2, 1966, 59-94.

4450   Scharbach, A. "Aspects of Existentialism in Clackamas Chi-
       nook Myths." Journal of American Folklore, LXXV, January-
       March 1962, 15-22.

       Sclochower, Harry. see 820.

       Upchurch, N. see 401.

NAUSEA

4451   Arnold, Werner. "Ennui-spleen-nausée-tristesse: Vier Formen
       literarischen Ungenugens an der Welt." Die Neueren Sprach-
       en, April 1966, 159-173.

       Dionne, René. see 471.

       Malhotra, Ashok K. see 340.

       Miro Quesada, Francisco. see 3023.

4452   Portilla, Jorgé. "La nausea y el humanismo." Filosofía y
       Letras, XXX, April-June 1948, 243-265.

       Poulet, Georges. see 491, 492.

NECESSITY

  Stack, George J. see 2116-2120.

NEGATION

4453 Paci, Enzo. "La negazione in Sartre." Aut Aut. No. 136-137.
      July-August 1973, 3-12.

NEGATIVITY

4454 Ricoeur, Paul. "Negativity and Primary Affirmation." History
      and Truth. Trans. into English by Charles E. Kelbley. Ev-
      anston, Illinois: Northwestern Univ. Pr., 1965, 305-328.

NEGRITUDE

4455 Jackson, Irene D. "Négritude in Full Bloom: A Study in Out-
      line." College Language Association Journal, VII, September
      1963, 77-83.

4456 Jean-Pierre, W.A. "Sartre's Theory of Anti-Racism in his
      Study of 'négritude'." Massachusetts Review, VI, Autumn
      1965, 870-872.

NEGRO

4457 Jackson, Esther M. "The American Negro and the Image of the
      Absurd." Phylon, XXIII, Winter 1962, 359-371.

4458 Jeanson, Francis. "Sartre et le monde noir." Présence Afri-
      caine. No. 7, 1949, 189-214.

NIHILISM

4459 "Civilisation du néant." La Table Ronde. No. 182, mars 1963.
      Special number devoted to Sartre.

4460 Clava, Giorgio. Gratuito nihilismo di Sartre. (Sguardi su la
      filosofia contemporanea, 56). Torino: Editione di 'Filoso-
      fia', 1964.

  Feleciano de Ventosa. see 4930.

  Hofer, Hans. see 2888.

  Hubner, Kurt. see 2649.

Müller-Schwefe, Hans-Rudolph. see 2714.

Zehm, Günther Albrecht. see 2496.

NIHILATION (Néantisation)

4461 Fabro, Cornelio. "L'annientamiento in Sartre." Città di
Vita (Firenze), VII, 1952, 406-417.

NINETEENTH CENTURY

4462 Artinian, Robert W. "Sartre's Nineteenth Century: A Critic
of His Criticism." South Atlantic Bulletin, XXXVI, No. 1,
January 1971, 40.

NOBEL PRIZE

4463 Anonymous. "Une déclaration de l'Académie Suédoise." Le
Monde. No. 6150, 23 octobre 1964, 11.

4464 Anonymous. "Il y avait déjà deux couronnes sur la tête de
Jean-Paul Sartre." Le Figaro Littéraire, XIX, No. 966, 22
octobre 1964, 2,6.

4465 Anonymous. "Jean-Paul Sartre: Without Nobel or Lenin."
Times Literary Supplement, 5 November 1964, 989-990.

4466 Anonymous. "Reluctant Laureate." The New Statesman and Nation, LXVIII, 31 October 1964, 640.

4467 Anonymous. "Sartre: 'I always refuse distinctions'." The
Times. No. 56, 150, 23 October 1964, 12. Text of the
statement by Sartre released in Stockholm concerning his refusal of the Nobel Prize.

4468 Anonymous. "Sartre: L'écrivain doit refuser de se laisser
transformer en institution." Le Monde. No. 6151, 24 octobre 1964, 13.

4469 Bloch-Michel, Jean. "Jean-Paul Sartre premio Nobel." La
Fiera Letteraria, XIX, No. 37, 1 November 1964, 1-2.

4470 Bondy, François. "Sartre's Refusal." Atlas, IX, January
1965, 51-52.

4471 Breitbach, Joseph. "Sartres 'Nein'." Merkur, XVIII, No.
201, December 1964, 1210-1212.

4472   Brenner, Jacques. "Sartre et le Nobel." Journal de la vie
        littéraire 1962-1964. Paris: Juillard, 1965, 320-322.

4473   Breton, André. "Le rappel de Stockholm." La Brêche, décem-
        bre 1964. Cf. Les Ecrits de Sartre, 405.

4474   Buckley, William F. Jr. "Nobel Committee and Sartre." Na-
        tional Review, XVI, 17 November 1964, 1004.

4475   Charlot, Martine. "Le refus de Sartre." Réforme, 31 octobre
        1964, 12.

4476   Chiaromonte, Nicolà. "Jean-Paul Sartre, Premio Nobel." Tempo
        Presente, IX, No. 11, November 1964, 4-6.

4477   Chiaromonte, Nicolà. "Sartre and the Prize." Trans. by Mary
        McCarthy. Encounter, XXIV, February 1965, 55-57.

4478   Cusak, Dymphna. "Jean-Paul Sartre and the Nobel Prize."
        Meanjin Quarterly, XXIV, 1965, 244-247.

4479   Daix, Pierre. "Sartre, le Prix Nobel, et la littérature."
        Les Lettres Françaises. No. 1052, 29 octobre-4 novembre
        1964, 1, 10.

4480   Dorrlamm, Rolf. "Aber Jean-Paul Sartre sagte nein." Christ
        und Welt, XVII, No. 44, 1964, 19.

4481   Dumur, Guy. "Sartre, Prix Nobel malgré lui." Médecine de
        France, décembre 1964, 44-45.

4482   Fabrègues, Jean de. "Jean-Paul Sartre et le prix Nobel." La
        France Catholique, 31 octobre 1964, 2.

4483   Fenu, Eduardo. "I premi sbagliati." L'Osservatore Romano, 31
        octobre 1964, 3.

4484   Fouchet, Max-Pol. "Sartre Nobel." L'Express. No. 697, 26
        octobre-1 novembre 1964, 71-74.

4485   Holz, Hans Heinz. "Sartre und der Nobelpreis." Stimme der
        Gemeinde zum Kircht z. Pol. Wirtsch. u. Kultur (Frankfurt),
        XVI, 1964, 693-696.

4486   Jean, Raymond. "Non récupérable: Sartre prix Nobel." Cahiers
        du Sud. No. 380, novembre-décembre 1964, 307-309. Réimpri-
        mé La littérature et le réel: De Diderot au 'Nouveau roman'.
        Paris: Albin Michel, 1965, 307-309.

4487   Johannet, René. "Jean-Paul Sartre, juge de l'académie Nobel."
        La Revue des Deux Mondes. No. 22, 15 novembre 1964, 240-
        242.

4488   Juin, Hubert. "Tel est Jean-Paul Sartre." Les Nouvelles Lit-
        téraires, XLII, No. 1939, 29 octobre 1964.

4489   Kanters, Robert. "A Literary Letter from Paris." New York
        Times Book Review, 29 November 1964, 44.

4490   Kemski, N.L. "Sartre nous explique son refus." Paris-Presse-
        L'Intransigeant, 24 octobre 1964.

4491   Maheu, René. "Sur un refus." Le Figaro, 26 octobre 1964.

4492   Marcel, Gabriel. "Prise de position." Les Nouvelles Litté-
        raires, 29 octobre 1964, 5.

4493   Marra-Lopez, José R. "Jean-Paul Sartre, premio Nobel." In-
        sula, novembre-décembre 1964, 25.

4494   Misrahi, Robert. "Jean-Paul Sartre, prix Nobel de littéra-
        ture." L'Education Nationale. No. 30, 29 octobre 1964, 19.

4495   Ormesson, Jean d'. "Pourquoi Sartre a-t-il refusé le prix No-
        bel?" Arts, 28 octobre-3 novembre 1964, 3-4.

4496   Rebatet, Lucien. "Du côté de chez Nobel." Rivarol, 29 octob-
        re, 1964, 5.

4497   Revel, Jean François. "Lénine aurait pu accepter le Nobel
        sans être confondu avec Bergson." Le Figaro Littéraire.
        No. 966, 22 octobre 1964, 7.

4498   Ritzen, Quentin. "L'obsession du refus." Les Nouvelles Lit-
        téraires, XLII, No. 1939, 29 octobre 1964, 6.

4499   Saraiva, Maria Mannuela. "Sartre e o premio Nobel: as razoes
        filosoficas de una atitude." Brotéria, January 1965, 40-
        52; Ibid., March 1965, 295-308.

4500   Sartre, Jean-Paul. "Textes relatifs au refus du prix Nobel:
        L'Ecrivain doit refuser de se laisser transformer en insti-
        tution." Le Monde, 24 octobre 1964. Aussi Les Lettres
        Françaises, 29 octobre-4 novembre 1964. Cf. Les Ecrits de
        Sartre, 402-404.

4501   Sérant, Paul.   "Le prix Nobel de la littérature: suprême hommage rendu à l'anti-bourgeois' Jean-Paul Sartre par une 'bourgeoisie' dans le sens de l'histoire."   Carrefour.   No. 1050, 28 octobre 1964, 19-20.

4502   Simon, Gérard.   "Le philosophe."   Les Lettres Françaises, 29 octobre-4 novembre 1964, 1, 10.

4503   Simon, Pierre-Henri.   "Un lauréat de grande classe."   Le Monde, 24 octobre 1964, 1, 13.

4504   Tournier, Michel.   "La revanche de l'autodidacte."   Les Nouvelles Littéraires, XLII, No. 1939, 29 octobre 1964, 7.

NOTHINGNESS

Boudreaux, Michael.   see 265.

4505   Glicksberg, Charles I.   "The Myth of Nothingness."   Arizona Quarterly, XI, No. 3, Autumn 1955, 220-229.

Jaquette, William A.   see 318.

4506   Manser, A.R.   "Sartre and 'le néant'."   Philosophy, XXXVI, No. 137, Spring 1961, 177-187.

4507   Sontag, Frederick.   "Sartre and Nothingness."   The Existentialist Prolegomena to a Future Metaphysics.   Chicago: The Univ. of Chicago Pr., 1969, 137-146.

NOSTALGIA

Hoy, Nancy.   see 316.

NOVEL (see Part III: Novel)

4508   Cruickshank, John.   "The Novel in France Since 1945."   The Critical Survey, I, No. 2, Spring 1963, 65-69.

4509   Collins, R.G. and McRobbie, Kenneth, eds.   New Views of the European Novel.   Winnipeg: Univ. of Manitoba, 1972.

4510   LeSage, Laurent.   "Introduction to the New Novel."   The French New Novel.   University Park, Pennsylvania: Pennsylvania State Univ. Pr., 1962, 1-41.

4511   Macksey, Richard.   "The Artist in the Labyrinth: Design or Dasein?"   Modern Language Notes, LXXVII, May 1962, 239-256.

4512 Magny, Claude-Edmonde. "Sartre ou la duplicité de l'être: As-
      cèse et mythomanie." Les Sandales d'Empédocle: Essai sur
      les limites de la littérature. Neuchâtel: Editions de la
      Baconnière, 1945, 105-172. Partially trans. into English:
      Sartre: A Collection of Critical Essays. Edith Kern, ed.
      Englewood Cliffs, New Jersey: Prentice-Hall, 1962, 21-31.

4513 Matthews, H.J., ed. Un nouveau roman: Recherches et tradi-
      tions. La critique étrangère. Paris: Minard, 1964.

4514 Murdoch, Iris. "The Novelist as Metaphysician." The Listen-
      er, XLIII, 16 March 1950, 473-476.

4515 Nadeau, Maurice. French Novel Since the War. London: Me-
      thuen, 1963. Trans. into English of Le roman français de-
      puis la guerre. Paris: Gallimard, 1963.

4516 Peyre, Henri. "Existentialism and French Literature." The
      Contemporary French Novel. New York: Oxford Univ. Pr.,
      1955, 216-239. Reprinted Sartre: A Collection of Critical
      Essays, Edith Kern, ed. Englewood Cliffs, New Jersey:
      Prentice-Hall, 1962, 31-38.

OBJECT

4511 Bychowski, Gustav. "The Archaic Object and Alienation." In-
      ternational Journal of Psychoanalysis, XLVIII, Part 3, 1967,
      384-393.

4518 Fitch, Brian T. "Le monde des objets chez Malraux et chez
      Sartre." Bulletin des Jeunes Romanistes. No. 1, juin 1960,
      22-25.

4519 Greenberg, Alvin. "The Revolt of the Objects: The Opposing
      World in the Modern World." Centennial Review, XIII, No. 4,
      Fall 1969, 366-388.

4520 Massey, Irving. The Uncreating Word: Romanticism and the Ob-
      ject. Bloomington, Indiana: Indiana Univ. Pr., 1970.

      Pellegrin, Jean. see 490.

ONTOLOGY

4521 Balliu, Julien. "L'aliénation et les avatars de l'ontologie."
      Revue de l'Université de Bruxelles, 20e année, août-septem-
      bre 1968, 403-419.

      Bhadra, Mrinal K. see 260.

4522   Birault, Henri. "Pour ou contre l'ontologie: réflexions sur
        l'histoire de la pensée existentielle." Critique, XVI, No.
        153, février 1960, 139-157.

        Brufau-Prats, Jaimé. see 1892.

4523   Bucio, Francisco P. "De l'ontologie phénoménologique à la
        psychanalyse existentielle." Revista Mexicana de Filosofía,
        IV, No. 4, 1961, 55-85.

4524   Caruso, Paolo. "L'ontologie phénoménologique de Sartre." Aut
        Aut. No. 51, mai 1959, 138-156.

4525   Cavaciuti, Santino. L'ontologia di Jean-Paul Sartre. Milano:
        Marzorati, 1969.

4526   Croteau. "Notes sur l'ontologie phénoménologique de Sartre."
        Revue de l'Université d'Ottawa, XXIV, 1954, 53-60.

4527   De Brie, G.A. "Ontologie en ethiek bij Sartre." Tijdschrift
        voor Filosofie, XXIV, 1962, 180-188.

        Desan, Wilfrid D. see 285.

4528   Dubarle, D. "L'ontologie phénoménologique de Sartre." Revue
        de Philosophie. No. 2, 1946, 90-123. Dans un livre: L'Ex-
        istentialisme. Paris: Téqui, 1947.

4529   Ecole, Jean. "Les pièces maitresses de l'univers de l'être
        et l'échec de la théorie générale de l'être dans l'ontolo-
        gie sartrienne." Giornale di Metafisica, XV, 1960, 52-112.

        Fabro, Cornelio. see 1991.

        Flynn, Bernard C. see 299, 2856.

        Garcia Baca, J.D. see 1996.

4530   Garelli, Jacques. "Existence et ontologie dans l'oeuvre de
        Sartre." La gravitation poétique. Paris: Mercure de
        France, 1966, 52-57.

        Hartmann, Klauss. see 1999.

4531   Kaelin, Eugene F. "Merleau-Ponty: Fundamental Ontologist."
        Man and World, III, Fall 1970, 102-115.

        Luisi, Giuseppe M. see 3362.

4532   MacIntyre, Alasdair C.   "Sartrian Ontology." A Critical His-
       tory of Western Philosophy. D.J. O'Connor, ed. New York:
       Collier-Macmillan, 1964, 518-521.

4533   Natanson, Maurice. A Critique of Jean-Paul Sartre's Ontology.
       Lincoln, Nebraska: Univ. of Nebraska Pr., 1951.

4534   Natanson, Maurice. "Sartre's Fetishism: A Reply to Van Meter
       Ames." Journal of Philosophy, XLVIII, February 1951, 95-99.

       Natoli, Salvatore. see 2011.

       Netzky, Ralph. see 1861.

       Owens, Thomas. see 3010.

4535   Pires, Celestino. "Ontologia e metafisica." Revista Portu-
       guesa de Filosofia, XX, 1964, 31-61.

4536   Ramos, O.G. "La ontología fenomenológica de Sartre." Revista
       Universidad de Antioquia, XL, 1964, 31-61.

4537   Royle, Peter. "Weltanschauung and Ontology in Sartre's Work
       and Thought." Theoria, XXXVI, 1961, 59-66.

       Royle, Peter. see 817.

       Schlisske, Günter. see 382.

4538   Shalom, Albert. "Remarques sur l'ontologie de Sartre." Dia-
       logue, V, mars 1967, 541-554.

4539   Shalom, Albert and Yolton, John. "Sartre's Ontology." Dia-
       logue, VI, December 1967, 383-398.

4540   Sheridan, James F. "On Ontology and Politics: A Polemic."
       Dialogue (Canada), VII, December 1968, 449-460.

4541   Shouery, Imad T. "Reduction in Sartre's Ontology." South-
       western Journal of Philosophy, II, No. 1-2, Spring-Summer
       1971, 47-53.

4542   Varet, Gilbert. L'Ontologie de Sartre. Paris: Presses Uni-
       versitaires de France, 1948.

4543   Verneaux, R. "Esquisse d'une ontologie du créé." Revue des
       Sciences Religieuses, XXIV, No. 3-4, 1950, 301-314.

       Whittemore, Robert C. see 1887.

Zaner, Richard M.   see 3147.

OPTIMISM

4544   Ecole, Jean. "La création du moi par lui-même et l'optimis-
       me sartrien." Etudes Philosophiques, XII, No. 3, 1957,
       469-483.

4545   Jeanson, Francis. "Pessimisme et optimisme dans la pensée de
       Sartre." Les Ecrivains devant Dieu. Reprinted Sartre: A
       Collection of Critical Essays. Mary Warnock, ed. Garden
       City, New York: Doubleday, Anchor Books, 1971, 176-185.

The 'OTHER'

4546   Allers, Rudolf. "Existentialism." Existentialism and Psychi-
       atry. Springfield, Illinois: Charles C. Thomas, 1961, 29-
       49.

4547   Arntz, Joseph. "De verhouding tot de ander in het oeuvre van
       Sartre." Tijdschrift voor Filosofie, XXIII, 1961, 237-274.

4548   Caruso, Paolo. "L'existenza altrui in Sartre." Aut Aut. No.
       47, 1958, 240-246.

       Cottier, Georges. see 911.

4549   Kern, Edith. "The Self and the Other: A Dilemma of Existen-
       tial Fiction." Comparative Literature Studies, V, No. 3,
       September 1968, 329-337.

4550   Lopez, Salgado C. "El prójimo en el existencialismo de Sar-
       tre." Estudios de Teología y Filosofía, IV, 1962, 59-69.

4551   Manser, A.R. "Existence and Others." The Aristotelian So-
       ciety, Supplementary Vol XXVII, London: Harrison and Sons,
       1963.

       Mendoza, Esther C. see 2821.

4552   Peman, José Maris. "El otro." La Estafeta Literaria. No.
       393, 23 March 1968, 4-8.

4553   Presseault, Jacques. "L'être-pour-autrui: Problème de struc-
       ture ontologique dans la philosophie de Sartre." Revue de
       l'Université d'Ottawa, XXXVI, No. 1, janvier-mars 1966, 132-
       143; Ibid, avril-juin 1966, 272-294.

       Pressault, Jacques. see 134.

Romeyer, Blaise. see 2487.

4554   Schultz, Alfred. "Sartre's Theory of the Alter Ego." Collected Papers, I: The Problem of Social Reality. Maurice Natanson, ed. The Hague: Nijhoff, 1962, 180-203.

Shouery, Imad T. see 4294.

4555   Tiryakian, Edward A. "Sartre: The Subject's Relationship to
the Social Object." Sociologism and Existentialism: Two
Perspectives on the Individual and Society. Englewood
Cliffs, New Jersey: Prentice-Hall, 1962, 130-133.

Tollenaere, M. de. see 3875.

PAINTING

4556   Kaelin, Eugene F. "The Visibility of Things Seen: A Phenomenological View of Painting." Phenomenological Studies in
the Philosophy of Experience. James M. Edie, ed. Chicago:
Quadrangle Books, 1965, 30-58.

4557   Laporte, Paul M. "Painting, Dialectics and Existentialism."
Texas Quarterly, V, No. 4, Winter 1962, 200-224.

4558   Pingaud, Bernard. "Sur le Séquestré de Venise (Tintoretto)."
L'Arc. No. 30, décembre 1966, 35.

The PARIS SCENE

4559   Abel, Lionel. "Letter from Paris." Partisan Review, XVI,
April 1949, 395-399.

4560   Allen, Louis. "Son of Calepin: The French Scene." New Blackfriars, LI, No. 605, October 1970, 479-480.

4561   Alvarez, A. "The Paris Scene." New Statesman, LVIII, 21 November 1959, 704, 706.

4562   Alvarez, A. "The School of French Brilliance." The Spectator, CCXXXI, No. 7110, 2 October 1964, 441-442.

4563   Barga, C. "Carta de Paris." Realidad, II, No. 6, November-
December 1947, 395-401.

4564   Bishop, Thomas. "The Critical View from France." Saturday
Review, 17 april 1965, 47-48.

4565   Dukes, Ashley. "The Scene in Europe." Theater Arts, XXIX,
       March 1945, 145-151.

4566   Lenoir, Jean-Pierre. "The Season in Paris." International
       Theater Annual. No. 5, 1961, 84-102.

4567   Le Sage, Laurent. "Return to the Melodrama in Paris." Amer-
       ican Society Legion of Honor Magazine, XXV, No. 4, Winter
       1954, 337-347.

4568   Lottman, Herbert R. "Letter from Paris." New York Times Book
       Review, 22 August 1971, 6, 10-11.

4569   Lottman, Herbert R. "Paris Literary Letter." New York Times
       Book Review, 16 February 1969, 46-47.

4570   Lottman, Herbert R. "Where They Eat and Ate in Paris." New
       York Times Book Review, 21 June 1970, 8, 16.

4571   Mackworth, Cecily. "Letter from Paris." Twentieth Century,
       CLXVI, December 1959, 451-461.

4572   Mauriac, Claude. "A Letter from France." New York Times Book
       Review, 22 March 1954, 28, 31.

4573   Mauriac, Claude. "A Letter from France." New York Times Book
       Review, 23 May 1964, 18-19.

4574   Patri, Aimé. "Paris Letter." The Hudson Review, XVII, No. 1,
       Spring 1964, 89-94.

4575   Patri, Aimé. "Paris Letter." The Hudson Review, XVII, No. 4,
       Winter 1964-1965, 565-571.

4576   Slonim, Marc. "European Notebook." New York Times Book Re-
       view, 28 June 1970, 10-18.

4577   Todd, Oliver. "Paris Letter." Hudson Review, XII, No. 4,
       Winter 1959-1960, 586-592.

4578   Wall, Bernard. "The French Reviews." Twentieth Century,
       CLIII, April 1953, 276-282.

4579   Wall, Bernard. "The French Reviews." Twentieth Century,
       CLIV, October 1953, 282-286.

PAST

4580   Lynch, L.E. "Past and Being in Sartre." American Catholic
       Philosophical Association Proceedings, XXII, 1947, 212-220.

PEACE

4581   Schmidt, Egon. "Sartre und der Friede." Heute und Morgen.
       No. 1, 1953, 43-45.

PERSON

4582   Coates, J.B. The Crisis of the Human Person: Some Personalist
       Interpretations. London: Longmans, Green, 1949, 9-36.

       Hana, Ghanem-George. see 3691.

4583   Markus, R.I. "Existentialism and the Person." Humanitas, II,
       No. 1, Autumn 1947, 20-23.

       Morris, Phyllis A.S. see 352.

       O'Brien, Robert J. see 359.

PERSONALITY

4584   Sève, Lucien. Marxisme et théorie de la personalité. Paris:
       Editions Sociales, 1972.

PESSIMISM

4585   Guerard, Albert J. "French and American Pessimism." Harper's
       Magazine. No. 191, September 1945, 267-277.

       Jeanson, Francis. see 4539.

4586   Kirk, Hans. "Den Franske pessimisme." Athenaeum, I, No. 1,
       1946, 334-341.

4587   Siepmann, E.O. "The New Pessimism in France." Nineteenth
       Century and After, CXLIII, No. 855, 1948, 275-278.

PHASE

4588   Barry, Joseph. "Die Verwandlungen des Sartre." Amerikanische
       Rundschau (München), V, No. 24, 1949, 117-120.

4589   Barry, Joseph. "Sartre Enters a 'New Phase'." New York Times
       Magazine, 30 January 1949, 12, 18-19.

Heist, Walter.   see 3213.

PHENOMENON

Elveton, R.O.   see 294.

4590   Elveton, R.O.   The Concept of Phenomenon.   Evanston, Illinois:
Northwestern Univ. Pr., 1973.

PHENOMENOLOGICAL METHOD

4591   Rossi, Lino.   "Il método fenomenológico in Sartre."   Il Verri,
IV, No. 4, August 1960, 104-117.

PHENOMENOLOGY

4592   Cuervo, Jean Elina.   "Fenomelogía y psicoanálisis."   Philosophia.   Instituto de Filosofia de la Universidad Nacional de
Cuyo, Mendoza, No. 35, 1969, 162-169.

4593   Earle, William.   "Phenomenology and Existentialism."   Journal
of Philosophy, LVII, 21 January 1960, 162-169, 75-84.

4594   Edie, James.   "Recent Developments in Phenomenology."   American Philosophical Quarterly, April 1964.

4595   Edie, James.   "Sartre as Phenomenologist and as Existential
Psychoanalyst."   Phenomenology and Existentialism.   E.N.
Lee and M. Mandelbaum, eds.   Baltimore: Johns Hopkins Pr.,
1967, 139-178.

4596   Edie, James.   "William James and Phenomenology."   Review of
Metaphysics, XXIII, March 1970, 481-526.

Hanly, C.M.T.   see 3692.

4597   Izard, Georges.   "Une étape de la philosophie, l'être et l'in-
fini."   La Nef, II, No. 4, mars 1945, 60-73.

4598   Izard, Georges.   L'Homme est révolutionnaire.   Paris: Grasset,
1946, 140-186, 223-230.

4599   Izard, Georges.   "Sartre o una neuva etapa de la fenomenología."   Sur, XIV, No. 130, August 1945, 53-65.

Landgrebe, Ludwig.   see 2713.

4600   Lauer, Quentin. "Four Phenomenologists." Thought, XXXII,
       1958, 183-204.

4601   Lauer, Quentin. The Triumph of Subjectivity: An Introduction
       To Transcendental Phenomenology. New York: Fordham Univ.
       Pr., 1958; Harper Torchbooks, 1965.

4602   Lee, Edward N. and Mandelbaum, Maurice, eds. Phenomenology
       and Existentialism. Baltimore: Johns Hopkins Pr., 1967.

4603   Natanson, Maurice. "Phenomenology and Social Role." Journal
       of the British Society for Phenomenology, III, No. 3, Octo-
       ber 1972, 218-230.

       Piorkowski, Henry. see 2716.

4604   Rossi, Lino. "Fenomenologia e relazione in Sartre." Il Ver-
       ri, V, No. 6, December 1961, 32-47.

4605   Spiegelberg, Herbert. "Husserl's Phenomenology and Existen-
       tialism." Journal of Philosophy, LVIII, No. 2, 21 January
       1960, 62-74.

4606   Spiegelberg, Herbert. "The Phenomenology of Sartre." The
       Phenomenological Movement: A Historical Introduction, Vol.
       2. The Hague: Nijhoff, 1960, 445-515.

4607   Schaper, Eva. "Phenomenology and Social Role: A Reply to M.
       Natanson." Journal of the British Society for Phenomeno-
       logy, III, No. 3, October 1972, 231-234.

4608   Stack, George J. "Sartre's Social Phenomenology." Studium
       Generale, XXII, 1969, 985-1015.

4609   Thévenaz, Pierre. "La phénoménologie de Sartre." De Husserl
       à Merleau-Ponty: Qu'est-ce que la phénoménologie? Neuchâ-
       tel: Editions de la Baconnière. Trans. into English by
       James M. Edie: What Is Phenomenology? Chicago: Quadrangle
       Books, 1964.

4610   Thévenaz, Pierre. "Qu'est-ce que la phénoménologie?: III,
       La phénoménologie de Sartre." Revue de Théologie et de Phi-
       losophie, 3e série, Tome II, No. 4, 1952, 294-316.

PHILOSOPHY

4611   Anonymous. "Sartre und die philosophische Wissenschaft."
       Aussprache (Berlin), III, No. 4-5, 1948, 3.

4612   Arendt, Hannah. "French Existentialism." The Nation, CLXII,
       23 February 1946, 226-228.

4613   Arendt, Hannah. "L'existentialisme français vu de New York."
       Deucalion, II, 1947, 247-252.

4614   Arendt, Hannah. "La philosophie de l'existence." Deucalion,
       I, 1946, 217-248.

4615   Arnaud, Pierre. "Aftermath-A Young Philosopher's View." Yale
       French Studies. No. 16, Winter 1955-1956, 106-110.

4616   Barrett, William and Aiken, Henry D. Philosophy in the Twen-
       tieth Century, Vol. III: Contemporary European Thought. New
       York: Harper and Row, 1971.

4617   Baulkoh, Friedhelm. "Erwachsenenbildung frei nach Sartre."
       Volkschule in Westen (Wesfalen: Portmung), 1967, 21-22.

4618   Beck, Robert N. "Existentialism." Perspectives in Philoso-
       phy. New York: Holt, Rinehart and Winston, 1961, Chapter 6.

4619   Boas, George. "Sartre." Dominant Themes of Modern Philoso-
       phy. New York: Ronald Pr., 1957, 646-652.

4620   Bobbio, Roberto. The Philosophy of Decadentism: A Study in
       Existentialism. Trans. by D. Moore. New York: Macmillan;
       London: Basic Blackwell, 1948, 53-60.

4621   Bochenski, I.M. "Jean-Paul Sartre." Philosophisches Jahr-
       buch, LVIII, 1948, 282-283.

4622   Breisach, Ernst. "Sartre: Man-Master and Useless Passion."
       Introduction to Modern Existentialism. New York: Grove Pr.,
       1962, 94-106.

4623   Breton, Stanilas. Situation de la philosophie contemporaine.
       Lyon: Viatte, 1954.

4624   Brini, Pietro. "Sartre y la dialéctica de la libertad total e
       inútil." Existencialismo. Barcelona: Luis Miracle, 1957,
       11-137.

4625   Bukala, C.R. "Sartre's Dramatic Philosophic Quest." Thought,
       XLVIII, Spring 1973, 79-106.

4626   Callot, Emile. Von Montaigne zu Sartre: Die Entwicklung d.
       französosische Philosophie vom 16. Jahrhundert bis zur Ge-
       genwart. Meisenheim, Wien: Westkulturverlag, 1952.

4627 Castelli, Enrico. L'Esistenzialismo. Roma, 1946.

4628 Coolidge, Mary L. "Some Vicissitudes of the Once-Born and of
      the Twice-Born." Philosophy and Phenomenological Research,
      XI, 1950, 75-87.

4629 Copleston, Frederick C. Existentialism and Modern Man. Lon-
      don: Blackfriars, 1953.

4630 Deledalle, Gérard. L'existentiel, philosophies et littéra-
      tures de l'existence. Paris: Edition Renée Lacoste, 1949.

4631 Félix, Henri. "Un exposé du système sartrien." Valeurs. No.
      6, 1947.

4632 Fetscher, Irving. "Grundzüge der Philosophie Sartres." Stu-
      dentische Blätter, Tübingen, II. No. 5, 1948, 5-6.

4633 Flam, Leopold. La philosophie au tournant de notre temps.
      Bruxelles: Presses de l'Université de Bruxelles, 1970.

4634 Flew, Anthony. An Introduction to Western Philosophy: Ideas
      and Arguments from Plato to Sartre. London: Thames and Hud-
      son, 1971.

4635 Gehring, R.B. "Jean-Paul Sartre." Philippine Studies, VIII,
      July 1960, 82-98.

4636 Gillet-Stern, Suzanne. "French Philosophy Over the Last De-
      cade." Journal of the British Society for Phenomenology,
      III, January 1972, 3-10.

4637 Halper, Ralph. Existentialism: A Theory of Man. Cambridge,
      Massachusetts: Harvard Univ. Pr., 1948.

4638 Jarret-Kerr, Martin. The Secular Promise: Christian Presence
      and Contemporary Humanism. London: SCM Pr., 1964.

4639 Joad, CEM. "Jean-Paul Sartre." New Statesman and Nation,
      XXVI, No. 8, 1948.

4640 Jolivet, Jean. "Chronique philosophique." Recherches et Dé-
      bats. No. 43, June 1963, 145-157.

4641 Jones, W.T. Kant to Wittgenstein to Sartre: A History of
      Western Philosophy, 2nd ed. New York: Harcourt, Brace, 1969.

4642 Knight, Everett W. The Objective Society. New York: Brazil-
       ler, 1959.

4643 Koch, Adrienne. Philosophy For a Time of Crisis. New York:
       Dutton, 1959.

4644 Kropp, Gerhard. Von Lao-Tse zu Sartre: Ein Gang durch die
       Geschichte der Philosophie. Berlin: Gebrüder Weiss, 1958.

4645 Lacroix, Jean. L'Echec, 2e éd. révisée. Paris: Presses Uni-
       versitaires de France, 1965.

4646 Lewis, H.D. "Philosophy Surveys, X: The Philosophy of Relig-
       ion, 1945-1952, Part II." The Philosophical Quarterly, IV,
       No. 16, July 1956, 262-274.

4647 Marcel, Gabriel. "Situation de la philosophie française."
       Conjonction (Haiti), I, No. 6, 1947, 16-18.

4648 Marsak, Leonard. French Philosophy from Descartes to Sartre.
       Cleveland: Meridian Books, 1961.

4649 Meyer, Hans. Geschichte der abendländischen Weltanschauung.,
       Vol. V: Die Weltanschaung der Gegenwart. Wurzburg: F.
       Schoningn, 1951.

4650 Mihalich, Joseph. "Jean-Paul Sartre." Existentialist Think-
       ers and Thought. Frederic F. Patka, ed. New York: Philo-
       sophical Library, 1962, 126-137.

4651 Montefiore, Alan. "Conversation With Philosophers: Alan Mon-
       tefiore Looks with Brian Magee at the Work Done by Foreign
       Philosophers." The Listener, LXXXV, No. 2188, 4 March 1971,
       267-271.

4652 Mounier, Emmanuel. "Perspectives existentialistes et perspec-
       tives chrétiennes." Malraux, Camus, Sartre, Bernanos: L'es-
       poir des désespérés. Paris: Editions du Seuil, 1970, 111-
       143.

4653 Mueller, Fernand Lucien. L'irrationalisme contemporain.
       Paris: Payot, 1970.

4654 Muller, Max. Crise de la métaphysique: Situation de la phi-
       losophie au vingtième siècle. Paris: Desclée de Brouwer,
       1953.

4655 Muller, Max. Existenzphilosophie im geistigen Leben der Ge-
      genwart. Heidelberg, 1958.

4656 Murguia, Adolfo. "Acerca de la muerte de la filosofia." Re-
      vista de Occidente, XXXIX, No. 116, November 1972, 234-243.

4657 Nadler, K. "Die französische Existenzphilosophie der Gegen-
      wart." Die Tatewelt, September 1946.

4658 Natanson, Maurice. "An Introduction to Existentialism." The
      University of Kansas Review, XVII, No. 2, Winter 1950, 130-
      139.

4659 Nauta, Lolle W. "Sartre neues Position." Archiv für Philoso-
      phie, XIII, No. 1-2, December 1964, 141-172.

4660 Patri, Aimé. "Vues d'ensemble sur l'existentialisme." Paru.
      No. 26, janvier 1946.

4661 Querido, R.M. "A Philosophy of Despair." National Review,
      September 1947, 237-241.

4662 Revel, Jean-François. "Appendice 4: Le malheur d'être philo-
      sophe." Pourquoi des philosophes?: 2: La cabale des dévots,
      éd. augmentée. Paris: Pauwert, 1965, 284-290.

4663 Revel, Jean-François. Pourquoi des philosophes? Paris: J.J.
      Pauwert, 1964.

4664 Robert, Jean-Dominique. "Philosophie et sciences de l'homme
      selon Sartre." Archives de Philosophie, XXXII, avril-juin
      1969, 244-284.

4665 Ruta, Salvatore. Sintesi di storia della filosofia e della
      scienze, Vol. III: Dai Post-Kantiani à Sartre, 2nd ed. Mi-
      lano: Renon, 1960.

4666 Ruta, Salvatore. Storia della filosofia da Kant a Sartre.
      Milano: Renon, 1957.

4667 Ruyer, R. "Les observables et les participables." Revue
      Philosophique de la France et de l'Etranger, octobre-décem-
      bre 1966, 419-450.

4668 Sertillanges, A.D. "El mundo desesperado de Sartre." Lec-
      tura, LXXXIX, 15 October 1952, 103-114.

4669   Sève, Lucien. "Panorama de la philosophie française nou-
       velle." La Pensée. No. 88, novembre-décembre 1959, 51-80.

4670   Sève, Lucien. La philosophie française contemporaine et sa
       genèse de 1789 à nos jours. Paris: Editions Sociales, 1962.

4671   Simon, Yves. Par-délà l'experience du désespoir. Paris: So-
       ciété Internationale du Livre, 1946.

4672   Stumpf, Samuel E. Socrates to Sartre. New York: McGraw-Hill,
       1966.

4673   Trotignon, Pierre. Les Philosophes français d'aujourd'hui.
       Paris: Presses Universitaires de France, 1967.

4674   Van der Merwe, N.T. "Que via, philosophia?" Philosophia
       Reformata, XXXVIII, 1973, 84-96.

4675   Yovel, Yirmiyahu. "Lucidity and Synthesis in Sartre's Philos-
       ophy." Iyyun, XXIII, April-October 1972, 136-151. In He-
       brew.

PIERRE (Le thème de la pierre)

4676   Knabenhaus, Brigitte. "Sartre." Le thème de la pierre chez
       Sartre et quelques poètes modernes. Zürich: Juris Druck,
       1969, 5-58.

PLAY

4677   Netzsky, Ralph. "Sartre's Ontology Re-Appraised: Playful
       Freedom." Philosophy Today, XVIII, No. 2, Summer 1974, 125-
       136.

POETICS

       Benanou, Michel. see 2807.

4678   Erlich, Victor. "A Note on Sartre's Poetics." Bucknell Re-
       view, IX, May 1960, 123-129.

       Hahn, Paul. see 2427.

POETRY

       Bataille, Georges. see 1649.

4679   Grubbs, Henry A. "The Essence of Poetry: A Concept and a Di-
       lemma." Yale French Studies, Spring-Summer 1949, 43-52.

Ungar, Steven R.   see 400.

POLITICS

STUDIES IN ENGLISH

Alvarez del Vayo, J.   see 3855.

4680   Anonymous.   "Commentary." Ramparts Magazine, October 1969,
       48-49.

4681   Anonymous.   "Culture Goes to Court." Times Literary Supple-
       ment.   No. 3318, 30 September 1965, 851-852.

4682   Anonymous.   "In Defense of Violence." Newsweek, LXXV, 8 June
       1970, 57.

4583   Anonymous.   "The French Ecarians." Times Literary Supplement,
       23 September 1965, 826.

4684   Anonymous.   "News Points: France: 'Intimidation' of the Intel-
       lectuals." Tribune, 7 October 1960, 9.

4685   Anonymous.   "Print and Be Seized." Time, XCVI, 16 November
       1970, 76.

Barry, Joseph A.   see 4588, 4589.

Benichou, P.   see 3889.

Bertman, Martin A.   see 2505.

4686   Bondy, François.   "A New Sartre?" Encounter, XXXV, July 1970,
       61-63.

4687   Bondy, François.   "Sartre." The New Left. Maurice W. Cran-
       ston, ed.   New York: Liberal Pr., 1971, 51-82.

4688   Bondy, François.   "Sartre and Politics." Journal of Contem-
       porary History, II, April 1967, 25-48.

4689   Burnet, Mary.   "Revolutionary Democrats." New York Herald
       Tribune, Paris ed.   2 June 1948. On. R.D.R; Cf. Les Ecrits
       de Sartre, 201.

Burnier, Michel-Antoine.   see 8.

4690   Capoya, E.   "Free Self in a Captive Society." Saturday Re-
       view, 48, 12 June 1965, 40-41.

4691   Cranston, Maurice. _Jean-Paul Sartre_. New York: Grove Pr.;
       London: Oliver and Boyd, 1962.

4692   Cranston, Maurice. "Men and Ideas: Sartre." _Encounter_,
       XVIII, April 1962, 34-45.

4693   Cranston, Maurice. "Sartre and Violence: A Philosopher's Com-
       mitment to a Pledge." _Encounter_, XXIX, July 1967, 18-24.

       Cranston, Maurice. see 3193.

4694   Eskin, Stanley G. "The Political Themes in Sartre's Literary
       Works." _Midway_, IX, No. 4, Spring 1969, 69-98.

4695   Flanner, Janet (Genet). "Letter from Paris." _New Yorker_,
       XLIII, 13 May 1967, 170 ff.

4696   Flanner, Janet (Genet). _Paris Journal, 1944-1965_. New York:
       Atheneum, 1965.

4697   Gilman, Richard. "The Writer as the Conscience of France."
       Horizon, XI, No. 2, November 1959, 66-72.

4698   Gorer, Geoffrey. "Pompous Pilot." _The Listener_, XLIII, No.
       1117, 22 June 1950, 107.

4699   Hamilton, Kenneth. "Life in the House that _angst_ Built."
       Hibbert Journal, LVII, No. 224, October 1958, 46-55.

4700   Hampshire, Stuart. "Reply to Lionel Abel on Sartre." _Parti-
       san Review_, XXXIII, Winter 1966, 160.

4701   Hobson, Harold. "Judgment Day." _Sunday Times_. No. 7704, 31
       January 1971, 29.

4702   Howard, Richard. "Letter from Paris." _Evergreen Review_, II,
       No. 8, Spring 1959, 171-174.

4703   Kappler, Frank. "Dealing With Earthly Hells." _Life_, LVII,
       No. 19, 6 November 1964, 98-112.

4704   Karol, K.S. "Paris Undercurrents." _New Statesman_, LIV, No.
       1397, 21 December 1957, 846-847.

4705   Knight, Everett W. "The Politics of Existentialism." _Twen-
       tieth Century_, LXV, No. 930, August 1954, 142-153.

4706 Kurhnelt Leddihin, Erich von. "Catholic Leadership in Europe." Catholic World, CLXXI, No. 1026, September 1950, 413-419.

4707 Lüthy, Herbert. "France's New Parochial Nationalism." Commentary, XVII, May 1954, 435-437.

4708 Mayne, Richard. "Five Million French Reds?" The Listener, LXXXII, No. 2016, 7 August 1969, 190-191.

4709 McCarthy, Mary. "Sartre and the McCoy." Politics, VI, No. 42, Winter 1949, 49-51.

4710 Millar, Robert. "Don't Let Unity Die." Tribune, 31 May 1957, 12.

4711 Molnar, Thomas. "The Politics of Sartre." The Commonweal, LXVI, 2 August 1957, 439-442.

4712 Parisot, Paul. "Keeping Up With Mr. Sartre." Encounter, May 1954, 56-58.

4713 Roberts, Nesta. "Sartre's Search." The Guardian, 29 September 1970, 11.

4714 Sargeant, Lyman T. "Existentialism and Utopianism: A Reply to Frederick L. Polack." Minnesota Review, VI, 1966, 72-75.

4715 Seymour-Smith, Martin. "Thinking Pink." Spectator, CCXX, No. 7281, 12 January 1968, 43.

4716 Singer, Daniel. "Who's Afraid of Sartre?" New Statesman, LXXXII, 9 July 1971, 38.

4717 Singer, Daniel. "The Writing on the Wall." New Statesman, LXXX, No. 7281, 12 January 1968, 201-202.

4718 Somit, A. "Sartre's Existentialism As a Political Theory." Social Science, XXV, January 1950, 40-47.

4719 Thody, Philip. "Jean-Paul Sartre." New Statesman, 8 October 1960, 531-532.

4720 Thody, Philip. Jean-Paul Sartre: A Literary and Political Study. New York: Macmillan, 1961.

4721 Thody, Philip. "Sartre: A Writer's Politics." Twentieth Century, CLXV, No. 983, January 1959, 13-22.

Walzer, Michael. see 1035.

4722 Weinstock, H. "Crisis and Hope: Interview." The Nation,
       CCVII, 30 September 1968, 297.

4723 Wolheim, Richard. "The Political Philosophy of Existential-
       ism." Cambridge Journal, VII, October 1953, 3-19.

Woodle, Gary L. see 408.

STUDIES IN FRENCH

Adamov, Arthur. see 1469.

4724 Aimel, Georges. "La décomposition du 'sartrisme'." Ecrits
       de Paris. No. 201, février 1962, 42-55.

4725 Anonymous. "Conférence de presse après les incidents du
       Sacré-Coeur." Le Figaro, 16 janvier 1971, 12.

4726 Anonymous. "Congrès des peuples pour la paix." l'Humanité.
       12 décembre 1952.

4727 Anonymous. "Dans L'Idiot International, M. Sartre: 'Je me
       considère comme disponible pour toutes les tâches politique-
       ment justes qui me seront demandées." Le Monde. No. 7995,
       septembre 27-28 1970, 8.

4728 Anonymous. "L'émission des Temps Modernes a été interdite ou
       supprimé." Combat, 3 décembre 1947, 1.

4729 Anonymous. "L'enfer sartrien." L'Express. No. 1004, 5-11
       octobre 1970, 14-15. Concernant La Cause du Peuple.

4730 Anonymous. "L'esprit et la liberté." Le Nouvel Observateur.
       No. 204, 18-24 novembre 1968, 46.

4731 Anonymous. "Inculpé pour diffamation." Le Figaro, 21 juin
       1971, 10.

4732 Anonymous. "Jean-Paul Sartre parle de l'anticommunisme à la
       tribune des Temps Modernes." Combat, 28 octobre 1947, 1.

4733 Anonymous. "Manifestations devant le ministère de la jus-
       tice." Le Figaro, éd. departmentale, 18 janvier 1972, 8.

4734 Anonymous. "On en parlera demain; Sartre: Maintenant, Tout."
       Le Nouvel Observateur. No. 308, 5-11 octobre 1970, 23.

4735   Anonymous. On Sartre's resignation from the Rassemblement démocratique républicain. Le Monde, 27 octobre 1949.

4736   Anonymous. "Presse: Sartre dirige une nouvelle publication gauchiste, Tout." Le Monde. No. 7996, 29 septembre 1970, 11.

4737   Anonymous. "Le Rassemblement démocratique républicain, R.D.R." Franc-Tireur, 13 mars 1948.

4738   Anonymous. "Sartre: L'alibi." Le Nouvel Observateur. No. 1, 19 novembre 1964, 1,5.

4739   Anonymous. "Sartre convoqué au Palais pour diffamation envers la police." Le Figaro, 24 septembre 1971, 15.

4740   Anonymous. "Sartre défend 'J'accuse'." Le Figaro, 3 mars 1972, 12.

4741   Anonymous. "Sartre en prison?" Le Nouvel Observateur. No. 286, 4-10 mai 1970, 20.

4742   Anonymous. "Sartre fonde l'agence de presse 'Libération' avec Maurice Clavel." Le Figaro, 1 juillet 1971, 10.

4743   Anonymous. "Sartre inculpé de diffamation." Le Figaro, 18 janvier 1972, 9.

4744   Anonymous. "Sartre inculpé d'injures envers la Caisse d'Assurance vieillesse artisanale." Le Figaro, 15 mars 1972, 16.

4745   Anonymous. "Sartre n'est pas venu à la Mutualité hier, malade." Le Figaro, 1 juillet 1971, 10.

4746   Anonymous. "Sartre ouvre un dialogue." Peuple du Monde, 11 juin 1949.

4747   Anonymous. "Sur la plainte de la CANCAVA, M. Sartre est inculpé d'injures publiques." Le Monde. No. 8451, 16 mars 1972, 10.

4748   Beau de Loménie, E. "Les doctrines littéraires et politiques de Sartre." Chroniques de la quatrième. Paris: Denöel, 1956, 151-169.

4749   Bedel, Jean. "Sartre: 'C'est la première fois que je vois un espoir se dessiner parmi les hommes'." Libération, 18 dé-

cembre 1952. Interview. Concernant le Congrès de Vienne,
12-19 décembre 1952.

4750 Bergeron, Regis. "Sartre retour du Congrès de Vienne: 'Nous
avons, l'écrivain soviétique Korneitchouk et moi-même, dé-
cidé de poursuivre un dialogue fécond." France-URSS. No.
90, février 1952, 7-8. Cf. Les Ecrits de Sartre, 260.

4751 Boisdeffre, Pierre de. "Sartre, génie dévoyé." Nouvelles
Littéraires, 28 mars 1970, 1, 7.

4752 Boisdeffre, Pierre de. "Témoignages en marge d'une enquête."
Liberté de l'Esprit, Summer 1949, I.

4753 Bosquet, M. On Sartre's Conferences in Tchechoslovakia, décembre 1963. L'Express, 16 janvier 1964.

4754 Bosschère, Guy de. "Lettre à Sartre sur la non-violence."
Synthèses, XIII, No. 149, octobre 1958, 253-266.

4755 Boussinot, Paule. Interview with Sartre on his participation
in the 'Congrès de Vienne'. Défense de la Paix, numéro spécial, décembre 1952, 12-14. Cf. Les Ecrits de Sartre.

4756 Buin, Yves. "Sartre parle . . ." Clarté. No. 55, mars-avril
1964, 41-47. Cf. Les Ecrits de Sartre, 397-398.

4757 Burnier, Michel-Antoine. "Raymond Aron: L'opium des conserva-
teurs." Magazine Littéraire. No. 28, avril-mai 1969, 36-
39.

4758 Burnier, Michel-Antoine. "Un combat politique." Sartre aujourd'hui. No. 30, décembre 1966, 15-19.

Burnier, Michel-Antoine. see 78.

4759 Châtelet, François. "Sartre et la politique." La Quinzaine
Littéraire. No. 18, 15-31 décembre 1966, 22-23.

4760 C.G.L. "Le regret a refroidi Sartre." Le Figaro Littéraire.
No. 1236, 26 janvier-1 février 1970, 21.

4761 Escarpit, Robert. "Au jour le jour: Sartre au bûcher." Le
Monde. No. 6152, 25-26 octobre 1964, 1.

4762 Escarpit, Robert. "Au jour le jour: Les mauvais diables et
les bons dieux." Le Monde. No. 7929, 12-13 juillet 1970,
1.

4763   Etiemble, René. "Jean-Paul Sartre." C'est le bouquet: Hy-
        giène des lettres, V. Paris: Gallimard, 1967, 433-449.

4764   Etiemble, René. "Lettre ouverte à Sartre sur l'unité de mau-
        vaise action." Arts, 24-30 juillet 1953. Réimprimé Litté-
        rature dégagée (1942-1953): L'hygiène des lettres. Paris:
        Gallimard, 1955, 142-160.

4765   Fayard, Jean. "Procès-verbal: Le Tribunal populaire interdit
        est remplacé par une conférence de presse." Le Figaro,
        28 juin 1971, 1, 10.

4766   Fenzl, Richard. "Sartre: Debout les morts." Praxis des Neu-
        sprachlischen Unterrichts, 11 janvier 1964, 302-307.

4767   Frossard, André. "OPAM vient de prendre la direction au quat-
        rième journal d'extrême gauche." Le Figaro, 4 juin 1971, 1,
        6.

4768   Frossard, André. "Procès-tient à son procès populaire de la
        police, qui aura lieu le 27 juin." Le Figaro, 26 juin 1971,
        1.

4769   Frossard, André. "Tous en justice: 'J'Accuse' dans le mensuel
        de gauche où il collabore." Le Figaro, 16 janvier 1971, 1.

4770   Frossard, André. "Soldatesque: L'Armée française et la tor-
        ture." Le Figaro, 9 février 1972, 1.

4771   Hébert, Christian. "Répression: L'inculpation de Sartre."
        Le Nouvel Observateur. No. 346, 28 juin-4 juillet 1971,
        14-15.

4772   Hervé, Pierre. "Ce qui fait délirer Sartre." Le Nouveau Can-
        dide, 29 décembre 1961.

4773   Jeanson, Francis. "Lettre à Sartre." Les Temps Modernes.
        No. 169-170, avril-mai 1960.

4774   Jeanson, Francis. "Pris d'une nausée politique, Sartre quitte
        le R.D.R." Samedi Soir, 13 octobre 1949, 13.

4775   Joncret, E.F. "Sacré Jean-Paul Sartre." Tribune Française
        des Hommes de Progrès. No. 5, juillet-août 1970.

4776   Kahn, Jean-François. "L'épée de Sartre." L'Express. No.
        817, 13-19 février 1967, 37-38.

4777   Kanapa, Jean. Comme si la lutte entière . . . Paris: Nagel,
       1946.

4778   Kanapa, Jean. "Lettre au Directeur." L'Humanité, 24 mars
       1954. Cf. Les Ecrits de Sartre, 273.

4779   Kravetz, Marc. "Sartre et la politique." Magazine Litté-
       raire. No. 55-56, septembre 1971, 27-32.

4780   Lefebvre, Henri. "Le destin de la liberté est en jeu."
       Arts. No. 850, 3-9 janvier 1962, 1, 3.

4781   Legris, Michel. "M. Sartre à la Sorbonne: Pour l'Association
       du socialisme et de la liberté." Le Monde. No. 7263, 22
       mai 1968, 3. Cf. Les Ecrits de Sartre, 465-466.

4782   Lelong, H.M. "Sartre optimiste." Le Croix de Paris, 5-6 no-
       vembre 1945.

4783   Lemaitre, Gabriel. "Choisir l'espoir." Etudes, Tome CCLXII,
       1950, 216-226.

4784   Martin-Chauffier, Louis. "Où en est Sartre? En littérature,
       un grand; en politique, un enfant." Le Figaro Littéraire.
       No. 1280, 30 novembre-6 décembre 1970, 10-12.

4785   "Masses, spontanéité, parti: Discussion entre Sartre et la
       direction du Manifesto." Les Temps Modernes, XXVI, No. 282,
       juin 1970, 1043-1063.

4786   Mauriac, Claude. "Pour un dialogue de bonne foi." Liberté
       de l'Esprit, février 1949.

4787   Mauriac, François. "Le bloc-notes." Le Figaro Littéraire,
       29 octobre 1964, 26.

4788   Mauriac, François. "Le bloc-notes . . ." Le Figaro Litté-
       raire. No. 1262, 27 juillet-2 août 1970, 4-5.

4789   Mauriac, François. "Le bloc-notes de . . ." Le Figaro Lit-
       téraire. No. 1256, 15-21 juin 1970, 4-5.

4790   Mauriac, François. "Mauriac répond à ses critiques." Maga-
       zine Littéraire. No. 22, octobre 1962, 17-19.

4791   Mauriac, François. Le Nouveau bloc-notes, 1958-1960. Paris:
       Flammarion, 1961.

4792   Mauriac, François. Le Nouveau bloc-notes, 1961-1964. Paris: Flammarion, 1968, 54-57.

4793   Mauriac, François. "La politique de M. Sartre." Le Figaro, 25 avril 1949. Concernant Entretiens sur la politique. Réimprimé "Les tribulations d'un 'rat visqueux'," "La seconde épitre sartrienne." Mémoires politiques. Paris: Grasset, 1967. Cf. Les Ecrits de Sartre, 211-212.

4794   Mauriac, François. "La politique de Sartre." Le Figaro, 4 mai 1948.

4795   Mauriac, François. "Sartre." Opéra, XVII, No. 1, 1951.

4796   Mauriac, François. "La seconde épitre sartrienne." Le Figaro. No. 2578, 23 décembre 1953, 1.

4797   Molnar, Thomas. "Présentation de Sartre." Défense de l'Occident. No. 78, janvier 1969, 14-25; Ibid. No. 79, février 1969, 28-40.

4798   Monnerot, Jules. "Petit crayon de M. Sartre." Liberté de l'Esprit, V, No. 37, janvier 1953, 31-32.

4799   Mounier, Emmanuel. "Premier signe: R.D.R." Esprit, XVI, No. 3, 1948, 462-464.

4800   Naury, Jean-Paul (Pseudonym of Michel-Antoine Burnier). "Entretien avec Sartre." Tribune Etudiante, No. 5-6, janvier-février 1962, 6-7. Cf. Les Ecrits de Sartre, 276-277.

4801   Olguine, Constantin. "Le 'Kommounist' contre Sartre." Problèmes Soviétiques. No. 8, 1964, 47-62.

4802   Ollivier, Albert. "L'existentialisme au micro . . . Sartre vous parle . . . Et ce qu'en pensent . . . Paul Claudel et al." Carrefour, IV, No. 163, 29 octobre 1947, pp. i, 7.

4803   Ormesson, Jean de. "Libres opinions: Sic vos . . . " Le Monde. No. 8113, 12 février 1971, 27.

4804   Parain, Brice. "Il suffisait d'y penser." Cheval de Troie. No. 1, juin 1947, 17-18.

4805   Parquin, Jean. "Le cheval en est mort." La Table Ronde. No. 43, juillet 1951, 161-166.

4806   Pauwels, Louis. "L'affaire des Temps Modernes à la radio." Combat, 23 octobre 1947, 1.

4807   Pauwels, Louis. "A la veille de reprendre ses émissions à la
       radio, Sartre déclare à Combat: 'Il est nécessaire de faire
       compagne contre la croyances en la fatalité de la guerre
       russo-américaine'." Combat, 18 octobre 1947, 1, 3. Cf.
       Les Ecrits de Sartre, 169-170.

4808   Pauwels, Louis. "Tempepête à la radio: Sartre répond à Guillain
       de Benouville et à Henry Thores qui avaient refusé un débat
       contradictoire sur le R.P.F." Combat, 22 octobre 1947,
       1, 3. Cf. Les Ecrits de Sartre, 171.

4809   Périer, François. "Sacré Sartre." Caliban. No. 31, septem-
       bre 1949, 17-21.

4810   Périer-Daville, Denis. "Les 'tribunaux populaires': Une dan-
       gereuse parodie." Le Figaro, 5 juillet 1971, 4.

4811   Revel, Jean-François. "De l'insoumission philosophique."
       Contrecensures. Paris: J.J. Pauvert, 1966, 202-205.

4812   Revel, Jean-François. "Philosophie et politique chez Sartre."
       Contrecensures. Paris: J.J. Pauvert, 1966, 220-225.

4813   Rony, Jean. "Sartre et la politique." Sartre est-il marx-
       iste? La Nouvelle Critique. No. 173-174, mars 1966, 100-
       128.

4814   Roy, Claude. "La nouvelle Sainte Alliance." Le Nouvel Obser-
       vateur, 2-8 février 1970, 34-35.

4815   Sartre, Jean-Paul. "L'alibi." Le Nouvel Observateur, 19 no-
       vembre 1964, 1, 6. Cf. Les Ecrits de Sartre, 406-407.

4816   Sartre, Jean-Paul. "Pourquoi je refuse d'aller aux Etats-
       Unis: Il n'y a plus de dialogue possible." Le Nouvel Obser-
       vateur, 1 avril 1965. Cf. Les Ecrits de Sartre, 412-413.

4817   Schmidt, Albert-Marie. "Le procès." Chroniques de Réforme,
       1945-1966. Lausanne: Editions Rencontres, 1970, 35-38.

4818   Séailles, André. "Sartre va-t-il se renier?" Preuves. No.
       23, janvier 1953, 105-106.

4819   Sénard, Jean. "Sartre et son démon." Le Figaro Littéraire.
       No. 849, 28 juillet 1962, 2.

4820   Sérant, Paul. "Dénoncer l'injustice partout." La Parisienne.
       No. 12, décembre 1953, 1628-1632.

STUDIES IN OTHER LANGUAGES

4821   Abosch, Heinz. "Sartre und die Politik." Blätter für
Deutsche und Internationale Politik, VI, No. 1, 1961, 64-70.

4822   Alicata, Mario. Preface to Il Filosofo e la politica. Roma:
Editori Riuniti, 1964.

4823   Anonymous. "Contradditorio francese: Testimonianze di Sartre
et al." L'Europa Letteraria, II, No. 9-10, June-August
1961, 268-272.

4824   Anonymous. "Sartre kämpft um seinen politischen Prozess."
Die Welt. No. 143, 24 June 1971, 6.

4825   Bondy, François. "Die Grossmandarine-Rückansicht." Der Monat, XVI, No. 192, 1964, 24-29.

4826   Bondy, François. "Sartre und die Politik." Merkur. No. 233,
August 1967, 764-780.

4827   Bongarzoni, Oretta. "Sartre sui fatti di Praga." Paese Sera,
25 August 1968. Cf. Les Ecrits de Sartre, 470.

4828   Buhl, Wolfgang. "Der Finstere von Paris." Erlanger Universität, IV, No. 5, 1950, 3-4.

4829   Carlini, Armando. "Una difesa di Sartre." Idea, VI, No. 23,
6 June 1954.

4830   Cavalcanti de Albuquerque, Roberto. "Sartre e o problema politico." Symposium, (Pernambuco), I, No. 2-3, 1960, 196-
201.

4831   Ceñal, Ramón. "Existencialismo moral y revolución en la obra
de Sartre." Revista de Filosofía, VII, No. 24, February-
March 1948, 7-47.

4832   Cesa, C. and Vanni, I. "Sartre a confronto con la politica e
con se stesso." Il Ponte, July 1964, 981-983.

4833   Chiaromonte, Nicolà. "Ambiguità di Sartre." Il Mondo, XII,
No. 12, 12 April 1960, 14.

4834   Chiaromonte, Nicolà. "Attualità." Il Mondo, VII, No. 30, 26
July 1955, 15.

4835   Chiaromonte, Nicolà. "Il dogmatico senza chiesa." Il Mondo, IV, No. 45, 8 November 1952, 7.

4836 Chiaromonte, Nicolà. "Il fanatico immaginario." Il Mondo, XVI, No. 18, 5 May 1964, 17.

4837 Chiaromonte, Nicolà. "Sartre, il solitario." Il Mondo, XII, No. 7, 16 February 1960, 14.

4838 Chiaromonte, Nicolà. "Der verhinderte Sartre." Der Monat, March 1954, 657-659.

4839 Fagone, Virgilio. "Il filosofo e la politica delle mani spor- che." Civiltà Cattólica, 2 May 1964, 225-238.

4840 Faracovi, Ornella P. "Jean-Paul Sartre: Un compagno di stra- da?" Il Ponte. No. 4-6, 1971.

4841 Fortini, Franco. "Alcune domande a Jean-Paul Sartre e a Si- mone de Beauvoir." Il Politecnico (Milan), July-August 1946, 33-35. Cf. Les Ecrits de Sartre, 150.

4842 Jacomella, S. "La conversione di Pitigrilli e la condanna- zione di Sartre." Civitas (Immensee), IV, No. 4, 1948, 166- 174.

4843 Jaspers, Karl. "Der Philosoph in der Politik." Der Monat, XV, April 1963, 22-29.

Krosigk, Frederich von. see 160.

4844 Macciocchi, Maria A. "Sartre no va in U.S.A." L'Unità, 19 March 1965. Cf. Les Ecrits de Sartre, 412.

4845 Marmori, Giancarlo. "Le astuzie di Sartre." Il Mondo, IX, No. 49, 3 December 1959, 9.

4846 Menéndez, Manuel. "Sartre y las elecciones." Indice. No. 327-328, 1-15 April 1973, 46-47.

4847 Rossanda, Rossana. "Sartre e la pratica politica." Aut Aut. No. 136-137, July-August 1973, 13-40.

4848 Vigorelli, Giancarlo. "Dalle parte di Sartre." L'Europa Let- teraria, I, No. 4, 1960, 5-6.

4849 Wroblewski, Vincent von. "Frederich von Krosigk: Philosophie und politische Aktion bei Sartre. Deutsche Literatur Zei- tung, XCI, No. 10-11, October-November 1970, 875-880.

POTENCY

4850   Finance, Joseph de. "La négation de la puissance chez Sar-
       tre." Sapientia Aquinatis, I, 1947, 473-481.

PRAXIS

4851   Arregue de Dell'Oca, Cristino. "La praxis sartreanea como in-
       teriorización de reciprocidad." Cuadernos de Filosofía, V,
       1968, 17-59.

       Bernstein, Richard J. see 2977.

4852   Cortese, Luigi. Il problema della prassi in Sartre. Roma:
       Caltanisetta, S. Sciascia, 1966.

4853   Figuières, Leo. "Problèmes de la praxis et du socialisme."
       Revue Théorique des Partis Communistes, Prague, janvier
       1963.

4854   Gorz, André. "Jean-Paul Sartre: De la conscience à la prax-
       is." Livres de France, XVII, No. 1, janvier 1966, 3-7.

4855   Hartmann, Klaud. "Praxis: A Ground for Social Theory." Jour-
       nal of the British Society for Phenomenology, I, No. 2, May
       1970, 47-58.

       Petruzzelis, Nicolà. see 2215.

PREDICAMENT

4856   Ryan, C. "Philosophical Predicament." Blackfriars, XXXII,
       March 1951, 113-114.

PREJUDICE

4857   Sattler, Jerome M. "Existential Considerations in the Char-
       acterology of Prejudice." Review of Existential Psychology
       and Psychiatry, IV, Spring 1964, 180-185.

PROLETARIAT

4858   Aron, Raymond. "Jean-Paul Sartre et le prolétariat, ou la
       grande peur du mal-pensant." Le Figaro Littéraire. No.
       336, 27 septembre 1952, 1, 5.

4859   Aron, Raymond. "Jean-Paul Sartre, le prolétariat et les com-
       munistes." Revue de Paris, LXI, juin 1954, 88-89.

Grandrey-Rety, Jean.   see 1052.

4860   Soukhomline, V.   "Le prolétariat et la liberté d'expression."
        Cahiers Internationaux.   No. 45, avril 1953.   A propos d'un
        article de Sartre.

PRE-REFLEXIVE

Royle, Peter.   see 3316.

Zurro Rodriguez, Maria R.   see 3238.

PROMETHEE

Prémont.   see 4243.

PROGRESSIVE-REGRESSIVE METHOD

Egebak, Niels.   see 4117.

4861   Pagano, Giacoma Maria.   "Il metodo progressivo-regressivo di
        Sartre."   *Atti e Memorie delle R. Academia di Scienze, Let-
        tere ed Arti en Padova*, XVIII, 1968-1969, 171-182.

PSYCHE

Galler, Dieter.   see 1280.

PSYCHICAL DISTANCE

4862   Reiss, T.J.   "Psychical Distance and Theatrical Distancing in
        Sartre's Drama."   *Yale French Studies*.   No. 46, 1971, 5-16.

PSYCHOANALYSIS (see Freud)

4863   Coltera, J.T.   "Psychoanalysis and Existentialism."   *American
        Psychoanalytic Association Journal*, X, January 1962, 209-
        215.

4864   Barnes, Hazel E.   "Humanistic Existentialism and Contemporary
        Psychoanalysis."   *Sartre: A Collection of Critical Essays*.
        Edith Kern, ed.   Englewood Cliffs, New Jersey: Prentice-
        Hall, 1962, 149-160.

4865   Barnes, Hazel E.   "Introduction."   *Existential Psychoanaly-
        sis: Jean-Paul Sartre*.   New York: Philosophical Library,
        1953.

4866   Barnes, Hazel E. The Literature of Possibility: A Study in
Humanistic Existentialism. Lincoln: Univ. of Nebraska Pr.,
1959.

Brooks, Rolph P. Jr. see 268.

PSYCHOANALYSIS

Bucio, Francisco P. see 4523.

4867   Coltera, J.T. "Psychoanalysis and Existentialism." American
Psychoanalytic Association Journal, X, January 1962, 209-
215.

Cristaldi, Mariano. see 3678.

Cuervo, Jean Elina. see 4592.

4868   Dobsevage, Alvin. "Jean-Paul Sartre: Existential Psychological Analysis." Journal of Philosophy, LII, July 1955, 412-
418.

4869   Dubal, Georges. "La psychanalyse existentielle." Revue Française de Psychanalyse, XV, No. 4, octobre-décembre 1951,
478-489.

Edie, James M. see 4595.

Egebak, Niels. see 4117.

4870   Farrell, B.A. "The Logic of Existential Psychoanalysis."
New Society, VI, No. 160, 1 October 1965, 9-11.

4871   Hyppolite, Jean. "La psychanalyse existentielle chez Sartre."
Figures de la pensée philosophique: Ecrits (1931-1968), Vol.
2. Paris: Presses Universitaires de France, 1971, 780-806.

4872   Schrader, George A. "Existential Psychoanalysis and Metaphysics." Review of Metaphysics, XIII, 1959, 139-164.

4873   Stern, Alfred. Sartre, His Philosophy and Psychoanalysis,
2nd revised ed. New York: Delacorte, 1967.

4874   Stern, Alfred. "El psicoanálisis existencialista." Folia
Humanistica, VIII, No. 94, October 1970, 781-793.

Stern, Alfred. see 2416, 2417.

Tauxe, Henri-Charles. see 2663.

PSYCHOLOGY

4875   Bannon, John F.   "The Psychiatry, Psychology and Phenomenology of Sartre." Journal of Existentialism, I, No. 2, 1960, 176-186.

Borrello, Oreste. see 4110.

4876   Cecchini, Augusto. La Psicologia di Sartre. (Istituto di Filosofia dell'Università di Pisa). Pisa: Libreria Universitaria, 1966.

4877   Cumming, Robert D. "Existentialist Psychology in Action." Scientific Psychology. Benjamin B. Wolman, ed. New York: Basic Books, 1965, 384-401.

Dempsey, Peter. see 17.

4878   Gandillac, Maurice de. "Sartre: His Philosophy and Psychology." Erasmus, XI, September 1958, 13-15.

Grant, Nigel J. see 417.

4879   Lapointe, François H. "The Phenomenological Psychology of Sartre and Merleau-Ponty." A Bibliographical Essay." Dialogos, VIII, No. 23, 1972, 161-182.

4880   Lyotard, Jean F. "Phénomeménologie et psychologie." La Phénoménologie (Coll. "Que sais-je?"). Paris: Presses Universitaires de France, 1954, Chapitre 2.

4881   Muuss, Rolf. "Existentialism and Psychology." Educational Theory, VI, July 1956, 134-153.

Patocka, Jan. see 2869.

4882   Pervin, Lawrence. "Existentialism, Psychology and Psychotherapy." American Psychologist, XV, 1960, 305-309.

4883   Weigert, Edith. "Existentialism and Its Relation to Psychotherapy." Psychiatry, XII, 1949, 399-412.

PSYCHOPATHOLOGY

4884   Rabkin, Leslie Y. Psychopathology and Literature. San Francisco: Chandler, 1966.

4885   Weizsäcker, Victor von. "Die Widerstand bei der Behandlung von Organkranken: Mit Bemerkungen über Werke von Sartre." Psyche, II, 4 March 1949.

RACISM

4886 Champigny, Robert. Humanisme et racisme humain. Paris: Edit-
      tions Saint-Germain-des-Prés, 1972.

4887 Damiens, Claude. "Le racisme chez Sartre, Genet et Aymé."
      Paris-Théâtre, XV, No. 179, 1962, 16-17.

      Fanon, Frantz. see 2631.

      Jean-pierre, W.A. see 4456.

R.D.R. (Rassemblement démocratique républicain)

4888 Altmann, Georges. "La France peut proposer au monde une ré-
      volution à faire dans la liberté." Franc-Tireur, 10 mars
      1948. Interview. Cf. Les Ecrits de Sartre, 193-199.

4889 Anonymous. Franc-Tireur, 13 mars 1948.

4890 Anonymous. Le Monde, 27 octobre 1949. Concerning Sartre's
      resignation from the R.D.R.

      Burnet, Mary. see 4689.

      Jeanson, Francis. see 4773.

      Mounier, Emmanuel. see 4799.

RATIONALITY

4891 Cooper, David G. "Two Types of Rationality." New Left Re-
      view. No. 29, January-February 1965, 62-68.

REALIST

4892 Van de Pitte, M.M. "Sartre as Transcendental Realist." Jour-
      nal of the British Society for Phenomenology, I, No. 2,
      May 1970, 22-26.

REASON

4893 Sinari, Ramakant. Reason in Existentialism. New York: Human-
      ities Pr., 1968.

REBELLION

4894 Curtis, Jerry L. "The Absurdity of Rebellion." Man and
      World, V, August 1972, 335-345.

REDUCTION

Shouery, Imad T.   see 4541.

REFLECTION

Goldthorpe, Rhiannon.   see 438.

4895   Rodie, C. Christopher.   "Emotion, Reflection and Action in
       Sartre's Ontology."   Man and World, VII, No. 4, November
       1974, 379-393.

RELIGION

4896   Copleston, Frederick C.   "Existentialism and Religion."   Dub-
       lin Review.   No. 440, Spring 1947, 45-63.

4897   Diaz de Cerio, M.   "Neurosis, religion y cultura."   Indice.
       No. 189, October 1964, 25.

       Dickenson, Donald H.   see 793.

4898   Geiger, L.B.   "L'existentialisme de Sartre et le salut chré-
       tien."   Jeunesse de l'Eglise.   No. 7, Cahier 7, 1947, 64-84.

4899   Gibson, A.B.   "Existential Religion and the Existential Re-
       ligion."   Danish Yearbook of Philosophy, VIII, 1971, 94-114.

(La) RESISTANCE

4900   Debu-Bride, Jacques, ed.   La Résistance intellectuelle.
       Paris: Juilliard, 1970.

RESOLVE

Grene, Marjorie.   see 2711.

RESPONSIBILITY

Anderson, Adele B.   see 3226.

Bach, Max and Bach, H.L.   see 2494.

Cook, Gladys C.   see 3677.

Flynn, Thomas R.   see 300.

4901   Scanlon, John D.   "Intolerable Human Responsibility."   Re-
       search in Phenomenology, I, 1971, 75-90.

Scott, Nathan A.   see 4321.

REVOLT

4902   Cruickshank, John.   "Revolt and Revolution."   French Literature and Its Background.   London: Oxford Univ. Pr., 1970,
226-243.

Erickson, John.   see 2993.

Gershman, Herbert S.   see 2527.

REVOLUTION

4903   Bondy, François.   "Sartre et la révolution."   Preuves.   No.
202, décembre 1967, 57-69.

4904   Ceñal, Ramón.   "Existencialismo moral y revolución en la obra
de Sartre."   Revista de Filosofía, VII, No. 24, February-
March 1948, 7-47.

4905   Garot, J.C.   "L'intellectuel face à la révolution."   Le Point.
No. 13, janvier 1968, 18-23.   Trans. into English: "Intellectuals and Revolution."   Ramparts Magazine, IX, December
1970, 52-55.

4906   Lichtheim, George.   "Philosopher in Revolt."   The Concept of
Ideology and Other Essays.   New York: Random House, 1967,
282-288.

Margadat, Ted W.   see 419.

4907   McBride, William L.   "Sartre and the Phenomenology of Social
Violence."   New Essays in Phenomenology: Studies in the Philosophy of Experience.   James M. Edie, ed.   Chicago: Quadrangle, 1969, 290-313.

McBride, William L.   see 39.

RHETORIC

Campbell, Karlyn K.   see 273.

Genette, Gerard.   see 4139.

ROMANTIC MYTH

Andrews, Jeffery.   see 250.

ROMANTICISM

4908   Siciliano, Italo. Il romanticismo francese de Prévost à Sar-
           tre.

RORSCHACH

       Eeden, H. van. see 231.

ROUMANIA

       Kazanian, Sonia. see 324.

RUSSIA

       Bedel, Jean. "Les impressions de Jean-Paul Sartre sur son
           voyage en U.R.S.S." (see 4909-4913).

4909   Bedel, Jean. "La liberté de critique est totale en U.R.S.S.
           et le citoyen soviétique améliore sans cesse sa condition
           su sein d'une société en progression continuelle." Libé-
           ration, 15 juillet 1954.

4910   Bedel, Jean. "De Dostoievski à la littérature contemporaine,
           un grand débat est ouvert entre les écrivains pour ou con-
           tre le roman héroïque." Libération, 16 juillet 1954.

4911   Bedel, Jean. "Ce n'est pas une sinécure d'appartenir à
           l'élite car elle est soumise à une critique permanente de
           tous les citoyens." Libération, 17-18 juillet 1954.

4912   Bedel, Jean. "Les philosophes soviétiques sont des bâtis-
           seurs . . . le marxisme est pour eux ce que sont pour nous
           les principes de '89." Libération, 19 juillet 1954.

4913   Bedel, Jean. "La paix par la paix: L'Union Soviétique pour-
           suit sa marche vers l'avenir." Libération, 20 juillet 1954.
           Cf. Les Ecrits de Sartre, 279-280.

4914   Garat, Jacques. "Il viaggio di Jean-Paul Sartre in Russia."
           Fiera Letteraria, IX, No. 32, 8 August 1954, 4.

4915   Lentin, Albert-Paul. "Une interview de Jean-Paul Sartre."
           France-U.R.S.S. No. 107, août 1954; Ibid., No. 108, sep-
           tembre 1954, 4.

SACRED

4916   Abellio, Raymond. <u>Vers un nouveau prophétisme: Essai sur le rôle du sacré et la situation de Lucifer dans le monde moderne</u>. Paris: Gallimard, 1950.

King, Thomas M.   see 32.

SACRILEGE

4917   John, S.   "Sacrilege and Metamorphosis: Two Aspects of Sartre's Imagery." <u>Modern Language Quarterly</u>, XX, March 1959, 57-66.

SACRE-COEUR

4918   Anonymous.   "Conférence de presse après les incidents du Sacré-Coeur." <u>Le Figaro</u>, 16 janvier 1971, 12.

SACRIFICE

4919   Rostenne, Paul.   "L'exigence humaine du sacrifice." <u>Revue de Métaphysique et de Morale</u>, LXXV, avril-juin 1970, 217-252.

SADNESS

4920   Mengod, Vincente.   "El tema de la tristeza." <u>Atenea</u>, año 21, Tomo CXV, No. 348, June 1954, 239-254.

SAINT GERMAIN-DES-PRES

4921   Hannotaux, Guillaume.   "De Montparnasse à Saint Germain-des-Prés." <u>Magazine Littéraire</u>. No. 39, avril 1970, 9-10.

4922   Montanelli, Indro.   "The Twilight of Saint Germain." <u>Atlas</u>, VII, No. 3, March 1964, 174-176.

4923   Routier, Marcelle.   <u>Saint Germain-des-Prés</u>. Paris: Aux Editions R.P.M., 1950. Recollections of Jean-Paul Sartre.

SAMKHYA

4924   Gelblum, Tuvia.   "Samkhya and Sartre." <u>Journal of Indian Philosophy</u>, I, No. 1, October 1970, 75-82.

4925   Larson, Gerald J.   "Classical Samkhya and the Phenomenological Ontology of Sartre." <u>Philosophy East and West</u>, XIX, January 1969, 45-58.

4926   Srinivasan, G. "Sartre and Samkhya." The Aryan Path, XXXVII,
        No. 12, December 1966, 54-55.

SCHIZOPHRENIA

        Galler, Dieter. see 1279.

4927   Vernon, John. The Garden and the Map: Schizophrenia in Twen-
        tieth Century Literature and Culture. Urbana: Univ. of Il-
        linois Pr., 1973.

SCIENCE

4928   Cera, Giovanni. "Sartre e le scienze." Rivista di Filosofia,
        LXII, No. 2, April-June 1971, 177-194. Concerning the rela-
        tionship between philosophy and science in Critique.

4929   Lentin, André. "Sartre, le marxisme et la science." La Pen-
        sée. No. 9, octobre-décembre 1946, 112-115. Concernant
        matérialisme et révolution.

SCOTISH VOLUNTARISM

4930   Feliciano de Ventosa. "Voluntarismo escotista frente al ni-
        hilismo sartriano." Naturaleza y Gracia (Salamanca), XI,
        1964, 73-96.

SELF

        Archer, Raymond. see 251.

4931   Glicksberg, Charles I. "The Literary Struggle for Selfhood."
        The Personalist, XLII, Winter 1961, 52-65.

4932   Barnes, Hazel E. "Jean-Paul Sartre and the Haunted Self."
        Western Humanities Review, X, Spring 1956, 119-128.

4933   Bergeron, André. "L'autoposition du moi par la conscience
        morale." Dialogue, III, No. 1, juin 1964, 1-24.

4934   Denat, Antoine. "Le moi, le monde et Dieu." Vu des anti-
        podes: Synthèses critiques. Paris: Didier, 1969, 11-17.

        Hoche, H.U. see 2732.

        Kern, Edith. see 4549.

        O'Brien, Robert J. see 359.

4935   Rice, Philip Blair. "Existentialism and the Self." Kenyon
       Review, XII, No. 2, Spring 1950, 304-320.

4935a Rohatny, Dennis A. "Sartre's Critique of Kant." Indian Phi-
       losophical Quarterly, II, January 1975, 171-176.

       Soper, William W. see 393.

4936   Sypher, Wylie. Loss of Self in Modern Literature and Art.
       New York: Random House, 1962.

4937   Wood, Forrest Jr. "A Whiteheadian Concept of the Self." The
       Southwestern Journal of Philosophy, IV, Spring 1973, 57-65.

SELF-DECEPTION (see Bad Faith)

4938   Canfield, John V. and Gustavson, Donald F. "Self-Deception."
       Analysis, XXIII, No. 2, December 1962, 32-36.

       Connerton, Paul. see 2932.

4939   Fingarette, Herbert. "Sartre and Mauvaise foi." Self-Decep-
       tion. New York: Humanities Pr., 1969, 92-100.

4940   Gardiner, P.L. "Error, Faith and Self-Deception." Proceed-
       ings of Aristotelian Society, LXX, 1969-1970, 197-220.

4941   King-Farlow, John. "Self-Deceivers and Sartrean Seducers."
       Analysis, XXIII, No. 6, June 1963, 131-136.

SELF-KNOWLEDGE

4942   Gilbert, Margaret. "Vices and Self-Knowledge." Journal of
       Philosophy, LXVIII, 5 August 1971, 443-452.

4943   Pole, David. "The Socratic Injunction." Journal of the Brit-
       ish Society for Phenomenology, II, No. 2, May 1971, 31-40.

SEQUESTRATION

       Boros, Marie-Denise. see 264.

4944   Boros, Marie-Denise. Un séquestré: L'homme sartrien. Paris:
       Nizet, 1969. Etude du thème de la séquestration dans
       l'oeuvre littéraire de Sartre.

4945   Epting, Karl. "Das Motiv der Gefangenschaft in Sartres Schau-
       spielen und in seiner Philosophie." Christ und Welt, Stut-
       tgart, XIII, No. 21, 1960, 16-19.

Galler, Dieter.   see 1281.

4946   Simon, John K.   Review of Boros's Un Séquestré . . . Romanic
       Review, LXII, No. 1, February 1971, 77-81.

Witt, Mary Ann.   see 1299.

SEX (Second Sex)

4947   Cate, C.   "Europe's First Feminist Has Changed the Second
       Sex." New York Times Magazine, 11 July 1971, 38-44.

4948   Sutton, Nina.   "Sartre and the Second Sex." The Guardian, 19
       February 1970, 11. Interview.

SEX

Eck, Marcel.   see 3021.

Friedmann, Maurice.   see 2499.

4949   King-Farlow, John.   "The Sartrean Analysis of Sexuality."
       Journal of Existentialism, II, No. 7, Winter 1962, 291-302.

4950   Ramsey, Paul.   "Jean-Paul Sartre: Sex in Being." Nine Modern
       Moralists. Englewood Cliffs, New Jersey: Prentice-Hall,
       1964, 71-109.

4951   Rosa, Nicolas.   "Sexo y creacion: Sartre y Genet." Critica y
       significacion. Buenos Aires: Galerna, 1970, 101-143.

4952   Solomon, Robert C.   "Sexual Paradigms." Journal of Philoso-
       phy, LXXI, No. 11, 13 June 1974.

Taylor, Robert E.   see 2944.

4953   Taylor, Roger L.   "Sexual Experiences." Proceedings Aristo-
       telian Society, LXVIII, 1967-1968, 87-104.

SHAME

4954   Drevet, Claude.   "La honte." Revue de Métaphysique et de Mor-
       ale, LXXIV, octobre-décembre 1969, 446-453.

Lauder, R.E.   see 2477.

Shouery, Imad T.   see 4294.

SIGNIFICANCE of Sartre

4955 Astruc, Alexandre. "Signification de Sartre." Domaine Fran-
      çais (Genève), No. 1, 1943, 415-426.

4956 Jones, R. "The Significance of Sartre." Adam International
      Review, XVI, No. 179, February 1948, 14-15.

SINCERITY

      Franks, Thomas H. see 302.

      Kanters, Robert. see 2747.

4957 Olson, Robert G. "Sincerity and the Moral Life." Ethics,
      LXVIII, No. 4, July 1958, 260-280.

4958 Peyre, Henri. Literature and Sexuality. New Haven: Yale
      Univ. Pr., 1963.

4959 Santoni, Ronald E. "Sartre on 'Sincerity': Bad Faith or Equi-
      vocation?" The Personalist, LIII, 1972, 150-160.

'SITUATEDNESS'

      Wein, Hermann. see 3837.

SOCIAL

4960 Adler, Franz. "The Social Thought of Jean-Paul Sartre."
      American Journal of Sociology, LV, No. 3, November 1949,
      284-294.

4961 Anonymous. "Jean-Paul Sartre als Philosophie: Zue Sozialpsy-
      chologie des Existentialismus." Befreiung, Aarau-Schweiz,
      I, 1953, 229-231.

      Burkle, Howard R. see 2069.

      Hartmann, Klaus. see 2193.

4962 Hughes, Stuart H. The Obstructed Path: French Social Thought
      in the Years of Desperation 1930-1960. New York: Harper
      and Row, 1968.

      Jones, William A. see 321.

      Stack, George J. see 2118.

4963 Spiegelberg, Herbert. "French Existentialism: Its Social Phi-
      losophies." Kenyon Review, XVI, No. 3, 1954, 446-454.

      Theunissen, M. see 2739.

SOCIOLOGY

4964 Buehl, Walter. "Dialektische Soziologie und soziologische Di-
      alektik." Köelner Zeitschrift Soziologie, XXI, 1969, 717-
      751.

4965 Dufrenne, Mikel. "Existentialisme et sociologie." Cahiers
      Internationaux de Sociologie, I, 1946, 161-171.

      Reynaud, Jean-Daniel. see 2165.

4966 Topitsch, Ernst. "The Sociology of Existentialism." Partisan
      Review, XXI, No. 3, May-June 1954, 289-304.

4967 Weinstein, Michael and Weinstein, Deena. "Sartre and the Hu-
      manist Tradition in Sociology." Sartre: A Collection of
      Critical Essays. Mary Warnock, ed. Garden City, New York:
      Doubleday, Anchor Books, 1971, 357-386.

4968 Willi, Viktor. "Soziologie und Existentialismus." Kyklos,
      Bern, VII, 1954, 125-164.

SOI (Le)

      Grooten, Johan. see 2764.

SOVIET (opinion of Sartre)

4969 Krauss, W. M. "Sowjetrussische Meinung uber Sartre." Ber-
      liner Hefte für Geistiges Leben, II, 1947, 389-394.

SPACE

4970 Wavre, Rolin. La figure du monde: Essai sur le problème de
      l'espace des Grecs à nos jours. Neuchâtel: Editions de la
      Baconnière, 1950.

STRUCTURALISM

4971 Châtelet, François. "Sartre en question: Sartre répond comme
      un dépossédé! . . . " Le Nouvel Observateur. No. 103, 2-8
      novembre 1966, 32-33. Cf. Les Ecrits de Sartre, 435.

4972 Daix, Pierre. "Sartre est-il dépassé?" Les Lettres Fran-
      çaises, février 1967, 1168-1169.

      Gramont, Sanche de. see 2784.

4973 Krause-Jensen, Esbern. Den franske strukturalisme: Pa sporet
      af en teori for de humane videnskaber. Copenhagen: Berlin-
      gske Forlag, 1973.

      Lapouge, Gilles. see 2776.

4974 Lévi-Strauss, Claude. L'Homme nu. Paris: Plon, 1971.

4975 McNicholl, Ambrose. "Lo strutturalismo." Aquinas, XIII,
      1970, 262-308.

      Pouillon, Jean. see 2783, 2789, 2790.

4976 Revel, Jean-François. "Sartre en ballotage." L'Express. No.
      803, 7-13 novembre 1966, 47.

4977 Schiwy, Günter. Der französische Strukturalismus: Mode, Meth-
      ode, Ideologie. Reinbek bei Hamburg: Rowohlt, 1969.

4978 Schiwy, Günther. Neue Aspekte des Strukturalismus. München:
      Kosel, 1971.

4979 Scholes, Robert. Structuralism in Literature: An Introduc-
      tion. New York: Yale Univ. Pr., 1974.

4980 Weinrich, Harald. "Strukturalismus." Merkur. No. 254, June
      1969, 593-595.

STYLE

4981 Brock, Erich. "Zum Problem der Stilkritik." Trivium, Zürich,
      III, No. 1, 1945, 72-77.

      Campoux, Charles. see 2285.

      Cohn, Dorrit. see 531.

      Jameson, Fredric. see 317.

4982 Jameson, Frederic R. Sartre: The Origins of a Style. New Ha-
      ven: Yale Univ. Pr., 1961.

4983 Legros, Georges. "Sartre a-t-il un style?" Cahiers d'Ana-
      lyse Textuelle (Liège), IV, 1962, 97-109.

SUBJECTIVISM

Burkill, T.A.   see 2595.

Borrello, Oreste.   see 3047.

SUBJECTIVITY

4984 Paci, Enzo. "L'ultimo Sartre e il problema della soggettività." Aut Aut. No. 67, January 1962, 1-30.

SUBSTANCE

4985 Jimenez, V. Maria. "El concepto de substancia en la filosofía
de Sartre." Revista de Filosofía de la Universidad de Costa
Rica, IV, No. 15-16, 1965, 295-301.

4986 Prentice, Robert. "Phenomenological Substitute for Substance." Antonianum, XLVI, No. 1, January-March 1971, 80-
112.

SUICIDE

de Franco, Raffaella.   see 3276.

4987 Fornoville, Théodore. "Le suicide dans l'éthique sartrienne."
Revue Philosophique de Louvain, LVII, 1959, 80-95.

SURREALISM

4988 Bataille, Georges. "Le surréalisme et sa différence avec
l'existentialisme." Critique, I, No. 2, juillet 1946, 99-
110.

4989 Beaujour, Michel. "Sartre and Surrealism." Yale French Studies. No. 30, 1962, 86-96.

4990 Breton, André. "Seconde arche." Fontaine, XI, No. 63, novembre 1947, 699-703.

4991 Glicksberg, Charles I. "D.H. Lawrence, The Prophet of Surrealism." Nineteenth Century and After, CXLIII, April 1948,
229-237.

Plank, William G.   see 366.

SYMBOL

4992 Doubrovsky, J.A. "Existence and Symbol." Philosophy and Phe-
      nomenological Research, XXI, No. 2, December 1960, 229-238.

SYMBOLISM

Cawdrey, Michael. see 828.

4993 Prince, Gerald J. "Le symbolisme des noms dans l'oeuvre ro-
      manesque de Sartre." Papers on Language and Literature,
      IV, No. 3, Winter 1969, 316-321.

4994 Ricoeur, Paul. "Le symbolisme et l'explication structurale."
      Cahiers Internationaux de Symbolisme. No. 4, 1964, 81-96.

SWEDEN

4995 Périlleux, Georges. "Sartre et la Suède." Moderna Språk,
      LXII, No. 4, 1968, 400-418.

TECHNOCRACY

4996 Debray, Pierre. "Quand M. Sartre découvre la technocratie."
      Aspects de la France. No. 732, 25 octobre 1962, 2 ff.

(Les) TEMPS MODERNES

4997 Audry, Colette et Stéphane, Roger. "Lisez 'Les Temps Mo-
      dernes'." Arts. No. 378, 26 septembre-2 octobre 1952, 5.

4998 Cornell, Kenneth. "Les Temps Modernes: Peep Sights Across the
      Atlantic." Yale French Studies. No. 16, 1955-1956, 24-28.

4999 Gide, André. Terre des Hommes. No. 8, 17 novembre 1945.
      Attack against ideas expressed in 'Présentation' des Temps
      Modernes.

5000 Marchand, Jean-José. "Sartre et Les Temps Modernes." Maga-
      zine du Spectacle. No. 1, 1947, 135-143.

Ramwez, Alan D. see 373.

5001 Spanggard, Kristen D. "Sartres Programartikel." Athenaeum,
      I, No. 2, 1946, 133-147.

5002 Tortel, Henri. "Les vitrés fermés." Cahiers du Sud, XXIII,
      No. 274, 1945, 841-844.

THEATER (see Part III: General Studies)

THEOLOGY and THEODICY

5003 Guthrie, G.P. "Importance of Sartre's Phenomenology for
        Christian Theology." Journal of Religion, XLVII, January
        1967, 12-25.

5004 Rosado, Juan José Rodriguez. "Teodicea y nihilismo." Anuario
        Filosófio, VI, 1973, 241-257.

5005 Van Neftrik, G.C. "Sartre en zijn betekenis voor theologie."
        Nederl. Theologie Tijdschrift, IV, 1949-1950, 259-277.

THIRD

5006 Flynn, Thomas R. "The Alienating and the Mediating Third in
        the Social Philosophy of Jean-Paul Sartre." Studies in Phi-
        losophy and the History of Philosophy, Catholic Univ. of
        America, VI, 1974.

        St. Aubyn, F.C. see 2930.

THOMISM

5007 Gilson, Etienne. "Le thomisme et les philosophies existen-
        tielles." La Vie Intellectuelle, XIII, No. 5, juin 1945,
        144-155.

5008 Mihalich, Joseph. Existentialism and Thomism. New York: Phi-
        losophical Library, 1960.

5009 Reinhardt, Kurt. "A Thomist Answers Sartre." The Commomweal,
        XLIV, 11 March 1949, 545-546.

        Reinhardt, Kurt. see 3482.

THOUGHT

5010 Riese, Walther. "On Thought in Existentialism." Journal of
        Existentialism. No. 21, 1965, 89-98.

TIME

        Bluestone, Natalie S. see 262.

        Church, Margaret. see 2638.

5011   Cormeau, Nelly. "Révolte contre le temps chez les romanciers d'aujourd'hui." L'Age Nouveau. No. 61, mai 1950, 37-44.

5012   Jameson, Fredric R. "The Rhythm of Time." Sartre: A Collection of Critical Essays. Edith Kern, ed. Englewood Cliffs, New Jersey: Prentice-Hall, 1972, 106-120. Reprinted from Sartre: The Origins of a Style. New Haven: Yale Univ. Pr., 1961.

        Kenevan, Phyllis B. see 325.

5013   Lawrence, Nathaniel. "The Illusion of Monolinear Time." Patterns of the Life-World: Essays in Honor of John Wild. James M. Edie, et al., eds. Evanston, Illinois: Northwestern Univ. Pr., 1970, 298-314.

5014   Le Huenen, Roland et Perron, Paul. "Temporalité et démarche critique chez Jean-Paul Sartre." Revue des Sciences Humaines, Fascicule 148, octobre-décembre 1972, 567-581.

5015   Marchand, Jean-José. "Le temps et la technique romanesque selon Jean-Paul Sartre." Problèmes du roman. Bruxelles: Le Carrefour, 1945, 151-158. Soixantes-deux études publiés sous la direction de Jean Prévost. Publié dans Confluences, 1943.

5016   Mole, Jack. "Time and Consciousness: Sartre." The Time of Our Lives. London: Epworth, 1965, 62-73.

        Pütz, Peter. see 1548.

5017   Schnaith, Nelly. "Tiempo y subjetividad en Sartre." Cuadernos de Filosofía (Buenos Aires), X, January-June 1970, 99-100.

        Seel, Gerhard. see 170.

        Shattuck, Roger. see 2926.

        Skloot, Robert. see 390.

        Sutherland, Donald. see 2645.

        Tembeck, R. see 1294.

5019   Zimmerningst, Martin. "Das Tempus bei Sartre." Die Neuren Sprachen, XVII, 1968, 27-35.

TOTALITARIANISM

5020   Latouche, Serge.   "Totalité, totalisation et totalitarisme."
        Dialogue (Canada), XIII, mars 1974, 71-83.

        Werner, Eric.   see 146.

'TOUT'

5021   Anonymous.   "M. Jean-Paul Sartre dirige une nouvelle publica-
        tion gauchiste 'Tout'."   Le Monde.   No. 7996, 29 septembre
        1970, 11.

5022   Anonymous.   "On en parlera demain; Sartre: Maintenant,
        'Tout'."   Le Nouvel Observateur.   No. 308, 5-11 octobre
        1970, 23.

TRANSCENDENCE

5023   Barnes, Hazel E.   "Transcendence Toward What: Is the Universe
        Like Us?"   Religious Humanism, IV, Winter 1970, 11-14.

        Goldthorpe, Rhiannon.   see 437.

5024   Smith, Colin.   Contemporary French Philosophy.   London: Met-
        huen, 1964, 27-47.

TRUTH

5025   Balliu, Julien.   "De autofinaliteit der Vrijheid bij Sartre."
        Dialoog, VI, 1965-1966, 32-43; Ibid., 272-293.

5026   Beaufret, Jean.   "Heidegger et le problème de la vérité."
        Fontaine, XI, No. 63, novembre 1947, 758-785.

5027   Wieland, J.H.   "Vrijheid en situatie in de wijsbegeerte van
        Sartre."   Tijdschrift voor Filosofie, XXX, March 1968, 82-
        117.

ULTRA-BOLCHEVISM

5028   Anonymous.   "Sartre est un ultra-bolchéviste . . . déclare
        Merleau-Ponty."   Le Figaro Littéraire, 7 mai 1955, 1.

5029   Merleau-Ponty, Maurice.   Les aventures de la dialectique.
        Paris: Gallimard, 1955.

ULTRA-INDIVIDUALISM

5030 Beyer, Wilhelm Raimund. "Wieder den Ultra-Individualismus."
      Vier Kritiken: Heidegger, Sartre, Adorno, Lukacs. Köln:
      Pahl Rugenstein, 1970, 117-146.

UNCONSCIOUS

5031 Conkling, Mark. "Sartre's Refutation of the Freudian Uncon-
      scious." Review of Existential Psychology and Psychiatry,
      VIII, 1968, 86-100.

5032 Grimsley, Ronald. "An Aspect of Sartre and the Unconscious."
      Journal of Philosophy, XXX, January 1955, 33-44.

5033 Lapointe, François H. "Phenomenology, Psychonanalysis and the
      Unconscious: I, Sartre." Journal of Phenomenological Psy-
      chology, II, No. 1, Fall 1971, 5-26.

      Reboul, Olivier. see 2420.

5034 Trilling, Lionel. "The Authentic Unconscious." Sincerity and
      Authenticity. London: Oxford Univ. Pr., 1972, 134-172.

5035 Wysghorod, Michael. "Sartre, Freedom and the Unconscious."
      Review of Existential Psychology and Psychiatry, I, Fall
      1961, 179-186.

UNIVERSAL

5036 Kerkhoff, Manfred. "La controversia de los universales en la
      filosofía de Sartre." Dialagos, II, No. 4, 1965, 145-165.

VALUES

      Chentrens, Roberto C. see 1523.

5037 Delgado, Honorio. "La objectividad de los valores frente al
      subjectivismo existencialista." Mercurio Peruano, XXXVII,
      No. 351, July 1956, 319-326.

      Jaquette, William A. see 318.

      Jolivet, Régis. see 3698.

5038 Lauth, Reinhardt. "Versuche einer existentialistischen Wer-
      tlehre in der französischen Philosophie der Gegenwart: Sar-
      tre und Polin." Zeitschrift Philosophische Forschung, X,
      1959, 244-278.

VIOLENCE

5039 Aron, Raymond. Histoire et dialectique de la violence. Paris: Gallimard, 1973, 61.

5040 Pashman, Jon. "On the Learned Origin of Violence." Revue Internationale de Philosophie, XXVIII, 1974, 194-208.

WOMAN

Nahas, Helen. see 355.

5041 Quinn, Bernard J. "The Authentic Woman in the Theater of Sartre." Language Quarterly, X, No. 3-4, 1972, 39-44.

5042 Stern, Karl. "Jean-Paul Sartre." The Flight From Woman. New York: Farrar, Strauss, 1965, 123-142.

WORLD

5043 Allers, Rudolf. "Bemerkungen über das Weltbild in anankastischen Syndromen und in der Philosophie von Sartre." Jahrbuch für Psychologie und Psychotherapie, VI, 1958, 203-208.

Barnes, Hazel E. see 2063.

WOUND

5044 Douglas, Kenneth N. "Sartre and the Self-Inflicted Wound." Yale French Studies. No. 9, Spring 1952, 123-132. Reprinted Sartre: A Collection of Critical Essays. Englewood Cliffs, New Jersey: Prentice-Hall, 1962, 39-46.

WRITER

5045 Bonnefoy, Claude. "Les souvenirs de Jean-Paul Sartre: 'Ma vocation d'écrivain est né au sixième étage." Arts. No. 932, 16-22 octobre 1963, 5.

5046 Brenner, Jacques. "Comment Sartre est devenu écrivain." Journal de la vie littéraire, 1962-1964. Paris: Juilliard, 1965, 208-210.

5047 Gaulmier, Jean. "Quand Jean-Paul Sartre avait dix-huit ans . . . " France Littéraire, V, juillet 1958, 5. Concernant la contribution de Sartre à la Revue sans Titre.

Lucio, Luellen G. see 339.

5048   Panichas, G.A.   "The Writer and Society: Some Reflections."
       The Politics of Twentieth Century Novelists.   New York: Haw-
       thorn Books, 1971, xxiii-liv.

5049   Raillard, Georges.   "Sartre et l'écrivain."   Le Français dans
       le Monde.   No. 92, octobre-novembre 1972, 52-54.

5050   Rybalka, Michel.   "Les écrits de jeunesse de Sartre."   Le Ma-
       gazine Littéraire.   No. 55-56, septembre 1971, 14-15.

PART VI

BOOK REVIEWS

BOOK REVIEWS

5051 Anonymous. "Mary Warnock, ed. Sartre: A Collection of Critical Essays." New York Times Book Review, 13 June 1971, 28-
29.

5052 Apostol, Robert Z. "Sartre, by Hazel E. Barnes." International Philosophical Quarterly, XIV, No. 1, March 1974, 129-
131.

5053 Barnes, Hazel E. "Critic's Second Thoughts: René Marill Albérès, Jean-Paul Sartre, Philosopher Without Faith." Prairie
Schooner, XXVI, No. 2, Summer 1962, 174-177.

5054 Belkind, Allen. "G.H. Bauer. Sartre and the Artist." Journal of Modern Literature, I, No. 5, Supplement, 915-918.

5055 Bortolaso, G. "Existenzialismo ateo ed esistenzialismo teis-
tico de L. Stefanini." Civiltà Cattólica, CIII, No. 2453,
6 September 1952, 495-508.

5056 Busi, Frederick. "Philip Thody. Sartre: A Biographical Introduction." French Review, XLVI, No. 2, December 1972,
425.

5057 Champigny, Robert. "Four on Sartre." Contemporary Literature, XIII, Spring 1972, 261-266. Concerning Richter, Suhl,
MaMahon, and Kern.

5058 Copleston, Frederick. "Jean-Paul Sartre: His Philosophy by
René Lafarge." The Spectator, 16 January 1971, 83-84.

5059 Cranston, Maurice. "Sartre: Ideologue's Ideologue." Washington Post Book World, II, No. 43, 27 October 1968, 12. Molnar.

5060 Daix, Pierre. "Une biographie de la création: Les Ecrits de
Sartre de M. Contat et M. Rybalka." Les Lettres Françaises.
No. 1329, 8-14 avril 1970, 3.

5061 Daniels, Graham. "Sartre: La Nausée and Les Mouches by Keith
Gore." French Studies, XXVII, No. 2, April 1973, 229-230.

5062 Desanti, Dominique. "Mieux qu'une bibliographie, un portrait:
Les Ecrits de Sartre." Le Monde des Livres. No. 7845, 4
avril 1970, 1-2.

5063 Doherty, Cyril M. "Opening up the World of Sartre." L'Esprit
      Créateur, XII, No. 1, Spring 1972, 61-65. MaMahon.

5064 Dubois, E.T. "B. Suhl: Jean-Paul Sartre: The Philosopher as
      Literary Critic." Erasmus, XXIV, No. 19-20, 10 October
      1972, 738-742.

5065 Dufour, Michel. "Les Ecrits de Sartre by M. Contat et M. Ry-
      balka." Dialogue (Canada), IX, No. 2, septembre 1970, 279-
      282.

5066 Emond, Paul. "Gérald J. Prince: Métaphysique et technique
      dans l'oeuvre romanesque de Sartre." Lettres Romanes, XXIV,
      No. 3, août 1970, 298-300.

5067 Fabre-Luce, Anne. "Les Ecrits de Sartre." Le Nouvel Observa-
      teur. No. 283, 13-19 avril 1970, 43.

5068 Fabre-Luce, Anne. "A. Manser. Sartre: A Philosophic Study."
      French Review, XL, No. 5, April 1967, 721-723.

5069 Fellows, Otis. "Robert Campbell: Sartre ou une littérature
      philosophique." Symposium, II, No. 1, 1948, 127-131.

5070 François, Carlo. "Benjamin Suhl: Jean-Paul Sartre, The Phi-
      losopher as Literary Critic." French Review, XLVI, No. 4,
      March 1973, 844-845.

5071 Gabaude, Jean-Marc. "Zádor Tordai: Existence et réalité, po-
      lémique avec certaines thèses fondamentales de 'L'Etre et le
      néant' de Sartre." Dialogue, XII, No. 3, septembre 1973,
      597-580.

5072 Goldstein, Walter D. "Literary and Philosophical Essays: A
      Review." Chicago Review, XI, Summer 1957, 101-106.

5073 Goldthorpe, Rhiannon. "Métaphysique et technique dans
      l'oeuvre romanesque de Sartre by G.J. Prince. Jean-Paul
      Sartre by H. Peyre. Sartre and the Artist by G.H. Bauer."
      French Studies, XXVI, No. 1, January 1972, 95-98.

5074 Grene, Marjorie. "Critical Notice: Sartre, A Philosophical
      Study by A. Manser." Mind, LXXVIII, No. 309, January 1969,
      143-153.

5075 Guiney, M. "Sartre: The Philosopher as a Literary Critic by
      B. Suhl." Modern Language Journal, LVI, No. 1, January
      1972, 61-62.

5076 Hampshire, Stuart. "J'attaque." The Listener, LXIV, No.
      1645, 6 October 1960, 583. Concerning Philip Thody's Sar-
      tre, A Literary and Political Portrait.

5077 Jannoud, Claude. "Sartre à lire." Le Figaro Littéraire.   No.
      1246, 6-12 avril 1970, 30. Cf. Les Ecrits de Sartre.

5078 Jourdan, Henri. "André Espiau de la Maestre: Der Sinn und das
      Absurde." Romanische Forschungen, LXXIV, No. 3-4, 1962,
      435-439.

5079 Kelbley, Charles A. "Little Known Texts of Sartre." Inter-
      national Philosophical Quarterly, XIV, No. 2, June 1974,
      229-236. Cf. Les Ecrits de Sartre.

5080 Kern, Edith. "G.H. Bauer, Sartre and the Artist." Modern
      Language Quarterly, XXXI, No. 2, June 1970, 263-266.

5081 Leotta, Massima. "G.M. Pagano: Sartre e la dialettica." Ri-
      vista di Studi Crociani, VIII, No. 3, July-September 1971,
      342-345.

5082 Lepschy, G.C. "Benjamin Suhl: Jean-Paul Sartre: The Philoso-
      pher as a Literary Critic." Modern Language Review, LXVIII,
      No. 2, April 1973, 425-427.

5083 Lorris, Robert. "The Theater of Sartre by D. McCall." Roman-
      tic Review. No. 3, October 1972, 244-246.

5084 Marcel, Gabriel. "Sartre est-il possédé? par P. Boutang et
      B. Pingaud." J'ai Lu, mars 1947.

5085 Marks, Elaine. "Robert Champigny: Humanisme et racisme hu-
      maine." French Review, XLVII, No. 2, December 1973, 447-
      448.

5086 Mayer, J.P. "Die Praxis der 'littérature engagée' im Werk
      Jean-Paul Sartres: 1938-1948 by Henning Krauss." French
      Studies, XXVII, No. 2, April 1973, 230-231.

5087 McKenna, Andrew. "B. Suhl, Sartre, The Philosopher as a Lit-
      erary Critic." Modern Language Notes, LXXXVI, No. 4, May
      1971, 604-606.

5088 Merry, Bruce. "R.D. Laing and D.G. Cooper, Reason and Vio-
      lence." Philosophical Studies (Ireland), XXI, 1973, 243-
      249.

5089   Morot-Sir, Edouard. "Existential Thought and Fictional Tech-
       nique: Kirkegaard, Sartre, Beckett by Edith Kern." Romantic
       Review, LXIV, No. 4, November 1973, 319-321.

5090   Morot-Sir, Edouard. "Benjamin Suhl, Sartre, The Philosopher
       as a Literary Critic." Romantic Review, LXIII, No. 3, Oc-
       tober 1972, 242-244.

5091   Nemo, Philippe. "Sartre et la grâce." Le Nouvel Observateur.
       No. 396, 12-18 juin 1972, 60. Concernant Berstraeten,
       Ethique et violence.

5092   Niess, Robert J. "Edith Kern, Existential Thought and Fic-
       tional Technique . . ." Modern Fiction Studies, XVII, No.
       2, 1971.

5093   Palmer, J.N.J. "The Theater of Sartre by D. McCall." French
       Studies, XXVI, No. 1, January 1972, 98-99.

5094   Picon, Gaëtan. "Sartre par lui-même par Francis Jeanson."
       Mercure de France. No. 1107, novembre 1955, 491-496. Ré-
       imprimé L'Usage de la lecture, Vol. 2: Suite balzacienne-
       suite contemporaine, Paris: Mercure de France, 1961, 131-
       137.

5095   Pleydel Pearce, A.G. "Sartre's Ontology by Maurice Natanson."
       Journal of the British Society for Phenomenology, L, No. 5,
       January 1974, 86-89.

5096   Roudiez, Leon S. "H. Peyre, Jean-Paul Sartre." Romantic Re-
       view, LX, No. 3, October 1969, 228-229.

5097   Schoell, Konrad. "G. J. Prince, Métaphysique et technique
       dans l'oeuvre romanesque de Sartre." Romanische Forschun-
       gen, LXXXI, No. 4, 1969, 649-652.

5098   Schulz-Buschhaus, Ulrich. "Henning Krauss: Die Praxis der
       'littérature engagée' im Werk Jean-Paul Sartres 1938-1948."
       Archiv für das Studium der Neuren Sprachen und Literatur,
       1973, 470-474.

5099   Simon, John K. "Un sésquestré: L'homme sartrien by Marie D.
       Boros." Romantic Review, LXII, No. 1, February 1971, 77-
       81.

5100   Spanos, William V. "J.F. Sheridan: Sartre: The Radical Con-
       version." Journal of Modern Literature, I, No. 5, 1971,
       919-922.

5101   Thody, Philip.   "Bauer: _Sartre and the Artist_."   _Modern Fiction Studies_, XVI, No. 4, Winter 1970-1971.

5102   Uribarri, Rafael.   "_Apuntes de literatura contemporanea_ by Maria Alonso."   _La Estafeta Literaria_.   No. 477, 1 October 1971, 710.

5103   Urmson, J.O.   "His Own Place."   _The Spectator_, XXII, No. 7327, 29 November 1968, 773.   Concerning R.D. Cummung's _The Philosophy of Sartre_.

5104   Warnock Mary.   "_Essays in Aesthetic_, trans. by Wade Baskin."   _British Journal of Aesthetics_, V, 1965, 88-91.

5105   Weightman, John.   "Sartre Catologued."   _Adam International Review_, XXXV, No. 343-345, 1970, 24-28.   Cf. _Les Ecrits de Sartre_.

5106   Williams, Raymond.   "The Need for Sartre."   _The Guardian_.   No. 38,067, 29 November 1968.   Concerning R.D. Cummings' _The Philosophy of Sartre_.

5107   Wilson, Colin.   "_Sartre, A Biographical Introduction_ by Philip Thody."   _Mediterranean Review_, II, No. 2, Winter 1972, 38-40.

APPENDIX

ADDITIONAL ITEMS

APPENDIX: ADDITIONAL ITEMS

5108   Aaras, Hans. "Sartres fornektelse." Edda, LIV, No. 2, 1954,
         138-157.

5109   Aarnes, Asbjorn. "Glimt fra Frankrike." Vinduet, I, No. 5,
         1947, 373-375.

5110   Ahlenius, Holger. Svenskt och Franskt: Studier och inlagg.
         Stockholm: Bonniers, 1950.

5111   Anonymous. "Von Emmanuel Hiel tot Jean-Paul Sartre." Nieuw
         Vlaams Tidjschrift, XIV, 1961, 1093-1094.

5112   Apostel, L. "Ondervraag over Sartre." De Vlaamse Gids, XLIX,
         124-125.

5113   Aspelin, Gunnar. "Sartres livsaskadning." Quo Vadis, 1948,
         34-38.

5114   Bakker, Reinout. "Jean-Paul Sartre." Wijsg. Persp. Maatch.
         Wet., IV, 1963-1964, 67-81.

5115   Balota, Nicolae. "Procesul lui Jean-Paul Sartre." Romania
         Literaria, XXII, March 1967.

5116   Bierling, R.F. Het Existentialisme. The Hague, 1947.

5117   Boer, Jo. "Aantekeningen over het hedendaagsche Fransche to-
         oneel." Erasmus, I, 1945, 38-52.

5118   Egebak, Niels. "Sartres filosofiske dilemma." Exil, II,
         1966-1967, 37-45, 105-111.

5119   Engfeldt, Birgit. "Jean-Paul Sartre." Vadringar Med Bocker
         (Lund), XIV, 1965, 1-4. With bibliobraphy of translations
         into Swedish.

5120   Flam, Leopold. "Jean-Paul Sartre in onze tijd." Nieuw Vlaams
         Tijdschrift, X, 1965, 257-265.

5121   Flam, Leopold. Ontbinding en protest: Van Marquis de Sade tot
         Sartre. Antwerpen: de Sikkel, 1959.

5122   Flam, Leopold. Profielen van Plato tot Sartre. Antwerpen:
         de Sikkel, 1957.

5123   Groot, C. de. "Sartres literaire zelfkastijding." Raam. No. 9, 1964, 57-66.

5124   Hellesnes, Jon. "Jean-Paul Sartre og emosjonane." Samtiden, LXXV, No. 8, 1966, 493-501.

5125   Holm, Soren. "Jean-Paul Sartre et moderne faenomen." Frie Ord, II, No. 2, 1947, 79-95.

5126   Huizen, P.H. van. "Sartre voor de spiegel geleid." Merlyn, I, No. 3, 1963, 65-73.

5127   Itterbeek, Eugene van. Tekens van leven: Beschouwingen over het schrijverschap. Bruxelles: Manteau, 1969.

5128   Johansen, Hans Boll. Den moderne roman i Frankrig: Analyser og synteser. Copenhagen: Akademisk Forlag, 1970.

5129   Kieffer, Rene. "'Acklet' av Sartre." Credo Katolsk Tidskrift (Uppsala), XLVII, 1966, 13-21.

5130   Kwant, Remy C. "Jean-Paul Sartre." Filosofen van de 20e eeuw. Assen, Amsterdam: Van Gorcum Intermediair, 1972, 113-123. Onder redactie van C.P. Bertels en E. Petersma.

5131   Martinson, Helga (Svarts). Karlek mellan Krigen, noveller och skisser av Moa Martinson. Stockholm: Tiden Forlag, 1947.

5132   Moe, Per. "En ny skapende kunstner, dikteren Jean-Paul Sartre." Samtiden, LVIII, No. 6, 1949, 368-379.

5133   Myhre, Amund. "Pa vei mot tabor: Et mote mellom en moderne Sisyfos og tre franske forfattere." Vinduet, X, No. 1, 1956, 72-77.

5134   Nordentoft, Soren. "Sartres tanker om frihed." Dansk Teologisk Tidskrift, XXI, 1958, 33-58, 100-111.

5135   Norwid, Tadwusz. "Legitymacja partyjna i Sartre." Wiadomosci, II, No. 53-54, 13 Kwietnia 1947, 3.

5136   Ottesen, Otto. "Fransk og Amerikansk litteraturmuljo." Vinduet, III, No. 7, 1949, 529-536.

5137   Popivic, D. "Zan-Pol Sartr: Obzivna bludnica." Letopis Matice Srpske, Novi Sad., No. 377, 1956, 277-279.

5138   Pos, H.   "Sartre in protestantse belichting."   Nieuwe Stem
       (Amsterdam), IX, 1954, 200-217.

5139   Prag, Siegfried E. van.   "Fransche Literatuur van 1940-1950."
       Critisch Bulletin, XIII, March 1946, 97-100; Ibid., April
       1946, 145-150; Ibid., May 1946, 193-198.

5140   Robbers, H.   "Sartre de vigheid van un verlaters."   Hedendaag-
       se visies op den mens.   Amsterdam, 1955, 117-128.

5141   Rutten, Willy.   "Het probleem van de vrijheid bij Sartre."   De
       Vlaamse Gids, XLV, No. 2, February 1961, 107-114.

5142   Spier, J.M.   Van Thales tot Sartre.   Kampen, 1959.

5143   Tassing, Einar.   "Jean-Paul Sartre."   Perspektiv (Copenhagen),
       X, No. 3, 1962, 43-47.

5144   Ustvedt, Yngar.   "Jean-Paul Sartres budskap."   Samtiden,
       LXXIII, No. 9, 1964, 517-526.

5145   Vestre, Bernt.   "Sartre: Den Trofaste forraeder."   Vinduet,
       XVIII, No. 3, 1964, 185-190.

5146   Vloemans, Antoon.   "Sartres mensenbeeld en het einde van het
       Existentialisme."   Nieuw Vlaams Tijdschrift, June 1969,
       359-361.

5147   Volkaert, Walter.   "Jean-Paul Sartre en de realiteit van de
       schilderkunst."   De Vlaamse Gids, XLV, 1961, 359-361.

5148   Votgovor, R.   "Na Sart."   Literaturen Front (Sofija), XII, No.
       48, 1956, 1, 3.